BES-127

SLAVISTIC PRINTINGS AND REPRINTINGS

edited by

C. H. VAN SCHOONEVELD

Indiana University

269

RUSSIAN HESYCHASM

The spirituality of Nil Sorskij

by

GEORGE A. MALONEY S. J.

1973

MOUTON

THE HAGUE · PARIS

LIBRARY OF CONGRESS CATALOG CARD NUMBER: 72-88188

Printed in Hungary

TABLE OF CONTENTS

Introduction   9
Abbreviations   15

PART ONE
THE TIMES IN WHICH NIL SORSKIJ LIVED

I. A Nation in Flux   19
 A. Historical and Intellectual Development   19
 B. Monasticism of the Period   25

II. Biography of Nil   33

PART TWO
SPIRITUALITY OF NIL SORSKIJ

I. Ascetical Ideal   51
 A. Purpose of Life   51
 B. Divine Writings, Guide to Perfection   54
 C. Meaning of Divine Writings   56
 D. A Spiritual Guide, Stareč   62
 E. Self-Study and a Spirit of Criticism   63

II. The Way Back to God   73
 A. The Struggle for Self-Perfection: an Internal Battle   73
 B. Psychology of Thoughts   78
  1. Presentation of the Thought-Image   79
  2. Conversation of Intercourse with the Thought-Image . . .   80
  3. Acceptance   80
  4. Capitivity   81
  5. Passion   81

C. Analysis of the Eight Sources of Passions 83
    1. Gluttony 84
       a. Measure of Food 85
       b. Time of Food 86
       c. Various Foods 87
    2. Fornication 88
    3. Avarice 91
    4. Anger 92
    5. Sadness 94
    6. Acedia 95
    7. Vanity 97
    8. Pride 99

III. Hesychasm of Nil 103
  A. Hesychasm in General 103
  B. Purity of Heart and *Nepsis* of Nil 110
    1. Solitude and Silence 111
    2. Emptying of Thoughts: *Apostasis Noimaton* 113
    3. Hesychia 117
    4. Vigilance and Sobriety *(Nepsis)* and Observance of Commandments 118
  C. *Penthos* 124
    1. Thought of Death and Last Judgement 125
    2. Gift of Tears 127
       a. A Gift of God 127
       b. Necessity to Pray for This Gift 128
       c. Self-Activity as Preparation 130
       d. Effects of Tears 132
  D. The Jesus Prayer 134
    1. Means to Combat Thoughts and Gain Purity of Heart 136
    2. Preparation for Infused Contemplation 141
  E. Appraisal of Nil as Hesychast 144

IV. External Practices 149
  A. Obedience to the Rule 149
  B. Poverty 155
  C. Work 158
  D. Apostolate 161

V. Sources of Nil's Teaching 173
  A. The Fathers Quoted by Nil 174
  B. Question of the Texts Used by Nil 176

C. Dependency on His Sources 180
D. Independence in the Use of the Patristic Writings 193

VI. Influence of Nil on His Contemporaries 199

Epilogue 239

Appendix I: Letters of Nil Sorskij 245
    1. Letter to Vassian Patrikeev 245
    2. Letter to Gurij Tušn 249
    3. Letter to German Podol'nij 253
    4. Letter to Kassian Mavnukskij 256
    5. On the Remembrance of Death 262
    6. Excerpt: "There is no good which can please all men".. 263
    7. On the Proper Way to Examine Oneself 263
    8. How to Overcome Vanity 264
    9. On Overcoming Evil Thoughts 266
    10. Letter to a Brother in an Eastern Country 267

Appendix II: The Hesychastic Method 269

Sources 281

Particular Bibliography Dealing with Nil Sorskij 285

General Bibliography 289

Index 297

INTRODUCTION

In trying to describe the complexity termed vaguely "the Russian soul", various authors have stressed the extreme character of this Slavic people. Dostojevskij's theme of the Russian Christian finding God only through sorrow for a lifetime lived away from God in sin is familiar to us all. But if this extremism could lead the Russians to a life of *pecca fortiter*, climaxed by a poenitential return of the Prodigal Son, it could also lead them to a life of extreme dedication to God, even without the necessity of tasting sin by passing through Dostojevskian orgies.

Nil Sorskij will remain always in the annals of Russian hagiography as a perfect example of complete dedication to the all-important task, that of self-sanctification. His spirituality will remain a mystery, grossly impractical, unless one understands Nil's attitude of complete dedication to a lifetime of contemplation.

Never officially canonized by the Russian Church, he always was a favourite among the simple Russian Christians, as well as for the more contemplative-inclined monks; both groups found in his treatise on "mental activity" or his *Ustav* a unique source of spiritual richness. Yet his greatness lies not in that he put in writing an ideal common to one race of people and to none other, but rather lies precisely in the universality of that ideal. In the latter half of the 15th century when he composed his two main works, the *Predanie* and the *Ustav*, Russia's feudal appanages were dissolving and giving way to a united Moscow empire under Ivan III. Along with the building-up of a strong spirit of nationalism, there developed also a religious chauvinism, embodied finally in Philotheus' "Third Rome" doctrine. It was Nil's strong love for Apostolic tradition that made him insist on building his spirituality on the one, universal spirituality of Chrisianity, that flowing directly from the Gospels and Apostolic letters, and commented on and lived by the Holy Fathers of the Church through the early centuries. He avers over and over that his doctrine is not his own, but that his one Master is Jesus

Christ; that his doctrine is the same as the Holy Fathers' who passed on through the ages directly from the Apostles, the one, continuous Christian ideal. In this consists Nil Sorskij's true genius, that in a time of nascent nationalism, he rose above narrow, arbitrary boundaries and based his spiritual teaching on the universal doctrine of the Gospels as presented by the early Fathers. In this age of exaggerated subjectivism and novelty seeking, the ordinary Christian yearns for a spirituality that is timeless and universal. In this age of ecumenism Catholic, Orthodox and Protestant can find in the spirituality of Nil Sorskij the source of universal Christianity, going back to a common fount, the Holy Fathers, who developed their evangelical spirituality, not merely for the Orient or the Occident, for the Egyptians or Greeks or Syrians or Romans, but for all men made to the same image of the Father and redeemed by the same Christ, who remains ever the one Head of whose Body we are the members.

This present work is concerned primarily with the exposition of Nil's spirituality as he himself presents it in his writings. Besides his writings, not excessively numerous, we have practically no other sources from which to draw. Shortly after his death (1508), his biographies were burned by the Tartar hordes invading northern Russia in the 1530's and 1540's. The Sorskij hermitage that he founded handed down no living tradition except what he himself had written. This scarcity of biographical detail made it easy for later historians either to dismiss him with a few curt lines about his writings and his skete ideal or to stress to exaggeration certain points such as his attitude towards the Judaizer heretics or his uncompromising stand against monastic possessions; of times: a result of failing to distinguish the teaching and activities of his later disciples from his own. In the 1860's and 1870's Russian writers of history and literature began to investigate Nil Sorskij, but only too often their Slavophile tendencies predetermined their conclusions which they too easily found in his writings. N. M. Nikol'skij complained that the historians were much too concerned with Nil's social doctrine, especially his attitude towards monastic property which issue remained always for Nil secondary, while they forgot completely the main point of all Nil's writings – to trace the way of pure contemplation as the primary aim of the monastic life.[1]

In this period of a single century from 1860 until the present time there have appeared several short works about Nil, but most of the authors

[1]   *Istorija russkoj cerkvi* (Moscow, 1931), p. 107.

basically relied on A. Arxangel'skij's pioneer work.[2] But even in this first serious attempt at scholarly investigation of Nil and his writings, little space is devoted to formulating Nil Sorsky's spirituality of asceticism and mysticism. One promising student, George Levickij, in 1889 gave a report on the research that he was doing on Nil's writings and their patristic sources,[3] but unfortunately his work was never finished. M. S. Borovkova – Majkova published the one critical edition of the *Predanie* and the *Ustav*[4] which we use in this work for all citations made from these two works.

Outside of these works, the other shorter articles produced nothing original[5] and so it was felt that there was a need for an orderly presentation of Nil's spirituality, drawn so heavily from the Fathers of the Desert and the Sinaite school of spirituality. Our principal sources remain always Nil's *Predanie*, *Ustav* and the four main letters that we know for certain were written by him.

The *Predanie* and *Ustav* are sufficiently the same in all the mss. so we can be assured of a uniform reading. A scholarly treatment of these manuscripts would be impossible, not having these available in the West and, besides, M. S. Borovkova-Majkova already has done this masterfully in the introductory article to her critical edition. The two works, in the 100 mss. which she examined in 15 libraries in Moscow and St. Petersburg (c. 1912) remain as two separate works. Arxangel'skij seems to err in his supposition that the *Predanie* was a shortened form, a first edition of Nil's later *Ustav*.[6] The two compositions treat a matter completely different and serve different aims.

Nil's *Predanie*, numbering only nine pages in the critical edition, was written quite early,[7] and gives concrete rules and norms of practical

[2] "Nil Sorskij i Vassian Patrikeev, ix literaturnye trudy i idei v drevnej Rusi. Istoriko-literaturnyj očerk. Part I. Prepodobnyj Nil Sorskij", in *PDP*, no. 25 (St. Petersburg, 1882).

[3] "Otčet professorskogo stipendiata G. Levickago o zanjatijax v 1889–90 g." in *Xrist. Čtenie*, part 2–3 (1895), p. 288–345.

[4] "Nila Sorskago Predanie i Ustav s vstupitel'noj statej", in *PDP*, no. 179 (St. Petersburg, 1912).

[5] After I had finished writing this work, I was able to read the work of Dr. Fairy von Lilienfeld's doctoral dissertation: *Nil Sorskij und seine Schriften – Die Krise der Tradition im Russland Ivans III* (Berlin, 1963). She shows a high sense of scholarship and critical judgement; her work will prove to be for future historians what Arxangel'skij's work was for those of the 19th century. As her approach is mainly historical, the theological presentation of this present work still has relevance.

[6] *Op. cit.*, p. 53.

[7] The Soviet expert, J. S. Lur'e, says it was probably written before 1491. Cf: *Ideologičeskaja bor'ba v russkoj publicistike konca XV – načala XVI veka* (Moscow–Leningrad, 1960), p. 300.

conduct for his disciples of the Sorskij skete hermitage. Here Nil touches briefly on the necessity of following the evangelical tradition as handed down by the Holy Fathers, on the need for physical work, on absolute poverty, personal and communal, on obedience to the superior, on rules for eating and drinking and finally on rules of cloister.

The *Ustav*, though, so called by Nil's followers and meaning the "monastic rule", is really no rule at all. It is an ascetical treatise on "mental activity" or what we would call today on perpetual or continuous prayer. One has the impression of a work tremendously compact, with not a citation or a superfluous thought and only after several readings does the unity of the whole composition of less than one hundred pages appear in its full clarity. We can get a summary view of Nil's basic spirituality by looking at the contents of his work.

Introduction: From the Writings of the Holy Fathers on Mental Activity.

Chapters: 1. Of the various interior (mental) battles waged against us, of the victory and defeat and how one must diligently struggle against the passions.

2. Of our struggle against these mental temptations and how they are to be conquered by the thought of God, through guarding of the heart, that is to say, through prayer and interior tranquillity and how to perform these. Also on spirituality gifts.

3. How and by what means we are to be strengthened in repelling the attacks of mental temptations.

4. On the observation of the common rule in our monastery.

5. On the different ways we must fight and conquer the eight principal temptations of the flesh and others.

6. On all evil temptations in general.

7. On the remembrance of death and the Last Judgment, how to learn to keep these thoughts ever in our hearts.

8. On tears and how one should act who desires to obtain these.

9. On maintaining the spirit of tears.

10. On renunciation and true freedom from all cares which consists in dying to all things.

11. On the need to do all these things at their proper time and with becoming moderation and on prayer for these and other needs.

Nil's letters reveal a warmth and love for his fellow-men, flowing from an affectionate nature of a monk who had left the world in order to love God more and found true charity towards his fellow-men in his supernatural quest for God alone. Because these four main letters of Nil, hitherto have not been translated from any edited ms., I have done so and presented them in an English version in Appendix I.

I appended in English translation other compositions, as given in the Elagin 1846 St. Petersburg edition of Nil's *Ustav*, not because all of them were original compositions written by Nil, as the editor of this edition erroneously claims, but because some are disputed as rightfully belonging to Nil, while others, as M. S. Borovkova-Majkova clearly proves, were merely translations done by Nil.[8] Nevertheless, the fact that Nil did do translations of these works shows a kindred spirit with the thoughts therein contained. I have quoted also from Nil's last testament as presented in the cited critical edition of the other two main works. The other small excerpts attributed to Nil I have preferred to ignore for they offer us no special insight into Nil's spirituality.

I felt that as an introduction to Nil's spirituality a chapter on the times in which Nil lived plus one on the available data of his biography were necessary to appraise properly Nil's contribution to Russian spirituality and the general spiritual heritage of all Christians in all the world and of all times.

Many thanks are due to Mr. J. S. Lur'e, the Soviet's expert on Nil Sorskij and his period. I have profited greatly from his scholarship.

In 1969 I was given a grant as an exchange post-doctoral scholar by the International Research Exchange Board (IREX) to spend three months working in the Moscow Lenin Library and the Ščedrin-Saltykov Library of Leningrad. There I was able to work with the original manuscripts of Nil Sorskij's writings and other valuable sources not easily available in America. I wish to express my gratitude to Drs. A. Novickij, J. S.Lur'e and N. A. Kazakova who were most helpful in directing my research.

And his free access to the manuscripts now found in Moscow and Leningrad. Thanks are due to Dr. Lilienfeld, especially for her encouragement and advice given over long months of correspondence. And finally,

---

[8] As is Letter V, Appendix I, on the remembrance of death. This is a translation done by Nil Sorskij of Nil Sinaite's work to Archimandrite Nikon. Cf: Migne, *PG*, 79, 437. M. S. Borovkova-Majkova: "K literaturnoj dejatel'nosti Nila Sorskago", in *PDP*, CLXXVII (1911).

deepest thanks to my Professors of Oriental Spirituality, Fr. Irenaus Hausherr, S. J., and Fr. Thomas Spidlik, S. J., both for their lectures and their writings which, if not always directly acknowledged, implicitly form the basis of this work.

Fordham University, New York
April 1, 1971

ABBREVIATIONS USED

AAE	*Akty Arxeografičeskoj Komissii.*
AI	*Akty Istoričeskie.*
BV	*Bogoslovskij Vestnik.*
Xrist. Čtenie	*Xristianskoje Čtenie.*
Čtenia	*Čtenia v Obščestve Istorii i Drevnosti pri Moskovskom Univ.*
Dict. A. L.	*Dictionnaire d' Archéologie et de Liturgie.*
Dict. Sp. A. M.	*Dictionnaire de Spiritualité, d'Ascése et de Mystique.*
DTC	*Dictionnaire de Théologie Catholique.*
DRB	*Drevne rossijskaja Biblioteka*
È. d'Or.	*Èchos d'Orient.*
Elagin Ed.	*Prepodobnyj Nil Sorskij, pervoosnovatel' skitskago zitija v Rossii i Ustav ego o zitel'stve skitskom* (St. Petersburg, 1864).
IRI	*Istorija rossijskoj Ierarchii sobrannaja byvšim novgorodskoj Seminarii prefektom Ep. Amvrosiem* (Moscow).
Istor. V.	*Istoričeskij Vestnik.*
Izd. OLDP	*Izdanije Obščestva ljubitelej drevnej pis'mennosti.*
Jbb. GO	*Jahrbucher für Geschichte Osteuropas* (München).
NRT	*Nouvelle Revue Théologique.*
OC	*Orientalia Christiana,* Pontificium Institutum Orientale.
OCA	*Orientalia Christiana Analecta,* Pontificium Institutum Or.
OCP	*Orientalia Christiana Periodica,* Pontificium Institutum Or.

PDP	*Pamjatniki drevnej pis'mennosti.*
PG	Patrologiae cursus completus, *Series graeca,* ed. Migne.
PL	Patrologiae cursus completus, *Series Latina,* ed. Migne.
Prav. Sob.	*Pravoslavnyj Sobesednik.*
Prib. k Tvor.	*Pribavlenija k Tvorenijam Svjatyx Otcev v russkom perevode.*
PSRL	*Polnoe sobranie russkix letopisej.*
RAM	*Revue d'ascétique et de mystique.*
RÉS	*Revue des Études Slaves.*
RHE	*Revue d'Histoire Ecclésiastique.*
RIB	*Russkaja istoričeskaja biblioteka.*
ROC	*Revue d'Orient Chrétien.*
SGGD	*Sobranie Gosudarstvennyx Gramot.*
TODL	*Trudy Otdela drevnerusskoj literatury, Akademii Nauk.*
Velik. Chet'i-Minei	*Velikija Chet'i-Minei,* izd. Arxeografičeskoj Komissii.
Vie Sp.	*La Vie Spirituelle.*
Zeitschr f. Kirch.	*Zeitschrift für Kirchengeschichte.*
Zeitschr. f. S.	*Zeitschrift für Slawistik.*
Z. M. N. Pr.	*Zurnal ministerstva narodnago prosvesčenija.*
Z. M. P.	*Zurnal moskovskoj Patriarxii.*

PART ONE

THE TIMES IN WHICH NIL SORSKIJ LIVED

I

A NATION IN FLUX

A. HISTORICAL AND INTELLECTUAL DEVELOPMENT

The age in which Nil Sorskij lived, the latter half of the 15th and the beginning of the 16th century, was one of unquiet ferment. The Russia of this time seemed like a sleeping giant awaking and slowly wiping away the stupor of centuries of heavy sleep. It was gradually realizing its potentialities under the strong autocratic rule of the Moscow Princes. In 1480 Khan Akhmad redrew his Golden Horde from the banks of the Ugra River and Mongol domination was officially terminated. Under the Mongols, Russia had been split up into numerous little princedoms ruled by feudal princes. The end of the 15th century saw the emergence of the first central autocratic state, drawn together out of the various princedoms. It was no sudden change or revolution but a gradual engulfing of the private holdings of the petty princes and boyars by the Grand Prince. Nor was the process a peaceful one, altogether desired by all, especially by the aristocrats. Through years of violence and intrigue, one by one the smaller kingdoms were swallowed up, leaving the alternative of a resettlement near the favour of the Grand Prince at Moscow or flight into Lithuania. The boyars looked on their new rulers as "ruined capitalists look on the sons of a fortunate magnate into whose hands their ancestral wealth has passed".[1]

The noble class which always looked upon the Church for support now saw the Church backing solidly the autocratic Grand Prince and saw it encouraging and blessing him even in his most doubtful deeds. In 1453 Byzantium was conquered by the Turks. The Second Rome had fallen just five years after it made its reconciliation with the First Rome in the Florence Council. Having learned well its lesson from its mentor, especially in relations with the State, the Russian Church did not hesitate to submit to the power of Muscovite absolutism and it threw its influence to support the ambitions of the Grand Prince. This could not but have

[1] V. O. Ključevskij, *Bojarskaja duma drevnej Rusi* (St. Petersburg, 1919), p. 270.

caused much dissent in its ranks, along with a seething reaction against the religious formulas and ritualisms that were growing up in this time and displacing genuine religious piety.

Under the tight reign of Ivan III and Vasily III, the Muscovite State continually pushed its frontiers farther. Against this political background of violent evolution into an autocratic state, the religious-intellectual development presents a tragic picture. There were no schools organized, not even of the most elementary type. There is no early document that indicates their existence. Any information mentions only private teachers, but no school-organizations.[2] Archbishop Gennadij of Novgorod writes to the Metropolitan Simon in Moscow (1495–1511) about the utter ignorance, illiteracy of his priests: "I respect the Ruler for that, that he has ordered schools to be built; by his intelligence and threats and your blessing, the matter has been improved. You should, our reverend Lord and Father, ask our noble princes to build a school. My advice on such should be one in which are taught the abc's and then a school for teaching the reading of the psalter. If they learn this much, they can read all books."[3] His words were not heeded apparently for we find some 50 years later in the famous Council of 100 Chapters *(Stoglav)* the assembled fathers complaining: "They teach students reading in a stupid manner."[4] "Candidates for the diaconate and priesthood are not able to read... When bishops ask candidates for orders why they cannot read, they give as answer: 'We learn from our fathers or from our masters and there is nowhere to go to learn more; as much as our fathers and masters know, so much they teach us...' But their fathers and masters know very little, especially do not know well Divine Scripture, for they never learned themselves."[5]

Thus the parish priests were the means to influence the religious-intellectual level of the society but that they were incapable of fulfilling their charge is only too evident. *Stoglav* paints the picture of contemporary priests "Priests and other church officers are always drunk and stand without fear and quarrel and every sort of speech pours from their mouths. Priests in church fight among themselves."[6] The Council orders that priests and deacons are not to be drunk when they come to the church of God and, while singing, they should stand orderly and not

[2] Golubinskij, E. *Istorija russkoj cerkvi*, 2nd ed. (Moscow, 1901), I, 1, p. 721.
[3] *AI*, I (St. Petersburg, 1841), no. 104, p. 147.
[4] *Stoglav*, 3rd ed. (Kazan, 1911), ch. 5, q. 6, p. 27.
[5] *Ibid.*, ch. 25, p. 59.
[6] *Ibid.*, ch. 5, q. 22, p. 33.

"beat and fight among themselves and use bad language, and not beat, even to the shedding of blood".[7]

Metropolitan Daniil summarizes this situation among the parish priests of his time (1523–1539): "All of our pastors, not only village, but also city priests, are hardly literate, not educated very much and in general quite ignorant... They do not understand what is necessary to be done, neither the faith which they have to teach people, nor even the holy functions. On the other hand, they are people generally poor, dreadfully in need, always dependent on their parishoners... What could be expected from such pastors?"[8]

It has often been said that the Divine Liturgy as transported from Byzantium became the book for the common person in Russia. Here in colourful pageantry he was supposed to have seen the mysteries of his faith re-enacted. Readings from the Old and New Testaments were supposed to have been his daily food. In the church Services he was to have learned the Christian ethics and his obligation to his fellow-men. Golubinskij asserts: "Divine Services in church were not for learning the faith by the ignorant, but for building it up in the already-knowers; it is not meant to be a preparation of the people or a beginning of their instruction in Christianity. It on the contrary demands excellent preparation and scientific fore-knowledge."[9]

The actual performance of church Services was far from the reported standard of Vladimir's legates to Byzantium where they avowed that they did not know, while assisting at the Byzantine Liturgy, whether they were "in Heaven or on earth".[10] Metropolitan Photius wrote to the priests of Pskov in 1428: "Some of you live on deceiving the people, you scandalize them in church with your carelessness ... you do not even consider or realize simply that your churches are the temples of God."[11]

[7] *Ibid.*, ch. 29, p. 62.
[8] Makarij (Bulgakov), *Istorija russkoj cerkvi*, 3rd ed. (Moscow), T. VIII, p. 337.
[9] Golubinskij E., *op. cit.*, T. I, 1, p. 740. He adds significantly: "The only school for the illiterate masses for us was the Church and its services. Our masses had decided advantages of having the services in their own language. But here we must make some pertinent remarks. Our liturgical language was not our own Russian language, but was the Bulgarian language. True, it was close to ours, but it was not understood by the masses, but only by the learned, as happens today... Christians in the West like the Germans knew that Latin was not their own and therefore were forced to study the Mass intelligently."
[10] Cf. D. S. Lixačev, *Provest' vremennyx let*, I, Academy of Sciences (Moscow, 1950), p. 274.
[11] *Pamjatniki drevne russkago kanoničeskago prava*, 2nd ed. found in *Russkaja istoričeskaja biblioteka*, T. I, no. 58, col. 494–496 (St. Petersburg, 1906–8).

We have already seen above the reprimands expressed by *Stoglav* at the drunkenness of priests and deacons in church and their quarrels, even unto blood. It adds about the laity: "They stand with no fear in their heavy boots and caps on their heads and sticks in their hands, as though they were in the market place ... and they talk and argue and speak about everything."[12] Not pressing further about the worthiness of conducting services, the Council goes on to complain that priests are negligent and lazy, some celebrating only every five or six weeks, even every half year, some once a year, on the feast of the church, although they "receive annual salary, money from molebens, panachidae, feasts, wheat for prosphora, wax for candles..."[13]

Metropolitan Alexis (1354–1378) complained about the coldness on the part of the laity towards church Services: "Be visitors, participators at church Services. Do not say, we sing ourselves at home. Such prayer cannot have any profit without church prayer..."[14]

Due to almost universal illiteracy, religion became for the masses a list of external rituals. This exteriorisation of religion appears early, already in the 11th and 12th centuries. The tendency to stress the ritual side of religion is common to any semi-barbarian society. We must never forget that Christianity was imported to Russia from Byzantium and Bulgaria by foreign priests and bishops and it was enforced by mass conversions on to the people by the ruling princes. Russia did not receive together with Christianity the classical culture of Byzantium. There was no need to teach the Russians Greek in order to give them the riches of the Byzantine rite. "Men of the West, barbarians, knew Latin and the Latin culture. The Slavs, converted by the Greeks, had no need for their Greek language, for they had the Bible and church Services in Slavonic translations. From a Slavonic library, Russia was spiritually fed. Upon this store of learning mostly from Bulgaria, Russia lived for centuries. The Slavonic literature had an overwhelmingly practical and didactic character. Theoretical interests were not awakened. The Russian intellect dwarfed in its development because of the absence of external occasions for exercise."[15]

Rules about when one fasts, what kinds of foods were permissible on what days designated as fast days, how many bows, whether waisthigh or to the ground were for the majority more understandable and intelli-

---

[12] *Stoglav*, ch. 5, q. 21, p. 33.
[13] *Ibid.*, ch. 5, q. 30, p. 35.
[14] Makarij, *op. cit.*, T. V., p. 161.
[15] Fedotov, G., *The Russian Religious Mind* (Harvard, 1947), p. 38.

gible. Already in the 15th century there were formulated the ideas of what made up "the ancient piety".[16] *Pravila* and *ustavy* written by founders of monasteries or members of the hierarchy attempted to formulate in writing the moral duties of Christians.[17] "Going on horseback, can one sing something spiritual? Can a wife of a priest bless him with her hand? Can one eat meat on the feast of the Exaltation of the Cross? In fasting time, a baby must not take cow's milk; in the second fast, not from the mother, and in the third nothing at all, neither from the mother, nor from cow. One should not sit with legs crossed in time of fasting. If a priest wants to celebrate, he must not eat onions for an entire day."[18]

Joseph Volokolamsk, a contemporary of Nil Sorskij, specified in his rule so many prostrations for the illiterate as so many arithmetical computations equaling so many read prayers of *kathismata*[19] or matins or from the hours. The force of prayer was measured by whole years, and the faithful could store up a supply for future time. One certain prayer given by Joseph equaled 300 prostrations a day. Naturally, such a prayer would be considered a great obligation, which, Joseph says, is relieved on feast days.[20]

It became universally understood that others could substitute in the doing of penance and propitiation for one's personal sins. Ten liturgies equaled penance done for four months, twenty for eight months and thirty for a whole year of penance. Monasteries became computing machines in determining how many liturgies, how many alms offered would equal how much God-pleasing penance. Not only for expiation penances for the sins of a person living, but to wipe away all unforgiven sins after death, required a "tax" to be paid in money or in immovable goods and the monastery complied with prayers said for the dead.

The benefices or donations consisted in arranging security or guarantee of post-death prayers for sins and the soul's salvation. Catechisms in explaining the eleven parts of the symbol of faith taught that prayers said for a soul were

---

[16] Makarij, *op. cit.*, T. VIII, p. 334, as outlined in the Sobornik of Metropolitan Daniel.

[17] *Ibid.*, T. III, p. 224–237.

[18] Cf. A. Arxangel'skij, *Nil Sorskij i Vassian Patrikeev ix literaturnye trudy i idei v drevnej Rusi*, Part I. (St. Petersburg, 1882), p. 221.

[19] The psalter is divided into 20 *kathismata;* each *kathisma* enduring approximately the same length of time, although having shorter or longer psalms. The word is derived from the Greek meaning to sit down.

[20] Cited by B. Grečev, "Nil Sorskij i zavolžskie starcy" in *Bogoslovskij Vestnik*, 1907, no. 2, p. 503, "Poslanija iosifovi ob epitimijax". Cf. S. Smirnov, *Drevne russkij duxovnik* (Sergiev-Posad, 1899), Append. VI, p. 109.

effective for the salvation of that one who did not fulfill the complete atonement for sins in this life, especially when these prayers were united with the unbloody Sacrifice of the altar... Thus the monasteries took on a very special function, to pray for others, especially for the dead. Various gifts were given at first. Then "deposits" for the deceased and benefices for perpetual remembrance. It soon became the norm, that, out of the property of the deceased, so much was reserved for the remembrance of his soul, even though he left no such mention.[21]

Joseph Volokolamsk, in a now famous letter to the widowed Princess Gočenin, recalls this system of remembered benefices. The princess in the course of fifteen years had given to Joseph's monastery for her father, husband, and two sons a great sum of money and thus she felt entitled to some special remembrance over and above a mere general one. She had been answered that a very special eternal remembrance would be a very special, costly benefice, much more than she had given. She condemns the practice as robbery and Joseph takes her to task for her inept use of the word and explains in great detail that for years her deceased ones were being remembered in the general requiem service *(panachida)* and in the daily Liturgy six times a day and that it would be impossible to sing in one day any more *Panachida* Services and celebrate more Liturgies.[22]

Amidst all this darkness of illiteracy there was a genuine cry for knowledge, at least for the ability to read. Reading books meant speaking with God and the holy Saints.[23] So there developed a reverence for the written word which was affectionately copied out by hand and passed on. Very little critical spirit in accepting and rejecting the good from the false was found among the masses. Legends and apocryphal writings often held the same authority as the Gospels. It was only in the 16th century that we find in Russia a canon of Bible books. Sokol'skij gives what could be a typical ancient Russian Bible canon. In the beginning the first Bible books included Genesis to Proverbs; then selections from Wisdom of Solomon; then sections of a chronology in which we read of the life and acts of Alexander the Great, king of Macedonia, climaxed by an apocryphal vision of a specious prophet Daniel. Other excerpts from a

---

[21] Ključevskij, V. O., *Kurs russkoj istorii* (St. Petersburg, 1918), T. II, pp. 331–332.
[22] Xruščov, Ivan P., *Issledovanie o sočinenijax Iosifa Sanina* (St. Petersburg, 1868), p. 98, and in Append., p. 488, Poslanie Josifa Volockago knjagine Marii vodove Kn. A. ф Godenina.
[23] "O čtenii knig v drevnija v vremena Rossii", in *Prav. Sob.*, 1858, II, pp. 173–198, 443–461.

paterikon[24] quotes from a sermon of John Chrysostom, and finally the Apolcalypse of St. John the Evangelist in full.[25] Thus there were woven into truly inspired writings much of the popular apocryphal writings, lowering the true knowledge that was available to the level of popular legend.[26]

B. MONASTICISM OF THE PERIOD

The first monks that came from Byzantium and Bulgaria brought with them the tradition embedded in centuries of Oriental Christianity that there was only one way of being sure to save one's soul: lead a monastic life. He who would take Our Lord's command seriously about becoming perfect as the Heavenly Father is perfect must strive to attain this through intimate union with God through perpetual prayer as St. Paul enjoined the Thessalonians[27] who were not monks. But the conviction was accepted universally that to do this meant separation from the world and the things of the world, to embrace solitude. The great masters of the spiritual life in the Orient were always monks who identified their monastic spirituality with that of Christianity. For St. Gregory of Nyssa, a Christian, not a monk, is one who strives to imitate the Divine nature.[28] The aim and the means are the same for all. "The Holy Scripture knows nothing of such a division (i.e. between a spirituality for monks and another one for laity). It wishes that all lead the life of monks, even if they are married."[29] So it would be only natural to expect this high esteem for monasticism in a newly christianized country such as Russia. Without a doubt the 15th century marks the high point of Russian asceticism[30] and

---

[24] *Pateriki* were various narrations from the lives of ancient ascetics containing sayings called from their writings and from those of the Holy Fathers and from the lives of the Saints. The most famous one dealing with the Russian Saints is the Kievo–Peskijer × the Saints. The most famous one dealing with the Russian Saints is the Kievo–Pečerskij Paterikon composed by the monk Polikarp and Bishop Simon of Vladimir in the 13th century.

[25] "Izučenie i upotreblenie biblii v Rossii" in *Prav. Obosr.*, 1868, no. 11, pp. 268–269.

[26] Golubinskij, *op. cit.*, T. II, p. 299, gives a bibliography of the chief apocryphal writings common in Russia at this period.

[27] I Thess. 5, 17.

[28] Migne, *PG*, V. 46, col. 244, St. Greg. Nyssa.

[29] St. John Chrysostom, "Adv. Oppugn. vitae monasticae" I, III, 15, *PG*, 47, col. 372. He says: "In Matt. Hom. VII" ... "All the precepts of the law are common to all of us as with the monks, with one exception, that of celibacy."

[30] Smolitsch, Igor, "Das altrussische Mönchtum (11–16. Jahrhundert)", in *Das östliche Christentum*, (Würzburg, 1940), p. 63.

the confirming once and for all of the spiritual asceticism of monasticism as the ideal for all, including the laity.

But in the 14th–15th centuries for the masses that entered monasteries[31] there were other motives activating them to leave the world. At the end of the 15th century, 1492 precisely, the conviction throughout all Russia was firmly held that the world would then end.[32] This had been worked out by mathematical calculations based on an apocryphal legend that put the end of the world at 7,000 years after the creation of the universe.

The social conditions of the times favoured the withdrawal to the security that the monastery walls gave. Almost continual bloodshed through Mongol invasions and the struggles between the smaller princes and the Grand Prince of Moscow made human life a cheap commodity. Solovjev reckons in the north-eastern part of Russia between 1228 and 1462 there were 90 internal and 160 external wars.[33] Force from the powerful, cunning treachery from the weak, and dishonesty among all created insecurity in society. In such insecure times the people hid their treasures under ground and in holy buildings, and for eternal salvation many felt their spiritual treasures had need of refuge in remote forests and caves.

Added to these social turmoils was a continuous series of physical hardships inflicted on the Russia of the 15th century. Solovjev claims that never did it seem that the Russian people suffered to such a degree as it did in that century. Catastrophes continually occurred. He quotes from the *letopisi* or ancient chronicles of the times:

In 1402 a plague in Smolensk; in 1403 one in Pskov; repeated in 1406. In the following years, a 'winged worm flew from the east to the west, eating up woods, trees and drying them up'. In 1409 in some places multitudes of people died from hunger; in others a pestilent epidemic of bloodspitting... In 1418: famine in all of Russia... It notes that in Novgorod for 10 years there was a famine and wheat shortage; there 'was a tremendous suffering and there was heard only weeping and wailing on the streets and in the market; many fell dead from hunger, children before parents, parents before children'.[34] To the security of monastic life the masses fled.[35]

---

[31] "Drevnija pustyni i pustynnožiteli na severo-vostoke Rossii", in *Prav. Sob.*, 1860, III, p. 202. Cf. also: Makarij, *op. cit.*, T. IV, p. 163.

[32] Ševyrev, V. P., *Istorija Russkoj slovesnosti* (Moscow, 1860), T. IV, p. 109. Cf. Tixonravov, N. S., *Sočinenija*, T. I, (Moscow, 1898), pp. 228–242.

[33] Solovijev, S. M., *Istorija Rossii*, 2nd ed. (St. Petersburg, 1894–1897), T. IV, ch. 3, col. 1218.

[34] *Ibid.*, col. 1219–1220.

[35] Aristov, Feod., "Nevol'noe i neknotnoe postriženie v monašestvo i našix predkov", in *Drevn. i Nov. Rossia*, 1878, VI, p. 142.

One must also remember that the only literature available to the Russians at the time was that of an ascetical nature. Practically all of the ancient literature found in Russia between the 11th to the 15th centuries is of a translated nature from southern Slavic countries through Slavonic translations.[36] For those who knew how to read, selections from the Fathers, from the various *Pateriki*, Lives of the Saints and Sayings of the Martyrs were the sole source of literature. A simple example of the history of Varlaam and Ioasaf carevič, founded on the idealization of the hermit life, translated into Slavonic and brought into Russia, had such popularity that it came down in folk-poetry in verses about Asaf carevič and in general of praise for the monastic life. People read some each day, learned verses by heart, which entered into their views and convictions and were expressed in their practical activities by establishing and spreading of monastic hermitages in unpopulated areas of Russia.[37]

It is no great wonder therefore that the Russian people formed the spiritual ideal of being transformed into that of angels, for their literary tradition emphasized strongly the ascetical side of life and the traditions of the great ascetics and their accomplishments were feats to be imitated by all.[38] Along with the canonization of monastic life among the majority of people, there went a conviction of the world and all that is found in it as seditious and evil. The ascetical tracts certainly painted the world in its worst colours, but what added peculiar strength to this conviction was the belief of the imminence of the end of the world and the widespreadth of mystical apocalypses.[39] With their thoughts so often centred on the destruction of this present world, the monastic life held out special appeal as the best preparation for the Heavenly Jerusalem.

As the monasteries of this period were the only centre of intense moral and intellectual life, it was only natural that also very noble and talented persons embraced the life.[40] Many "Lives" of the early Russian Saints mention that they left the world when quite young, during their years

[36] Ikonnikov, V., *Opyt issledovanija o kul'turnom značenii Vizantii v russkoj istorii* (Kiev, 1869), pp. 60–62. He gives a list of the Oriental ascetical writers who were translated into Slavonic and thus brought into Russia through Bulgaria and Serbia.
[37] Buslaev, ф. I., *Istoričeskie očerki russk. narod. slovesn. i iskusst.*, 4th ed. (Moscow, 1888), II. pp. 231–232.
[38] Cf. Nikol'skij, Nikolaj, *Materialya dlja povremennago spiska russkix pisatelej i ix sočinenij* (St. Petersburg, 1906), pp. 577–596. Also Sobolevskij, A. I., *Perevodnaja literatura moskovskoj Rusi XIV–XVII vv.* (St. Petersburg, 1903), pp. 9–13.
[39] Ščapov, *Russkij raskol staroobrjadstva* (Kazan', 1859), pp. 156–162.
[40] Ikonnikov, *op. cit.*, p. 120, gives a detailed list of some of the leading noble families from which came outstanding Russian ascetics. Included is Nil Sorskij from the noble family of Majkov.

of training, no doubt under the influence of ascetical literature. Here in the monasteries were found the only existing collection of books outside the royal libraries. The monks had to learn to read in order to read Holy Scriptures and the Fathers. They were at first occupied with books, copying, binding, painting them. But we must not think of these libraries as containing large numbers of books. In the middle of the 17th century during the *raskol* there was a call for the oldest Slavonic manuscripts.[41] Out of the 39 oldest monastery libraries there were collected only 2,673. In many places, especially large cities, there was a shortage of books. When Archbishop Gennadiij of Novgorod wanted to consult a complete Bible in his crusade against the heretical Judaizers, he had to send out a circular to the monasteries of Belozer, Ferapont and Spasov-Kamen'-. Prince Kurbskij complained that there was a great shortage of books and good translations and that the best and most ancient translations were kept in monastery vaults.[42] Six of the most eminent libraries were found in the monasteries of Troica-Sergiev, Čudov, Kirill-Belozerov, Rostov, Solovec and Volokolamsk. It is interesting to note that of these 2,673 ancient Slavonic manuscripts, 1,000 are devoted to pure asceticism.[43]

Another factor explaining the rush to monasteries is that of enforced tonsuring. Boyars who proved to be a bother to the Grand Prince were silenced by forcing upon them monastic vows and sealing them off in a monastery. Naturally these nobles did not always put off their worldly habits of thinking and living and could not but look upon more sincere monks of more humble background with haughty disdain and treat them as their servants.[44]

With all these various factors contributing, the spread of monasteries in northern Russia in the 14th and 15th centuries remains always a unique phenomenon is the history of Christian asceticism. Ključevskij gives some interesting facts to illustrate this phenomenon.[45] Of the 20 monasteries known up to the 12th century, only four of them were found in northern Russia. Of 50 new ones in the 12th century, only 2 are in the south.

---

[41] Makarij, B., "Kritičeskij očerk istorii russkago raskola izvestnago pod imenem
[42] "Poslanie Kurbskago", in *Prav. Sob.*, 1863, June, p. 571.
[43] Ikonnikov, *op. cit.*, p. 233.
[44] A typical case of enforced tonsure was that of Prince Vassian Patrikeev, Nil Sorskij's most famous disciple, who however seemed to have found a true monastic vocation under Nil's guidance. Vassian was found supporting, along with his father and Prince Rjapolovskij, the party of Ivan III's daughter-in-law Helen and her son Dimitrij when Ivan III changed favourites. Rjapolovskij was executed but father and son Patrikeev were forced to be tonsured.
[45] Ključevskij, *op. cit.*, p. 302 and ss.

Novgorod quickly took over from Kiev as the centre of monasticism. Many cities where before there was no prince, now had one and he felt it his Christian duty to decorate his city-residence with at least one monastery. Such a centre was not considered well-planned if it did not have a monastery and a cathedral.

But in the 14th century there begins an important change in the way of spreading monasteries, especially in the north. Up to then, nearly all of them, either in the south or north, were built in cities or in their neighbourhood. Perhaps due to frequent Mongol raids, prudence dictated such precaution. In the 14th century a movement began to move into wooded areas, both as protection from warring parties and as "deserts" of solitude. In this century we find 42 "desert" monasteries to the 42 new city monasteries. But in the 15th century, almost two times as many are founded in forests than in the inhabited areas, and in the 16th century one and a half times as many. In these three centuries in the province of Moscow there were founded 150 desert monasteries to 104 founded in cities or near them.

This movement did more than any other social phenomenon to colonize the vast woods of the North. A founder of a city-monastery would flee into solitude from the world. His strictness of life, fame as an ascetic would attract followers and benefactors. Peasants also settled around the monastery. Soon there arose a large, rich and noisy monastery and the true disciple of the teacher breaks away and founds a new hermitage. Thus a wide colonization movement was launched which in four centuries penetrated every corner of middle and northern Russia.

Thus there developed three types of monasticism; the coenobitic or community life, a strictly hermitical life, and that of the *skit* or skete type. This latter type often was the precursor for the coenobitic life. Two or three monks would live together; others would be attracted and soon a large monastery developed. Oftentimes in order to be faithful to the religious practices and ascetical ideals the founder of such coenobitic monasteries asked aid from the prince in terms of property and money. The system of benefices already described grew up as a source of livelihood. Hardly a prince died without first receiving the tonsure, and this often a few hours before his death.[46] Large benefices in landed property with peasants to work the land, fell into the hands of these monasteries.

---

[46] Karamzin, Nikolaj M., *Istorija Gos. Ross.*, 5th ed. (St. Petersburg, 1842), T. VIII, p. 104.

And in short time Russian monasticism was faced with dire consequences. Now monks were occupied in controlling the huge estates of land, entire villages with hundreds and thousands peasants working for them. Hermits who fled the world were now more than ever caught up with the world. Humility and obedience were difficult to practise in running such huge corporations. But the greatest source of scandal for the average Russian Christian was in the violation of the monk's vow of poverty. The monks tried to justify themselves by saying that the riches of the Church were the riches of the poor. Undoubtedly many monasteries really did help the poor and were the only social service-units to take care of the sick and aged. The Kirillo-Belozerskij monastery in time of one famine daily fed 600 men until the next harvest. Joseph Volokolamsk was supposed to have fed 600–700 hungry in his monastery each day.[47] 70,000 people were fed in one famine. Women threw their babies at his monastery door.

But for many monks and many monasteries, the ascetical life was often forgotten under the groaning dining tables. In one of Joseph's monasteries, in the first half of the 16th century, 51 days in the year were given over to feasts in honour of wealthy benefactors. In the Soloveckij monastery there were 191 feast days. And the menus were worked out with care as to what to eat and drink, the quantity and the quality.

The vices and classical ignorance of the secular clergy never called out such glaring dissatisfaction as appeared towards monks in serious protests against their defection from monastic ideals through excess riches. It was difficult for lay persons to reconcile the security of the monk and his poverty, his cutting himself off from the world and then his increased activity in managing the affairs of whole villages, difficult to reconcile the monk's vow of obedience with his unquenchable striving for power. In a period of awakening of popular self-consciousness, these contradictions put leaders of Russian society on the road to departure from the visible Church.

These are some of the many factors explaining the rapid growth in Russian monasticism in the 14th–15th centuries. Perhaps the greater part of the mass of monks did not exactly feel inclined to the hard demands of monasticism. And this led to rapid downfall, to bitter resentment among the people which culminated in various heresies and break-

---

[47] Cf. Ključevskij, V. O., *Kurs...*, *op. cit.*, T. II, p. 338.

aways from the official Church. But among the chaff that filtered into the monasteries of this time, there were found some few precious seeds of wheat which died to self and produced a hundred fold. These great *podvizhniki* or ascetics remained true to the ascetical ideal that they inherited from the Eastern Fathers and amidst much monastic corruption; perpetuated the true spirituality that alone can be worthy of the term often used to express the finest in Russian spirituality, "the Russian Soul". Among these great ascetics must be placed Nil Sorskij.

II

BIOGRAPHY OF NIL

Of all the saintly personalities who passed through early Russian history, leaving their imprint on posterity, Nil Sorskij is one about whose personal biography we know the least. Nil has been remembered by historians through his writings, especially his Rule, and by chance remarks handed down by tradition. Therefore to assemble the small pieces into a full and exact narrative of his life would be impossible. We can, however, piece together the main events of his life and through his writings gather a fairly concrete image of the man.

We know that he was born in 1433 and died in 1508. According to a legend there were Lives written of him up until 1538 when the chronicle reports a conflagration by the "Kazan' people",[1] meaning here the Golden Horde. But one cannot be quite certain, in view of the historical developments with the eventual victory of the Josephites under Metropolitan Daniil with the condemnation of the Trans-Volga hermits, whether the *žitie* of Nil too was not put to the flames by the opposition.[2]

Nil for centuries has stirred up interest in his personality and his ideas. Even after 300 years, his *Ustav* ("Rule") and letters are found being copied and spread all over Russia, reaching even the Novonjametskij Monastery in Moldavia where Paisij Veličkovskij did much to propagate Nil's ideas. The first printed edition of his *Ustav* took place in 1813 by Bishop Amvrosij,[3] then repeated from other manuscripts by Optyna and

---

[1] Barsukov, N., *Istočniki russkoj agiographii* (St. Petersburg, 1882), col. 406–407. Cf. also Konoplev, "Svjatye vologodskago kraja", in C*tenie imper. obšč. ist. i drev. russ.*, Moscow, 1895, p. 76.

[2] Cf.: "Pis'mo o neljubkax starcev Kirillova...", *op. cit.*, p. 508, where it is hinted that Joseph burned Kirill's monastery after removing all piety from there.

[3] *IRI*, T. V (Moscow, 1813). Cf. "Nila Sorskago Predanie i Ustav" and the introductory article by M. S. Borovkova-Majkova, St. Petersburg, 1912. This can be found as a separate work or as it first appeared in *Pamjatniki drevnej pis'mennosti i iskusstva*, CLXXIX (1913), p. 3 and ss. N.B. all citations from Nil's *Predanie* and *Ustav* will be made from this critical Slavonic text, without doubt, the most scientific which has the advantage of offering variant readings from all prior editions and practically 100 ma-

the Holy Synod. At the end of the first half and especially of the second half of the 19th century, there appeared much scientific literature dealing with Russian monasteries and their leading representatives and their relation to various social-religious questions in the 16th century.[4] Always a few words were devoted to Nil, recalling him or giving general information, but sometimes even devoting whole articles to him. About 200 manuscripts from the 16th to the 19th centuries contain his *Ustav* and letters. More than 30 authors either recall in general or in particular that in Nil's compositions there is to be found something that is different from the ordinary monastic writing and that they opened up a new beginning in ascetical writing in Russia. But unfortunately the mass of manuscripts are practically deprived of biographical data. The only manuscript giving the most detailed information about Nil is one found in Moscow dating from the 17th century.[5] We read:

> ...this saintly Father, our Nil, whose parents, who they were, or in what city he was born or in what year he left the world (to be tonsured), we do not know for sure. But we have received something about this from hearsay, that he was born and educated in the Tsar's city of Moscow and there also studied; he received the monk's habit in the Lavra of Kirillo-Belozerskij and from there travelled to Constantinople, then to Mount Athos. He then returned to Russia and came under divine guidance to the Sorskij hermitage. And living here some time, pleasing the Lord God with fasting and prayers and struggling against all evils, this holy starec, the blessed Father, our Nil, fell into eternal sleep in the Lord in the year 7017, Nay the 7th. And from here with the good. pleasure of God and the prayers of St. Nil, in this hermitage of Sorkij there grew up the skit monastery according to the *Ustav* and tradition of the Holy Ancient Fathers.

---

nuscripts consulted. The history of the manuscripts and editions need not detain us, for the reader can find a complete summary given in this work of Borovkova-Majkova, pp. I–III. Cf. also A. Arxangel'skij, *op. cit.*, pp. IV–XII and throughout the entire work.

[4] Cf. the interesting but necessarily biased remarks of the Soviet historian, J. S. Lur'e, in his "K voprosu ob ideologii Nila Sorskogo", Academy of Science USSR, *TODL (Trudy Otdela drevnerusskoj literatury)*, T. XIII (1957), pp. 182–183: "Up to the 1860's no historian bothered about Nil. He was considered "the great ascetic", the "man of spiritual power", but then the liberal slavophil historians of the 1860's and 1870's put Nil on a new soil. They saw in him their historical predecessor. In their eagerness to free the peasants to court reforms and others of a bourgeois nature, they appealed to pre-Peter the Great reformers. They needed to find two beginnings, two contrasts, dark and light. The Josephites became the antagonists and the trans-Volga hermits (Nil's followers) the preachers of meekness and patience."

[5] Ščukin Moscow Museum, manuscript No. 212, 17th cent., cited by Borovkova-Majkova in *Russk. Fil. Vestnik*, T. LXIV (1910), pp. 62–64.

Thus, having the date of Nil's death and from some manuscripts his age of 75, we can deduce 1433 as the date of his birth. From a letter written shortly after the death of Nil we learn his family name was Majkov. "There also came the Starec Paisij Jaroslavov, friend of the Grand Prince Vasilij II and with his disciple Starec Nil Majkov. This Nil was on the Holy Mount and the Grand Prince held both of them in great esteem..."[6] Authors dispute whether Nil was of the noble or peasant class.[7] It seems most probable that he came from the higher class of Russians of his day, judging from his wide familiarity with the great men of his time and also due to his extensive education.

At an early age, sick of the world and undoubtedly highly influenced by the ascetical tone of the current literature of his day, he turned to the monastic life.[8] That he was quite young can be discerned from his letter addressed to the prince-monk Kassian: "You, o lover of Christ, remember how you began your journey along the road of faith, your first zeal, your fervent thoughts when you first came to me in my nothingness, living in this unpopulated hermitage, alone, struggling, having dedicated myself to God from my youth."[9] With his intellect and his inclination towards a life of silence and introspection, he surely made good use of the books therein contained.[10]

The founder of this monastery, St. Kirill, had left a strict order of monastic life behind him after his death June 9,1427. Though there

---

[6] "Pis'mo o neljubkax starcve Kirillova i Iosifova monastryrja", in *Prib. k tvor.*, T. X, p. 505.

[7] Arxangel'skij, *op. cit.*, p. 3, quotes Nil's own words that he was a peasant, "*poselja-nin*". This surely from the text in the letter could be an expression of Nil's spirit of self-abasement and would not necessarily imply true peasant origin. Bishop Justin Poljanskij in his *Prepodobnyj i bogonosnyj otec naš Nil* (Moscow, 1892), p. 7, answers Arxangel'skij's reasoning: "It is true Nil calls himself 'unlearned' and a 'peasant', but illiterate he could call himself from his deep humility and peasant because he was born probably and lived on his family estate among farming inhabitants." The majority of authors place him as a member of the noble family of Majkov and make Andrej Majkov a contemporary of Nil engaged in diplomatic services, a brother of Nil. Cf. N. Nikol'skij, *Opisanie rukopisej Kirillo-Belozerskogo monastyrja*, ed. by *Obšč. ljubit. drev. pis'.*, St. Petersburg, 1897, pp. XXXVII–XXXVIII.

[8] Arxangel'skij, *op. cit.*, pp. 3–4, cites a manuscript from the Kirillo-Belozerskij monastery that mentions Nil as having worked as a book copyist before entering that monastery. In this capacity he would have been familiar with the current ascetical literature and would thus have developed his later interest in book-copying.

[9] "Letter to a sorrowing Brother", fol. 374B. All the available letters can be found in Appendix I of this work with a note on the manuscript. All references will be given according to the *folium*, A meaning left hand, B right of the *folium*. Fol. is used for *folium*.

[10] The only other library richer was that of Troica-Sergeeva Lavra which had 300 books. Cf. N. Nikol'skij, *op. cit.*, pp. XLV–XLVI.

remains no exact, detailed description of the monastic life lived in Nil's monastery upon his entrance, due mainly to the fact that Kirill himself did not commit to writing any rule or *Ustav*, we can gather what Nil's life must have been like by viewing the life in the Simonov monastery where Kirill had received his monk's training, and from a description of the common life as found in the life of Kirill by Paxomij.[11]

The Simonov monastery received its structure under the observance of St. Sergius and ... fulfilled the necessary demands of the coenobitic life: the brethren had all in common. Everything belonged to the community. No one could freely leave the monastery without permission. Each day the monks assisted at the Divine Services in the church and the rest of the time was spent in works for the common good according to the assignment of the superior.[12]

The beginnings of monastic property possession can be seen in the structure of the Simonov monastery[13] and this was brought into the Kirill monastery and would later cause dissension and great disagreement, ending in Nil's withdrawal to form his skete type of life.

Five months after the death of Kirill, a great epidemic hit the monastery and 30 of the 53 monks died. The unwritten tradition of Kirill was greatly weakened as new monks came in with different ideas. After the death of higoumen Innokentij and Xristofor, Trifon as chosen as the monastic head. He had been tonsured in another monastery and thus there began a struggle between those who witnessed Kirill's life and the new-comers, one in which Nil himself would take part, later on. Kirill left a strict common life, nothing personally owned, but with the principle of possessing land for the common good of the whole monastery. A conservative part stood firmly for the common life, but ever inclining to increasing the numbers of vocations and possessions. Others stood adamant against possessions, thus neglecting the demands of common life and tending more towards an evangelic, hermitic life.[14]

---

[11] Nikol'skij N., "Obščinnaja i kelejnaja žizn' v Kirillo-Belozerskom monastyre", in *Xrist. Čtenie*, 1907, p. 163.

[12] *Ibid.* Nikol'skij bases his facts on a manuscript of Pachomius' life of Kirill which Nikol'skij personally possessed in his private library. Cf. p. 157.

[13] For a more complete account of life in the Simonov monastery, cf. "Duxovnaja gramota S. Jos." in *Velik. Čet'i, Minei*, Sept. 9, col. 551 (St. Petersburg, 1883).

[14] In northern Russia where population was sparse, tilling the soil would not be enough to support a large coenobitic monastery. It became necessary to have other income if the monks were to fulfill other duties proper to their monastic state. Cf. St. Sergius, in *Velik. Cet'i Minei*, Sept. 25 (St. Petersburg, 1883), col. 1571.

It was Trifon who caused the eruption of the tradition by accepting properties far from the monastery, the very same properties that Kirill in his lifetime refused to accept.[15] Under the new higoumen Kassian,[16] matters returned to normal, but the seed of dissension had already been sown. Kassian had been tonsured in the Spaso–Kamennij monastery where the great friend and spiritual director of Nil, Paisij Jaroslavov, had been higoumen. Most probably both of these two deeply spiritual monks were living in Kirill's monastery when Nil was undergoing his first years of monasticism.[17] In Spaso–Kamennij, the *Ustav* of Mt. Athos was observed in its pristine fervour.[18] And under the guidance of Kassian a small group eager to dispossess the monastery of all possessions on the principle that riches and possession were not in keeping with the monastic ideal, was formed. The older element, and especially those who knew Kirill and his tradition were insistent on a strict common life with necessary possessions owned corporately.

It is easy to imagine to which side Nil tended as we see from his later writings his complete insistence on absolute poverty, not only personal, but also non-possessing of property by the monastery. Paisij, so full of the Athos ideal, must have guided Nil in his reading of the Holy Fathers, especially Nil of Sinai, Simeon the New Theologian and Gregory of Sinai who favoured the hesychastic view that monks are to strive for continual prayer and to do so they must not be distracted by things of this world, not even to be engaged in agriculture, but they were to occupy themselves with "mental activity" in their cells.[19] Coming in contact with various views on the monastic life and the role of poverty in helping contemplation, Nil's ardent nature, seeking always greater perfection in contemplation, must have yearned to live the life he read about among the Fathers. When he actually left the Kirillo-Belozerskij monastery to begin his trip to Constantinople and then on to Mt. Athos is not known exactly. Nil records his journey quite simply in his *Ustav*, "as we saw

[15] We know most of this from the *Ustav* of Joseph Volokolamsk, ch. 10. Cf. *Velik. Čeť'i Minei*, Sept. 9, col. 550–551.
[16] Trifon kept money for himself, bought land on his own account, widened the buildings and monastery. The protesting group was led by Dosifej whose head Trifon once beat so violently on the table that he nearly beat him to death. Cf. *ibid.*, col. 550–551.
[17] Kassian was igoumen from 1448–1469. Cf. Stroev, Pavel, *Spiski ierarxov i nastojatelej monastyrej rossijskija cerkvi"* (St. Petersburg, 1877), p. 55.
[18] Ključevskij, V. O., *Drevnerusskija žitija svjatyx, kak istoričeskij istočnik* (Moscow, 1871), p. 190.
[19] Cf. "Skazanie o Spaso-Kam.", in *Prav. Sob.*, 1861, part 1, pp. 203–211, written by Paisij himself.

with our own eyes on the holy mount of Athos and in the lands around
Constantinople and in other places many such dwellings..."[20]

It was not a rare happening for Russian monks to travel to Athos and
Constantinople in those days. Chiefly behind most of these visits were
administrative affairs between the Russian hierarchy and the Patriarch
of Constantinople. But also there was a genuine conviction that the
true roots of Oriental monasticism were sowed on the Holy Mountain
and thus there grew up among sincere Russian monks, the desire some
day to live some time in these monasteries and explore their rich libraries.
Historical chronicles relate that this type of pilgrimage of Russian monks
to the East began in the 11th century.[21] But in the 14th and 15th century,
the number of eminent Russian monks increased. Among those who
lived there and practised the hesychastic life were Epifanij, the author of
the life of St. Serge, another disciple of S. Serge, Serge Niromskij, a
certain Savva, higoumen of Tver', Metrofan Byvalcov, an higoumen
Iona, plus Nil and his disciple Innokentij or Prince Oxlevinin.[22]

Nil and his companion arrived on Mt. Athos at a time when contemplation had reached a high degree of perfection. The writings of Simeon
the New Theologian and Gregory the Sinaite were put into practice after

[20] *Ustav*, p. 89. Cf. also Nil's letter to the Starec German, 1864 ed., St. Petersburg, p.
179. In the "Pis'mo o neljubkax..., *op. cit.*, p. 505, it is put briefly, "This Nil was on
the Holy Mount".

[21] In 1052 the Russian monastery of Pantelejmon was started thanks to the benefices
of St. Vladimir and Jaroslav I. In 1080 also the monastery of Ksilirgi was given to
the Russians. In the 13th century, the Archimandrite Dosifej of Pečerskaja Lavra
recommended the strict life of Mt. Athos as the model for his monastery and in this
time begins the move to import bishops from Mt. Athos for Russia. Cf. Gorskij, A. V.,
"O snošenijax russkoj cerkvi s svjatogorskimi obiteljami", in *Pribav. k tvorenijam
otcov*, VI, pp. 123–168, and "Russkie inoki na gore afonskoj" in *Xrist. Čtenie*, 1853,
II, pp. 290–317. Cf. also Mošin, V., "Russkie na Afone, russko-vizantijskie otnošenija", in *Byzantinoslavica*, no. 9 (1947), pp. 55–85; no. 11. (1950), pp. 32–71. Also
Arximandrit Leonid, "Afon i russkoe monašestvo", in *Zurnal Moskovskoj Patriarxii*,
no. 8 (1958), p. 60–64.

[22] Sergij Niromskij, Nil and Innokentij, all, on returning to Russia, founded similar
hermitages or sketes. Cf. Ikonnikov, V., *op. cit.*, p. 77: "But the one who best expressed the Athos tendency was Nil Sorskij." "Russkie inoki na svjatojgore afonskoj ot
perexoda X veka do poloviny XIX veka", in *Xrist. Čtenie*, 1853, Oct., p. 290. The
author gives Nil Sorskij and his disciple Innokentij among the Russian monks who
inhabited Mt. Athos and adds: "These two lived there for a long time like bees in a
paradise ... and Nil gave to our Russian monasticism rich compositions from his
pious pen from which flowed, not abstract and theoretical truths about skite solitude,
but truths learned from experience of life itself, freed from passions, angelic ... If we
owe to Anthony Pečerskij the first monastery founded in Russia, then more fairly to
Nil we owe the first skite asceticism." Cf. also G. Iljinskij, "Značenie afona v istorii
slavjanskoj pis'mennosti", in *Z.M.N.Pr.*, 1908, no. 11, pp. 1–41.

the triumph of Palamas over Varlaam of Calabria. Hesychasm reigned supreme on the peninsula.[23] The influence of Simeon the New Theologian and Gregory Sinaite, Nil Sinaite, Cassian, Climacus and Isaac the Syrian for Nil must have been great as we can judge from his frequent citations and evident familiarity with their writings. He must have been fluent in Greek and thus the riches of the libraries of Mt. Athos and Constantinople furnished him with great sources from which he could build a spiritual life in perfect harmony with the highest ideals in Oriental spirituality. His was not a mere study of the mind, but it engaged his whole being, giving him a deep experience of integrated theory and practice that would be seen so clearly in his writings. As a result of "living" rather than "studying" the Holy Fathers "he was not chained to their compositions in any exterior manner of repetition, but he freely used them to express his personal thought, but now he thought in a patristic manner and expressed himself in their language".[24]

It is impossible to know how long Nil stayed in the East, but it must have been a fairly long time[25] judging from the familiarity with the Fathers and the conviction of the perfection of the skete type of monasticism that he would later manifest both in his writings and in his personal life.

He returned to Russia and naturally enough went back to his monastery of Kirillo-Belozerskij. But great changes had taken place, not only in Nil's spiritual outlook, but also in the views of the monks in the monastery he left, when he was young.

We have a letter of Nil written to a fellow-brother in need, explaining why he left Kirill monastery and began his hermitical life. Perhaps he had returned at the time that Joseph of Volokalamsk describes, when many *starcy* left the Kirill monastery unsatisfied with the higoumen, until

---

[23] Cf. Meyendorff, Jean, *Introduction à l'étude de Grégoire Palamas*, Vol. 3 in the collection: *Patristica Sorbonensia* (Paris, 1959).

A short but adequate account of the quarrel between Palamas and Barlaam with the hesychast victory can be found in his *St. Grégoire Palamas et la mystique Orthodoxe* (Bourges, 1959). He gives also a history of its subsequent development, in particular, in Russia through the instrumentality of Nil Sorskij, pp. 154-155. Cf. Arximandrit Modest, *Svjatyj Gregorij Palama* (Kiev, 1860).

[24] Nikol'skij, N. K., *Materialy dlja istorii drevnerusskoj duxovnoj pis'mennosti* (St. Petersburg, 1897), III, p. 16.

[25] "St. Nil was tonsured in the Kirill monastery from which he left and spent not a short time on the holy mount of Athos and in the regions around Constantinople." B. G. Grečev cites this from a manuscript found in the Imperial Public Library, F. 1, no. 260, 1. 56. *Op. cit.*, no. 2, (1908), p. 66, ftn. 5.

he had been finally driven out by the Grand Prince himself.[26] If this is true, then Nil left his monastery between 1473–89 because it was during the reign of Metropolitan Gerontij that the difficulty described by Joseph occurred at Kirillo-Belozerskij. Nil writes in this letter:

Before we left the monastery, was it not only for spiritual benefits and not for any other reason that we were guided in our actions? Nowadays one does not see in the monasteries an observance of the laws of God according to Holy Writings and the tradition of the Holy Fathers, but rather we act according to our own wills and human ways of thinking... After returning from my wanderings, I came to the monastery of Kirillo-Belozerskij and close by I built myself a cell and there lived in solitude... Then I moved even farther from the monastery.

He explains how he sought more solitude "in order to live according to God's commands and the commentaries of the Fathers on Holy Scriptures, also in accord with the Apostolic tradition, and the lives and teachings of the Fathers and what was in agreement with my own conscience in order to glorify God better and profit spiritually".[27]

No doubt his ideal, developed on Mt. Athos, could not be satisfied, not even living nearby the monastery as a solitary hermit. He was filled with a greater desire for more complete solitude as he himself tells us in a letter: "Now I moved farther from the monastery where, by the grace of God, I found a place suited to my tastes, where few worldlings frequented."[28] This place that suited his tastes was about 15 versts (ten miles) from the monastery in a swamp near a creek called the Sor. A visitor to this area reports:

Wild, deserted, gloomy is the place where Nil founded his hermitage. It was on level ground, but quite swampy with woods around it with more pines than other leafy trees. The River Sor or Sorka does not flow, but stands still in that place and is more similar to a stagnant swamp than flowing water. Among the many advantageous spots offering abundant, cheerful natural beauties, it would have been difficult to find a place more morose and solitary than this place of hermitage. At first sight one understands what the saint was seeking and it completely corresponded to his character of spiritual contemplation.[29]

---

[26] This hypothesis is suggested by A. Muravjev, *Russkaja Fevajda na severe* (St. Petersburg, 1894), p. 248. Cf. also A. Arxangel'skij, *op. cit.*, p. 25. S. Šumakov in his *Obzor gramot kollegii ekonomii* (Moscow, 1900), pp. 88–89, claims that the Sorskij skete did not exist in 1482, therefore Nil could not have left earlier than between the years of 1470–1480.
[27] The entire letter is reproduced by A. Muravjev, *op. cit.*, pp. 249–252.
[28] Letter to ... Cf. *Appendix I* of this present work, Letter III to German, fol. 105B.
[29] Ševyrev, S., *Poezdka v Kirillo-Belozerskij monastyr'* (Mosc., 1850), II, p. 103.

Here Nil was left to engage in his "mental prayer" and his studies of Holy Scriptures, undisturbed by the world. But it was not long before other monks, undoubtedly those from the nearby monastery who knew and loved Nil and his Athos ideal and who were gradually becoming dissatisfied with the quarreling in the Kirill monastery came to him both seeking spiritual advice and conversation, and perhaps even wanting to stay and imitate his life, as he himself clearly states in his *Predanie*.

Many virtuous brethren came to me wishing to live with us, though I refused many, because I am a sinful and stupid person and so weak in soul and body. But some of those turned away by me insisted on staying and would not cease knocking on my abode and they gave me no rest. I then looked upon it, perhaps, this is the will of God that they come to us, perhaps they have a right to share in the tradition of the saints and keep the commands of God and live according to the tradition of the Holy Fathers... If any of them were not willing to live according to the commands of God and the tradition of the Holy Fathers, then they were to cease knocking at my humble abode. I sent away such as proved lazy and quarrelsome. For I did not go to those wishing to be their superior, but they came to me, forcing it on me.[30]

His only aim, as he continues, was to point out to these followers the will of God as presented in the Holy Writings and in the tradition of the Holy Fathers who interpret these writings. He would not take upon himself the terrible responsibility of directing these souls, but, living like an equal, he would indicate what he had learned from long years of seeking always in the Holy Writings, not his own will, but purely the will of God.

Thus Nil started with this small group to live the pure skete rule of life he had lived on Mt. Athos.[31] The skete consisted of a group of *cella* or huts in which the monks or *kelliotai* lived. The cells were scattered about a centrally located community church to which the monks came

---

[30] *Predanie*, p. 3–4.

[31] We can hardly say that Nil was the first to have lived the skete type of monasticism in Russia. We know that it existed in the Novgorod region before Nil's time, but it never reached the Mt. Athos purity as found in Nil's skete and in his *Ustav*. Evprosin of Pskov (+1481) in the middle of the 15th century had brought back from his journey to Mt. Athos and Constantinople the skete usages. There was a skete rule in Russia but one which stressed more the church services according to the Athonite custom. Cf. Smolitsch, I., *Das russische Mönchtum*, *op. cit.*, p. 250. Also cf. Makarij, *Isto-rija...*, *op. cit.*, T. VII, p. 77 and foll.

For a treatment of the idiorhythmic life in Russia of ancient times cf. *AI*, I, no. 26, p. 181.

for common liturgical services. The monks lived in groups of two or three, often an older monk and a younger, a starec with one or two disciples. From the common "cloister" they received food for a week and on Saturday or vigil of feasts they would come together for services. Each monk lived in a certain sense according to his own needs. He cared for himself, providing his own food and clothing. He set his own daily order and prayer order as he wished.[32]

The number of actual skete monks living with Nil is not known, but it must have been a very small number as we can judge from the number in 1515, just seven years after Nil's death. At this time there were one hieromonk (priest), one deacon, and 12 starcy unordained monks.[33]

The order of the skete monastery and the activities of the monks will be touched on later. We can be sure that Nil and his monks spent most of their time in continual prayer and in the study of the Holy Writings. Nil writes in one letter: "I will tell you about myself, for your love of God makes me indiscreet so that I babble on about myself... I do not do anything without having proof from Divine Writings and then I follow them as far as I have strength to do so. When I must do something, I search before in the Divine Writings and if I do not find anything agreeing with my conscience, I lay my work aside until I can return and do find something with God's grace; then I do it boldly, as it has been made known to me..."[34] This meant long hours of prayerful study over Holy Scripture.

We know that Nil also with his monks took up the art of copying books and also of correcting the glaring errors that existed in many of the manuscripts of an ascetical nature, especially the Lives of the saints. There was no leaving the skete and no preoccupation with the world. A monk's charity towards fellow-men was to be shown by his prayers for them and his freely giving of spiritual advice. This was for Nil the highest type of charity.

Amidst these literary activities, there came forth from Nil's pen his two chief works, his *Predanie* and his *Ustav*, plus several letters which

---

[32] For a complete description of the Athos model upon which Nil based his *skit* cf. Ph. Meyer, *Die Haupturkunden für die Geschichte der Athos-Kloster* (Leipzig, 1894); also Sokolov I., "Vnutrennee sostojanie monašestva v vizantijskoj cerkvi s poloviny IX i do načala XIII veka (842–1204)", in *Prav. Sob.*, 1893, III.

[33] Letter of the Grand Prince Vasilij Ivanovič to Nil's hermitage, in *AAE*, I. no. 227, p. 394, *Dopolnenija*.

[34] Letter to Gurij, fol. 102B–103A.

we have intact to-day.[35] Through his letters he gave spiritual comfort and advice to all classes of men, especially to other monks and nobles. Our historical documents give us light only twice when we learn that Nil interrupted his contemplation to busy himself about two of the central questions of his day: the problem of the heretics and that of monastic possessions.

In the region around Novgorod there grew up in the 14th and 15th centuries a spirit of rugged individualism, freedom and self-enterprise. Its remoteness from the central control of power, both religious and political, plus its development of commerce and trade with many foreigners, built up in the people a spirit of criticism against any and all authority. It is not to be wondered then that the first noticeable heresy in Russia, the *Strigol'niki*, began in Novgorod, demanding moral reform from church leaders, and not long before its fall, arose the heresy of the Judaizers which had great effects for the Church in Russia in the 15th and beginning of the 16th century.[36]

Archbishop Gennadij, appointed to the see of Novgorod in 1484, started immediately a crusade to crush the heretics. By this time it had invaded even the court of Moscow and held a particular fascination for intellectuals and nobles. The Grand Prince Ivan III with the Metropolitan Gerontij of Moscow did not give the full importance to the danger,

---

[35] The *Predanie* of Nil is his earliest attempt to give to his disciples a written, but very simplified, rule of *skit* monasticism. A *Nadslovie* or foreword prefaces it in very few manuscripts. The author is unknown but in a late manuscript the name of Innokentij Oxlebinin is given as its author. The author explains Nil's purpose in writing the *Predanie* and makes it clear that the latter was written by Nil before he wrote his *Ustav* and that both were meant to be separate works. Cf. the St. Petersburg 1864 edition *Prepodobnyj Nil Sorskij, pervoosnovatel' skitskago žitija v Rossii i ustav ego o žitel'stve skitskom, Introduction*, pp. XXXIX–XL. Also A. Arxangel'skij, *op. cit.*, p. 60; Borovkova-Majkova, *op. cit., Introduction*, p. II. She examined over 100 manuscripts found in Russia and found that 97 gave the *Predanie* and *Ustav* and 52 the letters of Nil. But unfortunately no critical edition of the letters has been so far edited. Through the kindness of Dr. Fairy Lilienfeld I was able to secure photostat copies of five letters of Nil from original manuscripts found in the Lenin Library of Moscow. Cf. the *Appendix* of this work where a translation is given. Other sources of the letters are: the St. Petersburg 1864 edition which gives four main letters along with five other works dubiously attributed to Nil, pp. 161–203; and A. Arxangel'skij, *op. cit.*, who gives only excerpts from nine letters attributed to Nil, pp. 48–138.

[36] The rise of this heresy will be treated more in length later on. Suffice here to say that there were many shades of heresy including open denial of the Blessed Trinity, the Divinity of Christ and His very existence on this earth. As there was no single heretical "school" with one set of teaching, opposed to the official Russian Church's teaching, it was most difficult to determine the guilt of each individual heretic and to find the most effective way of blotting out these often vaguely formulated contrary teachings.

at least so thought Gennadij. So the latter began to take things into his own hand; the first step was to write in 1489 a letter to Ioasaf, Archbishop of Rostov, in whose diocese were living Nil and his teacher Paisij Jaroslavov. He asks him to visit Paisij and Nil and get their opinion about the popular rumour that the world would end in 1492. He continues: "Write to me if it is possible for Paisij and Nil to come to me and to discourse with me about the heretics (i.e. Judaizers)."[37]

Whether Nil and Paisij went to Novgorod and gave their views to Gennadij about the heretics we do not know, but we do know that in the following year both of them are found present at the Synod of 1490 in Moscow. Concerning what stand they took towards the heretics we do not have any document. We can guess from Nil's gentleness and tolerance pervading all his writings that he must have pleaded for mercy rather then death-penalty towards which Gennadij inclined. Nil, in his writings, stressed always that those "who have strayed from the path of virtue should not be reviled or reproached". Monks should not be concerned with their punishment, but "that this should be left to God, for God is strong enough to correct them".[38]

The members of the Synod passed a very lenient sentence contrary to the instructions sent by Gennadij[39] by depriving two or three heretical priests of orders and sending them back to Gennadij. Undoubtedly Gennadij quickly enough saw that Nil and Paisij were not of his thinking, for *he never* bothered to consult the two again.

The last public act of Nil before he retired into oblivion to await death in 1508 was to attend the Synod of Moscow in 1503 and there to raise his voice in protest against the scandalous abuses in monasteries throughout all of Russia, due to the vast property possessions held by monks. The Synod was called principally to deal with the problem of whether widowed priests and deacons would be forced to retire into monasteries and other ecclesiastical questions. The Synod was apparently breaking up and some of the members actually had left, among who was Joseph Volokalamsk, when Nil quite unexpectedly brought up his protest about monastery properties.

---

[37] This letter in full is found on pp. 315–320: Kazakova, N. A., and Lur'e, J. S., *Antifeodal'nye eretičeskie dviženija na Rusi XVI-načala XVI v.* (Moscow–Leningrad, 1955).
[38] Cf. Nil's letter to Gurij, fol. 101B.
[39] This letter is given in *Pamjat. drevnerussk. kanon. prava*, I, pp. 782, 784, *op. cit.* Gennadij pleads that the Fathers be not swayed by their (heretics) deceits, but that the Fathers remain firm and condemn them to the stake to be burned.

And when there was held the council about the widowed priests and deacons, the starec Nil got up and said that monasteries should not have villages, but that monks should live in solitude and be fed by the fruit of the work of their hands. And with him sided all the hermits of Belozerskij. And hearing this, higoumen Joseph began to upraid them, calling as testimony St. Theodosius, the founder of the coenobitic life, and St. Athanasius of Mt. Athos and St. Anthony and St. Theodosius of Pečerskaja Lavra, the miracle workers and fathers of many monasteries and they all had villages...[40]

Nil was supported by the Trans-Volga hermits, but, when Joseph began to present his arguments, the Russian Church saw the beginnings of a polemic war that would separate the two camps into the Josephites and the Trans-Volga Starcy. It would be Joseph and his followers who would be eventually triumphant and thus they would set the official policy for monasteries in Russia. But Nil, foreseeing the battle and possibly the futility of fighting for his pure form of monasticism where already formalism, ritualism and above all, greed and politics had taken over religion, retired from the lists. "It is not befitting", writes Nil, "that a monk becomes entangled with those who would contend with him, but that he should rather retire."[41] And this is exactly what he did after the Synod of 1503. In his Sorskij skete Nil hides himself and there he dies May 7, 1508 at 75 years old.[42] Before dying Nil wrote his last testament which gives us an insight into his deep kenotic spirit:

I, unworthy Nil, entreat my superiors and brethren who are of the same spirit as myself to carry out this last will of mine. After my death, throw my body out into the desert so that there the animals and birds may devour it, for it has so basely sinned against God and is unworthy of a burial. If they do not do this, then dig a hole on the place where we live and bury me in it with every kind of abuse. Fear the words which the great Arsenius commanded his followers, saying: 'I will call you before judgment if you give my body to anyone.' It has always been my earnest striving as far as my strength allowed to receive no honour or praise in this monastery in life, so be it after my death. I beg all to pray for my sinful soul, and I ask pardon from all as I forgive all. May God pardon us all.[43]

---

[40] "Pis'mo o neljubkax", op. cit., p. 505. We will treat both these topics of Nil's attitude towards heretics and monastic property in fuller detail later on.

[41] Ustav, pp. 86–87.

[42] "In the years 7016, in the week of the Myrrhbearing Women (second Sunday after Easter), on the 7th day of May, died Nil Starec of the Sorskij hermitage." Manuscript of Moscow ecclesiastical Academy, XVI Century, no. 185, fol. 375.

[43] Nil's Testament can be found in the manuscript no. 188, formerly in the Troice-Sergieva Lavra, now in the Lenin Library, Moscow. Also found in St. Petersburg 1864 edition, pp. XXXII–XXXIII; also Borovkova-Majkova, op. cit., p. 10.

These are the few facts that Providence has allowed us to know about Nil's life. There has never been a formal canonization of Nil in the Russian Orthodox Church.[44] One document speaks of Liturgies and Panachidas (funeral services for the burial or remembrance of the dead) offered up for Nil's soul in his *skit* even as late as the 18th century.[45] But by the 19th century Nil's cultus is firmly established throughout all Russia and his name is found in the calendar of the Saints with his feast day celebrated on May 7.[46]

If the people of Russia were deprived of biographies telling them in detail about the sanctity of Nil, they had nevertheless his writings. They were not excessively numerous, but from their rich content one can judge much about the personality of their author. These writings establish without a doubt an author of exceptional merit, especially when judged according to his times and the circumstances in which Nil lived. But above all, they delineated for the ordinary people, eager to save their souls, a soul immersed totally in the Absolute that for Nil was the beginning and the end of all life. His spirituality, although never worked out as a completely progressive system, has always had great influence

---

[44] "We do not even know whether he (Nil) was formally canonized... There are no known details about Nil Sorskij. It is true that in two thirds of the manuscripts we find traces of a church Service to him, tropar, kondak, ikos; it would even be possible to show approximately the time of its composition, but it seems to have been only a local attempt and this does not prove anything conclusively." (A. Arxangel'skij, *op. cit.*, pp. 45–46. The 1864 St. Petersburg edition of Nil's *Ustav*, *op. cit.*, states simply that in the course of time the Holy Church placed Nil among the choir of saintly Fathers and his memory is celebrated in the Church calendar on the 7th of May. Nil has no proper office of his own but is honoured by the common one of "*prepodobnyj*" found in the Minei. Cf. p. XXXIII. Kologrivov, I., S. J., says that it is from 1903 that we find Nil's name in the official ecclesiastical calender for the Russian Church. Cf. *Essai sur la sainteté en Russie* (Bruges, 1953), p. 198.

[45] From the *Novgorod-Sophia Collection of the 17th century*, no. 1519, fol. 33, now found in the Saltykov-Ščedrin Public Library in Leningrad.

[46] Nil's tropar, the special prayer of intercession in honour of the saint read during the Liturgy or the Divine Office, reads: "Rejecting a worldly life and fleeing from the snares of the world, O confessor and God-bearing, Father Nil, you were most diligent in gathering heavenly flowers from the writings of the Fathers. Living in the desert of your monastery, you flourished as a wild lily; and from there you finally arrived in the heavenly mansion. Teach us also, those who reverently honour you, to follow your royal way and pray for our souls." His kondak, a second commemorative prayer in honour of the saint of the day, recited or sung during the Liturgy and the Divine Office, reads: "With patience you bore the vain habits and worldly morals of your brothers, you found undisturbed peace in the desert, O Blessed Father, through your fastings, watchings, and constant prayer in the labours you underwent, you showed the right paths to follow to the Lord through your teachings. With them we also honour you, O most blessed Nil." Cf. Bishop Justin Poljanskij, *Prepodobnyj Nil Sorskij i ego ustav o éitelstve skitskom* (Berlin, 1939), p. 114.

in Russia. As he repeated so often, he was a mere channel through which passed the riches of the Holy Fathers to Russian monasticism and hence to the Russian people. In his humility he never felt himself as an original writer or spiritual director. He was gathering "crumbs" that fell from the table of the Holy Fathers and he was passing them on to those who cared to profit from his teaching.[47] But perhaps in this lies his true greatness, that Nil, in so doing, passed on the rich heritage of the early Fathers of the Church who formed for both the East and the West the one common ancient monastic tradition plus the Fathers of the later hesychastic mysticism.

[47] *Ustav*, pp. 14–15.

PART TWO

THE SPIRITUALITY OF NIL SORSKIJ

I

ASCETICAL IDEAL

A. PURPOSE OF LIFE

In his writings Nil is not concerned with giving his readers a *pandecta* of all that had ever been written of importance about the spiritual life. In his two main writings, his *Predanie* and his *Ustav*, he was giving his followers a monastic ideal, the principles which would lead the monk to obtain his ascetical ideal: union with God in this life, as far as grace and the individual's cooperation would allow, and life eternal hereafter. Therefore, the end of man is in the main presupposed. But occasionally Nil's soul opens to us his deep conviction of the emptiness of this present life and his every yearning for the fulfilment of God's plan.

Nil, in a letter to the Prince Vassian Patrikeev, one of his faithful disciples who finds himself outside of the monastery, back among his former friends and his former way of living, points out to him the emptiness of all that is temporal and of this world.

...and you, reflect for a moment from your own experience. How many sorrows, sufferings has this world that passes by so rapidly and how much evil it accords those who love it. But for those who leave the world ... what a sweetness is theirs ... And when you have to depart from this world, think, what does it profit those who during their lifetime ruled it? If you have much honour, fame, riches, all that, what is it but a shadow that passes by and as smoke that soon disappears? So many, seeking to gather in all the goods possible of this world, lovers of the world, but then in their very youth died, like flowers of the fields in full bloom they fell. And how they did not want to leave this life. But when one is living in the world, he doesn't think of its deadly evil, but strives ever for honours and bodily comforts. But you the loving God has mercifully called from the world and placed you in His Service by His Goodness. For this sake, you must give thanks for so great a mercy and do all in your power to please Him and to save your soul, forgetting the past which is no longer useful and stretching forward to acquire future virtue and with that eternal life.[1]

---

[1] Letter to Vassian, fol. 94A–B–95A. Cf. *Appendix I.*

This life has meaning only in relation to the future life. It is a returning to God. It is living according to His 'divine commands', seeking in all things only His will.

Woe to us. We do not understand the dignity of our souls, we do not un-derstand to what a life we are called, as St. Isaac says. Our life in this world, its sorrows, its goods and all the rest we consider as something important, but about the life of the soul, the mind, so burdened by sloth, love of the world and petty worries, we say that was only for ancient saints, but not needed by us; in fact, such asceticism we say is impossible to-day.[2]

Man remains essentially the same. His end remains the same. Therefore man has need of the same means that all saintly men have ever used to attain salvation. To attain one's final end, to return to God, the Christian must keep himself holy. Sanctity is not merely a consequence, but a necessary condition for attaining God. The soul that loves God adheres to God alone. And the first step for Nil in the long process of returning to God is to cut oneself off from all extrinsic attachments and then to tie the self to God in one's heart. But before there can be attachment to God there must be detachment from the world.[3] "Full activity in our chosen way of life should consist in this, that always and in every detail, in every undertaking, in soul and body, word and deed and thought, as far as there is in us the strength, to remain in the work of God, with God, and in God."[4] Man must leave the "natural" worldly way that he had been living and now occupy himself with "probing our thoughts and feelings so that all our actions be in harmony with God's will. Shun what is human".[5] All effort must be focused on purifying our mind and heart from every human taint. "Thinking of God, that is, mental prayer, is above all other actions and is the chief of all the virtues, for it is the love of God."[6]

For the soul, according to Nil, whose one insatiable desire is to see God, the most secure, most noble way is the monastic life. In the whole Oriental tradition, to be a monk was to be an integral Christian, one who took seriously the end of all men, to give glory to God and to save his soul. The monk was he who responded with his whole heart to Christ's challenge, "Be ye perfect as my Heavenly Father is perfect."[7] Isaac the

[2] *Ustav*, p. 31.
[3] Cf. Isaac Sinaite, *PG*, 86A, 811.
[4] *Ustav*, p. 35.
[5] *Ibid.*, p. 55.
[6] *Ibid.*, p. 86.
[7] Matt. 5, 48.

Sinaite, in explaining how man should be a pilgrim on this earth, striving, longing always for his true heavenly home, instinctively equates the pilgrim and the monk. "A pilgrim is one who in mind is placed outside the whole world and mourns, one who in hunger and thirsting leads all his life out of hope for the future rewards... And the monk is he who sits outside of the contagion of the world always supplicating God to obtain the future rewards."[8] This is in substance the advice Nil gives to his friend Gurij in answer to the latter's question, "What must a pilgrim journeying to salvation do?"[9] For Nil, the monastic state was none other than assuming the form of angels.[10] The sublimity of this calling to participate in the life of angels who look continually on God and sing His praises should be a motive strong enough to overcome impure thoughts.[11]

Among the three common types of monastic life in Russia, the most perfect for Nil was without a doubt the skete type. He had seen this life at close hand on Mount Athos and in the countries near Constantinople. And it was this type of monasticism he developed along the shores of the Sora River. The skete type is the middle way as St. John Climacus teaches.

He (Climacus) tells us that there are three excellent forms of monastic life: the life of solitude, living with one or two brothers in silence, and the coenobitic common life... The middle way, that is, living in silence with one or two according to the opinion of John Climacus, was much more promising for many. For he says, woe to the hermit when acedia hits him or he is overcome by sleep or indolence or despair, there is no one near to pick him up and encourage him.[12]

This middle way is not to be undertaken too soon for it requires great preparation. "And this fitting time is after we have acquired wisdom by living among other men. Climacus says, 'Who is not clean, not yet delivered from passions, but, ignoring this, tries to lead the life of silence is like a man who leaps from a boat and with one board thinks he will easily get to shore. But those who are fighting their passions, they can live alone, but only in due time, and only if they have a superior; for solitude demands the fortitude of an angel.'"

[8] Isaac Sinaite, *loc. cit.*, 831, B–C.
[9] Letter to Gurij Tušin, fol. 101A–B.
[10] *Ustav*, p. 44.
[11] *Ibid.*, p. 44.
[12] *Ibid.*, p. 87. Cf. *PG*, 88, 642B–643A.

B. DIVINE WRITINGS, GUIDE TO PERFECTION

Having left the world to serve God, the monk who wishes to follow Nil's direction must divest himself of his own will and follow only the will of God. "We have but one teacher, Our Lord Jesus Christ, who gave us the Holy Scriptures and sent His Holy Apostles and Venerable Fathers to teach the way of salvation to the human race."[13] There is no central point more insisted on by Nil than this: that to know the way of perfection leading to God, man must study the Divine Writings. And in so doing he was merely repeating what had always been the basic belief among the great Oriental Fathers. St. John Chrysostom puts it succinctly: "It would be good if we had no need of recourse to Holy Scriptures, but rather if we led a life so pure that the Holy Spirit holds in our souls the place of the inspired books and as those were written with ink, so our hearts would be written by the Holy Spirit. But because we have rejected this grace, let us open our hearts to this second means of navigation."[14]

The greatest danger to perfection, Nil points out, is to follow one's own will, that will which inclines so to the things of the flesh and imprudent judgments. Act rather according to Holy Writings and the way of life pointed out by the Holy Fathers and you will not, with the grace of Christ, sin. Don't take these words harshly. They come from Holy Writings and not from me. It is indeed difficult and cruel for those who do not wish to be humiliated in the fear of the Lord and to give up their earthly wisdom. They act according to their passionate wills and not according to Holy Writings. Such do not search the Holy Writings with a humble spirit. Some do not even want to hear these sacred writings, let alone not wanting to live according to them for they say, 'they were not written for us and it is impossible for the present generation to keep them.' But for true ascetics in ancient times as well as our present times and for all times, 'the words of the Lord are pure as purified silver and furbished seven times and His commands are illuminating and more desired than gold and precious gems.'[15]

When other disciples came to his cell in the wilderness of the Sora River, Nil's first question was whether they wanted to live according to the Divine Writings.[16] If they were not satisfied to spend the rest of their lives in searching the Holy Writings for the will of God, then "they must cease to harrass me". The big danger of his times among other monasteries is:

---

[13] *Predanie*, p. 2.
[14] J. Chrysostom, Hom. 1 in Matt. 1, 1, *PG*, 57, 13.
[15] Letter to Starec German, fol. 107B.
[16] *Predanie*, p. 3.

They are not keeping God's Laws according to Holy Writings, and the tradition of the Holy Fathers, but they follow their own wills and human ways of interpretation. They do many corrupting things, thinking at the same time they are acting in a virtuous manner. This comes from not governing themselves according to the Holy Writings, from not being careful with Godly fear and humility to search them, but rather we ignore them and indulge in human affairs.[17]

In this same letter, Nil shows how he always acted.

When we lived together in the monastery, you yourself know full well how I ever fled from the wordly enticements and strove only to live according to Divine Writings. I always sought out the Divine Writings, above all, the laws of God and their explanation of them by the Fathers, and the apostolic traditions, then the lives and teachings of the Holy Fathers, and I gave my whole attention to these and so I gradually learned. In them I lived and had my respirations... And if there was something to do to improve myself, if I did not find it immediately in the Holy Writings, I laid it aside until I could find some teaching on this point. And if anyone from out of spiritual love came to me for advice, I advised him to do just as I have advised you. For this reason, I advise you for the good of your soul, as I have striven ever to do so myself... Observe the commands of the Word and the traditions of the Holy Fathers and tell your brethren to do so also. But especially if you are in your hermit cell or find yourself back in the monastery among your brother monks, always give attention to the Holy Writings and follow in the footsteps of the Holy Fathers, for so do the Divine Writings command us to do.[18]

Thus we see how the Divine Writings contain for Nil the way and the only way to salvation, because it is God speaking and the Holy Fathers interpreting the Word of God for us. Not only do they give us the general doctrine necessary to be saved, but in all practical difficulties of daily life one can find a comforting reassurance of what he should do to please God. One need not search in other sources, for the Holy Writings given by God for our salvation are adequate.[19]

---

[17] Letter to German, fol. 104B.

[18] *Ibid.*, fol. 105A–B–106A.

[19] T. Spidlik: *L'autorità del Libro per il Monachesimo Russo*, in *OCA, Il Monachesimo Orientale* (Roma, 1958), p. 153, quotes Starec Silvan, a monk who died on Mount Athos in 1938. "When a monk studies Sacred Scripture, the works of the Holy Fathers, liturgical books, these inexhaustible founts of dogma and prayer, he finds a treasure so great that he has no longer need to write on these matters, to say something new. But when, in the life of the Church, there is manifested a true necessity, then new books are written." Cf. Sofronij, *Starets Silvan* (Paris, 1942), p. 39.

C. MEANING OF DIVINE WRITINGS

From the few short citations from Nil's writings it is evident at once
that he does not refer only to the inspired writings contained in the Bible
under his term "Divine Writings". Not only he and his contemporaries as
Joseph of Volokalamsk[20] extend inspiration beyond the actual writings
found in the Bible to include also writings of Holy Fathers, but we find
they are only following the Byzantine tradition.[21] The Byzantine monks
and theologians fought to establish the true teaching of the two natures
in one person; Christ Jesus, during the heresies of Nestorianism and
Monophysitism by quoting the writings of earlier Fathers as "inspired".
Theodore Studite praises St. Basil because Christ spoke through his
mouth and those who follow him follow the same Holy Spirit.[22] And St.
Basil himself gives us the reason why we can have confidence that the
Holy Spirit also guided the Holy Fathers. "Because they have followed
the true meaning of Scripture."[23]

Nil in his *Ustav* writes: "It is not from my wisdom but from the God-
inspired writings of enlightened Holy Fathers that I teach. For what I
have written here is not without authority from the Holy Writings."[24]

What is the basis for this assumption that the Holy Fathers are also
inspired? Nil simply gives the sanctity of the Fathers as the sole criterion
why others less holy should listen to their inspired words.

Because the saints, by practising perfection, labour in the vineyard of their
heart both as regards to their sentiments and as regards to their mind because
they have purified their mind from passions, because they have found the
Lord and have spiritualized their intellect, now command us that we, inflamed
with the fires of passions, attain living water from the fount of the Divine
Writings.[25]

---

[20] Spidlik, T., *Joseph de Volokolamsk, un chapitre de la spiritualité russe* (Rome,
1956). Joseph extends the name "Holy Writings" even to include certain civil laws.
Cf. p. 12. He goes so far as to lay down the principle: "Whoever writes in his own time
for the Church is moved by the Holy Spirit."
[21] *Ibid.*, p. 14. This tradition was carried over to the Hesychast spirituality of Sinai.
Cf. *Discours de Syméon le Nouveau Theologien:* "... tout ce que dit ou fait ou écrit
un tel homme, ce n'est pas lui, mais l'Esprit Saint parlant en lui qui le dit et l'écrit,"
p. 174. Cf. also p. 202: "Il faut pourtant admettre que s'ils sont d'accord eux aussi
avec les anciens Péres, remplis de Dieu, c'est évidemment qu'ils parlent eux aussi dans
le même Esprit," *OC*, T. IX (1927), author: Hausherr, I., S.J.
[22] Cf. Epist. II, 164, *PG*, 99, 1520C.
[23] S. Basil, *Liber de Sp. Sancto*, 7, *PG*, 32, 96A.
[24] *Ustav*, p. 90.
[25] *Ibid.*, p. 14.

This development of the conviction that a Father possessed the Holy Spirit and the gift of inspiration in proportion to the degree that he was spiritual goes back to the earliest days of the Church.[26] In the strict doctrinal sense of the term "Fathers of the Church", handing down true teaching from the deposit of the Church after the close of the period of public revelation, we find only in the 5th century under the influence of St. Basil and St. Gregory Nazianzen during the Christological controversies of the Council of Ephesus (431) and of Chalcedon (451).[27] A certain amount of sanctity was required but surely not heroic virtue. The important element was conformity to the traditional teaching found in the universal Church. But in the field of spiritual and mystical writings the Holy Fathers received a different and wider interpretation. All those were included under the title of Holy Fathers who by their writings or personal lives gave testimony of a life of integrated orthodox doctrine with the most intense Christian life. Speculation was not stressed as much as the living faith that was expressed by a life lived under the guidance of the Holy Spirit. Thus Holy Fathers became synonymous with the "Spiritual Fathers". "The spiritual father is anyone who due to the mortification of the passions and the *apatheia* that results from charity has equalled the interior knowledge of divine things and the discernment of human things, so as a result he can without danger to himself wisely guide others in the ways of God."[28]

The spiritual persons become associated with the perfect, the saints, those in whom the fullness of the Holy Spirit resides. Our Lord said to His Apostles: "It is not you who speak, but the Spirit of your Father who speaks in you."[29] And again, "Who hears you, hears me."[30] Therefore the spiritual persons, the perfect ones, the saints who teach others as the Apostles because they lead the "apostolic life", not in the sense of travelling to all corners of the globe, in a geographical, quantitative sense, but rather in the qualitative sense that they imitate the Apostles in their sanctity and thus the Holy Spirit speaks through them as through the first Apostles.

Finally, the meaning of these "Holy Fathers" takes on for the Sinaite hesychastic school of spirituality, and directly thence to Nil and the

[26] For a scholarly development of the term "spiritual" and its relationship with the Holy Spirit, cf. Hausherr, I., S.J., *Direction spirituelle en Orient autrefo is* (Rome, 1955), p. 39–55.
[27] Cf. Cayre, F., *Spirituali e Mistici dei primi tempi* (Catania, 1957), p. 19.
[28] Hausherr, I., "Direction...", *op. cit.*, p. 52.
[29] Matt. 10, 20.
[30] Lk. 10, 16.

Russian tradition, the meaning as given by Nicetas Stethatos, biographer of Simeon the New Theologian:

The sign of perfection, by which we can recognize the perfect man who has reached 'that maturity proportioned to the completed growth of Christ' (Ephes. 4, 13), and completely possessed by the Holy Spirit is the infallible knowledge of God from which there flashes, bestowed from high on by the Spirit, the word of superior wisdom, from which comes the ability to act as theologian to scrutinize the depths of God, to pronounce in the midst of the Church good words flowing from a good heart, to resolve the difficulties of the parables, of the enigmas and the hidden words of the Spirit, from which follows the foresight, the prediction of things to come. From which knowledge come revelations, the visions during vigils and during sleep, from which flows the ecstasy of the intellect, the enrapture by the hidden beauty of the kingdom of Heaven, the discovery of the mysteries of God, the desire to be united to Christ and to mingle with the life of the powers on high, the appetite to enjoy the joys reserved for the saints, and the contemplation of the divine light of the glory of God, according to the sacred versicle: 'Blessed are the pure of heart, for they shall see God'.[31]

Thus for the Russian monks, a Father of the Church was a teacher of the Truth because he was first of all a saint in whom the Holy Spirit gave testimony, first through the actual life he led of purity and prayer and, secondly, through his writings. What these Fathers write is from the Holy Spirit because they are united with the Holy Spirit in their holiness. We see this in Nil's repeated assertions that his doctrine is holy, inspired, of the Holy Spirit, not because it comes "from my wisdom, but God inspired the writings of enlightened Holy Fathers, that is what I teach".[32]

The Holy Fathers were first purified and then made a fitting instrument through which the Holy Spirit spoke and still continues to speak to us.

The saints, who have laboured bodily and have exercised themselves in the vineyard of the soul, and have purified their minds of sensuality, have found Our Lord and have attained spiritual wisdom. As for us, who are inflamed with desires, we are told to draw the waters of life from the sources of the Divine Writings which will quench the fires of our concupiscence and guide us towards the grasping of truth. And so, even though I am a sinner, and without great intelligence, I have applied myself to the Holy Writings, following the advice of the spirit-bearing Fathers *(duxonosnye otcy)*. Like a dog picking up scraps from under the table, I have gathered the words uttered by those

---

[31] Nicetas Stethatos, *Logos par demande et réponse, OC* (Rome, 1928), XII, p. XXIV.
[32] *Ustav*, p. 90. Cf. Article of Archimandrite Porphirij: "On the Authority of the Holy Fathers of the Church and the Importance of Their Writings", in Russian, in *Pribavlenie k izdanju tvorenij svjatyx otsov*, 1863, pp. 1–59.

blessed Fathers and have written all this down as reminder to us to be their imitators, if only in a small way.[33]

Nil pleads unworthy to be able to teach due to his sinfulness.

You asked me a sinner. We are a sinner and unworthy, how can we dare to pose as having a gift to teach? But yet we fear the judgment of God by hiding truth because of laziness and of our sins. And so I dare to answer ... but not because I am powerful in deeds and words, you know my weakness and my poverty... but I forget my nothingness and lack of learning and recalling your faith and seriousness and diligence for good, as you requested, I have dared to write you about divine rules (pravila)...[34]

In the *Pandectes* of Nikon of Montenegro,[35] a work certainly known to Nil and Joseph Volokalamsk, Nikon gives as the reason why we fall into the snares of the devil and are given over to perdition, because we do not know Divine Writings.[36] He makes no distinction between the inspired writings of the Bible and the writings of the Holy Fathers, but he puts them all into the one category as does Nil. But Nil does make a distinction and a gradation of "inspiration" when he gives an insight into how he conducted his own personal search into the Divine Writings. "I always sought out the Divine Writings, above all, the laws of God and their explanation by the Fathers, then the Apostolic traditions, then the lives and teachings of the Holy Fathers..."[37] We have already quoted Nil's statement that "we have one teacher, Our Lord Jesus Christ, who gave us the Holy Scriptures, and sent the Holy Apostles and Venerable Fathers to teach the way of Salvation to the human race".[38] Therefore the only real teacher upon whom Nil wishes to base his teaching is Our Lord Jesus Christ and the Gospels and the Epistles of His direct Apostles

---

[33] Ibid., p. 14. It is interesting to note that Climacus uses the same phrase: "...Having gathered what fell from the lips of those learned and blessed fathers as a dog gathers the crumbs that fall from the table..." *Scalae*, PG, 88, *Gradus 25*, 988D.

[34] Letter to an unknown Starec, manuscript quoted by Arxangel'skij, *op. cit.*, p. 79–80.

[35] This was an encyclopedic work motivated by the Turkish invasion to summarize all that was deemed necessary for the spiritual life. Nikon, its author, was a monk living in the 11th century in the monastery of Montenegro in Syria. Cf. Beneševič, V. N., *Taktikon Nikona Černogorca*, in *Zapiski Ist. Filol. Fakul'teta Petrogradskago Universiteta*, CXXXIX (St. Petersburg, 1917), 1st vol. Cf. also De Clercq, C., "Les textes juridiques dans les Pandectes de Nicon de la Montagne Noire", Venice, 1942, p. 9 and foll. in *S. Congreg. per la Chiesa Or. Codificazione Canonica Or. Fonti* Serie II, Fasc. XXX.

[36] De Clercq, C., *Ibid.*, ch. II, p. 23.

[37] Letter to German, fol. 105B.

[38] *Predanie*, p. 2.

will furnish him the first sources. "God's word to us is something alive, full of energy, it can penetrate deeper than any two-edged sword, reaching the very division between soul and spirit, between joints and marrow, quick to distinguish every thought and design in our hearts."[39]

For Nil, God is still speaking and making known to each man His Will. The Word of God is being addressed to each man, personally destined to enlighten him. The Word is the Light that illuminates every man born into the world.[40] There is no man to whom God does not address His Word. And yet Christians, those in Nil's time, believed in a revelation made once and a deposit kept by the Church. What once was a living, direct communication between God and a few chosen souls, for those Christians of later times remained a deposit. "When you cannot find a teacher, then the Holy Fathers tell us to turn to the Scriptures and to listen to Our Lord Himself speaking. Study the Scriptures and you shall find eternal life in them."[41]

The Gospels are not just a dead deposit, but Christ Himself is speaking and telling those who listen "with fear of God and humility"[42] how to find eternal life. The letter kills, but the spirit lives because the Spirit is living and breathing into the words of Scripture a direct communication with God. Nil compares our souls with the virgin soil ready to receive the seeds of the Word of God. "Take the seeds of the Word of God and do not turn your heart into stone nor briars, but into good soil, producing manifold fruits for the salvation of your soul."[43]

After the Gospels and Epistles of the New Testament, together with the other books of the Old,[44] for Nil the most important writings were the commentaries of the Holy Fathers on the books of the Bible. "I always sought out the Divine Writings, first the commandments of God and their explanation of them by the Fathers." The Apostolic Fathers were aware of his guidance of the Holy Spirit in their explanation of the revealed truth of God. St. Clement in his first epistle to the Corinthians clearly expresses this conviction that was in the early Church:

Through Christ we turn our regard to the high heavens, through Him we reflect as in a mirror His face without blemish, but all sublime; through Him

[39] Heb. 4, 12.
[40] Jn. 1, 9.
[41] *Ustav*, p. 14.
[42] Letter to German, fol. 104B.
[43] Letter to Gurij Tušin, fol. 103B.
[44] We have already quoted on p. 6 that until Archbishop Gennadij of Novgorod in 1499 ordered his first complete Bible, there was no full canon with all the inspired books of the Bible as we know them. Cf. footnote 25 of Part I, chapter I.

the eyes of our heart are opened. Through Him our intelligence, so incapable and obscured, reflourishes in turning towards His light; through Him the Master has wished to make us taste the 'gnosis' immortal.[45]

And the patristic writers who followed the Apostolic Fathers were guided by the same action of the Holy Spirit, producing writings "of an universal wisdom, which is as a synthesis of the theological virtues and of the superior gifts of the Holy Spirit. Here is the essence of the evangelical spirit which animated the Fathers and which had to be the true support of their action."[46]

Not only the commentaries of the Holy Fathers on the words of Christ as found in the New Testament, but also their various writings and their very lives became a witness to that continuous tradition of the unfolding of the Word of God through the action of the Holy Spirit in God's holy souls.[47] Thus Nil places in the third place the Apostolic traditions, followed by the lives and teachings of the Holy Fathers.[48] This may seem a bit too vague and too inclusive to classify all under the general term "Divine Writings". We must remember that this was the common terminology handed down by the Fathers of the Sinaitic spirituality, such as Isaac the Syrian, Climacus, Nilus Sinaite, Hesychius, and later on Simeon the New Theologian, and Gregory Sinaite.[49]

And ancient Russia, so meagre in speculative thinking, was extremely gifted in historical thinking. Their physical remoteness from the then great centres of culture and learning, especially from Byzantium, made them cling all the more conscientiously to the historical documents that gave them a sense of continuity with past ages.[50]

Thus the importance as a guide to one's life of perfection varies among the various writings that Nil puts under the general term of "Divine Writings". The writings of the Fathers and their lives had value in proportion as they mirrored faithfully the teachings found in the words of Our Lord in the Gospels and in the Apostolic traditions, especially as

[45] "First Epistle of Clement to the Corinthians", *PG*, I, 271C.
[46] Cayre, *op. cit.*, p. 26.
[47] "It is necessary to reflect and have common sense in order to comprehend what is intended by each sentence (of Holy Scripture). But we need also Tradition, for in the Holy Scriptures we do not find all." Epiphanius, *Pananrion*, 61, 6, *PG*, 41, 1048B.
[48] Letter to German, fol. 105B.
[49] An example, cf. Simeon the New Theologian: "Hear the Word of God, hear the Apostles, hear the teachers of the Church. The Apostles and the teachers all cry out as one, 'here is the Holy Spirit. Christ must be received if you wish salvation'," *PG*, 120, 539B. Also, *Ibid.*, 550A.
[50] Cf. Fedotov, *op. cit.*, pp. 39–43, 92.

found in the letters of St. Paul. Towards the writings of the Fathers and their lives what would be the criterion? Who would decide for a monk whether this or that given writing partook of the inspiration of the Word of God because it was faithful to the evangelical message as taught us by Christ? How in practice would this mass of patristic writings serve as an infallible guide for a monk's quest of perfection?

D. A SPIRITUAL GUIDE, STAREC

Nil's writings always have as a presupposition the skete life, the middle way of John Climacus where a monk lived with one or two brothers in silence.[51] And such a life of silence, solitude and continual prayer can only be embraced by those who have learned to overcome their basic passions by solid formation in a regular community life where discipline would be enforced by rule. He recommends the skete solitude only after the monk has progressed sufficiently in the way of prayer and perfection. But Nil insists that such a life be not undertaken because of its intrinsic difficulties unless the monk finds a spiritual adviser, "for solitude requires the power of an angel."[52]

Under the expert guide of a spiritual father, a starec, with whom the beginner is supposed to live, the novice to the skete life comes to learn the secrets hidden in the Divine Writings and arms himself through the discretion and sanctity of his holy guide from error and his own faulty human way of thinking. "In order to learn these Divine Writings one can follow the oral instructions of some experienced starec who is a witness in word and deed and through his spiritual discernment (duxovnym razymom) and so live one's life in harmony with his virtuous example."[53] Again he exhorts his disciples to "seek the true readings and adhere to them and converse with intelligent and holy men. Not all judge Divine Writings with right reason. And without proof of such correct writings, do not perform anything."[54] "So for those having understanding of Divine Writings and spiritual wisdom and a life giving witness by their virtues, to such strive to subject yourself and strive to be an imitator of their lives."[55]

[51] *Ustav*, p. 87. Also *PG*, 88, Climacus, *Gradus 1*, 642B, 643A.
[52] *Ibid.*, p. 88.
[53] Letter to German, fol. 106B.
[54] Letter to Gurij, fol. 102B.
[55] Letter to Gurij, fol. 103A–B.

One cannot err by following the example of a starec who has integrated into his life the teachings of the Gospels and thus by his sanctity is able to judge the right from the wrong writings. For, in an often quoted line from one of his letters, Nil succinctly says: "There are many writings, but not all are divine."[56] The first duty of the starec will be to guide the novice in discerning the true writings from the false. "Those pilgriming to salvation must first obey the Divine Writings. Only by immediate study of these writings can we know how not to wander from the true path. Follow the example of good starcy but again only of such about whom it is well-known "that their life and their wisdom are in agreement with holy writings".[57] Thus the life of the starec and his words are the same as the Holy Writings. There is only one Holy Spirit guiding both the authors of the writings and the spiritual guide who interprets them.

E. SELF-STUDY AND A SPIRIT OF CRITCISM

Nil stands out in sharp relief from his contemporaries, especially in direct opposition to Joseph Volokolamsk, in his constant insistence on the principle of self-development. The individual personality of each monk contained the secret of a loving service to God and no mechanical, external obedience alone could ever "extort" this loving submission to God's will. It was the intellect and will developed properly according to the indications of God's plan of salvation in the Divine Writings that alone could insure a conscious, active, loving service. In complete conformity with the ancient Eastern asceticism as found among Climacus, Macarius, Isaac the Syrian, Nil looks upon the monastic life as a form of life with the individual personality of the monk as the centre of this life. The external side was reduced to a minimum and the personality of the monk as the only living element became their chief occupation. The external side has meaning only as an expression of the means most suitable to aid the monk's interior life. Perfection for them could never consist in mere routine performance of external practices. There had to be a conscious understanding of the goal of perfection and the means to arrive there with a conscience willing to embrace at each and every means which would best lead to the end. Therefore the individual monk must think out, consciously understand and be convinced of the instructions; then, by

---

[56] *Ibid.*, fol. 102B.
[57] *Ibid.*, fol. 103A.

force of conviction, put them into practice in his concrete life. Encouragement, incentive, exhortation do not come from the pens of these great ascetics. As with these Fathers, so with Nil, no step of perfection was reached unless the monk had grasped for himself with his intellect the importance of a given teaching and then with his will moved his whole being to attain the proposed goal by choosing the best means.

A monk must go about his perfection with consciousness. And it was precisely in following the prescriptions of Holy Writings that the monk found the greater possibility to develop his rational powers. The first exercise of one's rational powers came in putting off one's "human" way of thinking and judging. "Do not do things according to human judgment, but according to Divine Writings and according to the Tradition of the Holy Fathers."[58] Nil, in his letters and also in his *Ustav*, often returns to this theme that his followers should not imitate those in other monasteries who do not keep God's laws as found in Holy Writings, but rather seek only their own wills and human ways of interpretation. "Not like others who follow their own will, so inclined to the flesh and to imprudent judgment."[59] For those, following the writings is cruel, stupid, suppression of all that is noble in man. "Yes, it is difficult and cruel for those who do not wish to be humiliated in the fear of the Lord and do not want to give up their earthly wisdom, but want to act according to their passionate wills and not according to Holy Writings."[60] The monk, stripped of his own "passionate" way of thinking and judging, is now exhorted by Nil to "bind yourself to the laws of the Divine Writings and follow them".[61]

The second step in the liberation of the full personality of the monk comes in choosing his guide, the starec who will, by his oral instructions and example of life, interpret the Writings for him as the voice of God. The monk does not come to the monastery and submit himself to the guide of any superior whosoever he be, but he chooses freely that one who will by his learning and sanctity best lead him along God's ways. S. Smirnov gives the traditional teaching of the Fathers, so assiduously followed by Nil, in regard to this complete liberty in the choice of a spiritual guide. "The choice of the starec was considered as an inalienable and essential right of the novice ascetic."[62] As for the qualities that a monk should seek in his future spiritual guide, St. Basil suggests:

[58] Letter to German, fol. 104A.
[59] *Ibid.*, fol. 104B.
[60] *Ibid.*, fol. 107B.
[61] Letter to Gurij, fol. 102B.
[62] Smirnov, S., *Duxovnyj otec v drevnei vostočnoj cerkvi* (Sergiev-Posad, 1906), p. 25.

Take great care and circumspection to find a man who knows how to lead those who march on the road to God, who is adorned with all virtues, who offers testimony by his own works of his personal love for God, who possesses knowledge of the Divine Writings, a man who does not search distractions, who does not love money, does not mix in affairs of others, one who is pleasing, a friend of God and of the humble, without anger, rancour, of great edification for those who approach him, without vanity and pride, insensible to flatteries, inaccessible to inconstancy, who puts nothing above God. If you find such a man, bind yourself to him, rejecting far from you your own will, as one expectorates undesired spittle.[63]

But to find such a guide, Nil forewarns the novice, will be a most difficult task. A trustworthy guide, they (Gregory of Sinai and the other Fathers explain) should be one who has acquired practice and wisdom which harmonize with the Holy Writings and who has acquired spiritual discretion *(rassuzdenie duxovnoe)*. "If in those times, in such ascetical times, it was difficult to find a good director, what now in these spiritual crises, how much more difficult, yet how much more needed is a good director and with what greater diligence should he be sought."[64]

What is to happen to the monk should he not find the guide his sincere will seeks out? Nil suggests: "When no guide can be found, the Fathers have us turn to the Holy Writings and listen to the Lord Himself speaking. Study the Holy Writings and you shall find eternal life in them."[65] "Live in harmony with the example of your spiritual guide. But if no such guide can be found, the (next) best of all is to follow God according to the Divine Writings."[66]

Therefore Nil is handing the monk the words of Christ, the writings of the Apostles, the commentaries of the Fathers on these, these writings and Lives of the Holy Fathers and telling him to make these the object of intense study. He is to dig out the necessary direction for his own moral perfection. This presupposes much previous preparation of purification and instruction in a more stable life than that offered by a skete hermitage, it means a fairly solid mastery over one's passions and a solid acquisition of the fundamental virtues. "We are told to draw the waters

---

[63] *PG*, 32, 296B.
[64] *Ustav*, p. 13–14. Cf. also Gregory Sinaite, *PG*, 1342B: "It is not for everyone to guide others. But great discretion of spirits is demanded. It is not easy to find a guide who does not err in his works, or thoughts. Who wants to attain pure prayer of quiet, must walk in trembling and struggle under the expert questioning of the spiritual guide."
[65] *Ustav*, p. 14.
[66] Letter to German, fol. 106B.

of life from the sources of the Divine Writings which alone can extinguish the passions that plague us and set us on the road to intellectual truth."[67]

But Nil wisely adds to his first injunction to study diligently the Holy Writings, another obligation: to separate the Divine Writings from the many false writings of those days. In his *Ustav* there is not found this injunction, undoubtedly because he felt that it would be clear from his often repeated command to "learn the Divine Writings". But in his letters he often returns to this theme of developing a spirit of criticism, of discerning the true from the false writings. "Writings are many, but not all are divine."[68] "Bind yourself to the laws of Divine Writings and follow the *true* Divine Writings. For there are many writings, but not all are Divine. You, seek the *true* from the many readings and stick to them. Converse with prudent and spiritual men, for not all men are able to judge prudently these Divine Writings. And without proof that these are true, do not do anything."[69]

It has already been pointed out: the general widespread lack of learning, inability to read, shortage of books, and the general *mélange* of canonical Biblical books with apocryphal writings and purely historical, secular books, were regarded as forming the truly inspired Bible.[70] From faulty translations made from Greek and other Oriental languages into Slavonic either by Bulgarian or Russian monks to errors that crept into the work of transcribers, from the overabundance of apocryphal writings that were handed down and regarded with a certain amount of reverence as making up a part of church tradition, from the fanaticism of clinging to the letter of Holy Scripture, liturgical texts, and patristic writings which resulted from excessive, external ritualism with not much interior spirit or intelligence guiding it, there developed a sacred awe for the printed letter. To correct any text that had been good enough for the great saints of early Russian Christianity was bordering on heresy. One can understand this exaggeration of the letter when the Russian Church took upon itself the responsibility after the fall of Constantinople to the Turks in 1453, to preserve Orthodoxy from the slightest change. Deprived of a full teaching body and not having yet established its own Patriarch, Russian Orthodoxy had to cling to the letter in order to insure teaching the same as

---

[67] *Ustav*, p. 14.
[68] Letter to Gurij, fol. 102B.
[69] *Ibid.*
[70] Cf. *supra*, pp. 2–6 of text. For a typical ancient Russian Bible canon, cf. text on p. 6 and footnote 25. Golubinskij, *op. cit.*, gives the back ground to the formation of the first Bible in Russia (of Gennadij), T. II, 2, 1911 ed., p. 263.

their ancestors had taught. *Stoglav* showed the necessity of correcting
books, but did not know how to go about it. It recommended measures
that surely would have been favoured by Nil 50 years earlier: to copy
books from faithful translations, going back to the original copies as far
as possible and to forbid the selling of uncorrected books.[71]

But the Fathers of the Synod were incapable of determining the criterion of a good translation. We need only cite the pathetic case of
Dionisij, the higoumen of the Troickaja Lavra who had been commissioned in the beginning of the reign of Tsar Michael Fjodorovič (†1645)
along with fellow-monks Arsenij and Antonij to correct the errors in the
Trebnik, the book dealing with all the rites of administering the sacraments and sacramentals, blessings and any special service outside of the
Liturgy and Office. If this happened 100 years after Nil's lifetime, it gives
us an idea of the situation during Nil's time. In gratitude for their corrections made, the three had been tried in the *Sobor* of 1618; their
corrections were declared heretical. Dionisij was excommunicated from
the Church, imprisoned in Novospasskij monastery, beaten and tortured
with physical cruelties and mental humiliations.[72]

What were the limits Nil placed on his principle of self-criticism of
writings? There are two points to remember in viewing Nil's principle.
Firstly, as has been already pointed out, he presupposes a certain level of
spiritual maturity on the part of the beginner of the skete life. In this
maturity he presupposes already developed a prudential judgment, the
ability to judge among good, bad, and indifferent and to avoid extremes.
The whole last chapter of his *Ustav* is devoted to summarizing the *Leit-
motiv* that should guide the monk in his spiritual striving for perfection.
"St. Basil teaches that all these good and edifying things should be done
in good time and with proper measure. Do all things with prudence and
discretion because without discretion even good frequently is changed
into harm, if time and measure are not observed. But when reason

---

[71] *Stoglav, op. cit.*, pp. 60–61.
[72] These three correctors had compared 20 different manuscripts, five of them in
Greek. When their corrections were presented to the Metropolitan Iona, he was irate
because they were done without his permission. The Moscow clergy were against
them because none of them had been on the correcting commission. Even Dionisij's
own monks were against him. In the *Sobor* the corrections were found to be errors.
A typical example of the corrections made: in the formula of blessing water, the
correctors dropped out the words "and by your fire" which they found were faultily
added to the true formula "bless this water with your Holy Spirit". For their labours
to remove error, they were branded heretics. Cf. Pypin, A. N., *Istorija russkoj lite-
raturi* (St. Petersburg, 1911–1913), T. 2, ch. VII, p. 252.

determines the time and the measure, then the result is indeed wonderful."[73]

Secondly, Nil limits freedom of investigation of Sacred Writings to the area he calls "the lives and teachings of the Holy Fathers".[74] His one teacher remained always Jesus Christ. Therefore there could not be any criticism of what clearly was the Word of God. The writings that came after the Apostolic age, from the Holy Fathers, would be "true" writings if they were in harmony and agreement with the teaching of Christ and His divinely inspired Apostles.

In regard to this last, practical application by Nil of his spirit of criticism, B. Žmakin says: "His principle of free critical investigation of ecclesiastical sources of right teaching and morality Nil employed by checking and correcting the Lives of the saints. He skeptically regarded the tales of some saints as for the most part fabricated in later times."[75] In proof of this statement he offers the words of Vassian Patrikeev, Nil's disciple, in answer to Joseph's charge that Nil and his pupil slandered not only the miracle-workers of Russia but also those of ancient times and in other lands by not believing their miracles and by changing the miracles found in the written Lives of those saints: "Joseph, you lie against me and my starec Nil. Nil did not change any miracles in their Holy Writings, but rather corrected them with correct manuscripts..."[76]

A. Arxangel'skij produces what he claims as conclusive proof of Nil's critical emendations. Two manuscripts,[77] containing Lives of saints, have places in the texts filled in with corrections and in the margins such notices as "from here in the copies not correct", "in the copies, here an omission", "here it is not sufficient", "if here one checks in another translation, he will find a much better reading than this". In the second

---

[73] *Ustav*, p. 85. Cf. also *Evagrius. Practica Ad Anatolium, PG*, 40, VI, 1224B.
[74] Letter to German, fol. 105B. Cf. Manuscript no. 23/1262, fol. 1–2 quoted by Arxangel'skij, *op. cit.*, pp. 124–125.
[75] Zmakin, V., *Metropolit Daniil i ego sošinenija* (Moscow, 1881), p. 33.
[76] "Polemičeskija sočinenija Vassiana Patrikeeva", in *Prav. Sob.*, 1863, part 3, p. 208. Zmakin also maintains that he saw in a collection of manuscripts possessed by Graf A. C. Ivarov a manuscript of the 16th century in handwriting, of the Lives of the Saints and in the foreword, mention is made that these Lives of the Saints have been "corrected by Starec Nil". He claims that most likely it is our Nil who in his *Ustav* claims that he chose from the compositions of the Holy Fathers and others only those that agreed with his intelligence. Cf. Zmakin, *op. cit.*, p. 33, footnote 34.
[77] Manuscrits no. 684 from the Troice-Sergieva Lavra, now found in the Lenin Library of Moscow and no. 23/1262 from the Kirillo-Belozerskij monastery, formerly in the St. Petersburg Ecclesiastical Academy, now found in the Saltykov-Ščedrin Public Library in Leningrad. I was able to check these mss. myself in the USSR in 1969.

manuscript we find these words: "These Lives of the saints and martyrs were copied over from a manuscript copied by Starec Nil with his additions and corrections, over which Nil worked much."

In the first manuscript, originally belonging to the Kirillo-Belozerskij monastery, the preface reads

...I wrote using various copies. I strove to find the correct one. I found in the various texts many uncorrected things. As far as my weak intellect could, I corrected these, for I could not let them stand. Let those having more intelligence than we, correct the still uncorrected and make up any deficiencies. If that which I have written is not in accordance with truth, I beg pardon of him who must copy or read this. Let him not copy it or read it, but let him write only the truth and speak the truth for only such is pleasing to God and helpful to souls, because that is all even a sinful person as myself would want. But it was all written here in this manner, and, if left, it would not have been pleasing to God, nor profitable for souls. Because of my weak intellect and ignorance, I hope that someone else will be able to do better than I have, thus being pleasing to God and a profit to souls, and I should thus rejoice in that... I beg for those reading or hearing that they may receive some profit; may they pray, please God, for me that I will have mercy from Him, for I have worked hard at this labour. Such for me is the fulfillment of the command to love God and my neighbour. May we, taking these Lives of the Holy Fathers, be zealous for their deeds and with them possess eternal life. This is true love for one's neighbour: to move his conscience to love God and keep His Commands according to His true divine words, and, according to the life and teachings of the Holy Fathers, to live as far as possible and thus be saved. If I am sinful and wretched and incapable of doing any good, at least I wish the salvation of many of my neighbours.[78]

This citation gives clearly the purpose of Nil in criticizing and correcting the erroneous texts. He wants himself and others to follow only the "true", as God sees it, for only in following the true can we give full glory to God and find profit for our souls. K. V. Pokrovskij checked the two mentioned manuscripts and made further investigations by comparing corrected Lives of saints done by Nil with the Lives copied over by contemporaries and even in earlier copies and concluded:

The criticism of Nil was purely scientific, referring to the given text, and not to the contents of the Lives, so that the three mentioned omissions (touching ideology, confer footnote n. 78) cannot be proof that Nil made changes for ideological motives against such sufficient and persuasive proof from entire series of omissions of a completely different character. ...The words of Joseph that Nil 'changed the miracles of saints' are founded on nonsense if one refers to the works of Nil. Referring with rare attention to the quoted text and leaving

[78] Quoted by Arxangel'skij, *op. cit.*, pp. 124–125.

free places to be filled in with the corrected citations, Nil, according to the opinion of the speaker, must have possessed a great knowledge of Greek Lives. In one place it can be proposed that Nil, by memory, supplied an omission of the Russian original on the basis of his knowledge of Greek hagiographical literature.[79]

J. S. Lur'e, the Soviet specialist on Nil Sorskij and his times, gives in detail examples, using the same mss. as Arxangel'skij and Pokrovskij used. He shows clearly the critical correction of texts made by Nil. Taking two mss. which he was able to investigate at length, the Kirillo-

---

[79] Pokrovskij, K. V., *K literaturnoj dejatelnosti Nila Sorskogo*, in *Drevnosti. Trudy Slavjanskoj komissii Moskovskogo arxeologičeskogo obščestva*, T. 5 (Moscow, 1911), *Protokoly*, pp. 32–34. The author wished to ascertain whether Nil omitted things that were left in texts of his contemporaries due to Nil's ideology or rather due to his scholarly bent on seeking the true reading. He compares the two Lives of Simeon Stylites and Chariton as found in the Troickaja Lavra manuscript with the text used by Makarij for his *Čet'i Minei* (September tome, Sept, 1, col. 8–19; Sept. 28, col. 2192 respectively), (St. Petersburg, 1868). "Except for the phraseology there are no important differences. What touches the omissions mentioned by Nil and scattered throughout the texts of both manuscripts, 23 in the Troickij and 17 in the St. Petersburg manuscript, they generally coincide with each other, and in a few small insignificant points they do not agree, and these are not in point of ideology... We can see the delicate attention of Nil. In the Minei text in one place it was incorrectly written 30 for 13, as found in the Greek text. Nil corrects the figure. In the Life of Chariton there may be omitted now and again a full word; in other cases, omissions equal to one or several phrases. Again their content has nothing to do with polemic, rationalistic thought. Only three omissions could touch ideology: (1) Ideas of Kirjak to build a coenobitic monastery; (2) Narration of the asceticism and fast of Hilarion the Great; (3) The receiving by Savva the Holy of 1,000 gold pieces for the upkeep and building of his monastery." But pressing further and making comparisons from contemporary manuscripts of the same Lives and even earlier copies, e.g. manuscript of Ivarov, no. 1054 (now found in the National Historical Museum of Moscow), Joseph Volokolamsk, no. 637, and Troickaja Lavra, no. 685 (both now found in the Lenin Library of Moscow) and the Greek Lives, the author comes to the conclusion quoted above in the text.

But J. S. Lur'e in his work: *Ideologičeskaja bor'ba v russkoj publicistike konca XV – načala XVI veka* ("Ideological Struggle in Russian Polemical Literature") (Moscow–Leningrad, 1960), pp. 328–330, insists that Nil's spirit of criticism at times touched also points of ideology and seeks to refute Pokrovskij's evidence by re-examining the three places cited by Pokrovskij. His conclusion is that Nil changed the texts in these three places because the original went contrary to Nil's ideology, i.e. the ideas of Kirjak on coenobitic monasticism, Hilarion's severe asceticism and fasting, and Savva's receiving of 1,000 gold pieces from the emperor for the upkeep of his monastery. The strongest testimony for Nil's scholarly criticism remains his own scope and method given in the cited preface of one of his copied works (Kir.-Bel. Ms. 23/1262, fol. 1–2B, cited by Arxangel'skij, *op. cit.*, p. 125) joined with the above proofs, offered even by Lur'e, and coupled with Vassian's defense of him before the attacks of Joseph Volokolamsk: "Nil did not change any miracles from their (the Holy Fathers') writings, but rather corrected them with correct manuscripts." (Cf. fnte no. 75 *supra*).

Beloz., no. 23/1262 and the Troick. Ms. no. 684 which practically co-
incides with that of the Kir.-Beloz., he compares the apparent corrections
through omission or addition to the text used by the composer of these
two mss...[80] Comparing them with the similar passage retained by the
composer of the *Velikija Cet'i Minei*, we find clear proof to support
Vassian's assertion against Joseph's accusation that Nil falsely changed
the Lives of the saints. Specific points cited by Lur'e that individual
lacunae and corrections by addition show that the centre of Nil's attention
was purely textual. First he cites from the *Zitie* of St. Theodore Studite.
Both Mss. no. 23/1262 and no. 684 omit in the same place where the
author speaks of the age of the saint when he was elected higoumen.
"Having *(lacuna)* years of age and having already been a monk for
thirty years..."[81] The text in the *Velik. Četi' Minei* gives the same version
as the common text used by Nil and the composer of the *Velik. Čet'i
Minei*: "Having five and thirty years of age, having already been a monk
for thirty years".[82] If Theodore was thirty-five years when he was chosen
higoumen and had been already a tonsured monk for thirty years, this
would make him five years old when he entered. And the text previously
had mentioned that he entered the monastery as an adult.

This seems a clear case of Nil's evident prudence and hardly a question
of changing a text because he was motivated by his religious ideology.
The Greek text, continues Lur'e,[83] gives the reason for the error. Theodore had been tonsured at the age of thirteen and not thirty, and this
explains the apparent *lacuna* in Nil's work while the composer of the
Minei retained the mistake. Thus throughout these two manuscripts
copied by Nil (or by his followers, perhaps from a work of Nil; the two
mss. carry the date 1509) there appear in the margin the quoted remarks
cited by Arxangel'skij above, telling of the motive for the *lacuna*.

Lur'e gives a further example illustrating Nil's completion of a text
by addition. In the Life of St. Ioannikij the text speaks about his military
undertakings before he actually leaves the world and gives himself to the
guidance of an "experienced man".[84] In both mss. there is inserted an
addition that makes a correct reading in conformity to a more exact
translated text. But in the *Minei* the story of the saint's military exploits

---

[80] Lur'e, *Ideologičeskaja...*, *op. cit.*, p. 326–328. We presuppose that Nil is the author
of the Mss. or at least that of Kir.-Bel. which has written on it: "From the book of
Starec Nil."
[81] No. 23/1262, fol. 172; no. 684, fol. 125.
[82] *Velik. Čet'i Minei*, November 1–12 (St. Petersburg, 1897), col. 373.
[83] Lur'e, *op. cit.*, p. 327.
[84] Ms. no. 23/1262, fol. 50; no. 684, fol. 85.

is mixed absurdly with the account of Ioannikij's leaving the world and seeking advice from a skilled director of souls. It is clear, concludes Lur'e,[85] that in the original used by Nil and the composer of the *Minei* there was some clear omission, a blank which Nil (or his followers) bravely filled in, while the author of the *Minei* had not the courage and hence retained a confused and senseless reading.

We could close this section by citing a modern textual critic of Lives of saints, the Bollandist Paul Devos, S.J.:

Un esprit critique s'était cependant assez tôt éveillé, dans un skit au nord de la Volga, et nous acheverons ces lignes sur la vision du sympathique S. Nil de la Sora, que nous retrouvons, consultant, comme il le dit, différents manuscrits des Vies de saints en tâchant de découvrir l'authentique, y rencontrant beaucoup d'erreurs et corrigeant ce que sa 'faible intelligence' lui permettait de rectifier, ailleurs encore, inscrivant dans la marge les remarques qui lui semblaient nécessaires. N'est-il pas intéressant de voir germer de pareilles préoccupations chez un homme qui mourut tout juste un siècle, à quelques mois près, avant que ne fut lancé dans le monde savant le manifeste de Rosweyde?[86]

---

[85] *Op. cit.*, pp. 327–328.
[86] Devos, Paul, S.J., *Chronique d'Hagiographie Slave, II, La "Sainte Russie", du Baptême de Vladimir jusqu'à l'Epoque Moderne*, in *Analecta Bollandiana*, T. LXXXIII, Fasc. I–II (Brussels, 1955), p. 236.

II

THE WAY BACK TO GOD

A. THE STRUGGLE FOR SELF-PERFECTION: AN INTERNAL BATTLE

Nil, under the influence of Macarius and the early Fathers of the desert, plus the strong effect exerted on him by Isaac the Syrian and the Sinaite school of spirituality with such Fathers as Climacus, Nilus, Simeon the New Theologian and Gregory, views the spiritual life of a Christian as a constant battle. "There is a great battle, a double one, in soul and body and there is nothing more necessary for one's existence. For this reason, one must be attentive with all strength and observe carefully and courageously one's heart, keeping it from these thoughts and having the fear of God ever before one's eyes..."[1] One's whole spiritual welfare depends on the way we wage this battle against the common enemy of all mankind, the demons. And the war is fought both in the body and in the soul.[2] But the heart or the mind is where the battlefield is marked off, and where victory or defeat is had.

Nil complains that "many do good actions, but neglect the mind; they know nothing of the spiritual contests, the victories and defeats. They neglect the mind which is the eye of the soul."[3] Thus a person may pass his whole life never entering into his mind and meeting the devil in direct combat, never aware that the crown of eternal life is only given to those who "fight the good fight" of St. Paul.

The monk, according to Nil, perfects himself by battling the devils with God's help. It is not merely a negative process of cutting out the evil presented by the devils to the mind, but the positive virtues are supposed to be developed during the fray. One, in fighting against all the

---

[1] Letter to Gurij, fol. 99A–B.
[2] For the divisions of passions rooted in the body and those in the soul cf. Cassian, *Conférences* (Sources Chrétiennes), Dom. E. Pichery (Paris, 1935), V, 3 and 4, pp. 190–192. St. Basil, *Reg. Fusious Tr.*, 16, *PG*, 31, 958A–C. Diadochus, *Capita de perfectione spirituali*, *PG*, 65, Ch. 99, 1210.
[3] *Ustav*, p. 12. No doubt Nil is quoting here Evagrius: "What the eye is to the body, that the mind is to the soul." Cf. I. Hausherr, *Les Leçons...*, pp. 181–188.

passions, acquires all the virtues at one time.[4] Nowhere does Nil develop logically this positive side as clearly as he depicts the battle of uprooting the evil thoughts suggested by the devils. This glaring absence in his system of asceticism will be treated later on. But even in this he was only being faithful to the great Fathers of the desert. Suffice to point out here that Nil, as they, emphasizes the battle element, the struggle to win back the heart in order that God may reign supreme as the only object of its love. "From the heart flows evil thoughts defiling the heart; therefore we must purify the inner vessel and worship God in spirit and truth."[5] Nil quotes Hesychius of Jerusalem: "Just as it is impossible to preserve life without eating and drinking, so it is impossible to achieve anything spiritual without that guarding of the mind which is also called "vigilance" *(nepsis)* even for those who force themselves to avoid sin for fear of the pain of hell."[6]

The early Christians, especially under the guide of Ss. Peter and Paul in their epistles, were especially aware of the existence of the devil and his cohorts. "Be sober and watch well; the devil, who is your enemy, goes about roaring like a lion, to find his prey, but you grounded in the faith must face him boldly . . ."[7]

Draw your strength from the Lord, from that mastery which His power supplies. You must wear all the weapons in God's armour, if you would find strength to resist the cunning of the devil. It is not against flesh and blood that we enter the lists; we have to do with princedoms and powers, with those who have mastery of the world in these dark days, with malign influences in an order higher than ours. Take up all God's armour, then, so you will be able to stand your ground when the evil times comes; and be found still on your feet, when all the task is over.[8]

The devil is a reality and war with him is a prerogative of every Christian.

---

[4] By "mortifying" the self of all irregulated desires and inclinations, the monk would be forced in the process to acquire all virtues. Cf. Nil Sinaite: "First we must fight the passions with much prudence which comes only through fighting. Then from our victories we can give to others of our conquests," *PG*, 79, 751B. Also St. Athanasius: *Syntagma ad Monachos*, PG, 28, 835; *Vitae Patrum*, PL, 22, 857, Diadochus, *Capitula centum de perfectione spirituali*, PG, 65, 1167ss.; Cassian, *Conférences, op. cit.*, IV, ch. 3 and 8, pp. 169, 173.

[5] *Ustav*, p. 11. Cf. Arsenius: "That which one must purify above all is the interior man," *Doctrina et Exhortatio, PG*, 66, 1617.

[6] *Ustav*, p. 13.

[7] 1 Peter 5, 8.

[8] Ephes. 6, 10–13.

Macarius, many centuries earlier, put down in writing Nil's complaint and much more in detail about those who do not know of the existence of this interior battle with the devil.

He who wishes to please God and to wage true enmity against the adversary must wage two wars; one against the visible things of this life which hold us in bondage with their earthly distractions and love for this life and the other war against the affections of sin aroused internally by the hidden spirits of evil... It is possible that if one, in fighting, strips the self from all external, worldly bonds, material things, and carnal pleasures, and begins to adhere to the Lord, he certainly can learn about the war of affections, the internal battle of wicked thoughts. Unless he denies the world, he can have no knowledge of the deceits of the hidden spirits and of the affections for evil. All this remains unknown to him because he still gives himself to external things and wishes to be held by the attraction of this world. But if he casts off the world, he will find repugnance, his hidden affections, hidden traps, the hidden war, an internal contest. And so begging God, he receives the heavenly arms of the Spirit as St. Paul says (Ephes. 6, 14), the breastplate of justice, the helmet of salvation, the shield of faith and the sword of the spirit, God's word. Thus arrayed with these arms, he can stand up against the hidden strategems of the devil with all prayer, perseverance, petition and fasting, acquired through faith... Thus the enemies, the powers having been conquered by the help and goodness of the Spirit by one's own striving always for all virtues, one may be found worthy of eternal life, glorifying the Father, Son, and Holy Spirit for all eternity.[9]

The first step in Nil's return to God is to leave all worldly attachments and retire into solitude.[10] "It is characteristic of the strong to draw the sword, the Word of God (Ephes. 6, 14) and struggle in solitude against the demons."[11] Here in the desert the monk meets his enemy in a battle that no lay person, due to his worldly attachments and commitments, would be able to undergo. Like his great Master, "the Spirit sent Him out into the desert, and there He spent forty days and forty nights, tempted by the devil; there He lodged with the beasts and there the angels ministered to Him".[12] In the Life of St. Anthony[13] we perceive

---

[9] *PG* 34, 658, IVB, VD.

[10] Nil Sinaite says: "Let us strip for the battle. I exhort you all. The enemy is nude, nor do the fighters enter into the arena and fight vested. The law of sports demand those fighting in the stadium and arena be stripped... We are commended to fight and against the adversary who is much faster than those who fight visibly. We expect to run, but instead of stripping off, we throw on additional weights of 1,000 pounds on our shoulders. We try to fight and all the time we provide the adversary with many gripping points." *PG*, 79, 798B–C.

[11] *Ustav*, p. 86.

[12] Mark 1, 13. Cf. Matt. 4, 1; Lk. 4, 1.

[13] St. Athanasius, *Life of St. Anthony*, *PG*, 26, 951A–B. Also 861C, 856A, 904B, 920A.

the conviction that the early monks had that the desert was the *habitat* of the demons. Perhaps it derived from the idea of victory over the dead from which place the devil had driven out man. In this solitude the monk finds the demons of his interior world. He is given occasions of supreme heroism in fighting the devils in his interior, in the depths of his soul. The spirit of evil wrestles against the spirit of God for the possession of the heart of the monk. But the monk never remains passive. Nil over and over repeats phrases such as "purify the mind", "attain grace and purify the soul", "guard the mind", "keep the heart silent", "look into the depths of the heart", "enclose the mind and heart", "bring the mind under control", "gather the mind into your heart", "contain the mind in the heart, freed of all imaginings".[14] The monk's first concern is to destroy the source of bad thoughts by battling always against the passions. When he reaches this stage through purifying the heart of all imaginings, he acquires *apatheia*.[15] When the monk is "dispassioned", then he can occupy his mind and heart with the continual presence of God.

This is the "mental activity" that Nil proposes constantly for his monks, the same as the *noera ergasia* of the Fathers of old.[16] "Many of the Holy Fathers spoke of the 'heart activity', of the control of the thoughts and of 'guarding of the mind' in various discourses, using words as they were inspired by the grace of God, each according to his own way of understanding. But the Holy Fathers first of all agree on this activity which they learned from the Master Himself who commanded

[14] *Ustav*, pp. 13, 21–22.
[15] Cf. Nil Sinaite, *De malignis cogitationibus*, PG, 79, 1145–1164. The majority of ancient ascetical writers, besides Nil Sinaite, considered *apatheia* (in the full Christian sense) as an essential element of spiritual perfection. Cf. Macarius, *Liber de elevatione mentis*, PG, 34, 905; *Liber de libertate mentis*, PG, 34, 938ss.; Cassian, *Conférences*, I, 6, 7, pp. 83–85, *op. cit.;* IX, 2, pp. 40–41. Climacus, *Gradus 29, Scalae*, PG, 88, 1147ss. summarizes as best as any of the Fathers their teaching on *apatheia:* "By dispassion I mean no other than the interior heaven of the mind, which regards the tricks of the demons as mere toys. And so he is truly dispassionate, and is recognized as such who has made his flesh incorruptible, who has raised his mind above creatures and has subdued all his senses to it, and who keeps his soul in the presence of the Lord, ever reaching out to Him even beyond his strength. Some say that dispassion is the resurrection of the soul before the body; but others, that it is the perfect knowledge of God, second only to that of the angels... The soul has dispassion which is immersed in the virtues as the passionate are in pleasures."
[16] Nil uses the words: "*myslennoe delanie*" or "*delanie serdečnoe*" for mental activity or activity of the heart; or again, "*bljudenie myslennoe*", for mental control. Cf. *Ustav*, p. 11.

us to clean the interior of the vessel, for from the heart flow out evil thoughts which defile man."[17]

Nil, warring against the formalism found in the piety of his day, continues, linking up "mental activity" with the only pleasing and meritorious action done by us in the eyes of God. "They (the Holy Fathers) thus reasoned that it is proper to adore the Father in spirit and in truth.[18] They recalled the words of the Apostle Paul: 'If I pray with my tongue (i.e. with lips only), my spirit (i.e. my voice) prays; but my mind is without fruit. I will thus pray with my spirit and with my mind."[19] And thus they were particularly concerned with mental prayer according to the injunction of the Apostle, "I would rather speak five words which my mind utters than ten thousand with my tongue."[20] It is the interior activity of one's mind that is all-important in prayer. Was it not St. Agathon, Nil says, who described bodily activity and external prayer as the leaves, while internal, mental prayer is the fruit.[21] Every tree, says our Lord, not bearing fruit, i.e. mental activity, is to be cut down and cast into the fire. God cannot hear the prayer of one who prays only with his lips, for he is praying not to God, but to the wind. God looks to the mind alone. The way back to God is through mental activity, for all other external activity, unless the mind or heart accompanies, it is useless before God.[22] The external temptations of the devil, attractions of world and flesh cannot harm man unless he allows the evil spirit to

[17] Matt. 23, 25: "Woe to you, Scribes and Pharisees, you hypocrites that scour the outward part of cup and dish, while all within is running with avarice and incontinence. Scour the inside of cup and dish first, thou blind Pharisee, that so inside too may become clean."

Matt. 15, 18: "All that comes out of his mouth comes from the heart, and it is that which makes a man unclean. It is from the heart that his wicked designs come, his sins of murder, adultery, fornication, theft, perjury and blasphemy. It is these that make a man unclean."

[18] Jn. 4, 24: "God is a spirit, and those who worship Him must worship Him in spirit

[19] 1 Cor. 14, 14–15: "If I use a strange tongue when I offer prayer, my spirit is praying, but my mind reaps no advantage from it. What, then, is my drift? Why, I mean to use the mind as well as the spirit when I offer prayer, use the mind as well as the spirit when I sing psalms." It is evident that Nil is taking this interpretation of St. Paul from Gregory Sinaite: "The Apostle asserts the same when he says: 'If I pray in an unknown tongue (i.e. with my lips), my spirit (or my voice) prays, but my understanding is unfruitful...' " PG, 150, De Quietudine, 6, 1320B–C.

[20] Ibid., ch. 14, 19. Cf. Climacus, op. cit., Gradus 28, 1133B.

[21] Ustav, pp. 11–12. PG, 65, 112A–B.

[22] Ibid., p. 12. Nil quotes Barsanuphius: "If the interior action does not strengthen man with the help of God, then his exterior activities are all in vain." St. Isaac the Syrian writes: "Exterior action when the spiritual does not accompany, it is like barren loins and dry breasts, for to such God's wisdom is unapproachable."

possess his heart. Likewise, unless God possesses his heart, man can labour exteriorly for a whole lifetime and yet his labours will not be pleasing to God. Each one must in his thoughts wage war, that Christ illumine his heart and drive out the evil spirits.

Just as a cloth thrown into the fire cannot resist the flames, but must immediately burn, so the devils who try waging war against the man who seeks only the Spirit are burnt and consumed by the divine power of the fire within if only man adheres constantly to the Lord and places his confidence and hope in Him. If there were demons strong as mountains, yet they would be burnt by prayer as wax in fire. The great war is in the soul and against the devils.[23]

B. PSYCHOLOGY OF THOUGHTS

Before Nil searches the human mind or heart to find the basic thoughts that the devil is wont to stir up in us, he analyses carefully the five steps how a thought psychologically develops in us, from the first moment of its entrance into our consciousness to the last when it has made us complete slaves to it through passion. There are five steps: (1) The arising in our mind of a representation, a subject, an image *(prilog)*; (2) The coupling or conversation with the image (in Greek: *sunduasmos*) *(sočetanie)*; (3) Consent given to the thought *(slozenie)*; (4) Slavery to it *(plenenie)*; (5) Lastly, passion *(strast')*. The dependence of Nil on Climacus is evident.[24]

---

[23] Macarius, *PG*, 34, *Hom. XLIII*, 774B–C.
[24] *Ustav*, p. 16. It is most interesting to compare the teaching of the Fathers as presented by Climacus on the development of temptations. "In the rules laid down by the Fathers there is given a distinction between various things, such as attraction, intercourse, consent, captivity or struggle, and the so-called passion in the soul. And these blessed men define attraction as a simple conception or an image of something encountered for the first time which has lodged in the heart. Intercourse is conversation with what has presented itself, accompanied by passion or dispassion. And consent is the bending of the soul to what has been presented to it, accompanied by delight. But captivity is a forcible and involuntary rape of the heart or a permanent association with what has been encountered which destroys the good order of our condition. Struggle, according to their definition, is power equal to the attacking force, which is either victorious or else suffers defeat according to the soul's desire. And they define passion in a special sense as that which lurks disquietingly in the soul for a long time, and through its intimacy with the soul brings it finally to what amounts to a habit, a self-incurred downright desertion." *Scalae, PG*, 88, *Gradus 15*, 896D. Philotheus Sinaite follows quite literally Climacus in his presentation of the five steps in the development of a thought-temptation. Cf. *Dobrotoljubie*, T. 3 (Moscow, 1888), no. 34–36, pp. 459–460. N. B. Migne handed down the writings of Philotheus on the forty chapters on Sobriety in his tome 162, but this manuscript was unfortunately destroyed by

1. *Presentation of the Thought-Image*

The image rises suddenly in the heart and is presented to the mind. It can be a simple suggestion from the devil, as says St. Gregory Sinaite, "Do this or that" as Christ was tempted to change stones into bread."[25] Or, as most Fathers admit, it may be any sort of thought coming to man's mind, good, bad, or indifferent. And thus this stage is never sinful for it does not depend on us. It is a state that we can expect, considering our fallen natures. "It is impossible that there be no attack from the enemy after the devil and his wicked spirits received entrance into man's heart when man was evicted from Paradise and turned away from God."[26] Simeon the New Theologian affirms that, once man has removed himself far from God, the devil can agitate and stir up the thoughts and mind of everyone as he wishes. And how much more is this true among the more perfect and those who have reached already a high degree of sanctity. One can never remain confirmed and out of the reach of the devil.[27]

Macarius aptly gives the example of merchants sailing with full wind and in sails and peaceful sea, yet, as long as they are not safely in the harbour, must continually fear, lest sudden wind rise up and the waves of the sea threaten the ship's safety. Thus great diligence is required at every moment.[28]

---

fire, so one has to search for these chapters either in the Greek or Russian *Philokalia* or they can be found also in the Vatican Library manuscript 730. Philotheus' discourse, however, on the Commandments is found under the name of Philotheus, Patriarch of Constantinople, *PG*, 154, 729–746. Others who have handled the psychology of temptation development in a similar way are: Hesychius of Sinai, *PG*, 93, *De Temp. et Virtute, Cent. I*, 46, 1496C; J. Damascene, *PG*, 95, *De Virtute et Vitio*, 93; Mark the Hermit, *PG*, 65, *De Baptismo*, 1013–1021; St. Nil, *PG*, 79, *De Monast. Exercit.*, 768B–D; Peter Damascene, *Philokalia, op. cit.*, T. 3, pp. 109–111.

Western asceticism, under the influence of St. Augustine and St. Gregory the Great, has preferred the simple scheme of three stages: suggestion, delectation, consent. Cf. article of Brouillard, B. in. *DTC*, "Tentation", T. XV, I, col. 116. Interesting also is a comparison of the Imitation of Christ with Nil's scheme: (1) simple thought enters mind; (2) vivid imagination; (3) pleasure or delight; (4) evil motion; (5) consent; (6) enemy enters totally. Lib. I, ch. XIII.

[25] Matt. 4, 3.

[26] *Ustav*, pp. 16–17.

[27] Cf. Isaac Sinaite: "It is impossible that man have peace in this life from the war waged through thoughts, but always as long as he lives in this flesh he must wage the war." These thoughts, he explains, arise from four causes: from natural desires of the flesh, from imagination, through stored up sense phantasms; from anticipated opinions and calling forth of them by the mind; and lastly from the insults of the devils waging war against us and forging us to vices. *PG*, 86A, 886B.

[28] Macarius, *Hom. XLIII, PG*, 34, 774D.

2. *Conversation of Intercourse with the Thought-Image*

The Fathers describe this second step as the becoming aware of the image-content with the will allowing the image to stay in the sphere of consciousness. This stage they consider as yet not sinful;[29] it can even at times be praiseworthy if one considers the thought in a manner pleasing to God, e.g. a thought against purity suggested by the devil would be held for some reflection, seeing how the flesh inclines ever to the sordid and how much more desirable is the possession of God than the possession of this momentary pleasure. But this, Nil warns, is only for those strong in virtue and perfection, because the devil can easily turn the thought into a passionate temptation. Therefore, the best advice Nil gives is to turn the thought to one of its contrary, to a good thought, or turn immediately to the contrary virtue.

3. *Acceptance*

In the acceptance there can be two degrees of development. After the will has already allowed the presence of the thought-image to remain, the mind wavers, but inclining ever more towards the action suggested by the devil. In the first degree of development, the will has not moved itself completely to actuate the suggestion. The mind however wants to act in this suggested way, playing with the idea.

The Fathers always judge the culpability in this stage according to the degree of perfection already achieved and the graces and helps given by God. If one receives from God great help to reject evil thoughts, but refuses, due to laziness or carelessness, he would be at fault. But if a beginner, almost without power before such a temptation (no temptation is ever beyond our power with God's grace which is always sufficient to overcome it), inclines for a short time to desire the evil proposed, but then quickly repents when he catches himself and calls to God for help, God will forgive him according to His mercy and the man's weakness and helplessness.[30]

But the gravity comes in the second degree of development, when the will makes a clean decision to actuate the suggested thought. He no longer fights against the suggested passion, but he decides to do all according to the suggestion. If for some reason beyond his control he cannot actuate his desire, he has sinned all the same and must confess his sin and do penance.

[29] *Ustav*, p. 17.
[30] *Ibid.*, pp. 17–18.

4. *Capitivity*

Nil sees two degrees. The first captivity comes when a soul completely involuntary is subjected to the attacks of an unwanted thought. The second is a desired, sustained preoccupation with the thought. In the first case, the soul can return to its peace and calm, calling on God's help. In the second it cannot return to its calm, because here the will has been at fault. Perhaps the will has not been guilty in the effect, in wanting to stay with the thought, but it has been guilty in the cause which produced the thought, i. e. through its own dissipation and superfluous, unprofitable conversations.

If persisting, enslaving thoughts occur during our prayer and we do not seek to become freed from them, this is very reprehensible and guilty because "during prayer the mind should be all turned to God and attentive to the prayer, quick to turn away any other thought".[31] But Nil sees the possibility of such persisting thoughts arising outside of prayer from unavoidable situations necessitated by our attending to the lower demands of our nature; this would not be sinful, for it is a necessary situation and the Fathers tell us that if we keep our mind in a reverent frame of thought, united with God, we will be delivered from such evil thoughts.

5. *Passion*

This is the result of wilful habits of sin when the temptation becomes rooted in the soul by frequent yielding to it and thus ingrained, burned into the soul, fed upon, it becomes a habit by which the enemy unceasingly torments and excites within the soul passionate inspirations. Thus the devil proposes some person or thing and that is enough to feed this passion and enflame the soul with exclusive love and longing for this object, so that, now, willing or unwilling, the man is mentally enslaved to these images and desires. But ultimately, the person alone is to be blamed for his freely yielding to the thoughts in the beginning stages. And for this reason he must be repentant in proportion to his guilt and pray for deliverance from this passion because passion merits only future punishment due to its preventing true repentance.

The Fathers counsel all strength to ward off and fight such passions. Nil gives the example of one subjected to the passion of lust. If he has this passion for some person, he must break off completely from any contact with him, from all conversation and even from being in his

---

[31] *Ibid.*, pp. 18–19.

presence. He must avoid any touch of his garments, even smells associated with him. Otherwise, he will only intensify the passion. "He enflames in himself the fire of passions and like animals he lets loose in his soul evil temptations of all sorts."[32]

What pertains to the guilt of the person in each step, Nil is not perfectly clear. Of the first step, the mere representation present in the mind, there can be no sin, for it is totally outside of our deliberation. The second is not always without sin, especially if the thought is not turned to God or its opposite good, but is received with a will-act to accept it and retain it. The third stage depends on what graces and knowledge we have received from God. Here we are faced with a full will-act on the part of one who has already advanced far in the way of perfection; for him to accept the evil thought would be very grievous; for a beginner who does not have much knowledge of the process or has received very few graces, he may be momentarily seduced to accept the thought, but quickly repents and thus there would be no grievous sin. In the fourth step, the captivity, if we are responsible for these agitating thoughts that destroy our peace, especially in prayer, it would be sinful. If, however, in the first degree of captivity, these evil thoughts arise completely involuntarily and unwanted, they are not sinful, but the person, turning humbly to God, can turn this momentary captivity into merit. In the last, that of passion, it is always due to one's own wilful sinfulness and must be repented and corrected or future punishment in the life to come awaits the soul.

This is the psychological process through which a soul, in the heart and mind of the affections, turns away from God and its one task of seeking ever its own salvation and becomes absorbed in "non-godly" objects.[33] And this process, due to ignorance on the part of human beings of the way the devil operates, of this psychological process of thought-development from the most elementary stage up to complete enslavement by passions, is the reason why we sin. No one sins unless he wants to do so; no one turns away from God unless he substitutes another god in His place, and this he must do willingly. But Nil insists that we be aware of this thought-process, of the strategy of the devil so that we may

---

[32] *Ibid.*, p. 20.
[33] "Where your mind is, there also is your treasure" (Matt. 6, 21). To whatever thing the heart of one is attached, drawn to and by desire goes after, that thing becomes his god. If the heart desires everywhere the Lord, He is the Lord of his heart... Where his heart is attached and the mind captivated, that is his god." Macarius, *Hom. XLIII, PG*, 34, 774B.

recognize his tactics at his first attack and resort to the efficacious means to overcome his attack. "The Fathers teach that we should oppose the enemy with a proportionate resistance to his attack, having in view that we will win or lose in our mind. The results of the combat will be either crown of victory or punishment of torments."[34]

C. ANALYSIS OF THE EIGHT SOURCES OF PASSIONS

Nil follows the ancient Fathers in his treatment of the principal causes of all temptations. "The Fathers say that there are eight principal vices of the soul of which numerous temptations are the offspring: gluttony, fornication, covetousness, anger, sadness, acedia, vainglory, and pride."[35] Nil is not eager to present any new teaching, but is determined to present that traditional teaching of the Fathers, confirmed by his own solitary life of asceticism, on the primary sources of evil in man. Lacking is any psychological dissertation on the relationship among the temptations. The number, order and reality are all taken for granted as known by all his monks from reading the Fathers and from their own personal experience in the ascetical life. Nil thus focuses his attention on "the different ways of fighting and conquering the eight principal temptations."

He says there are in general many ways of resisting these temptations and of conquering them, depending greatly on the strength of the one struggling. One can pray against the evil thoughts, striving for the opposite virtue, or enter into direct battle with the temptation, or else in contempt, as one who is occupied with a greater love and interest and thus

---

[34] *Ustav*, pp. 20–21.

[35] *Ibid.*, p. 39. For a scholarly summary on the origin of the theory of the 8 capital sins, cf. Hausherr, I., S. J.: "L'origine de la théorie orientale des huit péchés capitaux," in *OC*, XXX (1933), pp. 164–175. The author makes a comparison with the Stoics' system and rules it out as the basis for Evagrius' enumeration. He carefully explains (1) why there are eight; (2) the names of the eight evil thoughts; (3) the order of these thoughts. He concludes that Evagrius took his teaching from his master Origen and reduced the scattered teaching into a compact system of eight, following Origen's exegesis of Deuteronomy on the eight enemies of the Chosen People, and assigned the order of these thoughts. Cf. also Cassian, *Conférences*, lib. V, especially ch. 17–18, p. 210. Also his *De Instit. Coenob.*, Liv. V, 1 (Corp. Script. Eccl. Latin., M. Petschenig) (Prague–Vienna, 1838), pp. 81–82. Evagrius, *De Octo vitiosis cogitationibus*, *PG*, 40, 1272–1277. Nil Sinaite, *De octo Spiritibus malitiae*, *PG*, 79, 1145–1164. Hesychius, *De temperantia et virtute*, *PG*, 93, 1535D; *Vitae Patrum*, Lib. V, VII, *PL*, 73, pp. 851–992, 1025–1066. Cf. also Vogtle A., "Woher stammt das Schema der Hauptsunden?", in *Theologisches Quartalschrift*, 122, 1941, pp. 217–237; Blomfield, M. W., "The Origin of the Concept of the Seven Cardinal Sins", in *Harvard Theol. Review*, 34 (1941), pp. 121–128.

cannot be bothered with such baseness. Beginners should rather pray evoking good thoughts in place of the bad ones, for only the most perfect souls can with success treat the devil with scorn.

1. *Gluttony*

It is surprising in what horror the ancient Fathers and monks held this vice.[36] Perhaps this constant difficulty came, oddly enough, from their fasts. Because they ate rarely, usually one meal at about 3 o'clock in the afternoon, they were constantly tempted to overeat, to exceed the limits of moderation. They were thus on the guard, not only to check the quality but also the quantity of food consumed. For, once sobriety was exceeded in eating and drinking, then the way to impurity was easy.[37]

Nil cautions the monk about thoughts of gluttony, either by imagining and desiring delicious, delicate foods, or by desiring to eat more than we need and out of the proper times.[38] His suggested remedy is to recall the words of Holy Scripture "Do not let your hearts grow dull with revelry and drunkeness and the affairs of this life, so that that day (last day of life) overtakes you unaware."[39] And one had to pray to the Lord for His help. Meditation on what the Fathers said about this being the root of all evil, especially of fornication, is most helpful.[40] From this passion of gluttony came the fall of our first Father Adam and "from that time until now, many are enslaved by gluttony and fall with a great

---

[36] Serapion the monk is typical of those who starved themselves to get rid of this temptation but, even in the excesses of starvation, still were not able to be totally freed. "From my youth I have been bothered by avarice, gluttony and lust I have rid myself of two, avarice and lust, so that they no longer bother me. I cannot get rid of the tendency towards gluttony. I did not eat for four days and my stomach continues to make demands and to insist on its habitual nourishment without which I cannot live." *Hist. Laus.*, *PG*, 34, 1186A.

[37] Cf. St. Basil, Reg. Fusius Tract., 18, *PG*, 31, 966B–D. Nil Sinaite, *De octo spirit. malit.*, 4, *PG* 79, 1147D: "Gula est mater intemperantiae."

[38] Cassian gives a similar triple division of the temptation of gluttony: (1) temptation to eat before the fixed time; (2) desire to gorge oneself, regardless of the quality of the food; (3) search for delicate morsels. Cf. *Conférences*, ch. XI, p. 199.

[39] Lk. 21, 34.

[40] Cassian, *De Instit. Coenob.*, Lib. V, 6, pp. 85–86: "It was not excess of wine, but bread taken in too great abundance that caused the crimes and destruction of Sodom. God Himself reproached Jerusalem through His prophet: 'What sin did your sister Sodom commit, if not that she overindulged in an abundance of bread,' (Ezech. 16, 49). And because this satiety of food had ignited in their bodies the fire of a frightful impurity, they merited through a just judgment of God that this fire of sulphur descended from Heaven to consume them . . ."

fall as is known in the Holy Scripture and from experience".[41] Another help is to reflect, as suggests Barsanuphius,[42] on the fleetiness of delicate and delicious foods, how quickly they decompose and shortly there is nothing left. From such considerations, the monk should be convinced of the necessity of using food and drink in the proper measure and at the proper time.

a. Measure of Food

Here we see the balanced judgment and prudence of Nil in his practical norms on the quantity of food the monk should take. And he is doing nothing more than to repeat the prudential norm of the early Fathers.[43] No one amount of food can be ordered for all monks, because the needs, both physical and spiritual, are different. "...bodies have different degrees of strength and power like honey, iron, wax".[44] First, the monk should consider his physical needs. Each monk is to determine for himself and is not to have his amount of food prescribed by rule, common to all. To do this he must seek by experimenting to find his "golden mean" between too rigorous a fast with inability to perform spiritual and manual works and oversatiety. "Let each one, say the Fathers, determine for himself the daily measure and quantity of food so that if something seems superfluous and produces heaviness, then he should lessen the amount. When he sees that that amount taken is not enough to keep up the body, then he should add a litle and so finally by experience he can come to a right quantity needed daily for his strength of body, not serving

---

[41] Qstav, p. 40. Cf. also Cassian, Conférences, Lib. V, 4, pp. 190–191.
[42] Barsanuphius, Dobrotoljubie, op. cit., vol. 2, 1884, no. 30, p. 607.
[43] Cf. St. Basili, Reg. Fusius Tract., 16, 18–20, PG, 31, 958–959, 966–970. Cassian, De Instit. Coenob., Lib. V, 5, pp. 84–85: "This is why we cannot give a constant and universal rule for everyone concerning the fast, because all have not the same force, strength, and that the fast cannot as the other virtues be practised independent of the body and through the soul alone. Here are the rules which we have received from the Fathers on this subject: they believed that still one had to observe some difference in the time, quantity and quality of food, according to the different strength, force of age or sex; nonetheless each one ought to propose for himself a rule of mortification and the subjection of the flesh according to the solidity of his virtue and strength... Many persons who labour under infirmity or old age, cannot fast even to the setting of the sun without harming themselves considerably. All cannot also be satisfied with legumes boiled in water or with simple, ungarnished herbs or with dry bread. There are some who eat two pounds of bread without feeling full. Another finds great difficulty eating even one pound or even six ounces. But all should propose as the end to regulate their food according to their temperament, so that they never feel complete satiety."
[44] Ustav, p. 41.

his lower concupiscences but his true needs."[45] The monk, especially the beginner, should observe the rule of leaving the table always a bit hungry, never eating to full satiety.

But Nil sees that not only the needs of the body, but also those of the soul must dictate the amount of food taken.

> He who has a sound and healthy body, he must tame it insofar as it is possible, in order to be delivered from the plague of passions and Christ's grace will permit him to subject it to the spirit. He with a weak body ought to indulge in some relaxation so that he may not be totally incapacitated for activity. To an ascetic, total deprivation is not necessary, but rather some deprivation and want must be imposed so that one gives the body only the needed amount of food and drink according to good judgment; in time of temptation, the body must be held in check from attacks of the enemy. . . . When the stomach is under control by prudent, intelligent constraint, then there comes into the soul a whole array of virtues. As St. Basil the Great says, 'If you restrain the stomach, you enter into paradise; if you do not, you have eternal death'.[46]

And he adds another practical point according to his prudent norm laid down above: "If someone for reason of a burdensome journey or from other heavy work feels that the body needs more and gives it more above the usual measure in food, drink or sleep, that is not to be reprimanded, for he acts with good judgment and according to praiseworthy needs."

It is this freedom from blind observance of any exterior from without the interior prudence dictated from the individual's intellect under the guidance of the inspiration of God that distinguishes greatly the spirituality of Nil from his contemporaries. His balanced prudence comes from his proper subjecting all means to the final end which he never loses sight of. Fasting is good and necessary, but always remains a means and as such is relative to the individual needs of each person.

b. Time of Food

Here again we see Nil's adaptability to the written tradition among the Fathers of monasticism. They usually enjoined the monks to fast until the day began to decline calling the hour of meals the ninth, or 2 or 3 o'clock

---

[45] *Ustav*, pp. 40–41. On this point it is interesting to compare the Rules of St. Ignatius of Loyola in his Spiritual Exercises on Food, § 217. Cf. Gregory Sinaite, *PG*, 150, 1338B: "Do not exceed the limits you have determined beforehand. Nourishment has three possibilities: temperance, frugality and satiety. In temperance the eater still has hunger; in frugality he has neither hunger nor is heavy; in satiety he is heavy."

[46] *Ibid.*, pp. 42–43. Cf. St. Basil, *Reg. Fusius*, *PG*, 31, 968A–C.

in the afternoon according to Nil's reckoning. But because the length of day varied greatly in the northern zone of Russia depending on the season of the year, therefore he enjoined on the monk a reckoning, not blindly according to the fixed rule of the Fathers, but according to their good sense, trying to observe the fast for the same number of hours after awakening. For those who could fast longer, they were free to do so.

c. Various Foods

Of all the various foods presented at a table, one should be indifferent to whether they are tasty, sweet and pleasing or otherwise, and prudently eat a little of everything, for in so doing, the monk shows thanks to God for all His creatures and he preserves at the same time his soul from pride. He does not show disdain for any creature of God and still has not the natural satisfaction of showing to the others exaggerated austerity.[47]

For those who are weak in faith or virtue, it is profitable for them to abstain from certain meats, especially from the more pleasing to the taste, because they do not have the adequate confidence and persuasion in God's providence that they will be able to eat them without spiritual harm; for them the Apostle Paul enjoins: "One man can in conscience eat what he will; one who is scrupulous must be content with vegetable fare."[48]

Following St. Basil's injunction: "It is not proper to fight against the body with food which rather should serve to preserve it," Nil lays down the prudent norm: "When any food is harmful to anyone because of his sick condition or bodily temperament, let him not eat such harmful food, but only that which will be profitable to him."[49]

[47] Cf. Gregory Sinaite, *PG*, 150, 1338A: "Take a little of everything and thus avoid pride and do not abhor the beautiful works of God."
[48] Rom. 14, 2. Here seems to be an example of Nil's applying a literal text to quote his purpose. It is evident from Paul's context that he is speaking of those Jewish converts who had scruples about eating meat because either the meat put before them had not been killed in the Jewish fashion (cf. Acts XV, 20) or because they feared the meat had been offered in sacrifice to idols (Cf. I Cor. 10, 25). Nil however applies the text to those still weak in faith. Certain delectable meats aroused the carnal passions and for those of weak faith, it were better not to presume on the mercy of God to supply for their lack of faith but to remove the temptation by eating herbs.
[49] *Ustav*, pp. 42–43. St. Basil, *Fusius*, p. 31, 969A.

2. *Fornication*

All the Fathers, along with Nil, hold the struggle against this vice as the most difficult, because such temptations arise not only in our body as in the case of gluttony, but also in our mind.[50] Because our mind can conjure up these thoughts at any time under the suggestion of the devil, one can never stop fighting to drive these from him. Chastity and purity are qualities interior to the mind and heart as well as something relating to external life. The body will be kept in check by the moderation exercised in eating, drinking, and in the physical, ascetical practices that keep the body ever in fighting condition. But one of the best ways to drive from our minds impure thoughts is to fill ourselves with the fear of God and a deep realization of his omnipresence. "When such lustful thoughts attack, then fill yourself with the fear of God; recall that nothing can be hidden from God, not even the most delicate movements of the heart. The Lord is judge and sees all, even most hidden."[51]

One great help to overcome such debasing thoughts against impurity Nil suggests is to recall that as monks, they have been clothed in the habit of "angels", therefore they must conduct themselves as if they were angels. "How can we spoil our conscience and destroy the angelic-like image by impure lust?" Climacus had said fairly much the same: "Purity means that we put on the angelic nature. Purity is the longed-for house of Christ and the earthly heaven of the heart. Purity is a supernatural denial of nature, which means that a mortal and corruptible body is rivalling the celestial spirits in a truly marvellous way."[52]

Nil appeals especially to the vows taken before the angels and men to preserve purity and chastity. To keep them properly a monk could not merely observe them in his exterior conduct alone, but he had to practise purity in the secret depths of his interior. It was in the heart that the

---

[50] Cassian, *De Instit. Coenob.*, Lib. VI, 1, p. 115: "This enemy (fornication) attacks us on two sides and comes to the battle armed as two different passions. This is why we must oppose it with double resistance. As he takes strength from the weaknesses he finds in our body and soul, so we will not let him so conquer us if we bring together these two parts, body and soul, to terrorize him." Cf. also *Vitae Patrum*, *PL*, 22, Lib. V, lib. V, 2; Nil, *De malign. cogitat.*, *PG*, 79, pp. 1147–1151.

[51] *Ustav*, p. 43.

[52] Climacus, *Scalae*, *Gradus 15*, *PG*, 88, 879D. For the tonsured state as putting on the "angelic form" cf. Ranke-Heinemann, N., "Zum Ideal der vita angelica im frühen Mönchtum", in *Geist*[4] *und Leben*, 29 (1956), pp. 347–357.

personal oblation of the self to God was consummated.[53] And whoever permits such foul thoughts of fornication to enter and dwell in the mind, he fornicates in his heart. This is the constant teaching of the Fathers, which undoubtedly explains the extreme delicateness in this matter, which often led to gross exaggerations.[54] But it clearly illustrates the basic conviction of Nil and the Fathers of purifying the mind from the slightest impure thought. "Therefore it is best to cut off all impulse to thoughts of this kind."[55] This often led to a false appreciation of chastity which could easily place as an end in itself the arriving at a state of insensibility where the monk would no longer experience the slightest movement or thought, even though these be most involuntary. [56] Under such exaggeration the true excellence of chastity as a constant, voluntary dedication of one's heart and whole being to God, even in spite of the pull downward of fallen nature, could easily have been forgotten. The treatment of this subject by Nil is remarkable for his prudence and balanced judgment, especially in the means he proposes to overcome the impure thoughts.

When these thoughts are not so violent, Nil suggests again to think on one's monastic state, or the "angelic form" or picture the scandalous

---

[53] *Ustav*, p. 43. Cf. Cassian, *De Instit. Coenob.*, Lib. VI, ch. 9, p. 120: "One must then first of all purify with great care, every corner of his heart. We ought to want to have the same purity in the most secret thoughts of conscience that other persons strive to have in their external body. It is in this secret tribunal of our soul that God presides as a Judge and Arbiter of our combats. He is witness at each moment of our battle and our courage which we show Him. We ought to blush to allow such thoughts to enter into our interior which would make us blush before men. How much more we ought to be concerned with our interior which is exposed to the Saints and Angels and to the light of God to whom nothing is impenetrable."

[54] Abbas Paul could not even endure the sight of a woman's bit of clothing. Walking once with another monk he met a woman on the road. So shocked was he that he abruptly left his companion and the proposed work of charity and fled back to his cell, faster than if he had seen a lion or a monstrous dragon. Cassian, *Conférences*, Lib. VII, ch. 26, pp. 268–269. Climacus tells us to remember him who wrapped his hand in his cassock when about to carry his sick mother: *Scalae, Gradus 15, PG*, 88, 890D.

[55] *Ustav*, p. 45.

[56] Cf. Cassian, *De Instit. Coenob.*, Lib. VI, ch. 10, pp. 120–121: "An assured sign that we have purity is if, during our sleep, there be no suggestive image presented to us that would surprise us or disturb us with the least movement of concupiscence. For even though these movements are not sinful, they show nonetheless that the soul is not yet perfect and that purity is not yet in all its perfection." Climacus, *Scalae, PG*, 88, *Gradus 15*, 879D–882A. "He is chaste who even during sleep feels no movement or change of any kind in his constitution. He is chaste who has continually acquired perfect insensibility to difference in bodies... Truly blessed is he who has acquired perfect insensibility to every body and colour and beauty... If a sign of true purity is to be unmoved by dreams during sleep..."

example one would give to men if they saw him yielding to such thoughts. The chief and most powerful means to victory over these impure suggestions is to pray to God. Maximus the Confessor and Climacus suggest repeating short ejaculations from the Psalms such as "The enemy surrounds me now", "Thou art my refuge when the enemy besieges me", "O God, Thou art my God; how eager my quest for Thee."[57] Another great help is to turn to those saints who were known in their lifetime for their purity and their battles against the evil spirit in order to maintain their virtue.[58]

But when the temptations become more intense, the monk should beseech, storm heaven with arms outstretched, eyes uplifted and pray with confidence to God to be delivered. "Oh, monk, take warning, and never fail to pray during these assaults in the manner we have described." One should never trust in the self, but pray as St. Isaac suggests: "Thou art mighty, Lord, and this is Thy battle. Do Thou wage it and gain the victory for us."[59]

In regard to women, the monk need never have any conversation with them, their very sight must be avoided, along with youthful, beardless and effeminate faces, for these are snares laid by the devil.[60] Above all, the monk must exert every effort, even violence, not to be alone with

---

[57] Ps. 16, 11; 31, 7; 62, 1.

[58] Nil cites the advise of Daniel of Scete (Egypt) who exhorted a fellow-monk in time of temptation against chastity to call on the martyr Thomais who was martyred for her chastity. And the monk was immediately delivered from the temptation. *Ustav*, p. 44. The text in Greek is edited by M. Leon-Clugnt, "Daniel Scete", in *ROC*, no. 5, 1900, p. 66.

[59] Isaac the Syrian. *Logos 54, op. cit.*, p. 320. Cf. Climacus, *Scalae, Gradus 15, PG*, 88, 899D: "Those who have not yet obtained true prayer of the heart, can find help in violence in bodily prayer, I mean stretching out the hands, beating the breast, sincere raising of the eyes to heaven, deep sighing, frequent prostrations... Hide for a while in some secret place. Raise on high the eyes of your soul, if you can; but if not, your bodily eyes. Hold your arms motionless in the form of a cross, in order to shame and conquer your Amalek by this sign. Cry to Him Who is might to save, using no subtle expressions but humble speech: Have mercy on me, for I am weak. Then you will know by experience the power of the Most High..."

[60] *Ustav*, p. 46. Cf. also Nil's letter IX on overcoming evil thoughts: "To conquer this temptation do not in anyway whatsoever converse with women, nor look even on their clothing nor attend to their personal goodness but flee ever from women and youth. And so doing you will conquer the passion of the devil of fornication," p. 203, St. Petersburg edition, 1864, *op. cit.* Cf. *Appendix* of this work.

such because they could be the occasion of the soul's damnation and nothing is more essential than the soul for which Christ died and rose from the dead.[61]

3. *Avarice*

Nil follows very closely the teaching laid down by Cassian.[62] Avarice is a disease that comes from outside of our nature, i.e. there is no intrinsic principle in our human nature except our corrupt will that seeks inordinately the possessions of material things.[63] Thus the temptation coming from outside of our nature is easier to flee from in the beginning and especially for those filled with the fear of God and who sincerely seek to be saved. But once this disease takes hold of us, it becomes the root for all other evils. It spreads like a spider web over the soul and stirs up in us anger, sorrow and so forth, but also developes in us an idol worship, according to St. Paul's words: "The love of money is the root of all evil things, and there are those who have wandered away from the faith by making it their ambition, involving themselves in a world of sorrows." "You must deaden, then, those passions in you which belong to earth, fornication and impurity, lust and evil desire, and that love of money which is an idolatry."[64]

The devil ceases stirring up in us other passions because this one is sufficient for the monk who is so enslaved to it. Therefore it is most necessary that a monk not only avoids possessing gold and silver and other material possessions, but he should pray to God that He take away from him any spirit of avarice, and, rather, grant him the love of evangelical poverty so that he may trust in the providence of God the Father who provides for the monk's daily needs as He feeds the birds of the air who do not store up provisions for the future. Here Nil con-

---

[61] In a letter to Gurij Tušin Nil exhorts him to maintain recollection and preserve his heart from all impure thoughts that might suggest in him impurity or excitation; he must diligently drive from him everything that could call up in his mind and heart similar thoughts and desires. "Keep yourself from seeing persons and hearing such conversations that may arouse your passions and suggest impure thoughts and God will take care of you." Fol. 110A–B.

[62] *Ustav*, pp. 146–147. Cf. Cassian, *De Instit. Coenob.*, Lib. 7, pp. 130–149.

[63] Cassian, *ibid.*, pp. 131–132: "We nonetheless say that there are certain vices which do not have any foundation in nature, but have as the only source the corruption of the will as in the case of envy and avarice, which have no natural cause, but both of them come from an exterior reason and an outside force. However, these vices are sufficiently easy to flee from in the beginning, but are really burdensome if allowed to gain a footing. They make the soul miserable and make it almost incurable."

[64] I Tim. 6, 10; Col. 3, 5.

descends to a few practical details: "Not only should we put far from us all gold and silver and property, but also anything that would be beyond the mere necessities of life, as clothing, shoes, cell, dishes, instruments for manual work. And even these should not be of any value, nor decorated, nor be connected with any cares and preoccupations and worries so that we do not fall into contact with the world."[65]

Here we see the first glimpse of Nil's love for evangelical poverty which will formulate itself in the Synod of Moscow of 1503 into a protest against the custom of his contemporary monasteries to possess property. "True victory over avarice and the temptation to be attached to material possessions comes not only when we do not have anything, but when we do not even wish to possess anything. This gives us spiritual purity".[66]

4. *Anger*

In Nil's treatment of this vice we see how permeated he was with the spirit of "*kenosis*" and the evangelical teaching of Christ on being meek and humble of heart. Anger for him is the temptation to want to return evil to one who has inflicted some evil on us. This may be a reaction that is natural, from our fallen nature, through faith in the teachings of the Master, the monk must overcome this basic inclination and substitute it with loving forgiveness. "It is thus that my heavenly Father will deal with you, if brother does not forgive brother with all his heart." "When you stand praying, forgive whatever wrong any man has done you; so that your Father who is in heaven may forgive you your transgressions; if you do not forgive, your Father who is in heaven will not forgive your transgressions either."[67] One's forgiveness by God will be proportioned to his forgiveness of his neighbour, especially of those who have offended him. If we have offended God and need His pardon, we can only obtain this by obeying His command to pray as He taught us in the "Our Father", "Forgive us our trespasses, as we forgive them that trespass against us... Your heavenly Father will forgive you your transgressions, if you forgive your fellow-men theirs; if you do not forgive them, your heavenly Father will not forgive your transgressions either."[68]

[65] *Ustav*, p. 47. Cf. Letter IX on overcoming evil thoughts, *loc. cit.*: "If you seek to conquer avarice, love strict poverty and poor clothing and simple food and drink; and you will thus be victorious over the suggestions of the devil of avarice."
[66] *Ibid.*
[67] Matt. 18, 35; Mk. 11, 26.
[68] Matt. 6, 12–15. Cf Letter IX in *Appendix* where Nil expands his doctrine of forgiveness.

We cannot do any good before God while there remains rancour and hatred in our heart towards others.[69] To prove this Nil offers the example of the Fathers who said that should an angry person resurrect someone from the dead, his prayer would not be pleasing.[70]

Nil invokes a solid principle of Christian asceticism to overcome thoughts of anger. Not only should one not in deed or word, nor even by the slightest glance do anything to offend a brother, but he should seek to change these bitter thoughts into wholesome thoughts and the best way to do this and to overcome our selfish nature at the same time is to pray for the insultor. Not only should we pray for him who has offended us and thus show brotherly love and mercy, but we should overcome our repugnance by humbly asking God mercy for our sins through the prayers of this brother. Abbas Dorotheus suggests this prayer: "Help, Lord, my brother, and on account of his prayers, have mercy on me, a sinner."[71] This is nothing other than the command of Our Lord Himself, "Love your enemies, do good to those who hate you, pray for those who persecute and insult you, that so you may be true sons of your Father in heaven who makes his sun shine on the evil and equally on the good..."[72] Nil notes that for one showing such humility and mercy towards others, God promises him His divine sonship. And should there not be the infallible words of Christ moving us to such a conduct for hope of the great reward promised, the example of Christ Himself should be enough to spur us to imitation. How much evil He supported patiently, humbly from the Jews and finally, dying at their hands, He could pray to His Heavenly Father for their forgiveness: "Father, forgive them; they know not what it is they are doing."[73] And so did the saints who, in imitation of their Master, not only did not return evil for evil, but prayed for their enemies, covering over their faults and rejoicing when the enemies reformed themselves. They treated them always with mercy and love. Later we shall see how this spirit of charity and humility of Nil was manifested towards the heretics.

---

[69] Cf. Cassian, *De Instit. Coenob.*, Li. VIII, ch. 11, p. 158: "How can we believe that God would permit us to live in anger against our brothers, I do not say for several days, but only even till sunset since He does not permit us to offer Him our prayers (Matt. 5, 23) as long as one of our brother has something against us?"

[70] He immediately adds, "Not that an angry person could resurrect the dead, but rather to emphasize that his prayer would be dead." *Ustav*, p. 48.

[71] *Ustav*, pp. 48–49. Cf. Dorotheus, *PG*, 88, 1714C.

[72] Matt. 5, 44–45.

[73] Lk. 23, 34.

5. *Sadness*

Cassian, Nil's steady master in dealing with the eight temptations, has a clear exposition on sadness, but Nil leaves him and turns to Isaac the Syrian for a more spiritual approach to this vice.[74] For true sadness as a vice, Nil seems to hint, may come from many reasons without giving any but one: that which comes from people, especially those who insult us. The principle upon which he bases his attack against sadness, especially that type that tends to cast us into despair, is that of loving trust in Divine Providence. "...relying fully on this, that it does not happen to us without the Providence of God and that, in general, God sends all that happens to us for our aid and salvation of our souls. And if that sent to us does not seem at the time helpful in those circumstances, at least the following circumstances will clearly show the full picture and how it was truly helpful to us, not as we wished, but as God arranged and wanted it."[75]

One should not exaggerate with the human mind these hardships but accept them with great generosity, having "a deep faith that the eye of God sees all and that nothing can happen to us without His will. He sends us temptations according to His goodness that, bearing them, we receive His crown."[76] This is a sublime thought that is repeated often in his epistolary exhortations. He exhorts Prince Vassian to bear with patience the sufferings God sends him for these are gifts given him by God.

This makes a monk a participator in the passion of Christ. And in this the lovers of God are distinguished from the lovers of the world. One lives in sorrows sent by God, while the others rejoice in food and worldly comforts. This is the true way to bear trials of sorrows with virtue and remain ever on this path for thus God leads His sufferers to eternal life. Thus it is proper to go along this path of sorrows with joy, remembering the end of this sorrowful life and the future life of unending happiness. God will comfort your heart in your sorrow with every joy and consolation.[77]

In a letter to Prince Kassian Nil presents his conviction that there cannot be any crown, any true happiness, either in this life or in the next unless there be sufferings. These should be the things we desire with joy,

---

[74] *Ustav,* p. 50. Cf. Isaac the Syrian, *Liber de contemptu mundi, PG,* 86A, 823–824, where he deals with faith in the Providence of God as a strength for the martyrs and saints during temptations.
[75] *Ustav, loc. cit.*
[76] *Ibid.*
[77] Letter to Vassian, fol. 98A–B.

for "the way of misfortune and sorrows is the only way to eternal happiness... Do you not see how God blesses and wishes to send these sorrows to those loving Him. They considered themselves His favourites in this life. You, o lover of Christ, receive all these and bear all sorrows with strength."[78]

There is another type of sorrow that comes from our past sins and helps us to have a more perfect repentance.[79] This sorrow is based on the hope in God's infinite mercy which pardons all who are repentant and sorrowful. Nil quotes St. Paul: "Supernatural remorse leads us to an abiding and salutary change of heart, whereas the world's remorse leads to death."[80] This is sorrow, not sadness, and with this sorrow comes joy into the heart, of the repentant soul.[81] This is sorrow from God and must be fostered.

Nil recommends as a remedy against sadness coming from the devil much the same suggestions of Isaac the Syrian: "Sadness coming from the devil must be driven from the heart as all other evil passions, by prayer and reading, by contact and conversation with spiritual persons."[82] If this sadness is allowed to entrench itself in the soul, it becomes the root of all evil and quickly turns to despair, making the soul empty and dry, not responsive to such salutary remedies as prayer and spiritual reading.

6. Acedia

Again Nil leaves the thorough treatment given this vice by Cassian[83] and turns to Isaac the Syrian and Gregory the Sinaite chiefly. Nil considers acedia mainly as a temptation allied with sadness or one that

---

[78] Letter to Prince Kassian, fol. 374A.
[79] Cf. Cassian, De Instit. Coenob., lib. IX, ch. 10, p. 170.
[80] 2 Cor. 7, 10.
[81] Cf. Hausherr, I., S.J., Penthos, OCA, 132, Roma, 1944: "Pour entrer dans la pensée de nos auteurs, il convient d'abord de nous rappeler qu'au nombre des passions à vaincre se compte aussi la tristesse. Dès le premier instant de sa présence dans l'âme, la componction lutte contre cet ennemi, et elle ne se développe qu'en le métant de plus en plus, jusqu'à l'exterminer en lui coupant les vivres fournis par les sept autres 'mauvaises pensées'..." (p. 152). "Les réflexions de l'abbe Isaie: "Frère, monte une garde vigilante contre l'esprit qui apporte à l'homme la tristesse; il met en oeuvre de nombreux engins de chasse, jusqu'à ce qu'il t'ait élevé toute vigueur. La tristesse selon Dieu au contraire, c'est une joie, la joie de te voir dans la volonté de Dieu... La tristesse selon Dieu pèse pas sur l'âme, mais elle lui dit: 'Ne crains pas, sus! Reviens! Il sait que l'homme est faible, et il le fortifie' " (pp. 156-157).
[82] Ustav, p. 51. Cf. Isaac, op. cit., PG, 86A, 817C-D, 852D, 853A.
[83] Cassian, De Instit. Coenob., Lib. X, pp. 172-193.

follows as an acute development of it. He gives no definition of it, nor even a description of it as Cassian and Climacus give.[84] He presupposes that each monk has had personal experience of this temptation and its terrible effects, and as there was no need to describe the temptation of fornication, so too here. Its special victims are hermits.[85] He quotes Gregory of Sinaite that the spirits of fornication and *acedia* are the most savage of all temptations.[86] Yet on the other hand nothing so furthers a monk's perfection in grace as this spiritual "dark night" of the soul.[87]

Thus Nil handles this vice practically from the sole view point of how to combat it with spiritual means in order that this spiritual crisis may be of spiritual profit. The first means is to realize that God is inflicting this trial on those whom He loves for their own greater sanctification. Hence, the devil's temptations to despair, filling the monk with doubt, fear, desperation that there is no mercy from God and that his sins will be never forgiven, that hell awaits him, that he is lost forever, must be fought courageously with much effort and strength. The devil tries to move the monk to thoughts of ingratitude against the goodness and mercy of God and to blasphemy that these temptations either are sent by God, but are beyond the monk's strength and grace from God, or that they happen to him outside of God's Divine Providence.[88] This condition of dryness, desolation soon changes and the monk feels the consolation and reassurance of God's mercy and personal love. Then he should profit, looking back on the period of desolation and seeing how God has sent him that ordeal for his profit and instruction out of His love.

But in the midst of the battle against these two thoughts of ingratitude and blasphemy the monk is instructed by Nil to pray in earnest, "Begone, Satan, I will adore my Lord God and Him alone will I serve; and every bitter and sorrowful cross I accept with a spirit of thanks and obedience

---

[84] Cassian, *ibid.* Cf. especially his classical description in ch. 2, pp. 174–175. Also Climacus, *Scalae, gradus 13, PG*, 88, pp. 858–862.

[85] Climacus, *ibid.*, 859A.

[86] Cf. Gregory Sinaite: "Before all other passions the two most troublesome and most deeply rooted are fornication and acedia." *PG*, 150, 1278, no. 110.

[87] *Ustav*, p. 52. Cf. Climacus, *op. cit., Gradus 13*, 859C. "Spiritual heroes come to light at the time of despondency, for nothing procures so many crowns for a monk as the battle with despondency." Cf. Hausherr, I., "Les Orientaux, connaissent-ils les 'nuits' de saint Jean de la Croix?" in *OCP*, 12 (1946), pp. 5–46.

[88] *Ustav*, p. 51.

from Him for the cleansing of my sins as is written 'The anger of God I accept, for I have sinned against Him'."[89]

Besides fervent outbursts of prayer against Satan and to God for His help, a monk should busy himself with reading or with manual work.[90] If it is possible, adds Nil, it is better to suffer this ordeal in silence without leaving the cell, but by remaining there in tranquillity. Isaac the Syrian insists "sit in your cell and it will teach you everything."[91]

Nil shows his strong but tender confidence and trust in God, insisting that God will never allow that a soul, relying on Him, will fall, for He knows our weaknesses and our strength, He knows how much we can bear.

If a potter knows just how long to hold his vessels in the fire in order to form them, not too long, not too short; if human beings know how much of a burden a horse can carry, a donkey, a camel, and then load them according to their strength, how much more does the mind of God know the possibilities of a soul in bringing it through temptations to the heavenly kingdom, not only to merit future glory, but also even now to enjoy the consolation of the Holy Spirit. Knowing this, we must bear all with patience, tranquillity, sitting in our cells.[92]

7. Vanity

For Nil the various temptations presented to the mind are illegitimate objects of attractions which take the mind away from God its only true object. "For the mind which turns away from the thought of God and busies itself with inferior matters commits adultery."[93] The vice of vainglory is perhaps the most subtle in its deception and works on all types of monks, but especially the more perfect. Nil again is not interested in defining this vice but is satisfied with giving a nominal definition. "Instead of a monk ordering his actions only to God, they are motivated by the desire to please men."[94]

---

[89] Micheas 7, 9. Matt. 4, 10.
[90] Cassian devotes many pages to the necessity of manual work to overcome *acedia*. Cf. *De Instit. Coenob.*, Lib. X, pp. 181–192. Isaac the Syrian, *PG*, 86A, 852D: "In dryness in prayer, read books of the Fathers and bear with great patience." Cf. also Climacus, *op. cit.*, *Gradus 13*, 859D.
[91] Isaac, *op. cit.*, 849. I. Hausherr, *L'hésychasme...*, *OCP*, vol. XXII (1956), pp. 36–38, gives the historical development of this phrase: "Reste assis dans ta cellule: elle t'enseignera tout."
[92] *Ustav*, pp. 54–55.
[93] *Ibid.*, p. 27.
[94] *Ibid.*, p. 55.

Nil leaves Climacus on this point,[95] preferring to remain with Evagrius Cassian, and Nil Sinaite in their traditional listing of vanity, as numbe seven, but nowhere is the distinction between vanity and pride clearly presented by Nil. He is, as always, more concerned with the spiritual means of combat rather than a speculative treatment. And his method is one of replacing the vain thoughts that seek the praises of men with thoughts that humiliate. "This should be our method; when we feel rising up in us such vanity, then we should recall our tears and low condition before God in affectionate prayer. If we are unable to do this let us represent to ourselves our exit from this world and that shameless vanity will be driven away. If it still burdens us, we should fill ourselves with fear and shame, being convinced that the one who exalts himself now will in the future life not escape debasement.[96] "... Recall when someone begins to praise you, the many and grievous sins or only one of them, the most foul; picture it vividly in your mind and say then to yourself: 'Judge whether such actions are worthy of praise and honour?' Then we see at once the impossibility of any praise and the internal enemy is driven away."[97] For those who have no humiliating sins to recall, the thought of God's perfection and their own small progress to approach this perfection should fill them with a disdain for the praises of men. In the presence of God's perfections, a monk feels his own acquisition of virtues is a drop of water compared to the vast ocean.[98]

God alone therefore should be the only motive why we perform our actions.[99] But if one allows himself to waver, to seek the praises of men

---

[95] Cf. Climacus, *op. cit.*, *Gradus 22*, 850A, 947D: "Some like to distinguish vainglory from pride and to give it a special place and chapter. And so they say that there are eight capital and deadly sins. But Gregory the Theologian and other teachers have given out that there are seven; and I am strongly inclined to agree with them. For who that has conquered vainglory has pride within him? The only difference between them is such as there is between a child and a man, between wheat and bread; for the one is the beginning and the other the end."

[96] Climacus, *op. cit.*, *Gradus 23*, 976D: "No one in the face of blasphemous thoughts need think that the guilt lies within him, for the Lord is the Knower of hearts and He is aware that such words and thoughts do not come from us but from our foes."

[97] *Ustav*, p. 56. Cf. Letter VIII: "How to Overcome Vanity", in St. Petersburg 1864 Edition, *op. cit.*, pp. 200–202 or for my English translation, cf. *Appendix I* of this work.

[98] Compare the meditations of St. Ignatius Loyola in his *Spiritual Exercises* on personal sin, § 58 and § 59.

[99] Cf. Gregory Sinaite, *PG*, 150, 1326A: "But in spite of his (devil's) ceaseless striving and shameless attacks, you will not often be robbed by him if you keep to a firm determination to please God alone."

in his actions, such vain thoughts become rooted in us and they "will give birth in us to haughtiness and pride, the beginning and end of all evil".[100]

8. *Pride*

"God resists the proud." "God holds in abomination every puffed-up soul."[101] With these two texts Nil sharply delineates the plight of the proud soul. God is his enemy and his soul is dead, unclean before Him. How can he receive mercy; who can purify him? Without God we are abandoned; we carry in ourselves the seeds of our own destruction. We are as a leaf shaking in the wind or dust tossed about in a storm; thus we are mere puppets in the devil's hands.

Thus Nil moves on to the means of acquiring the opposite virtue of humility. The influence of Gregory Sinaite is most evident in this section. Gregory teaches that there are two kinds of humility: to deem oneself the lowest of all beings; and to ascribe to God all one's good actions. Those seeking humility are advised to keep in their minds three thoughts: (1) that they are the most sinful of all men; (2) that they are the most despicable of all creatures since their state is an unnatural one; and (3) that they are more damned than the demons, since they are slaves of demons.[102]

Nil, without mentioning Gregory, advises the monk "to hold the self lower than all, i.e. consider the self worse and more sinful than all others, viler than all creatures because we are addicted to unnatural vices, worse than the devils themselves who chase us and overcome us".[103] A monk can show this interior conviction by his exterior conduct. Here Nil stresses the exterior, but only because it is a reflection of a true interior disposition and because the exterior also helps to foster the interior. The Fathers, Nil says, have always maintained that for beginners the interior man is formed from the exterior. St. Basil observed that when a man is unguarded as to his exterior, there is little reason to believe that his interior disposition is different.[104]

---

[100] *Ustav*, p. 56. Cf. Cassian, *De Instit. Coenob.*, Lib. XII, ch. 1, p. 206: "This vice (pride) holds the last place in the order and arrangement of the eight vices, but it is the first in order of origin and time." Cf. also p. 209. Also Hesychius, *De temp. et virtute*, Centuria II, *PG*, 93, 100, 154D, gives egoism or self-love *(philautie)* as the source of all other vices. Cf. Nil Sianite, *De oct. spirit.*, *PG*, 79, 17, 1162C.
[101] Proverbs 3, 34; 16, 5.
[102] Gregory Sinaite, *PG*, 150, 1279C.
[103] *Ustav*, p. 57.
[104] *Ibid.*, 58. St. Basil, *PG*, 31, 1368A.

These exterior exercises that can foster the interior spirit of humility are: choose always the last place at table and in other gatherings of the brethren; wear the poorest garments, love lowly, menial works; when meeting another brother, make a low, sincere bow; love silence; be not loud in words and in conversation; avoid quarrels and contradictions; do not love show, demonstration, nor insist on your own words even though they may seem right.[105]

Nil goes on to quote directly from Gregory on how to develop in oneself the spirit of self-abasement from which is born and grows humility.

Are there in the world sinners whose sins are equal to mine, let alone exceeding mine? No, my soul, you and I are worse than all men, we are dust and ashes under their feet. How can I help considering myself the most despicable of all creatures, when they behave according to the order of their nature whereas I, owing to my innumerable sins, have sunk below my nature? Truly animals and beasts are purer than I, sinner that I am, for I am the lowest of all since I have brought myself down into hell and am lying there even before death. Who does not know or feel that a sinner is worse even than the demons, since he is their subject and their slave, even here sharing their prison in the outer darkness? A man possessed by demons is truly worse than the demons. You dwell in the abyss of hell even before death, how dare you delude yourself and call yourself righteous when through evil deeds you have made of yourself a despicable sinner and a demon? Woe to your delusion and your error, you offspring of the devil, you unclean dog, condemned for this to fire and darkness.[106]

Nil uses a bit of irony and gentle criticism of his contemporary religious in unmasking what he calls "a commonly accepted virtuous pride". This is not virtuous but shameful, for monks have left the world and now through subterfuges seek the praise of the world because of the good name of the monastery in which they live, or the great numbers of monks or the extensive lands and other properties their monasteries possess, or even by success these monks may have made in the world through their acquaintances. Others think it is virtuous to take pride in a beautiful voice, singing ability, or facility with languages, or in one's flawless pronunciation.[107] Others still become vain with their handiwork,

---

[105] *Ibid*. Cf. Gregory Sinaite, *PG*, 150, 1282B; Isaac the Syrian, *PG*, 86A, ch. 24, 851D and ss.; Climacus, *op. cit.*, *Gradus 25*, entire.
[106] Gregory Sinaite, *op. cit.*, 1279C–D.
[107] Cf. Gregory Sinaite, *op. cit.*, 1323D: "Let your reading be in solitude and not aloud, to avoid the temptation of boasting to yourself either about your voice, or about the refinement of your enunciation, or of imagining yourself reading to a gathering and entrancing everyone with your art."

others due to the fame of their parents or relatives or the rank of superiority they have acquired in the monastery. All this is extreme absurdity and should be hidden from others, for "seeking honour for a monk is not honour, but shame; their honour is a shame".[108]

These are God's gifts and it is utter folly to take credit for what belongs not to us, but to Him. Climacus had written practically the same: "It is shameful to be proud of the adornments of others, but utter madness to fancy one deserves God's gifts. Be exalted only by such merits as you had before your birth. But what you got after your birth, as also birth itself, God gave you."[109]

But such temptations will always be present to those striving earnestly to lead a life of perfection, an interior life. For the pious, harassed by proud thoughts about their good life, there is no other recourse than to earnest prayer to God for deliverance. Nil quotes Climacus who has the devils confess their weakness before such a strategy: "There is only one thing in which we have no power to meddle and we shall tell you this, for we cannot bear your blows; if you keep up a sincere condemnation of yourself before the Lord, you can count us weak as a cobweb."[110] Isaac the Syrian confirms that that is not pride when a proud thought enters the mind, without holding it in its power, for God will not judge one for unwilful temptations.[111]

These eight basic passions are the source of all sin. For Nil Sorskij, as well as for Evagrius, Climacus, Gregory Sinaite and other Sinaite Fathers,[112] all thoughts that enter the mind or heart, whether good or bad, are capable of turning into one of these eight passions. Therefore one's spiritual combat, with much sweat and labour, must consist in the control of the heart, purifying it of every element that might be used by the devil to turn it away from the continual remembrance of God. The end of the interior combat against these passionate thoughts is to expel or at least weaken them. Only when the heart is freed from these thoughts, when it is "purified", then only can it begin its ascent to God, to union with Him – the end of all spiritual strivings. This brings us to the subject of the best means of attaining purity of heart, of control of the thoughts in order to reach continual prayer or infused contemplation.

---

[108] *Ustav* p. 59. Cf. Isaac, *PG*, 86A, 851C–D.
[109] Clim,acus, *op. cit.*, *Gradus 23*, 967C.
[110] *Ustav*, p. 60. Cf. Climacus, *ibid.*, *Gradus 23*, 970D.
[111] *Ustav*, p. 60. Cf. Dorotheus, *Doctrina*, *PG*, 88, X, 1724D.
[112] *Ustav*, p. 21. Cf. Gregory Sianite, *PG*, 150, 1316, 1329, 1332; Evagrius, *De Oratione*, *PG*, 79, XI, 1169; CXVII, 1193; Climacus, *op. cit. Gradus 28*, 1132C–D.

III

HESYCHASM OF NIL

A. HESYCHASM IN GENERAL

Hesychastic spirituality has always been of interest to the Occidental mind, even if unfortunately sometimes with a great deal of ignorance at viewing an unintelligible phenomenon as "curious and quaint" and failing to penetrate to the essence. Many Western scholars[1] have done much of late to dispel ignorance in the West on this subject, but there still remains much confusion as regards historical points of development and clear distinctions of what are essentials from what are mere accidental aids. It would be a grave mistake to relegate hesychasm only to the mechanical recitation of the "Jesus Prayer" along with the technique of respiration, sitting posture and fixation on the navel. Father I. Hausherr, S.J. has added greatly to the appreciation of true hesychasm in four classical works.[2] According to him, the history of hesychasm can be divided into three divisions: (1) Sinaite hesychasm; (2) Hesychasm of the 11th century, Simeon the New Theologian; (3) The hesychast disputes of the 14th century.[3]

The Sinaite school of hesychastic tradition is represented chiefly by Nilus, John Climacus, Hesychius (not of Jerusalem, but of Sinai),[4] Philotheus. With their emphasis on the solitary life, on "guarding of the heart", on mental prayer of *theoria*, they transmit from Evagrius the synthesis he made of Origen and the Fathers of the Desert. The Fathers of the desert stressed the hesychasm of ascetical practices designed to develop *hesychia* or tranquillity, both exterior and interior.[5] This meant emphasizing flight from the society of other men, silence of lips and heart by reducing all cares *(amerimnia)* to only one, the evangelical

---

[1] I. Hausherr, S. J., G. Wundle, M. Jugie, L. Bouyer, F. Lilienfeld to mention a few.
[2] "Penthos", *OCA*, 132 (Roma, 1944); "Noms du Christ", *OCA*, 154 (Roma, 1960); "L'hésychasme: étude de spiritualité, *OPC*, Vol. XXII (1956), pp. 5–40, 247–285; "La méthode d'oraison hésychaste", *OC*, Vol. IX (1927), pp. 101–210.
[3] *OC*, Vol. IX (1927), p. 119.
[4] Cf. M. Viller, S. J., *La spiritualité des premiers èsicles chrétiens* (Paris, 1930), p. 93.
[5] Cf. J. Gouillard, *Petite Philocalie de la Priere du Coeur* (Paris, 1953), p. 16.

occupation of seeking only the kingdom of God. This interior struggle to live only for God was carried on by a constant vigilance or sobriety *(nepsis)* over one's thoughts. When, through attention *(prosoche)*, the mind or heart possessed *hesychia* or rest from passionate thoughts, it was able to contemplate God unceasingly.[6] To this *practica* Evagrius adds his notions of *theoria* from Origen. The mind, the mirror of God, now purified, would be able to contemplate the Trinity through its own divinization through grace. It became a temple of God and *apatheia* as a necessary condition allowed the possibility of continual contemplation of God. With the Sinaite hesychasts comes an important change. In place of Evagrius' "man is an intellect", they substitute "man is a heart"; ascetical practices or *practica* are still ordered as for Evagrius towards *apatheia*, the state where the passions, never extirpated fully, are controlled by the will of man so as to give complete freedom to contemplate God in man's heart. Corporal visions are to be discredited and the presence of God is to be guarded in the heart by *penthos*, abiding sorrow for one's sins, developed by continual thought of death, judgment, gift of tears, complete detachment from all creatures. The new element, already found among the Fathers, that of personal, warm devotion to Jesus, is now an habitual disposition.[7] Philotheus, following his master Climacus, says:

Sweet memory of God, that is, of Jesus, coupled with heartfelt wrath and beneficent contrition, can always annihilate all the fascination of thoughts, the variety of suggestions... daringly seeking to devour our souls. Jesus when invoked easily burns up all this. For in no other place can we find salvation except in Jesus Christ... And so every hour and every moment let us zealously guard our heart from thoughts obscuring the mirror of the soul, which should contain, drawn and imprinted on it, only the radiant image of Jesus Christ, who is the wisdom and the power of God the Father.[8]

Thus with the Sinaite hesychasts there is definitely added to the ascetical *practica* designed to guard the heart against any and all thoughts, good or bad, the ejaculation, indefinitely repeated, of the name of Jesus.[9]

[6]   Cf. I. Hausherr, "La Méthode...", *op. cit.*, p. 120.
[7]   *Ibid.*, p. 120c?
[8]   Philotheus of Sinai, *Dobrotoljubie*, T. 3 (Moscow, 1888), p. 454, no. 22–23.
[9]   "Flog your enemies with the name of Jesus, for there is no stronger weapon in heaven or earth." Climacus, *Scalae, PG*, 88, *Gradus 21*, 945B ss. Diadochus of Photike, *Philokalia ton ieron neptikon*, 3rd edition (Athens, 1957–1958), tome I, § 31, pp. 243–244.

Building on the solid doctrine of the Sinaite Fathers, Simeon the New Theologian (†1022) adds a new element, that of the necessity of supernatural consciousness. Diadochus of Photike, paradoxically in combatting the "mystical materialism" of the Messalians, ends up as the theorist of "sentiment" of conscious awareness of the supernatural operations of the Holy Spirit in the human soul.[10] From the life of Simeon written by his disciple Nicetas Stethatos we learn that Simeon had read Diadochus[11] but, in his application, he pushed the sentimental consciousness to views near to those held by the adversaries of Diadochus.

With the Sinaite hesychasts there was a stress always on the ascetical purification of the heart with a minimal description in terms intelligible to the ordinary person of the intimate joys of contemplation, coming from the conviction that a monk reached contemplation, not through instruction, but through interior combat. Thus contemplation was not opened to everyone, not even every monk who sought solitude, because it always remained a charism, a gift from God, given only when the soul was prepared through ascetical purification.[12] To desire or demand contemplation through any other way than the practice of virtue was forbidden; contemplation obtained through any other means than through virtue was exposed to illusions and pride. To speak about the joys of contemplation to one who experienced them was useless, so they thought; to speak about them to one who had not experienced them would have been absurd. But with the doctrine of Simeon, contemplation was opened to every Christian.

If a baptized Christian is not sensibly aware of the Divine inhabitation in his soul and of the operation of the three infused virtues, he does not possess sanctifying grace. We feel our body clothed with outer clothes, why should not the soul feel the "investiture" of Jesus Christ, His enveloping presence? If we have no realization of these realities, it is because we are cadavers or because God is for us a word only.[13] "A man, who consciously possesses in himself God the Giver of knowledge to men, has already studied all the Holy Scriptures and has collected, like fruit, all the benefit their reading can afford. So he no longer needs to

---

[10] Cf. M. Viller, *op. cit.*, p. 126. Also Diadochus of Photike and his type of supernatural consciousness: *Philokalia, op. cit.*, tome I, § 29, p. 242; § 33, pp. 243–244; § 36, p. 245.

[11] Cf. text edited by I. Hausherr, "Vie de Syméon le Nouveau Théologien", in *OC*, vol. XII (Roma, 1928), p. 6.

[12] Cf. I. Hausherr, "Contemplation et Sainteté – Philoxène de Mabboug", in *RAM* 14 (1933), p. 194.

[13] "Discourse of Simeon", text given by I. Hausherr, *OC*, vol. IX (1927), pp. 174–176.

read books."[14] One wonders what Diadochus of Photike would have done
had he lived in the time of Simeon for he had fought bitterly against the
Messalians on points that Simeon himself dangerously held:[15] he attributes to his own private revelations a superior authority to decisions of
the hierarchy; he judges as universally possible what his mystical gifts
from God have attained; the presence of the Holy Trinity in the soul is
seen by a material light. Above all, he describes the delights of contemplation in terms of material, sensible experiences, concretely so that even
the simple and those having had no spiritual experience can hunger and
thirst to share also such joys.[16]

It was actually Gregory of Sinai who had the greatest success in
promulgating hesychastic mysticism and in starting a period of "renaissance". Hesychasm had been known and practised on Mount Athos
before Gregory's arrival at the end of the 13th century, but Callistus, his
disciple, biographer, and later Patriarch of Constantinople, tells us that
when he arrived he found only three solitaries on the whole peninsula:
Isaias, Cornelius, and Macarius, who practised, besides the practica,
virtues, also mental prayer or *theoria*.[17] He brought the hesychastic
Fathers to the peninsula and started a movement that would establish
hesychasm as the central mystical doctrine of Orthodoxy.[18] He insists
greatly on the purification of the soul and the fight against the passions,
on the necessity of arriving at Evagrius' *apatheia*, the infusion of divine
light and supernatural knowledge of the created world with intimate
union of the soul with God, as taught his predecessors, especially Climacus and Simeon. He hands down quite faithfully the ascetical purification
of the "heart" of his Sinaite predecessors and builds up the tendency of
Simeon to concretize and localize the supernatural experience in man's
heart.[19] Thus we have the "Prayer of Jesus" stressed: "Lord, Jesus

[14] Simeon the New Theologian, "*Practica et Moralia*", *PG*, 120, n. 118, 668A.
[15] Cf. the text of the three methods of attention and prayer, edited by I. Hausherr,
OC, vol. IX (1927), pp. 164–165.
[16] "La Méthode...", *ibid*., p. 133.
   Pomjalovskij, Ivan V., "Žitie iže vo svjatyx otca našego Gregorija Sinaita" (text in
Greek) (St. Petersburg, 1894), p. 10.
[17] Bois, J., "Grégoire le Sinaite et l'hésychasma à athos au XIVe siècle", in *Èchos
d'Orient*, oct., p. 69.
[18] Bois, J., "Grégoire le Sinaite et l'hésychasma à Athos au XIVe siècle", in *Echos
d'Orient*, oct., p. 69.
[19] A Guillaumont has excellently traced the development in antiquity, especially
among the Semites, as found in the Old and New Testament above all, of the various
senses of the word "heart". Showing how Byzantine spiritual writers remained faithful
to the Semite traditional way of using the word heart, he comments: "la notion de
'coeur', fondamentale dans la méthode hésychaste, est tout à fait conformée aux

Christ, Son of God, have mercy on me a sinner," linked with the rhythm of controlled breathing. This was not only an oral prayer, but was to become spontaneously aligned with the heart's beating that, through it, thoughts would be controlled and the heart would "pray always" as St. Paul enjoins the early Christians. Through constant prayer the way was opened to contemplation of God. To attain a spontaneous "prayer of the heart", he specifies in detail the position of the body to be assumed so as to facilitate slow breathing and to aid the soul in entering the heart.

His method consists in these instructions: "In the morning force your mind to descend from the head to the heart and hold it there, calling continually in mind and soul: 'Lord, Jesus Christ, have mercy upon me' until you are tired. When tired, transfer your mind to the second half, and say: 'Jesus, Son of God, have mercy upon me.' After some time, change back to the first half, but you should not alternate too often through laziness..."[20]

But over and over again Gregory insists on the great danger of self-deception and the necessity of listening to other spiritual guides rather than following one's own inclinations.[21] All in all, he emphasizes, more than any single element in the material technique of performing the Jesus prayer, the necessity of accompanying prayer with "the following virtues: fasting, abstinence, vigil, patience, courage, silence, not talking, tears, humility which generate and preserve one another."[22]

---

usages bibliques du mot et repose sur les anciennes théories physiologiques qui faisaient du coeur le siège de l'intelligence; l'ardent défenseur de l'Hésychasma au XIVe siècle, Grégoire Palamas, fait de cette théorie la base de sa méthode d'oraison. Le mot "coeur" n'est plus pris ici au sens métaphorique, comme chez les spirituels de la haute époque chrétienne, dont les hésychastes se réclament volontiers. C'est le coeur, au sens propre du mot, qui est le siège de l'esprit, de la prière, de la grâce sensible et goutée, selon un enseignement constant du XIVe au XIXe siècle." He quotes from the method of Nicephor and also from Pseudo–Simeon's Method showing how these hesychasts insisted on making the mind enter into the heart, to keep it there, and to have the mind guard the heart; then he adds the just caution that we should have ever in mind when touching on the physical method: "On ne peut bien comprendre et bien juger de telles pratiques spirituelles, au premier abord singulières, que si on les rattache à des modes d'expression séculaires et demeures, vénérables, et à d'anciennes théories sur les fonctions physiologiques du coeur et leurs répercussions sur le plan psychique." "Le sens du nom de coeur dans l'antiquité", in the Ètudes Carmélitaines (1950), pp. 80–81. In order to understand the full meaning of "heart" as used among Orthodox today, cf. B. Vyšeslavcev, Serdce v xristianskoj i indijskoj Mistike, YMCA Press (Paris, 1929), and Th. Spacil, S.J., "Doctrina Theologiae Orientis Separati de Revelatione, Fide, Dogmati", in OC, XXXI, 2, pp. 173 and foll.

[20] Gregory Sinaite, "Instructio ad Hesychastes", PG, 150, 1329A–B.

[21] Ibid., no. 15, 1328D.

[22] Ibid., no. 13, 1325C–D.

He singles out the Fathers to be read with profit, all others could be momentarily left alone for these "neptic".[23] Fathers teach all that is necessary to attain perfect contemplation.

Always read about silence and prayer, namely St. John of the Ladder, St. Isaac, St. Maximus, the New Theologian and his disciples Stethatos, Hesychius, Philotheus of Sinai and others who have written on this subject. Leave for a time all other writings, not as something inadmissible, but as something not corresponding to your aim at the moment (gaining experience in prayer); for the subjects they treat may distract your mind from prayer.[24]

Thus we have the beginning of a "canon" of approved authors of the prayer of the heart, which would form the basis for the later *Philokalia* compiled in the eighteenth century by Macarius of Corinth (†1805) and Nicodemus Hagiorite (†1809) and first published in Venice in 1782.[25] The authors approved by Gregory became the chiefly quoted ones by Nil in his writings and undoubtedly were the constant source for his reading.

It was Gregory Palamas (†1359) who formed a theological and metaphysical explanation of what the hesychast Fathers had been trying to say down through the centuries, but they had always couched it in Biblical or at least in highly metaphorical language. His metaphysical distinction of the essence of God and the divine energies need not detain us in our rapid review of the hesychastic Fathers. Though he adds nothing new to the hesychastic method as such, his name is associated with the final form that hesychasm took: "the hesychastic renaissance, begun on Mount Athos at the end of the 13th and beginning of the 14th centuries to which Palamas gave an indelible mark."[26]

The Patriarch Callistus[27] and Ignatius of Xanthopoulos, in their *Directions to Hesychasts in a Hundred Chapters (Century)*, collected all

---

[23] This is used in the title of the *Philokalia:* "Philokalia ton ieron neptikon". Fr. I. Hausherr says: "It is impossible to translate the word "nepsis". However, there are synonyms that give us some intelligibility such as "attention", "silence of the heart", "custody of the heart". "Les grands courants de la spiritualité orientale", in *OCP*, Vol. I, no. 1–II (Roma, 1935), p.

[24] Greg. Sinaite, *PG*, 150, no. 11, 1324D.

[25] Paissij Veličkovskij (†1794) translated it into Slavonic and called it *Dobrotoljubie*. This translation did more than any other single factor to promote a rebirth of monasticim and the practice of the Jesus Prayer in the beginning of the 19th century. Bishop Feofan the Hermit (†1894) translated it into Russian.

[26] Gouillard J., "La Centurie", in *Echos d'Orient*, vol. 37, 1938, p. 459.

[27] This Patriarch Callistus II is not to be confused with the Patriarch Callistus I, the disciple of Gregory Sinaite and his biographer. Cf. Ammann, A. M., S. J., "Die Gottesschau im palamitischen Hesychasmus", in *Das östliche Christentum* series, Würzburg, 1938, pp. 12–13.

that the hesychast Fathers down through the centuries, including what the Apostles themselves, had to say about prayer, especially about the Jesus Prayer, and they worked the sayings into a detailed synthesis. This would become the manual and guide for all future hesychasts and, with its solid, ascetical teaching mingled with exacting details of technique, it would be the one treatise most relied on when a trustworthy spiritual guide was not available. Down through all the hesychast Fathers, from Evagrius, Macarius, Maximus, Diadochus, Climacus and the Sinaite Fathers, above all, from Isaac the Syrian, the authors assemble an overwhelming mass of teaching on the stages of progress from purification to *apatheia* to constant remembrance of God through the use of the Jesus Prayer and respiratory method, all climaxing in contemplation where "abandoning the many and the varied, we shall unite with the One, the Single and the Unifying, directly in a union which transcends reason, as the glorious Theologian says: 'When God unites with gods (that is, god-like men) and is known by them, then the heart is filled with radiance by the penetration of the Holy Spirit'."[28]

With the *Century* of Callistus and Ignatius, the two hesychastic tendencies are melded together for all time: the intellectual contemplative tendency of Evagrius, Diadochus, Maximus and the Sinaite Fathers, stressing control of all thoughts through solitude, sobriety *(nepsis)* and *penthos* so that the mind, freed from influence of the passions, could contemplate God within; the other tendency, presupposing the former and equivalating the remembrance of God to the prayer of the heart, i.e. the constantly repeated Jesus Prayer, stresses material techniques of breathing, posture, the Taboric *lumen* as visible to the corporal eyes.[29]

It would be most unjust to misjudge these latter Hesychasts. They always placed the material aids of a method subservient to the final contemplative end and presupposed a thorough purification through constant control over "passionate" thoughts. But from the new elements that they introduced, always as instrumental, succeeding generations who practised this method did not always distinguish and thus the over-materialization of a method led to many abuses and a general discarding of even the essentials. We need only say here as regards the accessories of the so-called Hesychastic "Method", that one should avoid, as the early

---

[28] *Century*, ch. 38, p. 91. Page references are given according to A. M. Ammann's text, *supra cit.*

[29] Because hesychasm has suffered greatly in the West from confusion about the method in relation to the essence of hesychasm, it was deemed best to treat the topic of the "method" in a separate part. Cf. *Appendix II* of this work.

hesychasts insisted so often in their writings, confusing true charity and spiritual perfection with sensible consolations, visions, lights and "warmth born in the heart".[30] Nor should ever be attached an infallible efficacy to any physical method as such, divorced from the necessary purification that always remains the basic condition for further union with God. In the Appendix II a brief history of the physical method is given. But one must keep ever in mind that historically the Jesus Prayer evolved through the deep penetration of the early hermit-monks of the transcendence of God and the corresponding conviction of their own sinfulness. Through their long years of asceticism that fed this *penthos* the prayer that arose to their lips, that summarized in an integral simplicity all of their spiritual aspirations, was the prayer: "Lord Jesus Christ, Son of God, have mercy on me a sinner." For hermits, coenobitic monks, lay persons, to take up the same prayer as a sure formula quick and easy success, with sensible delights guaranteed if one followed the physical side, with no solid preparation of the virtues that this prayer summarizes and presupposed as already having been acquired as habitual, this is to invite false mysticism, engender spiritual pride, and could lead to physical aberrations.

This has not been a complete history of hesychasm, but only a rapid review of periods of transition which added or stressed some feature in what we know after the 14th century as *hesychasm*. Thus Nil Sorskij, arriving on Mount Athos in the second half of the 15th century, through living successors of the hesychastic Renaissance period, and through the writings of the earlier hesychast Fathers, was able to know all faucets of this spirituality. It remains now to show in what points he was mostly influenced; in other words, from his own spiritual teaching, what did he consider as the essence of true hesychasm?

B. PURITY OF HEART AND "NEPSIS" OF NIL SORSKY

If Nil Sorskij, in the scattered writings that we possess of him, stresses too often, as G. Levickij asserts,[31] that the spiritual life is a battle, an internal war fought by the all-ness of God it is because the means to attain his end take on seemingly exaggerated proportions merely because for Nil,

---

[30] Ch. 54, *Century* of Callistus and Ignatius, p. 109.
[31] Levickij, G., "O nravoučenii prepodobnago Nila Sorskogo" in *Xrist. Čteniie*, vol. 2–3 (1895), pp. 338–339.

without the use of these means, continually and successfully for the whole of a monk's life, there is no attaining of the ultimate end: salvation of one's soul; proximate: intimate union with God through grace and prayer. Thus we can understand why, especially in the only two "formal" treatises on the spiritual life that Nil wrote, he stresses solitude, silence, control of thoughts, tranquillity or *hesychia*, sobriety or vigilance *(nepsis)* especially through observance of the "commandments". All of these means produce the purity of soul, mind or heart necessary to give the monk the only true God-like liberty of sons of God. This purity of heart only can assure charity or love of God for Himself. Hence we can examine Nil's spirituality under the subdivisions: (1) solitude and silence; (2) emptying of thoughts *(apostasis noimaton);* (3) *hesychia;* (4) *nepsis* through observations of commandments of God.

1. *Solitude and Silence*

Nil, in encouraging his disciples to follow him in solitude and silence, quotes Arsenius the Great as the model of a perfect hesychast *(bezmolv-nik:* one without disturbances) and gives as his authority for this Isaac the Syrian: "St. Isaac, above all the Fathers, esteemed *hesychia* and praised St. Arsenius the Great as the perfect hesychast; but even he (Arsenius) had his followers and disciples. So also Nil Sinaite and Daniel the Hermit and many others, as is confirmed in their lives, had disciples. And everywhere in the writings of the Fathers do we find praise and approval of "hesychia" *(bezmolvie),* living in communion with another or perhaps two."[32] Nil is making the love of solitude and silence of Arsenius his own, yet in harmony with a minimum of necessary companionship, "for solitude (absolute, hermitical) demands the fortitude of an angel".[33] Nil's ideal is found in the account given among the *Apophthegmata Patrum:*[34] "The Abba Arsenius, still at the imperial court, prayed to God in these words: 'Lord, lead me along a way of life where I can be saved!' And a voice said to him: 'Arsenius, flee men and you will be saved.' The same Arsenius, now become a hermit, in this new life made again his same prayer; and he heard a voice which said to him: 'Arsenius, flee, keep silence, remain tranquil' (fuge, tace, quiesce); these are the roots of impeccability."

[32] *Ustav,* pp. 88–89. Cf. Climacus, *Scalae, PG,* 88, *Gradus 27,* 1112D. Also, I. Hausherr, "L'hésychasme. Étude de spiritualité", *op. cit.,* p. 25.
[33] *Ustav,* p. 88.
[34] *PG,* 65, de Abbate Arsenio (1–2), 88.

This is the simple program that Nil reiterates over and over:

Isaac gives the following instruction to those desirous to observe true silence and to purify their minds through prayer: 'Retire from the sight of the world and cut off conversations; do not let friends enter your cell, even under the pretext of good intentions, unless they have the same spirit and intention as yourself and are likewise advanced in mystical prayer. Fear mixing with others; against this we can warn from experience. For, after we have emerged from intimate conversations, even when they have seemed to be good, our souls are troubled against our will, and these disturbances continue with us for a long time.[35]

There must be the flight from the world, the society of men, into the "desert", the commonly used by Nil in his patristic language to indicate the monastic life. In his letter to Starec German he recalls his own example of having fled the world and all wordly enticements to devote himself wholly to "living according to the divine writings".[36] In his letter to Gurij, he tells him that to cut oneself from the world, a monk must cut himself from that which especially binds him to it; a monk must sacrifice all his habits and cut himself off completely, irrevocably from the past, because otherwise former impressions will again arise in the soul. Once he has separated himself from the world, there must be only one purpose, one dedication: to strive for moral perfection.[37] To Vassian he advises strict redrawal from talking, hearing and seeing improper things that could stir up the soul to unrest. "Separate from all who do not live according to the writings of the Fathers."[38]

A monk, having withdrawn from the world, does not *ipso facto* acquire the necessary purity of heart, but strict silence, exterior and interior, of the heart, is absolutely necessary. "Strive with active concentration on the task of God alone. St. Basil the Great says that the beginning of purity of heart is silence. And St. John Climacus further defines silence as first of all, detachment from concern with regard to necessary and unnecessary things; second, as assiduous prayer; and third, as the unremitting action of prayer in the heart."[39]

Therefore the monk must guard from all unnecessary, exterior conversation and even those conversations which Climacus considers as belonging to the "necessary things" and which Nil interprets as "conversations with good and spiritual fathers and brothers which we may

---

[35] *Ustav*, pp. 82–83. Issac the Syrian: *Logos 23, ed. cit.*, p. 142.
[36] Letter to German, fol. 105A.
[37] Letter to Gurij, fol. 101A–B.
[38] Letter to Vassian, fol. 97A.
[39] *Ustav*, p. 81. Cf. Climacus, *op. cit., Gradus 27* 1108C–D. Basil, *PG*, 31, 136B–C,

think to be helpful for our spiritual improvement. But even conversations of this kind should be pursued within measure and at suitable times, for if we are unguarded in this matter, we shall involuntarily be disturbed with unnecessary, interior turmoil."[40] Agitation of the soul comes from "things displeasing to God". Therefore, to maintain exterior and interior silence, one must "live according to the commandments of God and in interior communion with God".[41]

Continuing on this theme of interior silence that comes from solitude cutting off from all unnecessary conversation, control of disturbing thoughts and images, Nil adjoins an important warning: not to drive out of one's soul this interior silence and *hesychia* by turning away from God present in the soul to pray to God outside of the soul through singing.

When you are conscious of the sweetness of divine grace working in you and when prayer operates in your heart, then you must continue in it. Do not interrupt it or rise up to sing psalms as long as God sees fit to leave its work in you, for to do so would be to leave God who is within, in order to call on Him outside yourself, as if one were to leave the heights to stoop down to the flats. Thus you would drive away prayer and deprive your mind of its silence at the very moment when hesychia, by the very meaning of the word, demands that the mind be preserved in peace and quiet tranquillity. God is peace and is foreign to all noise and disturbance. And so, when you are engaged in mental prayer, do not fall for the temptation of allowing any representations of any images or visions to enter, for powerful dreams and movements do not automatically cease to be when the mind enters into the heart and makes its prayer and only those can resist these disturbing thoughts and conquer them who obtain the fullness of the grace of the Holy Spirit and those who cling to Jesus Christ with unshakened mind.[42]

2. *Emptying of Thoughts:* Apostasis Noimaton

Nil follows the tradition begun by Evagrius in his asceticism to attain *hesychia* and insisted on by the Sinaite Fathers and others of the Palestinian tradition that the mind, in order to reach true contemplation, must begin by emptying itself of all thoughts, whether they be good or bad.[43]

[40] *Ibid.* Cf. Isaac the Syrian, *PG*, 86A, 854C–D. Also S. Basil, *Reg. Fus. Tract.*, PG. 31, 917A.
[41] *Ustav*, p. 90.
[42] *Ibid.*, pp. 25–26.
[43] Nil (Evagrius), *De Oratione, PG*, 79, (62) 1179C, (55) 1177D; Cassian, *Conférences, IC*, 3, *ed. cit.*, pp. 41–43. Climacus, *op. cit., Gradus 28*, 1136D. Hesychius Sinaite, *PG* 93, *Centuria* I, (5) 1481D, (14) 1485B, (21) 1487A, (44) 1496B; *Centuria* II, (3) 1512D, (61) 1532B, Gregory Sinaite, *PG*, 150, 1316, 1329, 1332.

"Especially should he strive to render his mind deaf and dumb in prayer, as Nilus of Sinai[44] says, keeping his heart silent and freed from any thought whatsoever, even should it be a good one, so says Hesychius of Jerusalem."[45] "For after the good thoughts, freed from passion, there come the passionate thoughts, as experience demonstrates, and it is to the entrance of the former that the latter owe their admittance. It is for this reason that we should strive to maintain our mind in silence, freed even from such thoughts as may seem legitimate."[46] Thus the process of purifying the inner vessel and worshipping God in spirit and truth is a difficult struggle, but at the first suggestion of a thought, it must be rejected at once. "For, by resistance in the beginning, we cut off the whole sequence."[47]

For those who have passed the beginning stage of fighting useless thoughts, especially evil ones by their opposites, those in "progress" and in a state of enlightenment, are not asked to recite psalms. "They must practice silence, abundant prayer and contemplation, for such souls are united with God and should not detach their mind from Him and permit it to be troubled; for the mind which turns away from the thought of God and busies itself with inferior matters commits adultery."[48] This latter is a reference undoubtedly to Simeon the New Theologian's phrase: "In the eyes of God who sees our hearts, such men (monks dedicated to God yet who seek praise of men) are equal to those who commit adultery. For a man who passionately wishes his life, name and works to be rumoured in the world commits adultery in the eyes of God just like the old people of Judea, according to David."[49] The concept of adultery applied to a monk who occupies himself with thoughts (not necessarily impure) other than God stems from Evagrius' teaching on a monk's complete absorption with God alone, or in other words, with continuous prayer.[50] This is further developed by Climacus in his doctrine about "emptying

---

[44] This is indeed Evagrius, De Oratione, PG, 79, (11), 1169C. For the problem of Pseudo-Nil consult: I. Hausherr, S. J., Les lecons d'un contemplatif. Le Traité de l'oraison d'Evagre le Pontique (Paris, 1960), Introduction, pp. 5–8. Also cf. M. Viller, op. cit., p. 94: "Le probleme de Nil".

[45] Hesychius, Century, I, PG, 93, (43) 1493D.

[46] Ustav, p. 21. Cf. Hesychius, ibid., Century, II, (61) 1532B.

[47] Ustav, p. 21.

[48] Ibid., p. 27.

[49] Simeon the New Theologian, Capita Moralia, PG, 120, (92) 653C.

[50] Evagrius, De Oratione, PG, 79, (34) 1173D, (44) 1175D, (49) 1177B, (53) 1177D, (54) 1177D, (62) 1179C, (118) 1193B, (120) 1193B.

the mind of thoughts"[51] or another name more evangelic, *amerimnia*.[52] The urge for "eliminating all thoughts" with Evagrius, Climacus, other Sinaite hesychasts and Nil Sorskij is prompted always by the totalitarianism of loving God alone. This asceticism to empty the mind of any thought that might turn the knowing and loving faculties of man from their one object, God, perhaps may be negative, but only insofar as it is a presupposed condition for the more positive. One eliminates all cares for the one great care, to seek perfection or to love and serve only God. To fully understand Nil Sorskij's teaching on the necessity of emptying the mind from all thoughts, worries, cares that could impede the mind from continual prayer and union with God, one must go to his master Climacus. In his 27th step, Climacus defines solitude or *hesychia* as the absence of care. "A small hair disturbs the eye, and a small care ruins solitude; because solitude (in Greek, *hesychia)* is the banishment of thoughts and ideas, and the rejection of even laudable cares."[53] Fr. I. Hausherr excellently translates this latter phrase as: "La grande affaire pour les hésichastes, c'est d'avoir à priori une parfaite indifférence pour toutes les choses humaines, si raisonnables qu'elles paraîssent."[54]

For Nil, as for Climacus and the whole Evagrian tradition, the eliminating from the mind of all thoughts, especially cares, worries or preoccupations (sinful or necessary and even laudable and legitimate) is a result flowing from the degree of indifference or detachment a monk has in his heart for all created beings. Nil must have been greatly influenced by the second step of Climacus on detachment.

The man, who really loves the Lord, who has made a real effort to find the coming Kingdom, who has really begun to be troubled by his sins, who is really mindful of eternal torment and judgment, who really lives in fear of his own departure, will not love, care or worry about money, or possessions, or parents, or worldly glory, or friends, or brothers, or anything at all on earth. But, having shaken off all ties with earthly things and having stripped himself of all his cares and having come to hate even his own flesh and having stripped himself of everything, he will follow Christ without anxiety or hesitation, always looking heavenward and expecting help from there ...[55]

[51] The Greek phrase *"apothesis noimaton"* which Nil Sorkij translates by the phrase *"molčašče* (to be silent) *ot vsjakogo pomysla"* is here used in a quotation from Hesychius of Sinaite: *Century* I, *PG*, 93, 1485B. Hesychius is undoubtedly quoting from Climacus, *op. cit., Gradus* 27, 112A, who uses this same phrase *"apothesis noimaton."* Fr. I. Hausherr explains this term in relationship to *"hesychia".* Cf. "L'hésychasme...", *op. cit.,* p. 263.

[52] I. Hausherr, *op. cit.,* p. 263.

[53] *Gradus 27,* 1112A.

[54] Hausherr, I., *op. cit.,* p. 269.

[55] *Gradus 2,* 653C.

In his letter to Gurij, Nil answers his third question: In what does true renunciation of the world consist? We find a fairly well summarized second step of Climacus, long-meditated on by Nil and breathing his personal conviction of the need for complete detachment in the heart from all worldly creatures and complete dedication to the service of God. A monk who has left the world must leave also the habits and attachments to these former affections. Now he must be intent only on his moral perfection. He must not see and hear things about the brothers, their secrets and activities, for this would

> make the soul empty from all good and set up an internal tribunal in your heart for the failures of your neighbour. This causes one to stop weeping for one's own sins... Do not engage in pleasant and common friendly conversations as worldly men do who busy themselves with absurd cares, such as various monastic customs, riches, possessions... One should not mingle with such, not even to correct them; leave this up to God who is powerful to effect even this.[56]

Nothing can dispel this over-preoccupation, especially for legitimate things like health, food, shelter, clothing, as can a deep faith in the Divine Providence. Nil gives a short but very succinct teaching on this in connection with means to combat the thought or vice of sadness.

> Nothing that happens to us is contrary to the will of Providence, and everything that is sent us by God is for our good and the salvation of our soul. Even if it does not seem helpful at the moment, we shall understand later on that it was willed so by God, and that it is not what we ourselves wish that is always useful to us. God sends us trials out of His mercy, so that after we have suffered, we may be crowned by Him. Without temptation it is impossible to receive a crown. This is why we should thank God for these sufferings, as our Benefactor and Saviour.[57]

Purity of spirit or of heart is had, according to Nil, "not when we possess nothing, but when, in addition (to such complete exterior poverty) we have no desire to possess anything".[58]

Thus for Nil, as for all his hesychast predecessors, the mind is emptied of thoughts, good or bad, when, not only the desire for such objects ceases in us, but when it is absorbed by the greater passion and one pre-occupation of loving God alone.

---

[56] Letter to Gurij, fol. 101B.
[57] *Ustav*, p. 50. Cf. Philotheus Sinaite, *Dobrotoljubie, op. cit.*, (20) p. 453.
[58] *Ustav*, p. 47.

3. Hesychia

This term which Nil usually translates as *bezmolvie*, literally meaning "without disturbance, without agitation", retains for him the full sense that it had for his predecessors.[59] Rather than an exterior action, it is the general term to indicate an interior state of the soul, arrived at through ascetical practices, especially of solitude, silence and the emptying of the mind and heart from not only all thoughts capable of disturbing the soul during continuous prayer, but also from all desires for everyone and everything other than God Himself. It is the necessary condition for continuous prayer and intimate union with God. It is death to the world and flesh, "the resurrection of the soul before the body",[60] through contemplative prayer. As Fr. Hausherr so well points out: "Hesychasm exists only for prayer and through prayer."[61] Nil gives advice that agrees with this.

Hence, we see for Nil, as well as for Evagrius, Climacus and other

If you cannot pray in the quiet of your heart and without thoughts and you see that temptations only multiply in your mind, do not be dejected at this but continue to pray. St. Gregory Sinaite, knowing full well that we ourselves, so laden with passions, cannot win victory over our disturbing, passionate thoughts, said, 'No one in the beginning stages can hold the mind freed from temptations if God Himself does not hold or support him and turn away such temptations. Only the powerful and much progressed in spiritual activity can hold the mind in this condition of 'thoughtlessness'. But even they do not drive them away by their own power, but do it with God's help and their opposing battle, always adorned with His grace and in His power...[62]

early Christian hesychasts, *hesychia* or *apatheia* differs from Stoic *apatheia* or a natural *ataraxi* because the Christian never forgets from his contemplation of the Holy Scriptures the real nature of man where original sin, removed by Baptism, still leaves its effect on a passionate nature which can never be extirpated, but can be controlled. A voluntary effort must constantly be exerted by the Christian, but always under the influence and help of divine grace. Nil summarizes well the place of all ascetical practices in the spiritual striving towards the final end: glory of God:

---

[59] Cf. Macarius, *PG*, 34, 905, 938 and foll.; Nil Sinaite; *De Malignis Cogitationibus*, *PG*, 79, cap. 3, 1204A–C; Cassian, *Conférences*, I, ch. 6 and 7, pp. 83–85; IX, ch. 2, pp. 40–41; Climacus, *Gradus 29* (entire), 1148B–1152C.
[60] Climacus, *Gradus 29*, 1148C.
[61] Hausherr, I., "L'hésychasme...", *op. cit.*, p. 270.
[62] *Ustav*, p. 22.

...may we remain in good works with strength, being supported always by the grace of the Lord God and Saviour Jesus Christ, through the prayers of the Queen and Mother of God, and all the Saints and being given ever to ascetical practices of virtue on our part. We must know that as we choose a place of tranquillity, so let us put away all useless, vain agitation, worry and the like, so unpleasing to God and let us remain in His commandments... Let us do all so as to please God: singing, prayer, reading, study of spiritual matters, manual labour and other work of any kind. So little by little, according to our strength we near to God, in the interior man; let us add by our good works to the glory of the Father, Son, and Holy Spirit, one God in the Trinity, now and forever, amen.[63]

This utter dependence on God's help to achieve with our cooperation a state of tranquillity is ever foremost in Nil's mind. When a monk has attained this state, "when the mind is motionless in the heart, generating prayer",[64] even then there arise dreamlike fantasies, "and only the soul that is perfect in the Holy Spirit, having achieved freedom through Jesus Christ, can exercise control over them".[65]

Some of the divine effects of this gift of *hesychia* Nil mentions, with an ardour and concreteness of detail common to Isaac who is here quoted.

The fathers call this condition prayer because this gift has its beginnings in prayer and is bestowed on the holy ones during prayer, but no man really knows how to define this phenomenon. When the soul undergoes such spiritual activity and subjects itself completely to God and through direct union nears the Divinity and is enlightened in its movements by an interior light from above and the mind experiences a feeling of future happiness, then it forgets itself, its temporal existence on this earth, and loses any attraction for the things of this earth; there is enkindled in it an ineffable joy, an indescribable sweetness warms the heart, the whole body feels its repercussions and man forgets not only his plaguing passions, but also even life itself and thinks that the kingdom of heaven consists of nothing other than this blissful condition. Here in this state he experiences that love of God is sweeter than life and intelligence, now in accordance with God's from which springs love, is sweeter than honey and the honeycomb.[66]

4. *Vigilance and Sobriety* (Nepsis) *and Observance of Commandments*

Having described this state of tranquillity as a necessary condition for persevering in prayer and which is further born in prayer and maintained through continual prayer, Nil follows the patristic tradition of his favour-

[63] *Ibid.*, p. 90.
[64] *Ibid.*, p. 25.
[65] *Ibid.*, p. 25.
[66] *Ibid.*, p. 28. Isaac the Syrian. *Logos 31, ed. cit.*, p. 197.

ite Fathers in exposing his doctrine on vigilance, by which the mind holds itself ever alert to reject at first impulse anything contrary to the intimate union achieved through constant prayer in the soul and to co-operate perfectly and instantly with the slightest inspiration of the Holy Spirit in leading the soul to greater perfection.

Nepsis, among the early Fathers who wrote about this type of asceticism, is described rather than defined.[67] The one who wrote the most in detail about it and had the greatest influence in this regard on Nil was Hesychius Sinaite, whom Nil erroneously calls Hesychius of Jerusalem.[68] His definition is classic:

Sobriety is a spiritual art, which with long and diligent practice and with the help of God, releases man completely from passionate thoughts and words and from evil deeds. As it proceeds, it gives a sure knowledge of God the Incomprehensible, as far as this can be reached; and it gives in secret a solution of Divine and hidden mysteries. It is the doer of every commandment in the Old and New Testament; and the giver of every blessing in the life to come. In itself it is, in essence, purity of heart; ...It is this which Christ calls blessed, saying: 'Blessed are the pure in heart; for they shall see God' (Matt. V, 8). Sobriety, if it be constant in a man, becomes his guide to a righteous and God-pleasing life. It is also a ladder towards contemplation; and it teaches us to govern rightly the movements of the three parts of the soul... and to guard the senses securely and increases daily the four great virtues, i.e. wisdom, courage, abstinence and justice.[69]

Nil quotes Hesychius further in speaking about the necessity of this virtue of sobriety:

Blessed Hesychius of Jerusalem says: 'It is impossible to live our present life without food and drink. So, too, it is impossible for the soul to attain anything spiritual and pleasing to God, or to be free of inner sin, without guarding of mind and purity of heart; in other words, without sobriety, no matter how much a man strives to refrain from committing sins in deed through fear of future torment'.[70]

On the very first page of his *Ustav*, Nil speaks about this "sobriety" using various general terms, all found among the Fathers. "The Monastic Rule: From the Writings of the Holy Fathers on 'Mental Activity', about its Necessity and How Proper it is to Seek it Ever with Zeal."[71]

---

[67] For a history of this word and various patristic descriptions cf. I. Hausherr, *op. cit.*, pp. 273–279.

[68] Cf. footnote *supra*, no. 4. Hesychius of Jerusalem died in 432–433 and this Hesychius whom Nil quotes obviously lived after Climacus († c. 649) upon whom Hesychius greatly depends, quoting him frequently.

[69] Hesychius, *Century I, PG*, 93, 1480D and foll.

[70] *Ustav*, p. 13. Cf. Hesychius, *op. cit.*, *Century II*, 1513B (7).

[71] *Ustav*, p. 11.

Thus reads the title to his *Ustav* and we can judge from this the importance Nil plans on giving this virtue which is so basic to Oriental spirituality. He thus begins, after his title:

Many of the Holy Fathers have spoken of the 'activity of the heart', the
'guarding of the spirit' and 'control of the mind', each using words inspired by
divine grace; but all understood one and the same thing by these different
expressions as expressed by the divine words: 'From the heart come forth
evil thoughts to defile a man; therefore we must purify the inner vessel and
worship God in spirit and truth'.[72]

Throughout the *Ustav* and Nil's other writings, there occur over and
over two phrases: "mental activity", or similar phrases, and "keeping
(or living according to) the commandments of God". Speaking of this
"mental activity" (Nil always uses the word "*delanie myslenoe*"), he
quotes again Hesychius and we see that Nil's *nepsis* is to be taken in
Hesychius' larger sense, as synonymous with Evagrius' "praxis": "The
practice of virtue (praxis) is the spiritual method for purifying the passionate part of the soul."[73]

Blessed Hesychius of Jerusalem prescribes four methods of this mental
activity: to guard oneself with attention against the assault of any thought;
or to keep the heart silent in its depths, free from all imaginings, and to pray
silently; or to call Jesus Christ to one's aid; or to think of the hour of death.
All these methods, says this father, conquer evil thoughts; whichever method
is chosen, all of them are called 'sobriety', in other words, 'mental activity'.
Examining all these methods, each of us has to fight according to his own
way.[74]

Often Nil refers to this "mental activity" as "this spiritual exercise",
"this spiritual operation", "prayer of the heart or mind", "containing
of the mind within the heart, free of all imaginings", "maintaining the
mind in silence", but always he means the same thing: "This life-giving
exercise" of guarding the mind in the heart so that no thought may catch
the heart unguarded and enter to multiply thoughts and take the soul
from union with God. This is the "science of sciences, and the art of

---

[72] *Ibid.*, Matt. 15, 19.
[73] Evagrius, *Practica*, *PG*, 40, cap. 50, 1233B. Fr. Hausherr notes: "Concluons que
le terme de nepsis a deux sens: un sens étroit, selon lequel il désigne cette partie de la
praxis qui consiste en la surveillance des pensées dès leur première suggestion, et un
sens large qui le fait synonyme de praxis. Il faut évidemment éviter de passer de l'un
à l'autre", *op. cit.*, p. 285.
[74] *Ustav*, p. 33. Cf, Hesychius, *op. cit.*, 1485B–C.

arts",[75] which like a door-keeper examines all thoughts and lets in only the "friends" and turns away the others as "enemies".[76]

If the virtue *nepsis* is the door-keeper, then discretion and moderation are the door through which only the God-pleasing thoughts are allowed to pass into the interior. But what is the norm for judging with the proper discretion and moderation the thoughts, words, deeds? Nil, over and over, insists on uniting our wills with that of God, seeking ever to please only God.

Every fulfillment of our activities in our chosen way of life consists in tnis, that always, in every detail, in every undertaking of soul, body, in thought, word or deed, as far as there is in us strength, we remain in the undertaking of God, with God and in God. Blessed Philotheus says that it is befitting such as us who are living yet in the world among its vanities, enslaved to the mind and all the senses by sinful vanities, that we begin to live for God; with our whole mind and all our senses to work for the living God, seeking His truth and will, to fulfill His holy commands and to remove all that is unpleasing to God according to the words of God: 'I have been directed by all your commandments; and I have ever hated the way of evil-doing'.[77]

A spirit of sobriety and vigilance is maintained by living in the presence of God and doing all for His glory.

In particulars ... the mind must always be persuaded of the reverence due to God and confidence in Him, so as to do all to please God and not for self vanity or to please men, knowing full well that God is everywhere and filling all, God is always with us, for He who gave us ears, hears all, and He who created the eye sees all. Thus if you speak with someone ... let your speech be pleasing in God ... So conducting yourself in this manner of keeping before your eyes God, as David said: 'Always I can keep the Lord within sight; always He is at my right hand, to make me stand firm', you can remain always in prayer.[78]

Again, Nil gives succinctly as the norm for all sobriety or moderation: "...we should constantly probe our thoughts and feelings, so that our actions may be in harmony with God's will".[79]

As concisely a definition as can be found among the Fathers, Nil defines his *nepsis* as "mental activity which consists in preserving the disposition of fear and trust and love of God".[80] Long before, Evagrius

---

[75] Hesychius, *Century II, op. cit.*, 1517B (19).

[76] *Ibid., Century I*, 1509B (96). Cf. also Anthony, "Texts on a saintly life", no. 20, in *Philokalia, op. cit.*, T. I, p. 26.

[77] *Ustav*, p. 36; Ps. 118, 128. Philotheus, *Philokalia, op. cit.*, T. II, p. 285, ch. 33.

[78] *Ustav, ibid.* Ps. 15, 8.

[79] *Ibid.*, p. 55.

[80] *Ibid.*, p. 37.

made his praxis synonymous with keeping the commandments of God, which praxis was guarded by fear of God and produced as offspring the love of God.[81] To understand Nil's insistence on observance of God's commandments and on its necessity in order to achieve union with God, one has to turn to Philotheus of Sinai who, of course, had been most dependent on Evagrius and Nil of Sinai. In explaining why the devil attacks us and wages against us mental war, he says:

Why and wherefore are those attacks and onslaughts directed against us? To prevent us from fulfilling God's will of which we pray: 'Thy will be done' (Lk. XI, 2), that is, God's commandments. Anyone, who sets his mind firmly in perfect sobriety in the Lord, free from wandering, and carefully observes those invasions (of the heart) by invisible enemies and the skirmishes with the sober mind which take place in the dreams of fantasy, will learn all this in "praxis". This is why evil demons are the target at which the Lord aims. Being God and thus foreseeing their plots, He established His commandments to oppose their aim, with threats against those who transgress them.[82]

Nil must have presupposed this text as known to his readers, or at least the same reasoning evident to them, for, although the necessity of living according to the commandments of God is ever stressed in his writings, he never clearly defines what he means by "commandments" or never reasons why such observation brings with it *hesychia* and the possibility of more intimate union with God through contemplation. He simply states: "Have this only before your eyes (to repent and to seek God with great love and fear) and obey His commandments, living constantly in prayer."[83] Hesychius much earlier had defined *nepsis* as the doer of every commandment of the Old and New Testament; it is in itself purity of heart, it is what Christ calls blessed, saying: " 'Blessed are the pure in heart; for they shall see God'. Sobriety becomes the guide to a God-pleasing life."[84]

If God came on this earth and spoke to us, revealing His Divine Will, man's first obligation is to fulfill as perfectly as possible that Will. This is why Nil's spirituality is mainly evangelic. Even in his stress of living according to the Fathers and the Holy Writings (including the Fathers) he is ever returning to the same argument: The Fathers are to be followed

[81] Evagrius, *Practica*, *PG*, 40, cap. 53, 1233C? Cf. also Hesychius, *Century I*, 1480D–1481A (1) who follows Evagrius in this matter and unites *nepsis* with observation of every command of the Old and New Testament.
[82] Philotheus, *Dobrotoljubie*, op. cit., (7), p. 446.
[83] *Ustav*, p. 32.
[84] Hesychius, *Century I*, 1481A (1).

because they lived the teaching of Christ in their own private lives and wrote under the same inspiration of the Holy Spirit as the Apostles. But where Evagrius makes the clear distinction between fulfilling the commandments of the law and forgetting them to follow what the more excellent "disposition established in him suggests",[85] Nil follows Philotheus and Hesychius of Sinai in using the more general term "commandments" to include the expressed will of God, whether that be found in the Old and New Law or in the natural law or in the more delicately perceived inspirations of the Holy Spirit, making known God's will in the ways of higher perfection and sanctity.[86]

For Nil, following Philotheus, the fulfillment of the commandments of God is the proof of true love of God. "If a man has any love for me, he will be true to my word; and then he will win my Father's love, and we will both come to him and make our continual abode with him; whereas the man who has no love for me, lets my sayings pass him by."[87] We can understand Nil's emphasis placed on the interior fulfillment of God's commandments and his later history-making rebellion against the "dead-formalism" of his contemporaries only if we understand Philotheus' doctrine on "commandments". According to him, God has created the human soul with three powers; in modern psychological terminology, the irascible (razdrazitel'naja), the concupiscible (pozelatel'naja) and the rational (myslitel'naja) appetites. God, in order that these powers may enjoy full "health" and attain their proper end for which He created them, gives commands for each power of the soul. The devil, in order to destroy this health and take the soul away from God, attacks the soul with temptations that violate the God-given commandments.[88] But some commands of God look only to exterior actions, such as corporal works of mercy. Other commands are more interior, spiritual and these are more comprehensive, containing in themselves many other exterior commands of God. Thus the fulfillment of

---

[85] Evagrius, *Practica, PG*, 40, 1232C (42).

[86] Philotheus, *Dobrotoljubie, op. cit.*, (16–18), pp. 449–452. Cf. his *De mandatis, PG*, 154, 731B and foll., especially 735B–D (7), 739B (12), 742A–C. Although this is listed in Migne under Philotheus Patriarch of Constantinople, Peter Possino, who first edited this treatise, insisted that it was written by a Philotheus who lived earlier, perhaps in the 6th century. Cf. *PG*, 154, col. 717, no. 22. A comparison of this treatise with Philotheus texts on Sobriety as found in the *Dobrotoljubie* or *Philokalia*, Russian or Greek versions, makes it clear that he is the author of both. Cf. also Hesychius on "Commandments", *Century I, op. cit.*, 1505D (84); *Century II*, 1513D (10), 1516A (11), 1532C (62), 1540D–1514A (89).

[87] Jn. 14, 23–24. Cf. Philotheus, *De mandatis, PG*, 154, 730B; also *Ustav*, p. 37.

[88] Philotheus, *Dobrotoljubie, op. cit.*, (16–18), pp. 450–452.

these interior commands of God insures the fulfillment also of all the exterior ones. Christ came to give us a new decalogue, the eight Beatitudes which are the commands of God for all, that centre around two interior, spiritual commands: the command of Christ to be pure of heart and to be humble of heart. All virtues are contained in these two, which further narrow down to one all-embracing command: "Love God with your whole soul, your whole heart and all your strength."[89]

Nil does not, as has been said above, elaborate so clearly his teaching on commandments, but this nevertheless does not detract from his insistence that only in keeping God's commandments can there be true charity of God. His master-virtue, rather than stressing either humility or purity of heart, is seeking to harmonize one's will with that of God, doing all, ever to please God alone.[90] He saw so clearly the teaching of his Master of the New Law that if he were to love Him, he must do His will. Thus, throughout Nil's *Ustav*, we find the short phrase, "keep the commandments", or "live according to His commandments" as a short summary of the way of perfection. His stress on reading, meditation and study of Holy Scriptures along with the commentaries of the Holy Fathers indicates the importance he placed on knowing each command of Christ. His emphasis on *nepsis* and control over all thoughts in order to pray continually shows his sincerity in wanting to know and be guided always by the will of God, made known through the delicate inspiration of the Holy Spirit, directing the purified soul.

C. PENTHOS

On reading Nil's writings, one is struck by the number of pages he devotes to the thought of death and of the last judgment and to the necessity of obtaining tears. In this, more than in any other spiritual phase, does Nil reffect the universal teaching of the early Fathers of the Desert whose doctrine on *penthos* requires these two: constant meditation on the last things and the gift of tears as a necessary means to retain the spirit of constant compunction.[91] By seeing what Nil teaches on the

---

[89] Philotheus, *De Mandatis, op. cit.*, 731B and foll.
[90] *Ustav*, pp. 55, 90.
[91] The best work written on this subject of "*penthos*" is that of Fr. I. Hausherr, S. J., "Penthos", *OCA*, 132 (Roma, 1944). For him, the nature of *penthos* consists in this: "c'est le deuil du salut perdu, et ce deuil doit être perpétuel, comme est perpétuelle la necessité de travailler à son salut", p. 34.

constant remembrance of death and on the gift of tears, we will be able to draw together his views on *penthos* and at the same time compare them with the traditional doctrine of the early Fathers.

1. *Thought of Death and Last Judgment*

In suggesting means to overcome temptations and remain faithful to the task of "mental activity" or interior prayer of the heart, Nil proposes: "The Fathers say that in our mental activity it is most helpful to have ever before us the remembrance of death and the last judgment."[92]
A quick glance at the writings of the Fathers shows this universal agreement that one should have this thought of death ever before oneself; it should be "if possible, as continuous as our breathing".[93] "He who with undoubting trust daily expects death is virtuous; but he who hourly yields himself to it is a saint."[94] One would never sin if this thought were ever present. No one doubted that it was most useful and most necessary to uproot sin and attachment to it, but as Nil asks: "How can we who are weak and tied to our passions learn to keep this thought ever present? Our inconsistency, our distractions cause a great impediment; we plainly forget to recall death, judgment, hell and eternal happiness... But even with our good will and unceasing efforts, only with God's help, work and time, along with patience, can we attain progress."[95]
One means, Nil suggests, to keep death before us is to recall various deaths that we have witnessed or heard of. He proposes that we reflect on how suddenly monks, often little expecting death, in various circumstances, were harvested by death, not even having time enough to say the prayers of the dying. Such reflections serve to fill us with fear. To intensify this fear, Nil gives a form of reflective meditation to the readers of his *Ustav*, showing how everything in this world vanishes before death: the famous and the great, the rich, are all the same as the poor and

[92] *Ustav*, p. 62.
[93] Hesychius, *Century, I, op. cit.*, 1509A (94–); *Century, II*, 1529B (53). Other Fathers who have touched on this matter: Anthony, *De Sanctitate* in *Philokalia* (Greek, *op. cit.*) (74), p. 14; (82) p. 15; (111), p. 19. *Apophthegmata Patrum, PG*, 65, Evagrius (1), 173B; Arsenius (51) 105D; Dioscorus (3) 161B. *Vitae Patrum, PL* 73, Lib. III, 740B. Paulos Evergetinos, *Synagoge* (Constantinople, 1861), I, ch. 5, p. 18. Climacus, *Gradus* 6 (all), 793C–800A. Philotheus Sinaite, *Dobrotoljubie*, (2), pp. 443–444, (6–) 445, (13) 447–448, (21) 453–454, (27) 456–457, (38) 461. Simeon the New Theologian, *Capita Moralia, op. cit.*, 605C (4), 637A (64), 637B (65), 640B (66), 641A (69).
[94] Climacus, *Gradus 6*, 793D.
[95] *Ustav*, pp. 63–64. Isaac the Syrian: *Logos 39, ed. cit.*, p. 248.

humble. All must face the same death, the separation of the soul from the body and then the judgment of God.[96] "In that bitter hour, we reflect: what a struggle for the soul to leave the body! What weeping! But nothing will help us. No one can have mercy on us. The soul will raise its eyes to the angels and beg for help, but in vain; the body will stretch out its hands to people but no help from anyone but from God and one's good works." He has us, in the best style of the Middle Ages' mendicant preachers, descend into the coffin and face the hard facts of reality with soul-searching questions:

Let us look into the grave and what do we see? We see our created beauty, now without form, without glory, nothing good remaining. Seeing our bones, do we know to whom they belonged? Was he a king, a beggar, honourable or without honour? All that the world considers beautiful, powerful, turns again into nothingness as a beautiful flower fades and dies, as a shadow passes by; thus all mankind must pass away. Feel this instability and call out to your soul: 'Oh, how strange, why does this remain ever for us a mystery? How were we brought into bodily existence? Why do we return to dust in death? Truly, this is the will of God, for so it was written, after Adam's fall, he fell under sickness, subject to every woe... Death entered creation and it overcame us too. But the foreseen death of the Lord and His ineffable wisdom teach us that, by His coming, He overcame the serpent and gave us resurrection, transferring His slaves and servants into life everlasting.'[97]

Then Nil focuses our attention on that last and universal judgment before the awful majesty of Christ. He recalls the text of Matthew and John where Christ's second coming as judge of the living and dead is described.[98] He depicts the terrible anguish of those unrepentant sinners whom Christ casts into eternal punishment, the graphic sufferings of Hell.

And from among these sinners am I not the first of the wretches?... What will we, guilty of so many sins, do then when we hear God call the blessed of his Father into the heavenly kingdom and He separates from them sinners, casting them into torments? What answer will we give? What will we say when all our acts are brought forward, all our secret words, thoughts, everything ever done secretly in day or night, now revealed to everyone? What shame will come over us? To deny the shameful deeds will be impossible ...Speaking of that fear and awfulness of the second coming of the Lord and His awful judgment, some Fathers say, that if it would then be possible to die, the whole world would die from fear.[99]

[96] *Ustav*, p. 65. Cf. Anthony, *Philokalia, op. cit.*, (80, 82), p. 15.
[97] *Ustav*, pp. 66–67. The ideas and language used here are similar to those found in the penitential canons sung in the Byzantine-Slav Church in various Lenten Offices.
[98] Matt. 24, 29–31; Jn. 5, 22–29; Matt. 25, 31–46.
[99] *Ustav*, pp. 68–69.

Nil ends his eschatological meditation with a deeply moving prayer, which he has his reader address to one's own soul, even should the soul be unwilling to hear such.

...But , oh soul, you still have time; turn away from evil deeds and begin a good life' turn to the Lord and cry out with faith: 'I have sinned, Lord. But I know your mercy and love for men. For this reason, I fall down and beg your goodness to grant me mercy, O Lord ...Save me from being cast into the depths of hell; stand before me and be my Saviour and Protector. Have mercy ... receive me cleansed by repentance and confession and with your power lead me to your divine judgment seat ... Lord, good and merciful Father, Son, only begotten, and Holy Spirit, have mercy and deliver me then from everlasting fire and grant me to stand at your right hand, oh most just Judge.'[100]

2. *Gift of Tears*

a. A Gift of God

Nil, as his noted predecessors whom he quotes so freely in touching on the gift of tears, stresses its supernaturalness and gratuitousness, but at the same time he strongly stresses what the individual must do to dispose himself for the advent of this gift. "Continue to meditate in this fore-said manner and if God should give us the grace of tears, we must not restrain ourselves, but weep as much as possible, according to our strength and power."[101] It is clear he is distinguishing the more "mystical" appearance of this gift from the general compunction and interior weeping that come under ascetical practices aimed to keep the soul in a constant frame of grief. The mystical gift of tears breaks on the soul suddenly like a "flood leaping over all the dikes set up by sin; the other type of compunction falls on the soul like rain onto the grass".[102] Nil rather simply describes its occurrence:

When we apply ourselves to preserving heartfelt affection and the interior power of prayer reacts on us with God's grace, moving us with a warming of our heart and making our whole soul glad with an ineffable, inflaming love for God and man, enlightening the mind and pouring out into our interior feelings of great joy, then tears pour out even without our own willing them

---

[100] *Ibid.*, pp. 70–71. Although Nil does not hint as to his source for this prayer, there are common elements found in the prayer of the martyr, St. Eustratius, *PG*, 116, ch. XXXII, 505B–C and in a prayer given in the life of St. Macrina, written by her brother, St. Gregory of Nyssa, *PG*, 46, 984CC–985A.

[101] *Ustav*, p. 71.

[102] Nicetas Stethatos, *Century, I, PG*, 120, ch. 70, 884B.

and they spurt forth without effort on our part. Then, as says John Climacus,[103] the soul, like to a baby, weeps and is physically affected, that is, the spirit rejoices and expresses this joy even on its face. God grant us these tears.[104]

Nil distinguishes this as the "perfect" gift of tears from the other gift of tears that comes to the monk through various spiritual exercises.

There are some who have not attained completely this gift of tears, but find it; some through contemplating the secret beauties of the Architect and Lover of mankind, God; others through reading the Lives of the Saints and their teachings; others by the Jesus Prayer; others come to this compunction from certain prayers, composed by Saints; others pray some canons and tropars; others through remembrance of their sins others from the remembrance of death and judgment; others through longing for the future joys of heaven, and so by various ways, they obtain the gift of tears. If anyone by any such subject is aroused to tears, he must meditate on how to retain this weeping until the tears no longer come; for one, wishing to be delivered from sins, is delivered from them by weeping and one, wishing to keep the self from sin, is kept so by weeping, said the Fathers.[105]

b. Necessity to Pray for This Gift

"Above all, pray for the gift of tears," enjoins Nil[106] and he follows with a most interesting quotation from "Blessed Gregory, Pope of Rome" on this subject of beseeching God for this precious gift. "Who does good works and has been deemed worthy to have received some gifts from God, but has not yet received tears, he must pray for this in order to weep, either thinking about the last judgment or longing for the heavenly kingdom or repenting over evil past deeds or kneeling before the Cross of Christ, seeing Him suffering for us, our Crucified Saviour."[107] Then, contrary to his usual custom, Nil offers a metaphorical analogy from Gregory the Great's scriptural analogy drawn from the account in the Book of Josue of Caleb and his daughter Axa.

Sitting on an ass, she sighs and asks her father for a piece of land with irrigation. 'You gave me dry land,' she tells him, 'Give me some with water as in the valley,' and the father gave her water in the mountains and water in the valley. By Axa, explains the holy Father (Gregory), is meant the human soul, sitting on the ass, that is, the bodily movements; he explains that Axa, sighing

---

[103] Climacus, *Gradus* 7, 816B.
[104] *Ustav*, pp. 77–78. Cf. Climacus, *Gradus* 7, 805D.
[105] *Ustav*, p. 76. Cf. Climacus, *Gradus* 7, 808C. Also, 805D.
[106] *Ustav*, p. 73.
[107] *Ustav*, p. 73. Cf. Isaac, *Dobrotoljubie, op. cit.*, Tome 2, pp. 754–755.

and asking of her father: land with water is how we must, with great grief of heart and with sighing, ask our life-giving Father for the gift of tears.[108]

We see here the continuous doctrine of all the early Fathers, especially of Pseudo-Nil (Evagrius) who summarized in a few short words the theology of tears that would ever afterwards be repeated by all who followed his spirituality of asceticism climaxing in contemplation. "Before all else, pray to be given tears, that weeping may soften the savage hardness which is in your soul and, having acknowledged your sin unto the Lord (Ps. 31, 5), you may receive from Him the remission of sins."[109] The same necessity of tears and hence the constant injunction to pray for this gift is reiterated on nearly every page of the *Apophthegmata* and *Vitae Patrum*.[110]

Nil offers, as testimony of this long-standing tradition, quotations from various Fathers to prove the necessity of this gift and of praying for it, with added instruction on the attitude one should have while beseeching God for this gift. Andrew of Crete whose penitential canon is sung in the Byzantine Oriental Churches on Thursday of the Fifth Week of Lent offers Nil the proper attitude in approaching God:

Where shall I begin to lament my wretched life's actions? What shall I set for first-fruit, of this my lamentation? O Merciful One, grant me, O Lord, tears of remorse that I may weep before You, the Creator of all and our Maker and our God. Before You, O Saviour, I lie completely revealed; how much I have sinned with my sorry soul and my brutish flesh; grant that with your help, I, strengthened, may throw off my past sinfulness and bring to You tears of repentance.[111]

St. Ephrem the Syrian, Germanos, Patriarch of Constantinople, St. John Damascene, Simeon the New Theologian are quoted, all insisting on the necessity of crying out with bruised soul to God for this necessary gift, without which the soul will neither be washed from its past iniquities, nor leave completely such passionate desires to cling only to God. Nil ends up by quoting Isaac the Syrian upon whose authority the whole Christian East relied for a systematized doctrine of the gift of tears: "And there are many other similar, prayerful verses found in the writings of the Saints about the necessity to ask with sincerity and from the depths

---

[108] *Ustav, ibid.* Cf. Josue 15, 18–19. Text Found in *PL*, 77, 819–880B: Letter of Gregory to Theoctista.
[109] Evagrius, *De Oratione, PG*, 79, (5) 1168D.
[110] Cf. *Apophthegmata Patrum, op. cit.* Anthony (33), 85C; Poeman, 353A, 357C. *Vitae Patrum, PL*, 73, Lib. V, *De Compunctione*, 861C–864C.
[111] "The Great Canon of St. Andrew of Crete", Canticle I, Stanza 2, 3. *Ustav*, p. 74.

of souls for tears and to pray often for this gift which Isaac the Syrian
judged better and more excellent than all other gifts and through which,
if we receive it, we come to purity of heart and become worthy of all
other spiritual goods."[112] Indeed, Isaac, upon whose teaching Nil relied
strongly in this matter of tears, vigourously claimed that "So long as
you have not reached the realm of tears, that which is hidden within you
still serves the world, that is, you still lead a worldly life and do the work
of God only with your outer man, while the inner man is barren; for his
fruit begins with tears."[113] Tears were a true indication that the mind
was leaving the prison of this world and entering on a new age. Tears
flow because the birth of the spiritual child is at hand, grace is about to
bring forth the Divine Image into the light of the life to come.[114]

c. Self-Activity as Preparation

The early Fathers, recorded in the Apophthegmata, did not know the
"gift of tears" with the connotation of being something reserved to a
few chosen souls of exceptional mystical calling. "According to the
hermits' understanding of it, they wept for sins for no other reason than
that they wanted to do so and they so wanted because they believed it
their duty."[115] Therefore it is a duty enjoined on all who are serious to
save their souls.

Nil approves the teaching of Simeon the New Theologian: one is not to
war against nature, forcing it to weep physically when it cannot; if
you force the body to accomplish a thing that is above its strength,
weakness ensues.[116] But on the other hand Nil approves the saying of the
same Simeon which is nothing more than a repetition from the Fathers of

[112] *Ustav*, p. 75. Cf. Isaac, *Dobrotoljubie*, *op. cit.*, T. 2, (219) pp. 775–776.
[113] Isaac, *ibid.*
[114] It is interesting to note Isaac's teaching on the *mystical* tears. "I am speaking of
tears such as flow unceasingly day and night. The eyes of a man who has reached this
degree become like a spring of water for up to two years and more, after which he
comes to the stilling of thoughts. After the stilling of thoughts, as far as nature permits it in part, there comes that tranquillity which St. Paul mentions (Heb. 4, 3) and
here the mind begins to contemplate mysteries." *Ibid.* It is interesting to compare
what St. Ignatius records on tears for a comparable period of two years. Cf. Giuliani,
M., S. J., *St. Ignace, Journal Spirituel* (Paris, 1959).
[115] I. Hausherr, "Penthos", *op. cit.*, p. 181. He traces the first appearance of the word
"gift" *(charisma)* of tears to St. Athanasius in his tract *De Virginitate*. Evagrius, in
his *Exhortatio ad Virginem*, summarizes Athanasius' doctrine of the gift, but obtained
by our prayers. Cf. also Evagrius, *De Oratione*, *op. cit.*, (7) 1169A, (8) 1169B.
[116] *Ustav*, p. 73. Simeon the New Theologian, *PG*, 120C–D, 490A. Cf. also Cassian's
doctrine on not forcing tears: *Conférences*, IX, ch. 30, pp. 65–66.

the Desert, from Gregory of Nyssa, through Evagrius and St. John Chrysostom, Theodore Studite, Barsanuphius, Climacus and all the Sinaite Fathers. "If our soul is in such a disposition (i.e. really understands its true nature and its actual fallen nature and is hence filled with deep sorrow and compunction at its estrangement from God), it cannot but weep bitterly with tears."[117] "It is impossible for one to live without tears who considers things exactly as they really are..."[118] Nil also held firmly that through considerations on death and judgment, on the inclinations of fallen nature through past sins and the "disobedience of Adam" towards the things of sense perception and away from union with God, the soul would naturally be filled with compunction and interior grief. It is here that the individual can force himself, to quicken these convictions, to make them become through lively faith a reality and thus the soul can remain in a state of continual grief. "Now if we cannot force out the smallest tear because of our weakness or our negligence, or for some other reason, we should not discontinue or be discouraged. Let us grieve and sigh, deplore our weakness in this endeavour but keeping up ever our hope and desire to weep interiorly, for grief of mind is superior to bodily actions, as St. Isaac tells us..."[119] And he quotes with special approval Climacus: "Indeed, St. John Climacus assures us, our good Judge judges tears, like all other things, according to a man's natural capacity: 'I have seen small teardrops shed with difficulty like drops of blood, and I have also seen fountains of tears poured out without difficulty. And I judged those toilers more by their toil than by their tears and I think that God does too'."[120]

We bring a grieving heart to God with the desire to weep bitter tears. We continually beg for the gift to weep. God will grant this gift eventually, if we "do not fall away or become discouraged".[121]

Nil insists along with Climacus that, man, convinced of the necessity of the gift of tears, must never cease doing all that lies in his power to ask and prepare for this gift:

---

[117] *Ustav*, p. 73.
[118] St. Gregory Nyssa, *De Beatit.*, III, *PG*, 44, 1224C and foll.
[119] *Ustav*, p. 72. Isaac the Syrian: *Logos 58*, p. 347.
[120] *Ibid.* Climacus, *Gradus 7*, 805C.
[121] A very apt passage on this point is Nil Sinaite's letter to the Deacon Agapet: "Who desires a thing, good or bad, already accomplishes it in spirit... If you cannot weep, imagine how you once wept and weep again through your intention and thus you will be purified from your sins. Through faith and prayer those who could not weep changed their rocky soul into a fountain of water." *PG*, 79, Epist. III, 257, 512. *Ustav*, p. 72. Cf. Climacus, *Gradus 7*, 812B.

Some, wishing and not finding tears, wail, beat the walls and interiorly weep and all this substitutes for tears... and so we must sorrow and grieve in thought and seek tears with a recollected spirit and humble heart. We must seek tears if we really want them ... without tiring the body excessively. For it is harmful to force too much the physical side, for if the supernatural strength is not given to the body, then you just add confusion, as says Isaac in complete agreement with the Fathers. But it is necessary to know that the Fathers consider here, true incapacity and not imagined, for against our sensual nature we must force ourselves, says Simeon.[122]

It is clear, therefore, that Nil distinguishes between the pure "mystical" gift of tears from God that comes upon the soul with little warning, where tears flow abundantly for a long time with no effort on the part of the subject and the other less perfect gift of tears that comes through immediate preparation by reflecting and moving the will by thoughts conducive to compunction. Below these gifts he clearly shows what is expected of each soul desirous of having these precious gifts of tears by way of ascetical practices conducive to purifying the soul from inordinate attachments and keeping it in a humble, contrite attitude before God. For Nil, the ascetical practices depend on us; the gift of tears comes wholly from God to be given to us when He deems us worthy of such and in what degree He wishes.

d. Effects of Tears

In his insistence on the necessity of receiving the gift of tears, Nil often adds the reason why he deems them so imperative. "Such tears should be preserved ... because they have great power and action in destroying and uprooting sins and passions..."[123] "For weeping delivers us from eternal fire and other future punishments, so the Fathers said."[124] "Ask and pray often to Our Lord for the gift of tears which, according to the words of Isaac the Syrian, is more excellent than all other gifts and through which, if we get it, we come to purity of heart and are made worthy of all other spiritual gifts."[125] Nil quotes Ephrem's petition for tears "in order to enlighten my heart so that I may pour out fountains of tears with sweetness in pure prayer so that ... the fires of retribution

---

[122] *Ustav*, p. 73. Cf. Climacus, *Gradus 7*, 804B, 808D, 813B, 816B–C. Also cf. Simeon the New Theologian, *Capita Moralia, op. cit.*, 645B (75). On excessive forcing of the body to tears see the examples given by I. Hausherr, *op. cit.*, p. 98.
[123] *Ustav*, p. 77.
[124] *Ibid.*, p. 71.
[125] *Ibid.*, p. 75. Isaac the Syrian, *Logos 75*, ed. cit., p. 508.

for my sins may be extinguished by this simple weeping".[126] Simeon the
New Theologian provides Nil with another reason for the necessity of
constant tears: "Clean the stains of my soul and give me tears of penance,
loving tears out of love, tears of salvation, tears that clean the darkness
of my mind, making me light so that I may see You, Light of the world,
Enlightenment to my repentant eyes."[127] St. John Damascene, in the
prayer for tears quoted by Nil,[128] prays that thus he may be cleansed
from all stain of passions and appear before God clean. "Give me tears,
O Christ God, as once of old You gave them to the repentant harlot."
Throughout all patristic literature the image of tears as a second baptism
is most frequently found. Tears remit sins and regenerate Divine life in the
soul. This is the reason for tears according to Evagrius: "... Pray to be
given tears ... that having acknowledged your sin unto the Lord, you
may receive from Him the remission of sins."[129] Climacus set it down
definitively for all successors:

> Greater than baptism itself is the fountain of tears after baptism, even
> though it is somewhat audacious to say so. For baptism is the washing away
> of evils that were in us before, but sins committed after baptism are washed
> away by tears. As baptism is received in infancy, we have all defiled it, but we
> cleanse it anew with tears. And if God in His love for mankind had not given
> us tears, few indeed and hard to find would be those in the state of grace.[130]

But Nil nowhere links tears up with baptism as such; he does, however,
as we have seen, stress the necessity of weeping for our sins in order to
receive forgiveness in this life before the general judgment when tears
will be useless to remit our sins.

From the quotations given above, we see how Nil approves of the
stress on tears as not only purifying the soul from sin and the attraction
of passions towards evil, but also illuminating the dark recesses of the
soul to the light of Christ's teaching. In seeking to do ever God's will
by performing as perfectly as possible all of God's known commandments,
the monk gradually prepares himself through the purification that comes
from such *praxis* to listen to the promptings of the Holy Spirit within

---

[126] *Ibid.* Ephraem the Syrian, *Sermo Asceticus*, ed. Assemani (in Greek), Vol. I, p. 61.
[127] *Ibid.* Cf. Simeon, *op. cit.*, 640D (68), 645B (75), 517D.
[128] *Ustav*, p. 75. This is another example of Nil composing from a penitential canon,
probably composed by Damascene. I could not find an exact corresponding passage.
[129] Evagrius, *De oratione, op. cit.*, 1168D.
[130] *Gradus 7*, 804B. St. John Damascene numbers tears among the many forms of
Baptism. Cf. "De Fide Orthodoxa", *PG*, 94, 1124C. Cf. also *Vie de Syméon, OC*, no.
45, tome XII, Introduction, p. XXXI, XLIV–L, by I. Hausherr, S. J.

and perform all "in harmony with the mind of God". But tears, for Nil, give the mind a deeper knowledge of God and of oneself; they fill the mind with "abundant food and it is sweetened in prayer".[131] This illumination received through tears "enlightens the mind and pours out into our interior a deep feeling of joy ... then the battle with the enemy becomes easier and temptations are quelled and calmed ... from the depths of the heart pours a certain ineffable sweetness, reacting on the whole body and every sick and diseased sense reacts on all the body members with an exulting joy."[132] Here we have Nil in complete conformity with the Fathers in their doctrine of re-integration of human nature through *penthos* and tears. It is nothing more than the summation of the evangelical plan of Christ or the restoration of the Divine Image through the eight Beatitudes, all enjoining a struggle against fallen nature, but all ending up with nature restored to its pristine place through the God-given joy. Tears restore the lost equilibrium between the body and the powers of the soul and the re-unification of human nature in perfect harmony with God's will brings joy, "joy at seeing the beloved and sorrow at being deprived for so long of that fair beauty".[133]

Nil ends his section on tears by quoting Isaac, his favourite guide in this matter: "This is the comfort of mourning in confirmation of Our Lord's Words that it is given to each individual in the measure of the grace that is in him. Then a man possesses a joy such as is not found in this world. This is completely unknown to anyone except those who dedicate themselves completely with their whole souls to this spiritual work."[134]

D. THE JESUS PRAYER

The only time that Nil explicitly treats of the Jesus Prayer is in his second chapter of the *Ustav* which chapter he entitles: "Our struggle against these temptations of the mind which are to be vanquished through the remembrance of the thought of God and through the guarding of the heart, that is to say, through prayer and interior silence..." For him, this ancient prayer serves two purposes and does so better than any other spiritual means: (1) It is the best means he knows to combat thoughts, all

---

[131] *Ustav*, p. 78.
[132] *Ibid.*
[133] Climacus, *Gradus 7*, 816B. Cf. also I. Hausherr, "Penthos", *op. cit.*, pp. 198–199.
[134] *Ustav*, p. 78. Isaac the Syrian, *Logos 75*, ed. cit., p. 503.

thoughts: good, bad, or indifferent which sooner or later could be used by the enemy to fill the heart with evil temptations; (2) After this negative purpose has been attained through faithful use of the prayer, Nil proposes it as the best preparation for what we can call "infused contemplation", a term that was surely unknown to Nil as such, but the phenomenon that he describes approaches what we mean to express by that term.[135]

The Jesus Prayer as given by Nil consists of the following formulae: "Lord Jesus Christ, Son of God, have mercy on me" or for variation sake: "Lord Jesus Christ, have mercy on me" resuming again, "Son of God, have mercy on me" or "Lord Jesus Christ, have mercy upon me, a sinner".[136] Nil is relying exclusively on his formulation from Gregory Sinaite who, in his instructions to Hesychasts, gives the following rules on how to say the prayer:

Some of the Fathers taught that the prayer should be said in full: 'Lord Jesus Christ, Son of God, have mercy upon me.' Others suggest saying only half, thus: 'Jesus, Son of God, have mercy on me', or 'Lord Jesus Christ, have mercy upon me', or they advise alternating, sometimes saying it in full and sometimes in a shorter form. Yet it is not advisable to yield to laziness by changing the words of the prayer too often, but to say for a certain time one formula as a test of patience. Again, some teach the saying of the prayer with the lips, others with and in the mind. In my opinion both are advisable.[137]

It is interesting to note with what great prudence and reserve (but with no less fervour and conviction) Nil presents his teaching on this prayer, especially when he describes the place, time, posture and manner

---

[135] We use the term in the sense of perception of God or of the mysteries of the faith in a manner exceeding the power of the human faculties. Cf. Hertling, L., S. J., *Theologia Ascetica* (Roma, 1939), p. 159.

[136] *Ustav*, pp. 21–22. It would be beyond the scope of this thesis to treat of the historical development of the formula of the so-called Jesus Prayer. Besides, there exist works already that have done just this. Cf. Hausherr, I., S. J., "Norms du Christ et voies d'oraison" in *OCA*, 157 (Roma, 1960); Un Moine de L'Église d'Orient, *La Prière de Jesus* (Chevetogne, 1951); Popov, K.: "Učenie o molitve iisusovoj blažennago Diadoxa (5ogo veka)", in *Trudy* Eccles. Academy of Kiev, 1902, T. 3, pp. 651–675 and Orlov, A. S., "Iisusova molitva na Rusi v XVI veke", in *Pamjatniki drevnej pis'mennosti* (St. Petersburg, 1914), pp. 1–32.

[137] Gregory Sinaite, *Praecepta ad Hesychastas*, *PG*, 150, 1329B. The last formula, "Lord Jesus Christ, have mercy on me a sinner" is not found as such in Gregory's instruction. Yet it is a formula, the first Jesus Prayer, uttered in substance by the Publican in the Lord's parable as found in Luke 18, 13, "Lord, have mercy on me a sinner." The same formula or idea is found over and over again among the Fathers of the desert in their quest for "*penthos*", cf. *Apophthegmata*, *PG*, 65, Alph. Agathon, no. 5, 190C; Alph. Apollo, no. 2, 136A. Also the same formula is found in the "Vie de Syméon le Nouveau Theologien", text edited by I. Hausherr, S. J., in *OC* (Roma, 1928), LIX.

of reciting it. "Recite the prayer as is most convenient, standing or sitting or reclining, but striving to enclose the mind in the heart. To achieve this, moderate your breathing so as to breathe as seldom as possible as Simeon the New Theologian teaches."[138]

1. *Means to Combat Thoughts and Gain Purity of Heart*

The hesychastic ideal of Nil, as we have already seen, following that of the early Fathers of the Desert, Evagrius and the Sinaite Fathers, aims to acquire a state of perpetual prayer where the mind is ever absorbed with God and His presence. The big enemy to this constant, interior union with God is the devil. Through his suggestions of thoughts, of any kind whatsoever, he can take the mind's attention from God and absorb it in passionate desires. That is why Nil prefaces his presentation of the Jesus Prayer with this sound psychology:

A wise and excellent way of battling against these temptations, the Fathers tell us, is to uproot the thought at the very first suggestion. ... And further in time of prayer it is necessary to bring one's mind to that condition where it is deaf and dumb, so says Nil Sinaite and to hold the heart freed from every thought, even though it may be a good one, so says Hesychius; for according to well-grounded experience, after the impassionate, good thoughts, the passionate, evil ones follow; the exit of the first open the door to the second.[139]

---

[138] His master Gregory, *loc. cit.*, *supra*, explicitly teaches, "Sitting in your cell..." Pseudo-Chrysostom, *PG*, 60, "Epistola ad Monachos", 751–6, but especially in 753, or as quoted by Callistus and Ignatius, *PG*, § 49, 725D, enjoins the prayer to be said in no special posture, but at all times "Eating and drinking, at home or on a journey, or whatever else he does, a monk should constantly call: 'Lord Jesus Christ, Son of God, have mercy upon me'." Nil is quoting from the *Three Methods of Hesychastic Prayer* which he attributes without having a doubt to Simeon the New Theologian, *PG*, 120, 707B. As to the author of this work, see *Appendix II*, footnote 8, and Fr. I. Hausherr, S. J., "Note sur l'invention de la méthode hésychaste", in *OC*, vol. XX (1930), p. 180. At this juncture, the Russian translation as found in *Dobrotoljubie, op. cit.*, vol. 5, p. 507, drops out of the text various "aids" including the one on controlling the breathing so as to respire as little as possible. One wonders whether Hesychius the Sinaite's expressions: "Let the Jesus Prayer cleave to your breath" ("De Temp. et Virt.", *Cent.*, II, § 80, 1537D) and "Combine sobriety and the Name of Jesus with your breath". (*Ibid.*, *Cent.*, II, § 87, 1540D), which were meant by him, not to be taken literally, but as an emphatic way of stressing the frequency of recalling the Name of Jesus, did not prepare the way for linking the prayer with the slow respiration. But much before even, Evagrius gives us the instruction to unite our breath with the name of Jesus. Cf. *PG*, 40, 1275C. Climacus would repeat it in his *Gradus 27, op. cit.*, 1112C.
[139] *Ustav*, p. 21. Pseudo-Nil Sinaite (Evagrius), *De Oratione*, *PG*, 79, 11, 1169C. Hesychius, *Cent.*, I, *PG*, 93, § 15, 1485B–C.

We see that Nil is consistent in his psychology of the "memory". His predecessors viewed the memory as a storebox of various sense impressions which at any moment could become "present" and command the attention of the intellect and will. Gregory of Nazianzen defined the memory as "the storing of impressions of the mind".[140] Nemesius followed Plato's philosophy saying: "Memory is according to Plato's definition the conservation of sense impressions and rational conclusions of the mind."[141]

One could not destroy these stored-up impressions, but one could forget them. One thinks and speaks, according to Nemesius, of the things he remembers.[142] For Diadochus, and for all the Sinaite Fathers, the secret of *nepsis* would be to "forget" these undesirable, passion-producing thoughts by becoming absorbed with the interior presence of Jesus Christ. Diadochus expresses very well the psychology that is behind Nil's use of the Jesus Prayer:

...for the one desirous to purify his heart, let him inflame it with the uninterrupted remembrance of the Lord Jesus, having this thought alone as the subject of godlike thought and as his constant spiritual activity. For he who wishes to get rid of his sordid self must not at one time pray and then at another not pray, but he must so exercise himself in prayer with attention of the mind, even though he may live far from a chapel of prayer.[143]

Thus, according to Nil, absorption with the Person of Jesus Christ living in the soul and constant union with Him made through reverent and interior pronouncing of the Holy Name was the best means to "forget" these other stored-up and unwanted images of the memory. He puts it succinctly: "So it is absolutely necessary to maintain our mind in silence from these thoughts, even those appearing good and to look ever into the depths of our heart and say "Lord Jesus Christ, Son of God, have mercy on me."[144]

But should one not be able to pray without thoughts but rather is aware of their increase, Nil gives the following advice: Do not be alarmed nor lose courage. It is only the strong and more perfect who can so control their mind with God's help that there be no imaginations present during their prayer. "But you, even if these representations seem to you good, should give no attention to them but, rather restrain your breathing, even with effort, and lock your mind in your heart. For a weapon, call

[140] *PG*, 37, 948: "Memoria retinet mentis impressiones."
[141] *De Nat. Hominis*, *PG*, 40, ch. XIII, 661A. "Soteria aistheseos kai noiseos."
[142] *Ibid.*, 661B.
[143] Diadochus, *Centuria*, in *Dobrotoljubie*, *op. cit.*, § 97, p. 74.
[144] *Ustav*, p. 21.

out to the Lord Jesus often and diligently and the imaginations will flee as though burnt invisibly by the fire of the divine name of the Lord Jesus."[145]

Through all this section where Nil exhorts the soul not yet confirmed in perfect union with God, in his insistence on using the Name of the Lord Jesus as the perfect weapon, even to the point of forcing one to continue in this practice at the cost of great effort, one sees the influence of Gregory and Hesychius of Sinai. No hesychast Fathers so insisted as they on the constant and sole use of this prayer to fight the attacking demons. In Hesychius' two Centuries on temperance, over and over one meets the name of the Lord[146] plus an exhortation to arm oneself with this Holy Name and thus do battle against the enemy. "And so every time it happens that wicked thoughts multiply in us, let us throw among them the invocation of Our Lord Jesus Christ and we shall see them at once disperse like smoke in the air, as experience teaches."[147] And again Hesychius says: "Let us compel ourselves to call out 'Lord Jesus Christ'. Let our throat be exhausted (lose its voice), but may our inner eyes never cease to look on high, waiting like David in hope for our Lord God" (Ps. 69, 3).[148]

In a similar manner Nil insists, even though the enemies increase their attack, the body grows weary and sluggish to "call upon God for help and compel yourself to go on praying with all your forces, never once turning away from the goal you have set for yourself and the imaginations will leave you soon enough with the help of God."[149]

When the evil thoughts are put to flight and there comes peace to the heart, he gives Hesychius' similar advice: "Then listen once more to your heart and to the prayer of the soul or the mind."[150]

---

[145] *Ibid.*, p. 23. Recall Climacus' expression that his successors were fond of quoting: "With the name of Jesus, flog your enemies, for there is not in heaven or on earth a weapon more powerful." *Gradus 21, op. cit.*, 945D. Cf. Gregory Sinaite, *De Quietudine et 2 orationis modis, PG,* 150, 1316C.

[146] Cf. I. Hausherr, "Noms...", *op. cit.*, pp. 254–255 where the author gives a list of all the variations of the Lord's name as found in Hesychius' work.

[147] *Cent.*, I, *op. cit.*, § 97, 1509C. Again another insistent text: § 99, 1509D–1512A: "Therefore, brother, do not from negligence sleep unto death, but scourge thy enemies with the name of Jesus; and as some wise man has said: 'Let His most sweet name be joined to thy breath; and then shalt thou know the profit of silence'." (St. Gregory Nazianzen).

[148] *Cent.*, II, § 5, 1513A.

[149] *Ustav*, p. 23.

[150] *Ibid.* Hesychius, *Cent.*, I, § 97: "And then, when the mind is left free (without confusing thoughts), let us start again with constant attention and invocation. So let us act every time we suffer such temptation."

Nil insists with Gregory of Sinai on the great importance of this prayer of the heart of the Jesus Prayer as the source of all good. Gregory earlier in his instructions to Hesychasts had written: "Works are many but they are individual; prayer of the heart is great and all-embracing, as the source of virtues[151] because every good is acquired thereby."[152] Nil phrases the importance of the prayer of the heart thus:

...turn again to the prayer of the heart, for exercises and works of virtue are many, but in relation to the whole, they are all only parts. The prayer of the heart *(serdecnaja molitva)* is the source of all good, refreshing the soul as cool waters sprinkle a garden, rejecting all temptations, not only evil, but any appearing good[153] for he calls that quietude *(bezmolvie)* when we remove the imaginations that arise in time, so that we may not be deprived of the most important by taking what seems to us to be good. Hesychia *(bezmolvie)* means to seek the Lord in your heart, i.e. to fix with your mind the heart in prayer and only with this to be continually occupied, so says Simeon the New Theologian.[154]

In spite of Nil's insistence on the invocation of the Jesus Prayer even to the point of extreme fatigue, he allows, as does his master Gregory, a certain relaxation. "If the mind and the body grow weary and the heart begins to ache from the effort and continued calling of the name of the Lord Jesus then change to singing so that one gives to the body some relief and rest."[155]

But always in the first rank of importance is the prayer of the heart, continued "even if there is the feeling of physical pain or weakness from the thought of interior crying and weeping." Singing of psalms is a means to relax, to drive away *acedia*; always a means, however, subordinated to the greater end, the prayer of the heart. If God rewards our efforts with His holy presence and sweetness and the Jesus Prayer begins to operate in the heart, we must not stop it to turn to the singing of psalms for this would be to leave God in our hearts to seek Him out-

---

[151] Gregory is evidently borowing from Climacus who uses the same phrase, "source of all virtues". Cf. *Gradus 28*, 1129B.

[152] Gregory Sinaite, *De Quietudine...*, *op. cit.*, 1320C.

[153] On rejecting even good thoughts, cf. Gregory Sinaite, *Praecepta ad Hesych.*, 1340C–D: "...if you see even the image of Christ or of an angel or some saint, or if an imaginary light pervades your mind, in no way accept it. ...Memories of good and bad things will often suddenly imprint their images in the mind and thus entice it to dreaming... Always be displeased with such images and keep your mind colourless, formless and imageless."

[154] *Ustav*, pp. 23–24. Hausherr, I., "La Méthode...", *op. cit.*, p. 159.

[155] This whole section on psalmody is quite literally taken from Gregory Sinaite, *Praecepta...*, 5, "Quomodo psallere oportet", 1333B–1336B.

side, to destroy that tranquillity that we had with so great effort sought in order to fill our minds with manifold imaginations.[156] Nil recognizes the difference in vocations as did his master Gregory who said: "The work of silence is one thing and that of a coenobite another; but each, abiding in that to which he has been called, shall be saved."[157]

Nil thus insists that for those whose vocation is properly one of "hesychasm", i.e. seeking tranquillity and undisturbed union with God, a different criterion of means to sanctification must be had than for those who bind themselves to perfection through perfect obedience in a community. Quoting Gregory, Nil claims for his hesychast followers exemption from long hours of psalm singing: "About those favouring singing and those favouring more illumination, the same Father (Gregory) says that is more proper to them, (i.e. those favouring illuminations) not to read psalms, but rather to keep silence, in uninterrupted prayer and contemplation for they are united intimately with God and they must avoid those things which would separate the mind from God and encourage confusion. A mind, leaving recollection and mental prayer about God and busying itself with things of lesser importance, commits adultery."[158]

Thus we see how Nil emphasizes the importance, along with Hesychius, Simeon the New Theologian and Gregory Sinaite, of the prayer of the heart or the Jesus Prayer. It should serve the hesychast monk, especially the beginner, to drive temptations away that the devils may suggest. It should serve the one already advancing in progress of prayer to concentrate the mind in the heart on God alone by removing from the focus of attention any other thought, whether good, bad or indifferent. The continual repetition of this prayer brings about the *hesychia* where

---

[156] *Ustav*, p. 25. Cf. Gregory, *Praecepta...*, 1333D: "According to the words of the Fathers, he who has tasted grace must psalmodise sparingly, and must concentrate on the practice of prayer. However, if he is attacked by laziness, let him psalmodise or read the writings of the Fathers. A ship has no need of oars when the wind swells the sails, for then the wind gives it sufficient power easily to navigate the salt sea of passions. But when the wind dies and the ship stops, it has to be set in motion by oars or by a tugboat."

[157] Gregory, *ibid.*

[158] *Ustav*, p. 27. Gregory, *Praecepta...*, 1333B and foll. Also *De Quietudine...*, 8, 1320D: "Those do right who wholly abstain from psalmody, if they are making progress. Such people have no need of psalmody, but should remain in silence, constant prayer and contemplation, if they have attained enlightenment. For they are united with God and must tear their mind away from Him and plunge it into turmoil (or a crowd of thoughts)... For if he relinquishes remembrance of God, such a man commits adultery, as if he were unfaithful to the bridegroom and lovingly seized the most unworthy objects."

passionate thoughts no longer exert any attention on the mind, allowing the mind to be absorbed completely with God. Having attained this "primitive state" where the mind, heart, all the powers of the soul and body are completely subjected to the disposition of God, absorbed in God and striving only to please Him, as the workings of the Holy Spirit will suggest interiorly, the monk is ready for higher prayer. Nil has already hinted at this in saying that when there is peace in the soul, the prayer of heart will begin to "work". It remains to see now what this "work" means for Nil. Climacus had briefly outlined the steps in prayer as following: "The beginning of prayer consists in banishing the thoughts that come to us by single ejaculations the very moment that they appear; the middle stage consists in confining our minds to what is being said and thought; and its perfection is rapture in the Lord."[159] For Nil, the Jesus Prayer accomplishes the first two steps, driving away of all unwanted thoughts and through the words of the prayer itself developing humility, the mother of all other virtues in the soul. These are the steps of preparation, the planting and pruning of the fruit tree; it remains now to see the harvest that such with labour with God's grace produces.

2. Preparation for "infused contemplation"

Nil's treatment of the higher stages of contemplation and mysticism is a compilation taken from his three favourite authors, Isaac the Syrian, Simeon the New Theologian and Gregory Sinaite. We are left wondering: Was it because Nil himself did not enjoy these special gifts of prayer, as I. Kologrivov suggests,[160] that he gives no hint about his own personal experiences in prayer? Or was it his great humility, that spirit of *kenosis* that he inherited from his teachers of hesychasm, the Fathers of the Desert and the Sinaite Hesychasts that the closer they approached God in contemplation and uninterrupted union, the more humble and self-abasing they became, the less inclined they were to speak about the hidden workings of grace in their souls? But we should also keep in mind Nil's purpose in writing his *Ustav*. As he mentions over and over, he is not writing his own ideas which he counts for little, but he is intent on giving what the holy and inspired Fathers wrote on the subject of "mental activity".[161] The choice of these three Fathers especially indicates Nil's teaching on higher contemplation, but also shows his own

---

[159] *Gradus 28*, 1132D.
[160] *Essai sur la sainteté en Russie* (Paris, 1953), p. 202.
[161] *Ustav*, pp. 14–15.

personal ideal that he himself strove to attain with God's grace. They can be called the "Doctors" of hesychast mysticism in its richest form, for they formed the synthesis between the intellectual mysticism of Evagrius and the conscious sentimentalism of Macarius and Diadochus. Especially Isaac was considered in the Orient, and is still so to-day, as the great teacher on mystical prayer.[162]

Nil gives a short description of this mystical contemplation from Isaac's writings where we see the influence of Evagrius' intellectual "nudity" brought to its fruition:

> When men experience such ineffable joy, this state suddenly cuts off all vocal prayer from the mouth; the tongue, the heart, the guardian of all thoughts, and the mind, the feeder of feelings, are all silenced along with the different thoughts that normally soar about like fast flying birds; now the thought does not govern the prayer, but it itself is directed by another power; it is held in secret captivity and finds itself in confusion, for it dwells on things ineffable and does not know where it is.[163]

Nil continues with Isaac's doctrine, describing this contemplation, no longer as prayer which has been abandoned for a superior good. The mind is in ecstasy, as St. Paul described it, not knowing whether he was "in the body or out of the body, God knows which".[164] No man knows the name of this state which defies adequate description in human terms.

> When the soul undergoes such spiritual activity and subjects itself to God and through direct union approaches the Divinity, it is enlightened in its movements by an intense light and the mind experiences a feeling of joy of the happiness that awaits us in the life to come. Then an indescribable sweetness warms the heart, the whole body feels its repercussions and man forgets not only any given passion, but even life itself and things that the Kingdom of Heaven consists of nothing other than this ecstatic state. Here he experiences that the love of God is sweeter than life and the knowledge of God sweeter than honey...[165]

What does the soul think about in this rapturous union with God? Nil has recourse to the master of mystical descriptions, Simeon the New Theologian. Permit the quotation of this classical description of hesychastic mysticism:

---

[162] Cf. Viller, M., op. cit., p. 139; Also cf. "Contemplation chez les Orientaux Chrétiens", in Dict. de Sp. Asc. et Myst., Tome II, p. 1762–1911. Also Viller, M., and Rahner, K., Aszese und Mystik in der Väterzeit (Freiburg Br., 1938), p. 161.
[163] Ustav, p. 27. Cf. Isaac, PG, 86a, 873C–874B, 880C.
[164] II Corin. 12, 3.
[165] Ustav, p. 28. Cf. Isaac, ibid., 864C–D. Also Simeon the New Theologian, in Dobrotoljubie, op. cit., p. 52.

I see a light which is not of this world. Sitting in my cell, I see within me the Maker of the world; I converse with Him and love Him and I feed on this one Divine Image. Uniting with Him I am raised to the heavens. Where is the body? I do not know, for God loves me and has received me into His very Being and hides me in his embrace and being in heaven and at the same time in my heart, He becomes visible to me. The Ruler of all appears to me in a way equal to the angels, yet in a way more advantageous, for to them God is invisible and unapproachable while by me He is seen and He unites Himself with my being. It is this state that St. Paul described when he said that 'eye had not seen nor ear heard'. Being in this state, I do not have any desire to leave my cell, but I long to hide myself in a deep hole in the ground and there, removed from the upper world, I would gaze on my immortal Lord and Creator.[166]

Nil exhorts those who have not received such mystical gifts not to become discouraged at hearing these sublime experiences of such mystics. The fact that we have not received them should not make us discouraged, says Nil. We must place all hope in the grace of God and fill ourselves with desire for greater union with God by keeping in our minds and reflecting on the words from the Holy Scriptures. We will thus become convinced of our own degradation in which we wallow. But he warns that it will be our doom if we forget the great dignity of our souls by becoming absorbed in the things of the world. Many think that this way of contemplation is impossible for souls to-day, all right for saints of old but to-day an impossible thing to acquire.[167]

Nil insists strongly that the monk must cooperate with God's grace that will always be present as long as there is a docile will. His chief occupation should be to empty himself of the vanities of this world, to be intent on ridding one self of passions, keeping the heart all the time free from evil temptations and performing always, as far as one's knowledge permits, the commands of God. The necessary means to "guard the heart" is to pray always. And thus faithful to God's command to pray always, the monk will be granted a higher type of prayer by God's grace when God in His designs so deems it.

---

[166] *Ustav*, pp. 28–29. Simeon the New Theologian, *Divinorum amorum Liber*, Hymn. 13, *PG*, 120, 526C–D.
[167] *Ustav*, p. 31. He seems to be quoting directly from Simeon who wrote: "A man who has not received this degree of perfection should blame only himself and not say in self-justification that such a degree is impossible, nor that it is possible for us to reach perfection, but of this we must remain always unaware. We should know from Holy Scripture that such is possible ... but that, through neglect and transgression of God's commandments, each one deprives himself of these blessings according to the degree of negligence." Cf. *Dobrotoljubie*, T. 5, p. 53, 150.

No, indeed, it is not so. It is not possible only to those who do not have a care and become enslaved by their passions, who do not want to do penance, who in substance do not want to belong to the Spirit of God. Thus they give themselves up to the useless worries of the world. But those, who sincerely repent and with great love and fear seek God, crying out only to Him and living according to His commands, will be received by God in His mercy. God will grant them His grace and will glorify them.[168]

E. APPRAISAL OF NIL AS HESYCHAST

As we have seen, Nil intended to present the doctrine of the Fathers on "mental activity". Yet very far is Nil from being a mere anthologist, collecting what some hesychast Fathers had to say on the subject. He shows a true synthetic mind, based on thorough acquaintance with the writings of these Fathers and, more important, a personal conviction derived from his own interior life of the possibility and the necessity of acquiring that about which he writes. Thus, convinced that these Fathers wrote from a special guidance of the Holy Spirit and that their holy lives were the best guarantee for the value of their writings,[169] Nil felt it useless to propound any new theory outside of the traditional doctrine handed down by these Fathers. His humility also rejected any such ambition on his part. Therefore Nil must be classified as a hesychast, faithful to the best tradition on that type of spirituality.

It must be said that Nil is the first important hesychast writer in Russia. Others like Dositheus, Archimandrite of Kiev, and Athanasius Rusin, long before Nil, knew the hesychast asceticism and the Jesus Prayer from their stay on Mount Athos,[170] yet as A. Orlov affirms: "It is well known that Nil observes more faithfully in his *Ustav* the testimonies of the Byzantine hesychasts, even in the details of expressions."[171] Nil it is who works into a synthetic treatise that which would have otherwise remained scattered throughout various *florilegia* of the Fathers. In this manner he not only bequeathes to Russian spirituality and monasticism a solid asceticism, but he blends in a manner of rare prudence and judgment the two leading lines of spirituality that in his times had influenced the whole Byzantine world, the spirituality of Evagrius along with the spirituality of Macarius, Diadochus, and Simeon the New

---

[168] *Ustav*, p. 31.
[169] Cf. the article already cited of Archimandrite Porfirij on the authority of the Holy Fathers of the Church and the importance of their writings.
[170] Orlov, A., *op. cit.*, pp. 2–3.
[171] *Ibid.*, p. 29.

Theologian. Evagrius, with his faithful followers, Isaac the Syrian and Climacus, stressed the pure intellectual contemplation. The whole asceticism was aimed at delivering the monk from the passions to arrive at the *apatheia*, where the soul would be able to return to the "primitive state" of Adam before the fall and in his soul find and contemplate God, purely, without any phantasm, without any thought. The line of Macarius' followers kept the strict asceticism of Evagrius with its stress on solitude and silence, emptying the mind of all thoughts, striving for *hesychia* but added the "heartfelt" element. The heart became the place where the mind contemplated God. To the external *ascesis* was added the interior one of "weeping" interiorly at the thought of death and last judgment, past sins and of remaining in this interior spirit of compunction or *penthos* as a means of purifying the heart from the influences of the passions. When the mind descends into the interior regions of the heart, the fruition of this *ascesis*, or *practica* as Evagrius calls it, is had in the continual contemplation of God within the heart. This is achieved by the use of the Jesus Prayer both as a means to grow in purity of heart and as a preparation for purer contemplation.

The two outstanding traits of Nil in his presentation is his fidelity to the outstanding hesychast Fathers whom he quotes so profusely and in his sense of moderation and proportion. His account flows with the complexity-unity found in any great masterpiece of symphonic music. We do not find any strident, exaggerated notes calling attention to themselves and destroying the one, single harmonious effect. Nil never forgets the end of all these interior struggles and asceticism: union with God. And he judges accordingly each step in the process of attaining this union. He thus pictures this process of moving ever closer to union with God as a constant battle; the precious soul, capable of the most intimate union with God is pictured as being ever under attack by the devils. The heart must be purified from all passionate thoughts through solitude, silence, constant vigilance and control *(nepsis)* and through observance of God's commandments. The thought of death and the last judgment, the gift of tears, purify the soul and the constant use of the Jesus Prayer allows the soul to live ever in the presence of God. If the enemies are conquered and the soul reaches union with God, it is the grace of God that ultimately conquers in the soul, "for it is not your own doing that you stand in virtue, but the result of grace, which holds you in God's hand and preserves you from all your enemies".[172] Yet

[172] *Ustav*, p. 35.

he never refrains from exhorting the individual to be diligent and constant in overcoming sloth and cowardice, to desire ardently to make spiritual progress and to do all that human effort with God's grace is capable of doing. Thus he maintains a perfect balance in relationship to man's cooperation with God's grace and the final gratuitousness of God's gift of grace, not only in extraordinary mystical phenomena, but also in all the ordinary God-pleasing actions of a monk's daily life.

Nil keeps a matured, detached judgment in presenting prayer helps, especially the use of controlled breathing and even the use of the Jesus Prayer. Never does he claim too much for these means; absent are all such phrases as one finds on the lips of a Nicephorus the Hagiorite or Pseudo-Simeon: "Sit in a corner and do as I tell you,"[173] followed by detailed, mechanical instructions. Nil stressed the basic, solid asceticism for all equally, but after the purification stages, he seems to allow great freedom to the individual workings of grace and personal temperament. He ends his second chapter on prayer as a means to combat temptations by quoting Hesychius of Sinai that to keep the mind free from imaginations, one could fight consciously against the unwanted thought, or keep the heart silent, void of all phantasms and pray, or to call on the Name of Jesus as a weapon of defence, or finally to think of the hour of death.[174] And Nil concludes that all these methods are good; all constitute that which he has been teaching, that is, "mental activity". "Therefore each one should study all these methods for each one must fight according to the way that fits him best."[175] We have seen him stressing the Jesus Prayer as "containing all goods, the source of all the virtues", but he also allows for other methods to be used when they will profit the monk more. At one time, even though weary and tired, the monk is exhorted to repeat the Jesus Prayer; at another time Nil tells him to turn to reading, when the mind wanders. "When our mind is distracted, we should busy ourselves with reading rather than with prayer, or we should take up some manual work..."[176]

Thus we see in Nil a flexibility and a freedom in choosing the aids that will best help a monk attain his desired end. His great principle in his hesychastic spirituality which we quoted already and with which he closes his Ustav always stands out bright before the disciple as a light-

---

[173] Hausherr, L., "La Méthode...", op. cit., pp. 164–165. Nicephor, "De cordis custodia", PG, 147, 963B–965A.
[174] Ustav, p. 33. Hesychius Sinaite, Cent., I, PG, 93, 1485B–C.
[175] Idem.
[176] Idem.

house giving security and direction so as to keep moderation and a hierarchy of values between the end desired and the means chosen to attain the end which Nil succinctly formulates as: "Let us do only what is pleasing to God, singing, praying, reading, studying spiritual things, doing manual work or any other labours. And so little by little let us approach God in the interior man, adding by our good works to the glory of the Father, Son, and Holy Spirit, one in the Blessed Trinity. Amen."[177]

From what has been said about Nil's type of hesychasm, above all, his fidelity to the Sinaite Fathers, it must be insisted on that Nil, as the first serious hesychast in Russia, transported to Russia the best in hesychastic tradition. It has been well pointed out by Fairy von Lilienfeld that Nil in no sense of the word can be associated with the "Palamistic" hesychasm, as many "neo-hesychasts" in Russia in the 19th century strove to do. Cf. F. v. Lilienfeld, "Der athonitische Hesychasmus des 14. und 15. Jahrhunderts im Lichte der zeitgenossischen russischen Quellen, in *Jbb. GO*, 1958, neufolge 6, pp. 436-448. "...So haben sich die russischen Neo-Palamiten des 19. und 20. Jahrhunderts auch immer auf die angeblich schon mit Nil Sorskij begonnene Tradition des Palamismus in Russland berufen! In einem gewissen Widerspruch zu diesem Bild Nils steht das Streben derselben Forscher, schon vor Nil die Wirkung des so verstandenen athonitischen 'Hesychasmus' in Russland aufzuspüren." (pp. 438-439).

[177] *Ibid.*, p. 90.

IV

EXTERNAL PRACTICES

A. OBEDIENCE TO THE RULE

To understand Nil's attitude towards a fixed religious rule, determining each action of the day for the monk and sanctifying perfect fidelity in all details to the rule through the exercise of the ruling virtue of obedience, one has to understand Nil's attitude towards the three types of monasticism practised in Russia of his day. We have already touched on this in explaining that Nil did not reject the other two types of monasticism, the coenobitic and anchoret way of life, in giving his preference to the exclusive skete type. But he suggests the "middle way", that of one or two brothers living in the company of an "elder", only when one had reached that stage of perfection necessary in order to profit from it. "We should undertake the middle way only at the proper time... And that is after one has acquired the necessary wisdom by living together with other men in a community... Those who are still stained with dung, i.e. with bodily passions, cannot enter upon the solitary life easily and properly and certainly not before the proper time and then only if they have a superior over them."[1]

G. Fedotov, in his book on Russian saints, unjustly gives the impression that Nil has no place for religious obedience. "This diffidence towards monastic obedience gives to Nil's teaching a character of spiritual freedom."[2] He goes on to explain that Nil does not allow for one's free following of his own will to perfection, but all direction is to come from the "Divine Writings".

Nil surely was not against monastic obedience, but, rather, held it as a necessary "purifying" means to prepare a monk for a life of greater solitude and more perfect submission directly to the inspirations of the Holy Spirit. When the monk had acquired the basic virtues, especially that of relinquishing his own selfish will, through living in a community,

---

[1] *Ustav*, p. 89.
[2] Fedotov, G., *Svjatye drevnej Rusi*, (Paris, 1931), p. 169.

as Nil himself did, then he could go on to a higher form of obedience to God where God's will was made known more delicately through the perpetual living in His presence and the seeking only to find His will. This theme of forsaking one's own will to find and accomplish perfectly God's will is stressed constantly; but, in Nil's *Ustav* and usually in his letters, he is writing for those hesychasts who are already leading the hidden life of contemplation. "Give yourself to obedience, imitating the way of life of the Fathers through their writings," Nil exhorts Vassian[3] and to his disciple Gurij he repeats the same, "Bind yourself to the Divine Writings."[4] To German he points out:

Keep the Lord's commands and the traditions of the Holy Fathers; tell also the brethren living with you. If you are in your hermit's cell or in the monastery with the brethren, give your attention to the Holy Writings and walk in the footsteps of the Holy Fathers because the Divine Writings so command us. Or give yourself in obedience to such a person who will prove himself spiritual in thought, word and deed... If such a guide is not found, then give yourself in obedience directly to God through Divine Writings and not so stupidly as some when they are in the monastery with the brethren and think that they are obeying, yet they are being fed innanely on their own self-will; they then leave and foolishly take up the life of solitude, guiding themselves all the time by their own carnal will and imprudent judgment, 'for they know not what they do'.[5]

Against egoistically following one's own will, especially in interpreting the one necessary rule, Sacred Scripture,[6] Nil writes:

We who are beginners and have not yet acquired prudence should teach and strengthen one another, as it is written: 'A brother helped by another brother is like a strong city' (Prov. 18, 19). But we have a master who will not deceive us: the God-inspired Scriptures. For this reason it is beneficial that we devote ourselves to the work of God, together with the faithful brethren, animated by the same aspirations, and that we dwell with one or two of them in searching out the will of God in the Divine Writings. If the Lord grant to one a greater understanding, let him aid the other brother, friend instructing friend.[7]

Thus we can conclude that Nil did not belittle monastic obedience, but rather he distinguished it according to the stage of spiritual progress

---

[3] Letter to Vassian, fol. 98A. Cf. *Appendix I.*
[4] Letter to Gurij, fol. 102B.
[5] Letter to German, fol. 106B. Lk. 23, 34.
[6] St. Basil also insisted on Holy Scripture as the only rule to follow. Cf. Dom J. Gribomont, "Obéissance et Évangile selon S. Basile le Grand", in *La Via Spirituelle*, Suppl. VI (1952), pp. 192–215.
[7] *Ustav*, p. 89.

of the monk. In living the skete form of life the monk was exhorted to live under obedience to a *starec*, one who could lead the other monk in discerning the will of God in the "Divine Writings". And only in the case of not finding a holy guide, but presupposed already an advanced stage of spiritual perfection, done in a community under strict obedience, could the monk search God's will directly from the writings. Nil encourages constantly spiritual conversations with holy, God-enlightened men who could share their discernment with others, even if they were not the constant spiritual Father.

In viewing Nil's attitude towards obedience, one must keep ever in mind two factors. First, the actual situation in Russia at the time Nil was living; more in particularly, in and around the Novgorod area where Nil's skete life was to find its stronghold. Considering the low level of literacy in Russia of the 15th century, the lack of books necessary to educate the monks in the full patristic tradition, the hitherto custom of only the higoumen in the Russian coenobitic monastery encharged with the duty and right to teach other monks, we should not be surprised that spiritual guides were scarce. Nil was not advocating free license on the part of each monk to follow whatever spiritual path most pleased him. Over and over Nil insists on the ideal: it is absolutely necessary to give up one's own will.[8] "To such as have understanding of the Divine Writings and spiritual wisdom and whose life is a witness to their virtues, to these strive to subject yourself and be an imitator of their lives."[9]

In the ideal order he would want to follow his guide Simeon the New Theologian who wrote: "Those who have planted their feet firmly on the rock of obedience to their spiritual fathers, receiving their teaching as though coming from the lips of God Himself, and on this foundation of obedience unswervingly and humbly practice what they are taught, speedily arrive at success."[10] But in an area like the Trans-Volga, quite uncultivated and conditions still primitive, Nil's words about the difficulty to find good spiritual directors are very understandable.[11]

The second factor to be kept in mind is the high spiritual, contemplative ideal that Nil was inaugurating in Russia, the skete form of hesychasm. After his own experience in the Kirill-Belozersky monastery and in various coenobitic and skete monasteries in Constantinople and on Mount Athos, he was completely convinced that God was calling him

[8] *Ustav*, p. 5. Letter IX: "On overcoming evil thoughts", Elagin ed., p. 204.
[9] Letrer to Gurij, foll. 103A–B.
[10] Simeon, *PG*, 120, 620D–621A, § 44.
[11] *Ustav*, p. 14.

to a very special life, as well as his disciples. That spiritual life was precisely a glaring contrast and protest to the external formalism that existed in Russian contemporary monasteries. That spiritual life demanded a more complete renuntiation of the world than was possible in any other Russian monastery of his day. It meant transplanting to the Russian "deserts" of Trans-Volga the spirit of the Fathers of the Desert, of Evagrius, of the Sinaite Hesychasts, of their followers on Mount Athos and that spirit was to be found in the New Testament and the writings of the Fathers. It required an internal asceticism similar to that of the anchorites of the desert, but lived in a community of two or three brethren so as to partake of the aids offered by communal life without at the same time forsaking the advantages in asceticism and continued contemplation of the solitary or hesychastic life. He had seen with his own eyes and had carefully read St. Basil the Great on the dangers of the anchoret life, above all, the danger of pride, self-deception, lack of reflection, self-centeredness, *acedia*.[12] In his small community of two or three, reuniting with the other monks each week-end for communal, liturgical services and recreation, he would retain the benefits that St. Basil and St. Theodore Studite found in the community of brothers united and living with "one mind".

It was unthinkable for Nil that, if he and his monks did all in their power to surrender their will and make it one with the Divine Will, God would not aid in guiding them. "When no guide can be found, the Fathers have us turn to the Holy Writings and listen to the Lord Himself speaking. Study the Holy Writings and you shall find eternal life in them."[13] "Live in harmony with the example of your spiritual guide. But if no such guide can be found, the best of all is to follow God according to the Divine Writings."[14]

Thus it is quite true that in the absence of a coenobitic life and a fixed rule with a superior to specify for each moment God's will, Nil's monk would be encouraged to greater human effort to determine God's will at each moment. But along with this "freedom from the letter" came the added necessity on the part of each individual monk to attain greater purity of heart and docility to God's workings through grace in the soul.

But what kind of a rule did Nil's monks follow? First of all, this so-called *Rule* or *Ustav* of Nil's is not an ordinary rule such as those we

---

[12] St. Basil, *PG*, 31, 928C–933B.
[13] *Ustav*, p. 14.
[14] Letter to German, fol. 106B.

know that came from the pen of St. Basil,[15] St. Theodore Studite[16] or even from Nil's contemporary, Joseph Volokolamsk.[17] E. Golubinskij gives a thorough history of the introduction into Russia of the Studite rule of St. Theodore (†826), especially under the more detailed version edited by the Constantinople Patriarch Alexis.[18] In speaking of reforming the rules of Russian monasteries he says that in the Russian Church there exists only one rule, i.e. that basically of Theodore Studite.[19] But Nil's contemporary, Joseph Volokolamsk, in writing his rule, complained of the many various interpretations and differences of customs existing in the Russian monasteries of his day. He was going to write a rule based on the typicon or rule of St. Theodore Studite and of St. Basil,[20] but he actually borrowed heavily from other sources to give a "rule according to Holy Scripture and the usages of ancient monasteries of St. Sabba of Jerusalem, of the great Athanasius of Mount Athos and above all of the most outstanding monastery of our country, that of St. Kirill of Belozerskij".[21]

When, however, Nil set about to put his ways of life into writing, he purposely ignored the traditional form of a monastic rule[22] because the skete life and his hesychastic spirituality were hitherto in Russia unorganized. He can be considered as the first one in Russia to embark on this task of writing a rule for a new type of spirituality and monasticism. Should we be surprised then if his "rule" does not follow the usual pattern of rules then known in Russia and all designed for the coenobitic life?

But, having seen already his hesychastic ideals and coming to know his own individual temperament and inclination, we can expect Nil's

---

[15] *Regulae Fusius Tract., PG*, 31, pp. 889–1052; *Regulae Brevius Tract.*, pp. 1080–1305; *Moralia*, pp. 700–869.

[16] *St. Theodore Studite, PG*, 99, pp. 1703–20, 1433–1758.

[17] Joseph Volokolamsk, *Ustav* or so-called *Duchovnaja Gramota*, found in Makarij, *Velikija Čet'i Minei*, Tome for September, col. 499–615 (St. Petersburg, 1868).

[18] *Istorija russkoj cerkvi*, tome I, 2nd half (Moscow, 1904), pp. 552–745. Cf. also Casey, R. P., "Early Russian Monasticism", in *OCP* (Roma, 1953), Vol. XIX, pp. 372–423.

[19] *Ibid.*, p. 726.

[20] *Duxovnaja Gramota, op. cit.*, col. 610.

[21] Savva Černij, "Zitie prepodobnago Iosifa Volokolamskago", found in Makarij: *Velikija Četii Minei*, Sept., col. 495.

[22] We can get a fairly good idea of a typical Russian monastic rule of Nil's time by studying that of Joseph Volokolamsk. He divides his rule into 14 chapters with such titles as "On what concerns good conduct in the refectory and on food and drink", "On what concerns communal and particular church services and the order to be followed", "That it is the duty of the superior to instruct and punish those under him", etc... Cf. *Duxovnaja Gramota, op. cit.*, col. 501–502.

rule to take a radically different form and spirit. Besides general indication found in his letters, the only two documents that present his way of life are his *Predanie* and his so-called *Ustav*. The *Predanie*, being a short draft of a few directives put down in writing at the beginning of the formation of his skete community, is hardly long enough or detailed enough to be considered a monastic rule as such. His *Ustav*, written much later,[23] perhaps near the very end of his life, in the manuscripts do not have in the title anything to indicate a rule. It is, rather, as we have already quoted, entitled: "On mental activity taken from the writings of the Holy Fathers – what is necessary for it and how one must diligently labour to attain it."[24] It is through tradition that his followers and writers referred to it as his *Ustav* or *Rule*. He himself clearly states in the opening lines of his *Predanie* that what he is writing is a "teaching profitable for my own soul and for my ever, reverend brethren who are one with me and share my spirit".[25] Nil's scope and whole spirit is radically different from any other legislator of monastic rules as can be seen in the closing lines of his *Ustav:*

> We, unwise and with the meagerness of our intelligence, with God's help have written this as a reminder to myself and to others of similar mind who are in need of instruction, if they so wish... If there is anything found here not pleasing to God and not helpful to souls because of my foolishness and ignorance, let it be not so, but may the will of God perfect it and make it well-pleasing. I ask pardon or beg this, that, if anyone should find anything else more practical and useful, then let him do it and we shall be glad and rewarded. If anyone should find from these writings some help, let him pray for me a sinner that I may obtain mercy before God.[26]

Nil does not pose as the higoumen or superior, but a brother among brothers. "I call you brothers instead of disciples. We have but one teacher, Our Lord Jesus Christ."[27] Each monk determines how he will dispose of his time in prayer and work. There are no fixed periods assigned for occupations. Murav'ev speaks of an order of church services that Nil composed for his monks, similar to that observed by the hermits of Mount Athos. It is understandable that Nil, who followed such a rule for many years on Mount Athos, would have been very familiar with such an order of carrying out the liturgical services and would have

---

[23] Cf. Arxangel'skij, *op. cit.*, p. 53. Dr. Lilienfeld, in her dissertation already cited, holds that the *Predanie* most likely was written after the *Ustav*.

[24] *Ustav*, p. 11.

[25] *Ibid.*

[26] *Ibid.*, pp. 90–91.

[27] *Predanie*, pp. 1–2.

used something similar rather than the fixed rules found in the Studite rule where the Liturgy and the Hours were the central feature running throughout the community's life.[28] According to the skete practice on Mount Athos, during the Liturgy the choirs or monks sang only the Trisagion, Alleluia, Cherubim Hymn, Hymn to Our Lady (Dostojna) and the common stiches or versicles. Except for feast-days, these were often rather recited than sung and after each Liturgy the monks left the central church and returned to their cells. It must be remembered that according to such usage, the monks came together, not each day, but only on Saturday and Sunday and on feast-days. For the remaining days they remained alone in their cells. Each Saturday night they celebrated the all-night service with many readings from the Fathers after each kathisma or group of psalms and long canons and prostrations. The solemn Liturgy with ornate singing was not known in these skete monasteries.[29]

Nil gives a few general rules sprinkled here and there but nowhere is there found an orderly rule worked out in detail. The chief care of the monk is to be directed only to attaining purity of heart and perfect tranquillity through active attention to God's presence. If now and again we come upon specific injunctions such as not leaving the monastery except with permission and grave necessity, not conversing with women or even looking at them, we can readily understand them in the context as "distractions" that impede the desired contemplation and thus to be avoided.

We have already treated under the eight passions Nil's teaching on chastity, bodily mortification with its norms for food and drink, fasting; in dealing with his hesychastic spirituality, we developed at length his doctrine on interior mortification and abnegation. It would be profitable still to see what guiding principles he lays down for poverty, work, and the apostolate.

B. POVERTY

Nil preaches the strictest evangelical poverty, both of spirit and of actual poverty. "We must resist and avoid like deadly poison the desire to possess earthly goods."[30] Thus he argues that monks, according to St.

---

[28] Murav'ev, A., *Russkaja Fivaida na Severe* (St. Petersburg, 1894), p. 292.
[29] *Ibid.*, p. 293.
[30] *Predanie*, p. 6.

Basil, not having anything to give or lend, are exempt from giving alms to the poor, for the monks are supposed to be the poorest of the poor. With complete honesty Nil's monks should be able to say: "We have left all to follow Thee" (Matt. 19, 27). By the work of their hands they must live, but if a monk is physically unable to gain his own living through manual labour, he can accept a few donations from the laity, but never in excess.[31] In the cell of the monk there are to be found no objects of value and the hermitage and lodgings are to be built of poor materials, always undecorated. In a letter on the remembrance of death,[32] he exhorts his disciple: "Clean your cell and the poverty of your possessions will teach you restraint, because when we possess a great many things we may have a sufficiency, but we are unable to control our desires. If you wish to have tears, love lowliness, poverty, and humility and do not strive to have fine things in your cell."[33]

In his teaching on avarice when treating the eight passions, we find his clearest principles on perfect poverty. Not only not having possession, but the very desire to possess them must be uprooted.

Not only gold or silver and property must be absent from our lives, but we should have only the barest necessities for life, as clothing, shoes, cell, dishes instruments for manual work. And these should not be of any value, not' decorated, not capable of arousing in us a fretting and preoccupation, and thus tempted to have contacts with the world. True victory over avarice and in general attachment to things consists in this that we not only do not have, but do not even wish anything. This leads us to spiritual purity.[34]

One of the best antidotes against a spirit of pride is to "wear the poorest clothes and prefer the most menial tasks".[35] Anything that would distract the mind, tie the heart to a disordinate attachment to creatures and away from God was to be avoided.

To aid the individual to acquire this poverty, actual and of spirit, there was to be an absolute "corporate" poverty. Here Nil stands out as one of the unique spiritual writers, perhaps the only one in early Russian times who advocated such extreme poverty in regard, for example, to the decoration of churches.[36] That there were innumerable saints who were of the same kenotic spirit as Nil cannot be doubted, but as a writer

---

[31] *Ibid.*, p. 6. St. Basil, *Reg. Fus. tr.*, *PG*, 31, p. 1031.
[32] Cf. Arxangel'skij, A., *op. cit.*, pp. 61–62.
[33] Text found in Elagin edition, pp. 196–197. Translation in *Appendix I.*
[34] *Ustav*, p. 47.
[35] *Ibid.*, p. 58.
[36] Fedotov, G., *op. cit.*, p. 172.

advocating this principle for others to follow, Nil seems to be a pioneer in Russian literature[37] and certainly a great exception and reaction to his times when the churches were laden with gold and silver; wherever the eye gazed, it feasted on the sumptuousness of an earthly duplicate of the heavenly Jerusalem[38]. Fearing to project his own spiritual ideals on others, he bases his teaching on the words and examples of the Holy Fathers. "In regard to church decoration, St. John Chrysostom writes: 'If anyone wants to donate sacred vessels or other adornments to the church, tell him rather to distribute them among the poor. For no one was ever condemned because he did not decorate the church. And other saints likewise taught.'"[39]

He argues that his monks should not have gold or silver or unnecessary ornaments in their possession, but only the bare necessities in the church by citing the example of the martyr of St. Eugenia, who, being a religious, would not accept silver vessels because it was not proper for religious to possess silver in any form.[40] The deed of the great Pachomius, father of all coenobitic monks, seems to have won the greatest of admiration from Nil. Not only would Pachomius not allow the interior of a church to be decorated, but, on the completion of a new church with brick pillars of too great beauty, he tied ropes around them and pulled with his monks until the pillars began to lean and thus the beautiful proportions were distorted; all to avoid vainglory and inordinate attachment to created beauty. Nil's simple conclusion: "If so great and saintly a man so spoke and acted, how much more ought we to do likewise in order to be preserved from similar things, we who are so weak in mind and enslaved by passions."[41]

There is an account of how Nil appeared in sleep to Tsar Ivan the Terrible when the latter visited the Kirill Monastery at Belozerskij. Out of reverence for Nil, Ivan wanted to build an extravagant church. But in the vision Nil forbade him to build the church of stone or to adorn it beyond the necessities from the danger of becoming too attached to

[37] Tixon of Voronež (†1783) was of a similar kenotic mind. Cf. his *Tvorenie*, 2nd ed. (Moscow, 1860) (15 vols.), tome VIII, p. 38.
[38] Golubinskij, *op. cit.*, pp. 286–291. Bishop Ignatius Brianchaninov in the 19th century still promoted this ideal: "The people are pressed like ants in their poor huts, yet are willing to build a high and beautiful temple to God... They walk practically in rags, but they want to see their church shining with gold and silver..." Quoted by L. Sokolov, *Episkop Ignatij* (Kiev, 1915), 2 vols., tome I, pp. 151–152.
[39] *Predanie*, p. 8.
[40] Cf. *Vitae Patrum*, Lib. I, *Vita S. Eugeniae, PL*, 73, pp. 627 and foll. Also *PL*, 21, p. 1113.
[41] *Ibid.*, pp. 8–9.

material beauty. For whole centuries the skete of Nil bordering the Sora retained its entire simplicity in wood.[42]

We shall see later on how his love for poverty formulated itself in a protest in the 1503 *Sobor* of Moscow against the abuses prevalent among his contemporary Russian monks due to excessive preoccupation with material possessions. We can only understand his austerity in this matter of poverty by understanding Nil's readiness to follow literally Our Lord's command to leave all, give all possessions to the poor and follow Him poorly. The Heavenly Father who feeds the birds of the air would provide in His Loving Providence for those who would seek first the Kingdom of Heaven. For Nil there was no other aim in life.

C. WORK

Nil, who drew his ascetical principles from the Gospel and the writings of the Holy Fathers, naturally would insist on the necessity of manual work. He quotes St. Paul: "If anyone will not work, neither let him eat," and he cites the example of Our Lord and His Immaculate Mother[43] who worked for their daily bread by manual labour and thus command us to imitate their example. "We have been instructed by the Holy Fathers to earn our daily bread and other necessities by manual labour." For the early Fathers of the desert, manual labor was first of all necessary in order that a monk would be self-supporting and independent of others.[44] "Mary has urgent need of Martha, for it is also because of Martha that Mary is praised."[45] Karl Heussi points out that manual work served not only for self-sustenance, but it was considered by the monks of the desert as a necessary ascetical means in the battle against the devil and in the acquiring of virtues.[46] By such work one practised patience and humility, fulfilled a command of God and fought off laziness, the spirit of *acedia*, and evil thoughts. Justinian in his Code of Civil Law confirms this tradi-

[42] Murav'ev, A., *op. cit.*, p. 241. He goes on to say that his follower disregarded his wish and built two stone churches, plus stone houses for the monks, as he saw when he visited in 1894. Bishop Amvrosij gives the same information. Cf. *IRI*, T. V, p. 213.
[43] *Predanie*, p. 5. 2 Thess, 3, 10.
[44] To cite merely from the *Life of St. Anthony*, cf. *PG*, 26, 3, 844C; 50, 916B–C; 53, 920A.
[45] *Apophthegmata*, *PG*, 65, § 5, 409. Cf. Völker, W., *Das Vollkommenheitsideal des Origenes* (Tübigen, 1931), p. 77.
[46] Heussi, K., *Der Ursprung des Mönchtums* (Tübingen, 1936), pp. 215–218. Cf. also Dörries, Hermann, "Mönchtum und Arbeit", in the collection *Forschungen zur Kirchengeschichte und kirchlichen Kunst für Johannes Ficker* (1931), pp. 17–39.

tion of the Fathers: "There are two kinds of work for monks: they can devote themselves to Holy Scripture or give themselves to so-called manual works..."[47]

This was therefore the tradition among all monks, be they anchorites or coenobitics, [48] so quite normally does Nil follow this monastic tradition. He also follows the Fathers in insisting on the necessary condition that the manual work be of a nature as not to disturb the mind in its quiet and constant prayer.[49] Nil insists that the work be done indoors, all the easier to avoid distractions, to remain recollected, but above all not to become too absorbed with cares and worries coming from outside work. "This work is to be performed indoors, for the Divine Writings hold that whereas those monks who live in a community may work with a pair of oxen in open fields to plough the land, this is not permitted in the case of hermits living separated from other men."[50]

Here Nil, if he applies this to his contemporaries, seems to be allowing them, the coenobitic monks, to possess or least to work land outside of the monastery because of the large number of monks to be fed. But for his followers there would be none of this. We know that Nil and his, monks busied themselves with the manual task of copying manuscripts. This work was quite in keeping with Nil's hesychastic ideal and in harmony with the Fathers' teaching on continual meditation on the Divine Writings. The monk could maintain perfect solitude, total separation from all earthly things, immersed in constant prayer, undisturbed contemplation of spiritual realities. And at the same time, considering the great need for books, this type of work was rendering invaluable service to the literary world of Russia of the 15th and 16th centuries. We have earlier shown Nil's critical attitude which he enjoined on his disciples in their study of the Divine Writings.[51] This work of transcribing was not merely to be a mechanical routine of copying manuscripts letter by letter. That there were many errors being transmitted through a lack of positive criticism we have already been at pains in an earlier chapter to point out. Thus Nil's work was to be prayerful study. The peculiar in Russia

---

[47] Schoelle, R. and Kroll, G., *Corpus Legum Justiniani* (Berlin, 1899), Vol. III, ed. 2, p. 675: "Oportet enim duplex hoc opus monachis esse, aut divinis vacare scripturis aut quae monachis deceant quae vocant manuum opera meditari et operari: mens enim frustra vacans nihil bonorum parit."

[48] Cf. Rezac, J., S. J., *De Monachismo Secundum Recentiorem Legislationem Russicam* (Roma, 1952), p. 122 and foll.

[49] Cf. John Colobos, *Apophthegmata*, PG, 65, 34, p. 216; *Pistamon*, 1. p. 376.

[50] *Predanie*, p. 5. Cf. also Cassian, *Conférences, op. cit.*, XXIV, 3, p. 174.

[51] Letter to Gurij, fol. 102B–103A.

circumstances at the time and one of the most charitable acts of apostolate Nil could perform dictated this swerving, if such it were, from the usual interpretation of his hesychastic forefathers on works. This will be commented on shortly in dealing with his ideas on the apostolate. This work of re-editing texts, comparing them with originals, finding the truth from among fictitious details and even errors of other transcribers, must have been absorbing and must have required a high degree of scholarship on the part of Nil and his monks. Whether Nil planned it or whether in the circumstances he saw it best to moderate somewhat his concept of manual work, the result is that Nil seems to mingle the theory of manual work of the Fathers of the desert with that of the "Hellenistic" Fathers, Clement of Alexandria and Origen. Both these Fathers urged the importance of cultivating the powers of the mind. Perhaps no Father stressed the importance of *meditari in lege Dei die ac nocte* and urged its daily practice more than Origen.[52] Also for Nil, such work, the study of Scripture, brought the mind into direct communion with the Divine Verbum and the spiritual world. The monk's mind was constantly being fed on divine thoughts and this proved to be the best and most powerful weapon against the demons. Nil and Origen agree perfectly in exhorting their disciples to learn the spiritual art from a study of the Scriptures, from the Lives of the Saints and from God.[53]

But surely there was also time and need for simple, hard, physical labour. Nil himself gives an early example by digging the well that would serve his skete and by constructing at the side of the pond a small mill to grind wheat for the monk's daily bread.[54] Nil insists that, even though the monks stay within the hermitage, those who are young and healthy should chastise their body in order, better to make it a docile instrument to the soul and this done: "by abstinence in eating and drinking and by work. The old and the infirm may be allowed some dispensation."[55] In his Chapter 4 of the *Ustav* on the general norms of the

---

[52] Cf. the citations from Origen given by Wilhelm Bornemann, O.S.B., *In investiganda monachatus origine quibus de causis ratio habenda sit Originis* (Gottingae, 1885), p. 80, n. 204.

[53] Letter to German, fol. 105B–106A. We do not wish to imply necessarily that Nil was directly influenced in his critical study of Holy Scripture by Origen; but surely there can be traced easily a continued influence exerted by Origen on Evagrius, Evagrius on Cassian, Cassian on Climacus and on the other Sinaite hesychast Fathers who were the main models for Nil's spirituality.

[54] Cf. Ševyrev, S. P., *Poezdka v Kirillo-Belozerskij monastyr'* (Moscow, 1850), part 2, p. 32.

[55] *Predanie*, p. 9.

skete life, Nil again touches on manual work as a necessity for taming the body.

One with a healthy body must wear it down by fasting, vigils and occupations demanding effort, e.g. by prostrations and heavy manual work so that the body will become subject to the soul and be delivered from its passions by the grace of Christ. If the body is weak, it should be treated in a way to strengthen it. As for prayer, one should never omit it, whether he be strong or weak, and even in performing necessary tasks the mind should be secretly absorbed in prayer. Bodily work is demanded from those healthy and strong of body according to their strength. But all interiorly can keep the mind concentrated in reverence and in hope and in love of God; this is an obligation on all, even those who are seriously ill.[56]

In such primitive surroundings such as the site selected by Nil along the Sora River, there never lacked the opportunity for this asceticism of physical work.

D. APOSTOLATE

The perennial problem of all contemplatives in regard to the apostolate did not escape Nil. His conclusions and principles are quite decisive, but there is no theory to explain his stand, perhaps because he and his monks saw this problem of apostolate through eyes quite different than ours. But we are nonetheless justified from our lack of asceticism and complete dedication to sanctification that Nil and his predecessors possessed to ask them certain questions in order the better to understand their ideal of the apostolate and to further enlarge our own view of true charity. How do these mystics who flee from every contact with their fellow-man fulfill the second great commandment so similar to the first: "Thou shalt love thy neighbour as thyself"? Is not their love for God a form of subtle egoism, a spiritual sensualism that hungers only for the delights of God with none of the burdens of distractions brought about by helping others to find and know God more intimately? Is it not a greater proof of love for God, those of concrete deeds and sacrifices done for others out of love for God than to remain only in the intentional order of interior prayer? Can there be a true love for God that does not necessitate an equal love for fellow-men? Is perfection to be measured by the standard Christ gave us: "Love one another as I have loved you." "Whatsoever you do to the least of My brethren, you do to Me"? And if so, how can this be

[56] *Ustav*, p. 37.

reconciled with the sayings of such Fathers that forbid all contact with people in the world?

For Nil and the Fathers, who is their neighbour? He is generally considered, if at all in particular, to be one's fellow-monk. This can be better seen by keeping in mind the patristic conception of how a monk was to exercise an apostolate among his neighbours.[57] Nil quotes Macarius, in dealing with the high flights of contemplation. "God in His mercy diminishes His grace for a time in His saints in order that they may concern themselves for their brothers through preaching and by their example, as St. Macarius says, speaking of those who had already reached perfection. And he gives this example:

> ...Such a man in that time of rapture prays out: 'O if my soul would only depart together with this prayer'. For he is like a man about to advance to the twelfth degree and then he would have attained complete perfection, but grace diminishes and this person descends one degree and stands on the eleventh grade of perfection and thus such souls do not reach the full measure of perfection in order that they may find time to be preoccupied with their brethren and provide them with the help of their preaching.[58]

The first way, therefore, that a monk according to Nil practises an apostolate towards his neighbour is by his *presence* whereby his neighbour, usually his fellow-monk, can come within his presence and thus, by seeing his example of virtue, holiness, perfection and hearing his spiritual words of wisdom as directed by the Holy Spirit, can be helped to greater perfection. The two features characterizing this presence is *passivity* and the *accidental role* or secondary role it plays in relation to the main one, that of self-perfection. The monk takes no initiative to make his holy presence seen or heard by his neighbour whoever he may be. Nil exhorts in a letter:

> Keep yourself from seeing persons and hearing such conversations for these stir up the passions and provide unclean thoughts and God will keep you from these... For if one does not cut himself completely from the world, he will be like one who habitually has intercourse with the world, for certain images and worldly habits, formerly acquired by him ... again are renewed and one cannot carefully continue in prayer seeking to find always God's will.[59]

---

[57] Cf. Hausherr, I., "La théologie du monachisme chez S. Jean Climaque", in the volume *Théologie de la vie monastique* (Paris, 1961), p. 405 and foll. Also cf. Bouyer, Louis, *Le Sens de la vie monastique* (Paris, 1950), p. 211.

[58] *Ustav*, p. 30; Pseudo-Macarius, *De Caritate*, *PG*, 34, 10, 916D–917A.

[59] Letter to Gurij, fol. 101B.

Towards sinners there should be passivity, no attempt to admonish, to correct them.

Turn away from hearing and seeing the affairs of the brethren and from their secrets and their actions. For that empties the soul of every good and makes one focus attention on the failings of the neighbour, while one leaves off weeping for his own sins. And do not be concerned to be engaged quickly in conversations with the brethren, even if they may appear to be helpful conversations... Do not have anything to do with such (sinners); it is not fitting even to converse with such, not even to reprove or correct them, but let God do this, 'for God is powerful to correct them.'[60]

In a letter on overcoming vanity he follows Climacus' teaching on avoiding any active apostolate before others because this serves so easily as a trap of the devil to lead the monk to vain glory.[61] "Do not correct another for some sin, not even if you see him doing such with your own eyes. Do not judge a sinner as guilty of judgment or torture, but attribute his sin to Satan... But rather think of yourself as the greatest sinner of all... do good secretly as our holy Father Vitalij did or as Simeon the Fool for Christ's sake did or as St. Andrew of Constantinople."[62] And he goes on to show how our passivity which demonstrates our complete dedication to the "work of God", that is, the only preoccupation that a monk should have, seeking always to please God and to avoid all that distracts from this work, at times turns into a "passive-activity" if we may so express it. One preaches the humility, the meekness, the forgiveness and mercy of Christ the Saviour to one's neighbour by showing forth control under abuse, joy when insulted, forgiveness and prayers shown to those who offend. "They (the saints) bore patiently all evils as though they were really not evil and prayed to God for those who inflicted on them insults. They did not reckon the sins of others as sins but as ignorance on their part."[63]

In his treatment of the vice of anger, Nil gives us two pages of directives on how to avoid this sin by opposing the tendency to anger with forgiveness of heart for injuries received, to reckon them as gifts from God and, by praying for the insulters, we assure our own forgiveness for

---

[60] *Ibid.*
[61] Climacus, *Gradus 3*, 665A–B.
[62] Letter on how to overcome vanity, Elagin ed., p. 201. Cf. *Appendix I* of this present work.
[63] *Idem.*

our many sins committed against God.[64] Another time Nil exhorts:
"Recall, brother, what great evil the Jews did to our Lord Jesus Christ,
but still, He, God, the lover of mankind, did not become angry with
them but prayed for them to the Father saying: 'Father, forgive them this
sin for they know not what they do'."[65]

This preaching by a Christ-like example, especially to one's brother-
monks is extolled by Nil in the rules he gives to Vassian. Here we see
how his rules of conduct when dealing with one's neighbour are based
on humility derived from a vivid realization of one's own sinfulness and
a keen faith in seeing Christ in each fellow-monk.

Hold every brother as a saint.[66] If you must speak or ask a question or give
an answer to anyone, do it with a pleasant tone and gentle speech, showing
spiritual love and true humility, and not with an indifferent, superficial manner.
Do not offend any brother... Do not judge anyone in anything, even if his
actions appear not good, but consider yourself as sinful and utterly useless...
Be an imitator of their (saints') way of life, showing patience in sorrows and
praying for those who offend you. Consider those as your benefactors. Understand that this which I am telling you is wisdom from Divine Writings which
tell us the wish of God in doing good.

He continues with an outline of perfection lived by the saints of old,
quite similar to that given by the Abba Isaias:[67] one progressing in perfection must bear hardships, the cross, even death, for this is a gift of
God. This makes man a participator in the Passion of Christ. By this
are the true lovers of God distinguished from those of the world. Thus
God leads His followers to eternal life through suffering. But such should
be borne then with joy and thanksgiving to God for the blessing and
grace to bear something for Him. One should recall the end of this life
of sorrows and the future life of unending happiness. Never forget one's
sinfulness and that all good done comes from God.[68]

Christ remains always the living example of this meekness of heart.
This *kenosis* would become a distinctive trait of Russian Christianity
and in the 18th and 19th century its great spiritual and literary authors,
including Bishop Tixon of Voronež, would make it shine through as

---

[64] *Ustav*, pp. 48–49.
[65] Treatise of St. Nil on overcoming evil thoughts, Elagin ed., p. 204. Cf. *Appendix I*.
[66] Letter to Vassian, fol. 97a. He probably is here quoting from various rules given
by Simeon the New Theologian. On the latter's doctrine of holding each brother as a
saint, cf. *PG*, 120, 123, 669D.
[67] Abba Isaias, in *Dobrotoljubie*, *op. cit.*, Tome I, pp. 281–283.
[68] Letter to Vassian, fol. 98A.

the ideal to be pursued by all classes of Russians bent on imitating Christ.[69]

The example and admonition of the Fathers to teach others (without necessarily going out to seek hearers who wanted to hear the word of God) did not escape Nil. Origen insisted always on the superiority of the life of contemplation to that of action, but he also insisted that one, on attaining perfection, through his asceticism, had a social obligation to share his knowledge with others.[70] And Climacus strongly insisted: "Who has a profitable word and does not communicate it to others liberally will not escape punishment. To what dangers do they not expose themselves who could work efficaciously to comfort people in times of trial and do not do it?... This surpasses before God all other action and all other contemplation..."[71].

Nil does not turn away either from those souls who come to him seeking for help. His own example bears out his deep charity in applying this principle. In his *Predanie* he tells us how he sought solitude and removed himself several miles from the Kirill Monastery. Yet a great many devout monks and others followed him there, begging to live with him and to learn from him how to grow in perfection. His humility sent them away on the grounds that a sinful person was incapable of teaching others about God. But when they insisted, he acquiesced: "I have no desire to be their master, yet they would force me to teach them."[72] But in writing a rule on this matter he cautions: "In our cells fellow-monks and visitors should be instructed only by monks in whom we have approved with confidence their ability to direct souls; they should have the power plus the art to listen well and give advice that will be useful."[73]

This is nothing but reiterating the doctrine of the Fathers of the desert that Nil had read in anthologies containing their *apophthegmata*. After God had healed their spiritual infirmities, He sent them out to edify and

---

[69] Cf. Gorodetsky, N., *The Humiliated Christ in Modern Russian Thought* (London, 1938). The author cites as typical of this kenotic spirit of forgiveness and meekness an example from Turgenev: "But what of the soldier whom a woman wrongly accused of having stolen her chicken and whom a general, passing by, condemned to be hanged? The woman was distressed – she had never expected such a result of her complaint. The soldier received the last sacraments and said: 'Please, sir, tell her not to take it so much to heart... I have forgiven her'." (p. 38.)

[70] Cf. Völker, W., *Das Vollkommenheitsideal des Origenes* (Tübigen, 1931), pp. 168–196. Also, Bettencourt St., "Doctrina Ascetica Origenis", in *Studia Anselmiana*, 16 (Romae, 1945), p. 85 and foll.

[71] Climacus, *PG*, 88, *Ad Pastorem*, 1193C–D.

[72] *Predanie*, p. 2.

[73] *Ibid.*, p. 8.

heal others, but never would one be encharged, as Ammonas asserts, to aid another to find God's will when he himself still was imperfect and followed not God's but his own.[74] The monks taught others only so as not to disobey their Creator; unless they saw clearly God's manifest will that they should go among men, they strove with all their strength to remain in their solitude. Nil cautions that, even though all are bound to help the neighbour by bearing with virtue annoyances, humiliations, rebukes and if they, even novices, do so with patience, this will be a great spiritual alms to the poor neighbour, yet only those who are capable of doing such are to dispense spiritual advice to those seeking it.[75] Thus for Nil the monastery's sole alms to be given should be the freely dispensing of religious instruction and advice to those who come to the monastery for this purpose. It becomes a moral centre where in times of spiritual necessity and sorrows, souls can come and receive spiritual guidance. But always he cautions the necessity of those giving advice, above all, of being deeply spiritual and purified from all earthly taint, so as the better to see God's will in all circumstances.

This love for all souls, despite its apparent passivity, or we could say, due to its apparent passivity, becomes more intense and more universal. Not expanding itself extensively in space, it can become rarified from all human, limiting elements and rise to a charity for men that becomes synonymous with the charity possessed for God. A total indifference towards all persons, whether rich or poor, learned or ignorant, monk or lay is the result.

Towards our neighbour in accordance with the command of God, we must show love. If they are near us we should show it in word and when this does not destroy our love of God; when they are far from us, in spirit we should stretch out this love to them, driving out of our hearts every evil remembrance of them. We should bend all our efforts towards them with a sincere desire to serve them. If God so sees us, He will then forgive our sinfulness, and our prayers will become a well-pleasing offering accepted by Him and He will pour on us His abundant mercy.[76]

Nil grasped this universal element and the relation of fraternal charity with the desire to do the greatest good in order that men may love God more and be more secured in their salvation. Thus he was convinced that one of the great outlets for the exercise of true fraternal charity was in

[74] Cf. Hausherr, I., "L'hésychasme...", *op. cit.*, pp. 32–33. On the charismatic gifts that God gave to monks to be used aiding others, cf. Climacus, *Gradus 25*, 1000B.
[75] *Predanie*, p. 7.
[76] *Ustav*, pp. 37–38.

the copying and making available to souls the Divine Writings, that is, Holy Scripture, the Writings of the Fathers and the Lives of the Saints. In a manuscript originally belonging to the Kirill-Belozerskij Monastery and cited by A. Arxangel'skij, we see Nil's love for his fellow-men and his eager desire to help them as best as he can. After explaining in the preface how he had corrected many errors as far as his weak intelligence gave him to understand, always having sought only to "please God and be helpful to souls", he enunciates his principle of charity:

> ... for I have worked hard at this labour. Such for me is the fulfillment of the command to love God and to love my neighbour... This is true love for one's neighbour: to move his conscience to love God and keep His commands according to His true Divine words, and, according to the life and teachings of the Holy Fathers, to live as far as possible and thus be saved. If I am sinful and wretched and incapable of doing any good, at least I wish the salvation of many of my neighbours.[77]

Another outlet for his fraternal charity and aligned with his unselfish teaching of other disciples was the apostolate of written correspondence carried on with people of all classes. We can imagine the shortage of spiritual guides of Nil's calibre in his days and hence the great demand for his epistolary guidance as second best to personal conversations. In the ten letters or excerpts from such, even more than in his two formal tracts on the skete life, do we see the soul of Nil, purified of all natural affections and bent on seeking only to aid others to love God more, reveal itself in a supernatural, fraternal charity that reminds I. Kologrivov of the ardent letters written by St. Francis Xavier to his brethren in Christ back in Europe.[78] To translate his expressions into English makes them seem somewhat effeminate, affected in tone, but in the original language and in the context they reveal nothing but the union between divine and human love. In one letter he catches himself speaking about his own interior life: "...see, your love for God makes me senseless even to the point of speaking about myself. But as it has been said: 'My secrets I open to those who love me'."[79] And a bit farther in the same letter he adds: "...I give thanks to God, seeing in you one who 'having heard the word of God, kept it'." In another letter he writes: "I send you advice, recalling you as my long, most dear friend, as it is

---

[77] Manuscript no. 23/1262, formerly found in the St. Petersburg Ecclesiastical Academy, but now found in the Saltykov-Ščedrin Public Library in Leningrad. Arxangel'skij, *op. cit.*, pp. 124–125.
[78] Kologrivov, I., *op. cit.*, p. 194.
[79] Letter to Gurij, fol. 102B.

written: 'I open my secrets to the sons of my house'. " He continues by
frankly admitting: "For that reason I now write you, speaking frankly
about myself because your love for God forces me and makes me irrational, even to the point of writing you about myself."[80]

In writing to the noble-monk Kassian who in his youth had suffered
many sorrows, both physical and mental, Nil seems to relive through
his intense sympathy and love for Kassian all that Kassian had suffered.
Such phrases appear often:

> For this reason, dear brother, am I deeply moved in soul, perplexed in
> conscience, interiorly rent as I recall even from your youth how many sufferings
> and misfortunes you had to bear, your imprisonment and exile from your
> native land of birth... I cannot bear, o my loved one, to keep my secret in
> silence, but I become foolish and lose my head *(ivrod)* when there is question
> of helping a brother, because this is true love; that one does not hide any
> secret from one's loved ones... O dear one... O lover of Christ.[81]

Nil's exercise of Christ-like forgiveness and clemency shown towards
heretics in contrast to Joseph Volokolamsk and Metropolitan Gennadius
of Novgorod we will treat later in a separate chapter.

Thus we see Nil is far from ignoring the intimate relationship between
love of God and love of neighbour, but his practice of this fraternal
charity is always in subordination and a means to further divine charity
in his soul. He concerns himself exclusively with one end–increase of
divine charity in his soul. His exclusive will to establish God's kingdom
in his soul forces him to cherish silence and solitude away from men.
This same end makes him prompt and ready to teach, advise, help in
any way, that is, spiritually, that will not only not diminish the internal
divine charity, but will even increase it in his soul and in the souls of
others.

Besides practising an apostolate of fraternal charity by one's *presence*,
either by actively teaching those who come seeking advice or passively
by mirroring one's virtues so as to be a concrete example to the world
of a faithful imitator of Christ,[82] there is another way of exercising the
apostolate. This second means is that of mere *existence*. The hermits

---

[80] Letter to German, fol. 104A, 105A.
[81] Letter to Kassian, fol. 365A, 374B.
[82] Climacus on this point preaching by example dedicates *Gradus 22* to warn the
monk of vain glory that comes often from this apparently wholesome desire. "Do not
believe the winnower when he suggests that you should display your virtues for the
benefit of the hearers... Nothing so edifies our neighbour as sincere and humble
speech and manners; for this serves as a spur to others never to be puffed-up And
what can be more beneficial than this?," 952C–D. Cf. also *Gradus 26*, 1020D–1021A.

and the hesychastic skete fathers whom Nil follows so closely in his spirituality had a greater realization than we do to-day of the truly good effected by such consecrated souls in the salvation of souls. Their departure from visible communion with other men must be seen through their deep faith and charity for God and men. The concept of *koinonia* was a reality that they meditated on constantly in their reading of the New Testament, expecially about the unfolding of Christian unity through fraternal love in Jesus Christ that they read about in the early Church founded after Pentecost. They separated from men in order the better to be united with them, for by concentrating all their efforts on loving God-Charity personified, they became intimately united with the children of God.[83]

The monks took literally St. Paul at his inspired word. They were united into a mystical unity with all other members under Christ their one Head. If one member was injured, the others came to the aid. No one member existed or laboured for himself alone, but for the "fulfillment of the whole body, that is Christ". Thus Nil, along with his predecessors, sought silence and solitude, refused to take any direct initiative to go out among men, not because they were self-centred and egoistic, but, rather, because they were completely Christ-centered they were drawn closer to one another. It would not be going astray from our topic to illustrate this important point by a quotation from Dorotheus. This will explain Nil's insistence on concentrating all attention on God while at the same time growing in more intense and more pure love for his neighbour.

Imagine a circle having a centre and radii jetting out from this centre. The farther these radii project from the centre the farther are they separated from other another. And conversely, the closer they come to the centre, the closer they are to one another. Take now this circle as the world; the very centre of the circle is God and the radii jetting out from the centre to the perimeter and from the perimeter back to the centre are the paths of men's lives. Here we can observe the same thing. In proportion as the saints move inwards towards the centre, desiring to approach nearer to God, so in that degree of their proximity, they come closer to God and to one another. Nearer to God they are nearer to one another; and inasmuch as they become nearer to one another, they become nearer to God. The same holds for drawing away. If they draw away from God, they withdraw from one another; and if they draw away from one another, so they draw away from God. Such is the characteristic of love.

---

[83] Cf. Hausherr, I., "L'hésychasme...", *op. cit.*, p. 22. Evagrius had written: "A monk is he who is separated from all and united to all." *PG*, 79, *De Oratione* CXXIV, 1194C. His instructor Origen earlier had written: "Saints through contemplation are united to God and are united one to another." *Prov.*, XVI, *PG*, 17, 196D.

When we are outside and do not love God, we are far from our neighbour. But if we love God and approach ever nearer to Him through divine love, so we become united by that same love with our neighbours. And in the degree that we are united with our neighbours, so we are united with God.[84]

This brings us to a principle that is found implicit in Nil's writings, but, as it was not expressed in such terms by the early Fathers, Nil also leaves it implicit, yet nonetheless quite evident to him and his followers: "Any progress made in perfection by one member in the Mystical Body of Christ has a salutary effect on the whole Body as a whole and on each individual member making up that Body." There is a repercussion in the whole Body, insofar as progress to restore all things in Christ is advanced by the sanctity of the individual member. An eye of perfect 20/20 vision must naturally add to the perfection of the whole being just as the defect of imperfect vision lessens the perfection of the whole. Nil in his hidden skete hermitage, far from the commerce of men (he confessed this was one reason attracting him to the swamps of the Sora), was contributing to the holiness of the whole Christ by growing daily in more intense, individual perfection. By the mere existence of such holy monks in the Church, the health of the whole Body was that much increased.

This point has been developed somewhat at length because we feel that herein lies one of Nil's chief contributions to Russian monasticism. True, all monasticism in Russia before and after Nil's lifetime had as its primary scope the glory of God and the sanctification of its members. But no one in Russia hitherto nor do we believe afterwards (except for individual saints who lived a similar life as Nil but who were not concerned primarily with founding a system of spirituality for others to follow) stressed as he did the importance of the individual perfection of the members as having more salutary effects by the mere ontological existence of their perfect union with God as opposed to the active presence of the monks working more or less in direct contact with souls.

Full activity in our way of life consists in this, that always in every detail, in every undertaking with soul and body, in word, thought or deed, as far as there is in us strength, we remain in the *work of God*, with God and in God. Blessed Philotheus says that it is befitting such as we living yet in the world, surrounded by its vanities, enslaved to the mind and all the senses with sinful vanities, that we begin to live for God, with our whole mind and all our senses, working only for the living God and seeking always His truth and holy will by fulfilling His holy commands and to remove all that is unpleasing to Him.[85]

[84] Dorotheus, *PG*, 88, 1696C–D; cited by Hausherr, I., "L'hésychasme...", *op. cit.*, pp. 22–23.
[85] *Ustav*, p. 36. Philotheus, *Philokalia*, *ed. cit.*, T. II, ch. 3, p. 285.

It is this perfection of the individual monk, preferably hidden from the sight of men, that must be sought after with avidity, Nil tells us in his general rules for his skete-life.

It should be noted that "the work of God" (delo Bozee) for Nil is the same as that for the Fathers of the desert and those who followed them, "Our hermits, monks, hesychasts ... love solitude only in order by means of it to accomplish "the work of God" – it is St. Anthony who was the first to use this phrase in the desert – and they believed that this work of God, as all the others, has for unique principle that of Charity for the unique end to establish the kingdom of God-Charity."[86]

The crucial issue that divided the camp of Nil's followers from the followers of Joseph Volokolamsk on the point of monastic poverty is basically one of seeking the best means to attain love of God through perfect fulfillment of love for the neighbour. For Nil, as we have shown at length, the most perfect service his monks could give to the neighbour was that of living as perfectly as possible the life of a monk, as he conceived him: one who left the world and all finite creatures in order to contemplate and glorify the Infinite. If men came to him seeking spiritual advice, or to be edified by his example, this was accidental to his primary purpose. And it was accidental also that by becoming as perfect as possible in his hidden life, he would become a light atop a mountain for all the world. But again it was God who would implant in the hearts of men the knowledge to understand their sins. "Let God alone admonish them for He is powerful to correct them."[87] It is not for the monk to call attention to God's workings in himself, but the obligation is entirely on the neighbour to open his eyes and not be blinded to the flaming light on the mountain top.[88]

---

[86] Hausherr, I., *op. cit.*, p. 23.
[87] Letter to Gurij, fol. 101B.
[88] Cf. Hausherr, I., "La Théologie...", *op. cit.*, p. 408. Cf. also the excellent article in the same volume written by Dom Adalbert de Vogue, O.S.B., "Monachisme et Église dans la pensée de Cassien", pp. 213–240. He makes the daring assertion that monks dedicated entirely to self-perfection, which means full charity where perpetual prayer flourishes in purified hearts as if in a natural state, are not to work through preaching the word in building up the Church, but rather in "*being*" the Church. They imitate the Apostles and such an "apostolic" life excludes an apostolate in our modern sense. (pp. 233 and foll.)

V

SOURCES OF NIL'S TEACHING

In the second half of the 19th century Russian scholars turned to the Greek Fathers as to the primary source of Russian spirituality. Especially was this true among the Slavophiles who were bent on showing a traditional teaching preserved in the Russian Church that had its beginnings in the primitive teachings of the early Fathers up through the later Byzantine writers, climaxing with Gregory Palamas. Scholars, such as A. Arxangel'skij, I. Sevyrev, Porfirij, Sreznevskij, Gorskij and Nevostruev, G. Iljinskij, and A. Sobolevskij, utilizing the oldest Slavonic manuscripts in Russia, tried to work out a history of translated works found in the Russia of the 11th till the 16th century.

Nil Sorskij is often dismissed with a few lines concerning his stay on Mt. Athos and his *Ustav* based on the "Skete Fathers".[1] The first Russian to discuss at any length Nil's dependence on the Fathers for his literary ideas was A. Arxangel'skij in a rather long chapter entitled: "The Literary Sources of Nil's Ideas".[2] The author contents himself with a general analysis of the main lines of doctrine found among such Fathers as Cassian, Climacus, Nil Sinaite, from whose works Nil drew most of his patristic quotations. Only in presenting Cassian's teachings on the eight vices as found in the last eight chapters of his *De Coenobiorum Institutis* does Arxangel'skij descend to particulars and proves the evident dependence of Nil for his fifth chapter on the eight passions.

The only other work, and quite superior as far as it goes, which treats the patristic influence on Nil's spirituality is a report given by a young doctorate candidate on the studies he made concerning the moral teaching of Nil Sorskij as found in the patristic sources of Macarius of Egypt,

---

[1] Cf. e.g. Radčenko, K., *Religioznoe i literaturnoe dvizenie v Bolgarii* (Kiev, 1898), pp. 5–8; and Syrku, P., *K istorii ispravlenija knig v Bolgarii v XIV v.* (St. Petersburg, 1898), T. 1, pp. 241–242.

[2] *Op. cit.*, pp. 137–184.

Isaac the Syrian, Basil and Cassian.[3] He shows a great deal of scholarship, especially in working out the moral teaching of Isaac the Syrian. But in any such detailed work, any author is necessarily confronted with the same problem: once one has checked the Fathers for the citations quoted by Nil, he is tempted to work out, as Levickij did, a careful moral system of the Fathers most frequently quoted by Nil and then to settle for the conclusion that these are the sum and substance of Nil's spirituality. As we have already taken pains to work out Nil's spirituality from his writings and, in every case where it could be checked, to cite the corresponding reference given by Nil or vaguely hinted at by him, it seems best to approach this subject by considering the following points: (1) the Fathers whom Nil quotes; (2) the question of texts available to Nil; (3) Nil's dependence; and finally, (4) Nil's originality.[4]

A. THE FATHERS QUOTED BY NIL

Nil approaches the Fathers much differently than other early Russian spiritual writers, as for example, his contemporary Joseph Volokolamsk.[5] Nil is not concerned with finding in the Fathers an authority to substantiate his own teaching, but he quotes them principally as a disciple quotes a master. He tells his reader over and over that what he writes is not his own, but that doctrine taught and lived by the Fathers.[6] His purpose is not to give new, original ideas of his own but to be faithful to the teachings of the Fathers, for their writings are the "waters of life" which will quench human concupiscences and guide men to the truth.[7]

Among the Fathers serving as a source of Nil's spirituality one can distinguish two categories. Firstly, those Fathers whom Nil quotes often and to whom Nil is evidently more inclined in regard to their general lines of spirituality, such as Climacus, Isaac the Syrian, Gregory Sinaite,

---

[3] Levickij, G., "Otčet professorskogo stipendiata G. Levickogo o zanjatjax v 1889–90", in *Xristianskoe Čtenie*, 1895, 2, 3, pp. 287–345. Lur'e, *Ideologičeskaja...*, *op. cit.*, p. 292, says that Levickij never published his work. This I was able to affirm for myself when I was in the USSR in 1969.

[4] A third work that treats the patristic influence on Nil's ideas is the work of Doctor Fairy von Lilienfeld, *Nil Sorskij und seine Schriften. Die Krise der Tradition im Russland Ivans III* (Berlin, 1963).

[5] Cf. J. Volokolamsk, *Prosvetitel'* (Kazan', 1857), p. 63. Cf. also Spidlik, T., S. J., *Joseph de Volokolamsk...*, *op. cit.*, p. 24: "Et ainsi en estil de tous les autres Pères... Ilsont pour lui le 'sable de la mer' oú il cherche et recueille ce qui lui plait ... quelque texte, quelque aphorisme dont le sens est plus ou moins bien interpreté."

[6] *Predanie*, p. 2.

[7] *Ustav*, p. 14.

Simeon the New Theologian. Secondly, other Fathers quoted a few times directly or not even cited, but whose ideas influenced Nil's thoughts. Taking his main literary works, the *Predanie* and the *Ustav*, we can readily see which Fathers were for Nil his favorite sources of spirituality. He quotes 31 patristic writers, but the names frequently repeated are few. The numbers in parenthesis indicate how many times Nil quotes the given writer in his two works: Climacus (35), Isaac (33), Gregory Sinaite (27), Simeon the N. T. (18), Basil the Great (10), Barsanophius (8), Nil Sinaite (6), Philotheus Sinaite (5), John Chrysostom (4), Ephrem the Syrian (4), Hesychius Sinaite (4), Peter Damascene (3), Maximus Confessor (3), Dorotheus (2), Arsenius (2), Nicetas Stethatos (2), Macarius (2), Anthony (2), Daniel the Hermit (2), Gregory the Great (Pope of Rome) (2), John Damascene (2), Pachomius (1), Agathon (1), Simeon Studite (1), Mark the Hermit (1), Diadochus (1), Theodore Studite (1), Gregory Nazianzen (1), Andrew of Crete (1), German, Patriarch of Constantinople (1), Eugenia Martyr (1).

In other parts of his writings, including all his letters, there is a constant repetition of the phrase "the Holy Fathers say", or, "as the Holy Fathers taught", or the equivalent, without any specific Fathers cited. When one reads the Fathers cited above, he is struck by a sameness of doctrine. Whether one searches in the *Life of St. Anthony* by St. Athanasius, or in the treatise on prayer of Evagrius, falsely attributed to St. Nilus Sinaite, or John Climacus' *Ladder of Christian Perfection*, in the writings of Isaac the Syrian, Simeon the N. T. or Gregory Sinaite on mystical prayer, one ever returns to key, fundamental principles about the spiritual life. The teaching about a monk's total devotion to the *unum necessarium*, his own perfection, complete withdrawal from the world, praise of solitude and silence, call to constant warfare against the evil spirits, constant remembrance and living in the presence of God, control of all thoughts as a necessary condition to arrive at *apatheia* without which contemplation of God in this life is impossible, all these points are touched on with the same insistence and with the same presentation by Nil's favorite Fathers. Thus when he introduces a new subject, he invariably begins with this general phrase of guarantee that this is not an original teaching of his own, nor of one individual Father, but "The Holy Fathers have spoken" thus.[8] This "sureness" that Nil manifests in attributing to the "Holy Fathers" a point in his spiritual doctrine indicates his com-

[8] Cf. the first paragraph of nearly every new chapter of his *Ustav*: pp. 11, 16, 20, 33, 36, 38, 61, 62, 71, 80.

plete familiarity with their writings, but, more so, with his spirit of the
Fathers. He had so integrated their common doctrine into his own spiritual life that, whether he was quoting them in general or as individual
Fathers or presenting his own spiritual experiences, there seems to be
little difference in the language or the thoughts expressed. Nil thinks and
writes patristically. Their vocabulary is his everyday speech as we can
see jetting out from the very personal, conversational tone found in his
letters.

B. QUESTION OF TEXTS USED BY NIL

P. Peeters has justly said that one can say generally that the Christian
literatures of the Orient are largely off-shoots of Greek Christian literature.[9] This can safely be applied as well to Slavic spiritual writings.
The newly converted Russians found a precious heritage of patristic
spiritual writings which had already been translated by the Bulgarians
from the original Greek texts in the ninth and tenth centuries. It was SS.
Cyril and Methodius' first preoccupation in evangelizing the southern
Slavs to give them the Holy Scriptures, the liturgical books, and the writings of the Fathers in their native, Slavonic tongue. Under the Bulgarian
king, Simeon, the 10th century ushered in the golden age of Slav-Bulgar-
ian literature, that is to say, translations of the Byzantine literature.[10]
Among these translated works, which formed the nucleus of early Slavonic literature, were the most important Byzantine hagiographical com-
pilations and ascetical treatises produced between the fifth and seventh
centuries: the *Apophthegmata Patrum*, the *Book of the Holy Men;* the
Lausiac History of Palladius; the *Historia Monachorum;* the *Historia
Religiosa* of Theodoret of Cyrus, the *Pratum Spirituale* of John Moschus,
and the *Scala Paradisi* of St. John Climacus.[11]

---

[9] Peeters, P., *Le Tréfonds oriental de l'hagiographie byzantine* (Brussels, 1951), p.
166, as cited by Heppell, M., cf. footnote 10 that follows here. Cf. also Priselkov, M.
D., *Istorija russkago letopisaija XI–XV vv.* (Leningrad, 1940); and Uspenskij, F. I.,
"Očerki po istorii vizantijskoj obrazovannosti", St. Petersburg, 1891.

[10] Cf. the article "Svedenija o drevnix perevodax tvorenij sv. otcev na slavjano-russkij
jazyk" ("Data on the early Slavonic-Russian translations of the works of the Holy
Fathers"), in *Prav. Sob.*, III (1859), p. 254 and foll. No author's name is given, but it
probably was written by by A. Arxangel'skij, because the article repeats in substance
the facts contained in Arxangel'skij's work: *K izučeniju drevnerusskoij literaturij tvo-
resnija otcov cerkvi v drevne russkoj pis'mennosti*" ("Towards a study of ancient Russian literature compositions of the Fathers of the Church in early Russian writings")
(St. Petersburg, 1888). This latter is found also printed in *Z. P.N.P.*, 1888.

[11] Heppell, Muriel, "Slavonic Translations of Early Byzantine Ascetical Literature",
in *Journal of Eccles. History*, 5 (1954), no. 1, April, p. 86.

In the other periods of translations made and transported to Russia, we find Greek monks in Russia itself, commissioned by Tsars and Princes to provide them with desired works translated from the Greek. Jaroslav, son of Vladimir, set up what we could call the first Russian library composed of books which the Greek and Bulgarian monks had translated into Slavonic.[12] Russian monks from the 11th to the 15th century in notable numbers journeyed to Constantinople and Mt. Athos to consult the works of the Fathers, especially various *typica* or monastic rules, as we learn in the history of Theodore of Pečerskaja Lavra near Kiev.[13] But the greater number of translations, especially of a strict ascetical and contemplative nature, come from the Russian monks inhabiting Mount Athos between the 12th and 15th centuries. The revival of hesychasm on Mt. Athos, due to Gregory Sinaite (†1360), insured the Slavonic translations of any Father who had written a treatise that touched on some phase of this spirituality. At the height of this translation activity Nil himself took up his abode on the holy mountain where these translations, plus the original Greek texts, were available to him. Added to these works of the Fathers translated directly from the Greek into Slavonic were numerous Slavonic manuscripts translated from the Greek *Pandectes* (Greek for 'collection') of the monks Antiochus and Nikon. Nikon's *Pandectes* and his *Taktikon* (lit. the book of order or discipline) were perhaps the two most famous and most consulted "collections" of patristic writings used in Russia. Nikon of Montenegro, a monk living in the 11th century, hoped to hand down to his Moslem persecuted Christian brethren an encyclopedia of citations from the Fathers and the church teachers on all topics touching Christian life, of importance both to the laity as well as to monks and clerics. With the scarcity in Russia of even Slavonic translations of longer works of the Fathers, this collection proved most practical. One need only to check the works of Joseph of Volokolamsk and Vassian Patrikeev, the well-known disciple of Nil Sorskij, to see how highly regarded was Nikon of Montenegro and how often he was utilized by contemporaries of Nil.[14] Nil himself must have been thoroughly familiar with Nikon's *Pandectes* and his

---

[12] "Svedenija o drev. perevod...", *op. cit.*, p. 355.

[13] Cf. Bodjanskij gives the 12th century ms. of the "Zitie Prep. Feodosija" written by Nestor (Slavonic) in *Čtenija Obšč. istor. i drevn. ross.*, 1879, I, p. 11A (Slavonic numbering).

[14] Cf. articles: " 'Prosvetitel' prep. Iosifa Volockago" in *Prav. Sob.*, III (1859), pp. 153–179. Also, "Polemičeskija sočinenija inoka knjazja Vassiana Patrikeeva (XVI)", ("The Polemical Compositions of the Prince-monk Vassian Patrikeev (XVI century)"), also in *Prav. Sob.*, III (1863), pp. 180–200, also p. 98.

Taktikon. Although he never mentions Nikon by name and there remains no way of checking his quotations due to inaccessibility of these *Pandectes* manuscripts found only today in Russia in Slavonic or in the satellite countries,[15] nevertheless it is safe to assume, along with the anonymous author of the article in *Pravoslavnyj Sobesednik*, that Nil relied heavily for his quotations upon Nikon's two works.[16]

It would be beyond the scope of this work, which is concerned primarily with the presentation of the spirituality of Nil, to present here a detailed research on the Slavonic manuscripts of the Fathers quoted by Nil.[17] But the above information provides a background for understanding the sources that were available to Nil in his patristic reading and writing. In the use of these sources did Nil quote directly from the Slavonic manuscripts or from the Greek originals? Surely during his stay (and it must have been a fairly long one[18] on Mt. Athos) he became quite conversant in Greek and could thus have had easy access to the Greek manuscripts as well as those in Slavonic translation. It would not be unplausible to think Nil also made copious citations in his own handwriting which he could have carried back to Russia. But during the actual writing of his *Rule*, considering the difficulty of getting original Greek manuscripts and also the nature of his literary work which was not a scientific, critical edition of the Fathers, but merely an "instruction" for his followers, we can incline more to the opinion that he used the Slavonic translations, either through his own personal notes written while on Mt. Athos and in Constantinople, or from available Slavonic translations that he had in his Sorskij skete.[19] A closer examination of his *Predanie* and *Ustav* text in Slavonic proves that in general Nil used in his quotations of the Fathers a Slavonic translation. To prove this,

---

[15] Sreznevskij, I. Z., *Svedenija i zametki o maloizvestnyx i neizvestnyx pamjatnikax* ("Data and notes about little known or unknown manuscripts") (St. Petersburg, 1874), pp. 96, 217 gives an adequate history of the *Pandectes* of Nikon and the Slavonic manuscripts with a detailed description of the latter. Some Slavonic mss. date from the XII century and hence have special importance in view of the fact that mss. of the same work in the original Greek language only date to the XIV century (as the Paris mss.). The *Taktikon* is even more important because there exist no Greek mss. Cf. *op. cit.*, p. 218.

[16] *Op. cit.*, pp. 384–385.

[17] This has already largely been done. Cf. Sreznevskij, E., *op. cit.*, footnote 14. Also his *Drevn. pam. russk. pis'm. i jazyka* (St. Petersburg, 1863). Cf. also Gorskij, A. and Nevostruev, K. I., *Opisanie slavjanskix rukopisej moskovskoj sinodal'noj biblioteki* ("Description of the Salvonic Manuscripts of the Moscow Synodal Library") (Moscow, 1855, 1857); Makarij, *Istorija...*, *op. cit.*, vol. V, pp. 247–248.

[18] Arxangel'skij, *Nil Sorskij...*, *op. cit.*, p. 181, footnote 44.

[19] Levickij, G., *op. cit.*, pp. 290–291.

one would have to consult the Slavonic manuscripts of the Fathers quoted by Nil, found in the Russian libraries. As these are unavailable I must rely on the few passages available from Slavonic manuscripts of Fathers quoted by Nil and compare them with Nil's Slavonic text along with the available Greek text.

Using a text from a 15th century manuscript provided by A. Arxangel'skij, a Slavonic translation from the Greek text of Gregory Sinaite's hesychastic instruction: *De Quietudine et duobus Orationis Modis*[20] and comparing it with Nil's Slavonic citation in the *Ustav*, we find the same words used and the same word order.[21] If we juxtapose this Slavonic citation translated into English alongside the same passage found in the Greek text of Migne we can see clearly that Nil used the Slavonic text rather than that of the Greek.

Old Slavonic Manuscript Text and

Nil's Slavonic Citation:

If you see, he says (Gregory), the impurity of the unclean spirits, that is to say, evil thoughts rising up in your mind, do not be frightened, nor do not wonder at this. If even good thoughts of certain things appear to you, do not attend to them, but hold your breathing as much as possible and locking your intellect in your heart, like a weapon, call out to the Lord Jesus often and with diligence...

Greek Text:[22]

If you indeed see unclean thoughts of the evil spirits, namely, the logismoi, rising up or taking the shape of images in your mind, do not be alarmed. And if good thoughts of things appear in your phantasm, do not pay heed to these, but, controlling the breathing as far as is possible and enclosing the intellect in the heart, frequently and perseveringly make the invocation of the Lord Jesus...

Another example is provided by the Old Slavonic text of Nil Sinaite (Evagrius), *De Oratione*, where Nil Sorskij's Slavonic text is an exact copy: "During prayer one should strive to render the intellect deaf and dumb."[23]

---

[20] We know that by the 15th century Gregory had been already translated into Slavonic. Cf. Gorskij and Nevostruev, *op. cit.*, II, 2, p. 446.

[21] *Ustav*, pp. 22–23. Arxangel'skij, *Nil...*, *op. cit.*, footnote 44, p. 180.

[22] *PG*, 150, 1316C. Gregory quotes from Climacus, *Gradus 21*, 945D. *Ustav*, p. 21.

[23] Manuscript no. 154 in the Moscow Synodal Library, Mss. of the XIV–XV cent., fol. 98, as cited by Arxangel'skij, *Nil...*, *op. cit.*, p. 179, footnote 44. The Greek text if found in *PG*, 79: *De Oratione*, 11, 1169C.

Oftentimes Nil, desirous to shorten a text, uses a quotation, not direct but in a general phrasing as he does for example with a quotation from Climacus. Not even recognizing Climacus as author, Nil merely says: "Like a dog picking up scraps from under the table, I have gathered the words uttered by these blessed Fathers..."[24] Climacus' phrase goes: "Having gathered what fell from the lips of those learned and blessed fathers as a dog gathers the crumbs that fall from the table..."[25] This might be an example of Nil, forgetting his source, but remembering the key-idea, which, meditated on frequently by him, became a part of his being. Looking for a "kenotic" expression of his unworthiness before the blessed Fathers, he instinctly chose that phrase of Climacus without ever giving heed to his master.

C. DEPENDENCY ON HIS SOURCES

If a writer such as Nil professedly sets out to reproduce what certain Fathers had written about various phases of the spiritual life, we cannot then blame him for being dependent on the Fathers for his ideas. But Nil was dependent on the Fathers in a special loyalty that stemmed from his basic premise in the spiritual order. To find the will of God, one had to explore God's revelation, the written or the oral word, which for Nil, in far-off Trans-Volga, was to be found in the Holy Scriptures and tradition, transmitted and commented on according to the true, apostolic teaching of the holy Fathers. Thus Nil, from this principle plus his deep humility, could hardly set out to write a spiritual instruction for his disciples and rely solely on his own original ideas. He was not creating new ideas, nor was he "plagiarizing" his sources; he was handing on the heritage of teaching common to the great Fathers on the spiritual life or at least some limited phase of it. This attitude is important to keep in mind in weighing Nil's merits as an original writer.

The 31 patristic writers whom he quotes in his *Predanie* and *Ustav* show his conscientiousness in citing his sources as much as possible. But he shows through his own citations his preference for Climacus, Isaac the Syrian, Gregory Sinaite, Simeon the New Theologian and Nil Sinaite. To ascertain the general lines of similarity in the doctrine of these Fathers as reflected in his two main works. I have, in presenting Nil's spiritual ideas in the earlier chapters, given, as far as I could, corresponding pas-

---

[24] *Ustav*, p. 14.
[25] *Op. cit., Gradus 25*, 988D.

sages of these Fathers in the footnotes, so it should not be necessary to repeat here each quotation in detail.

The dependency on Climacus is not only acknowledged by Nil in his numerous direct quotations, but also from his quotations drawn from other Fathers such as Gregory Sinaite who often, when Nil cites them, are themselves merely quoting from Climacus, or at least heavily influenced by his general doctrine.[26] The influence of Climacus on the Sinaite hesychastic Fathers was only too evident to Nil and hence he himself relied much more on him than on any other Father quoted.[27] The thoughts expressed by Climacus in his *Scalae* provide Nil not only with general thoughts, but specific quotations on renuntiation of the world and a perfect spirit of detachment (*Gradus 1, 2*).[28] On remembrance of death (6); on *penthos* (7); on freedom from anger and on meekness (8); on silence (11); on *acedia* (13); on gluttony (14); avarice (16); poverty (17); vainglory (22); pride (23); humility (25); discernment of thoughts and passions and their opposite virtues (26); *hesychia* (27); prayer (28); *apatheia* (29). It has already been pointed out the direct dependency of Nil on Climacus in the first chapter of the *Ustav* where Nil uses Climacus' doctrine on the various degrees of psychological development of thoughts, leading up to passion.[29] If the general lines are those of Climacus, nonetheless, we can see Nil's independence when Climacus' doctrine is inadequate or does not fit in with the general plan of Nil's total system. This is brought out clearly in the swerving from Climacus by omitting the psychological step of "struggle" (in Greek *pali*).[30] Nil begins this topic on the process in a thought-temptation by quoting Climacus and Philotheus Sinaite, mentions that "other Fathers" also taught similarly. Had he read Mark the Hermit's presentation against the Messalians, perhaps the first Father to give these distinct moments of a temptation?[31] Other Fathers who treated this topic, such as Peter

[26] An example of this is the passage in the *Ustav*, p. 23, where Nil quotes Gregory Sinaite that the prayer of the heart is the source of all good (virtues) and refreshes the soul as if it were a garden. Gregory is obviously taking his quotation and doctrine on mental prayer from Climacus, *Gradus 28*, 1129B.

[27] Climacus was early translated into Slavonic, perhaps between the X and XI centuries, first in Bulgaria, then later in Serbia in the 14th century. Cf. Arxangel'skij *K izučeniju...*, *op. cit.*, p. 90.

[28] Cf. Part Two, ch. II, B: Psychology of Thoughts, of this present work. The numbers that follow refer to Climacus' various *Gradus*.

[29] Levickij, G., *op. cit.*, treats well this point. Cf. p. 278.

[30] *Ustav*, pp. 17–18.

[31] *PG*, 65, *De Baptismo*, pp. 1013–1021. Cf. Hausherr, I., "L'hésychasm...", *op. cit.*, p. 278.

Damascene,[32] Hesychius of Sinai[33] and Philotheus Sinaite,[34] all followed essentially the presentation of Climacus. Yet in each Nil must have found some progression enabling him to modify Climacus' teaching. Peter Damascene clearly saw the inconsistency of Climacus in putting the "struggle" after the will had already been in "capture" *(aichmalosia)*, so he inserts it in a more naturally psychological position, between the "conversation" *(sunduasmos)* and the "consent" *(sugkatathesis)*. Hesychius simplifies even more, giving four principal moments: presentation *(prosboli)*; conversation *(sunduasmos)*; consent *(sugkatathesis)*; and sensible habit or sin *(aisthiti praxis-amartia)*.

Philotheus and Hesychius, being undoubtedly the last in this series of Fathers, go the next step and drop out completely the "struggle" moment *(pali)*. This is in complete keeping with Philotheus' exact mind and economy of words in giving definitions.[35] Here we see Nil's freedom in leaving Climacus and following the scheme of thought-temptation development given by Philotheus and Hesychius. Both Nil and Philotheus stressed the "active" side of the asceticism of thought-control and mental purification as a preparation for prayer. The whole spiritual life was a battle against thoughts, especially bad ones. It is clear why both Nil and Philotheus withdrew "struggle" from the psychological development of a temptation. A monk was to pass each moment armed and ready against the slightest introduction of a temptation. In the actual development of the temptation, "struggle" should be present in each moment, especially as Nil says: "A wise and excellent means of struggle, as the Fathers tell us, is to uproot the thought at the very first suggestion, that is, at the presentation when the thought comes to us."[36] Nil, after finishing in Chapter I the treatment of the five steps, goes back to Climacus' definition of "struggle" *(pali)*: "Struggle, according to their (the holy Fathers') definition, is power equal to the attacking force, which is either victorious or else suffers defeat according to the soul's desire;"[37] and brings it in the beginning of the second chapter on the struggle against these temptations of the mind.[38] Thus we have a good example of how Nil depends on a Father or several Fathers; yet, as will

[32] *Philokalia, op. cit.*, T. 3, pp. 109–11.
[33] *PG*, 93, *Cent.* I, § 46, 1496C.
[34] Dobrotoljubie, T. 3, *op. cit.*, no. 34–36, pp. 459–460.
[35] Cf. Hausherr, I., "La Méthode...", *op. cit.*, p. 141.
[36] *Ustav*, p. 20.
[37] *Gradus 15*, 879A.
[38] *Ustav*, pp. 20–21.

be pointed out in treating of his originality, Nil uses the ideas of the Fathers, but orders them according to his own preconceived plan, so as to attain the greatest unity and order in his presentation. Nil is far from being a mere "collector" or anthologist of patristic texts.

In general, one can say that Nil's general orientation towards a hesychasm of strict thought-control *(nepsis)*, leading to tranquillity *(hesychia)* through the means of perpetual mental prayer and the constant living in the presence of Jesus Christ, have their primary source in Climacus. On these lines, so characteristic of the Sinaite spirituality,[39] Nil depends also in his quotations on Gregory of Sinai, Simeon the New Theologian, Hesychius Sinaite and Philotheus Sinaite, but evidently their prime source remains always Climacus.

Nil's dependency on Cassian poses a unique problem as Arxangel'skij has taken such pains to point out. "In the *Ustav* of Nil Sorskij ... the Russian author takes direct borrowing (not large ones) from the composition of Cassian *(De Institutionibus Coenobiorum)*, using sometimes Cassian's own words (and not quoting his name);"[40] and in the footnote Arxangel'skij explains: "...Nil Sorskij, citing Cassian's words, never quotes his name, that which he usually does with great conscientiousness and accuracy in relation to the other ecclesiastical writers whom he quotes. How to explain this fact, we do not know... But the name of Cassian was well-known even in early Russian literature (seen by the manuscripts quoted ... and his closest disciple, Innokentij Oxlebinin, in his Preface to the *Predanie* many times quotes words of "Saint Cassian to support himself."[41] The places where Nil relies on Cassian in his central Chapter Five of the *Ustav* are indeed many and have been already cited and compared with the corresponding places in Cassian's *De Inst. Coen.*[42]

That Cassian was well-known, read and appreciated by the monks of the Sinaitic spirituality in the 7th century (and through Climacus in the following centuries) is clear from Climacus' statement: "From humility comes discernment as the great Cassian has said with beautiful and

---

[39] Cf. Hausherr, I., "La Méthode...", *op. cit.*, pp. 134–142.
[40] Arxangel'skij, *Nil...*, *op. cit.*, p. 150.
[41] *Ibid.*, footnote, no. 8. If however the "Nadslovie" or Introduction to Nil's *Ustav* was not written by Innokentij, but, as Borovkova-Majkova suggests, by Vasilij in 1767 (in Moravia in the monastery of Paisij Veličkovskij) then this frequent mention by name of Cassian would be quite understandable. Cf. her "Nil Sorskij i Paisij...", *op. cit.*, p. 32.
[42] Cf. this present work, Part II, Ch. II, C: "Analysis of the Eight Sources of Passions", footnotes, no. 38, 40, 41, 42, 49, 52, 53, 55, 60, 61, 67, 77, 81, 82, 88, 97.

sublime teaching in his chapter on discernment."[43] His *Institutiones* were early translated, perhaps even in his lifetime, from Latin into Greek,[44] but in an abbreviated version. Migne presents under Pseudo-Athanasius an abridgement of Cassian's *Institutiones*, from Books X–XII, dealing with the main 8 passions.[45] Was this Pseudo-Athanasius text the source of Nil Sorskij's fifth chapter on the 8 passions? In Migne the Greek text is mutilated between the fifth passion sorrow *(lipi)* and *acedia* and precisely in these two points does Nil clearly turn away from Cassian's teaching as found in Books IX and X of the *Institutiones*[46] and introduces divergent points either original or culled from other Fathers. This could have been the Greek text translated into Slavonic and used by Nil.[47]

Did Nil depend on Cassian and not cite his name as the source in the main for his teaching on the eight passions merely because he was using a Slavonic text that he knew was authentically not Cassian's but attributed to the supposed Pseudo-Athanasius or Nilus Sinaite? It is unimaginable that Nil, after having lived on Mt. Athos and in contact with Greek manuscripts and, above all, with hesychasts of Climacus' bent towards Cassian, should not have been aware of Cassian as having been the chief source for the teaching on the eight passions. Another hypothesis is that perhaps, because Cassian was a Latin who wrote the *Institutiones* for Latin monks in France, Nil did not want to quote by name the founder of Latin monasticism in France in an instruction for Russian monks. Though he personally may have realized how "Oriental" in spirit Cassian was through the latter's long travels in the East where he visited the various types of monasticism in Palestine, Egypt, Syria and Constantinople, yet Nil was bent on presenting traditional doctrine of Oriental asceticism as proposed by the well-known Eastern Fathers. And for the

---

[43] *Gradus 4, PG*, 88, 717; Cassian, *Conférences*, II, *op. cit.*, ch. X, p. 120. Cf. also, for Cassian's influence in the Orient, the article "Cassian" by M. Olphe-Galliard, S. J., in *Dict. Sp. A. et M.*, Tom II. col. 269 and foll.

[44] Arxangel'skij, *Nil...*, *op. cit.*, p. 149, footnote 7.

[45] *PG*, 28, 872C–D, under the title: *Second Letter to Castor*.

[46] *De Institut. Coen.*, *op. cit.*, pp. 166–193.

[47] Whether Nil Sorskij relied on the *De Octo Vitiis* attributed in Migne to Nilus Sinaite is greatly to be doubted. The scheme presented on the eight passions is too schematic, full of aphorism, and metaphors that found no room in Nil Sorskij's writing. Marsili, S., O. S. B., has compared the two texts, that from Ps.-Athanasius which is clearly an abridgement, as has been said, of Cassian, and that of Nil Sinaite, *De Octo Vitiis*, *PG*, 79, 1436–1464. The first part of each chapter of Nilus has the same phraseology and terminology as does Ps.-Athanasius and Cassian. His conclusion is that Nil is only an abridgement of Ps.-Athanasius which is an abridgment of Cassian. Cf. Marsili, S. O. S. B., "Resumé de Cassien sous le nom de St. Nil", in *RAM*, 15 (1934), pp. 241–245.

simple monks of the Trans-Volga, Cassian hardly was a name. If his works were known in Slavonic translations, as has been pointed out above and in footnote 45, the ordinary monk knew them as Athanasius or Nilus Sinaite. The fact that Innokentij, Nil's disciple, quotes Cassian often by name proves that he, like Nil, most likely became familiar with Cassian's works while on Mt. Athos and in the East the companion of Nil.

Nil quotes directly Basil the Great only ten times but this does not indicate by any means the great esteem Nil evidently had for him and a general dependency in many key points of Nil's spirituality. In his theory about monasticism and in his rules for external conduct and relations with fellow-monks, Nil was undoubtedly influenced greatly by Basil. The Cappadocian (†379) was in his day a reaction against the rigid, letter-of-the-law discipline that prevailed in Pachomius' monasticism. Nil found in his own Russian contemporary monasticism a spirit that stifled spontaneity, allowing no scope to the individual direction of conscience and he must have found support in the writings of Basil. Both of them stress the necessity of the individual monk to get in harmony with God's mind and will; thus the intellect seeks to know at each step what is God's will through His commandments; the will gives life and fecundity to all human activities, thoughts, desires, words or external actions by a free choice in performing the will of God out of Divine love.[48] Others, especially in the Sinaite hesychastic tradition such as Climacus and Philotheus,[49] stressed the fidelity to the commandments of God as the source of all asceticism and virtue and hence the guard over the mind, but even these authors were dependent on Basil, for he was the first to work the doctrine of the "commandments" into a system of asceticism. T. Spidlik, S. J. has well demonstrated Basil's doctrine on the commandments in his recent work, *La Sophiologie de S. Basile*.[50] Both for Basil and Nil, the commands of Our Lord in the New Testament were the sole and sufficient norm for action and conduct of life. These commands found in Holy Scripture freed the individual's highest potentialities for good. Faithful obedience to them was the only true sign of Divine life. When Nil wrote in one of his letters the following, had he not been putting into practice Basil's similar teaching? "I do not act unless I find proof in the Divine Writings... For when I must do something, I first search the Divine Writings and if I do not find anything

---

[48] Cf. Hom. in Ps. 48, 8, *PG*, 29, 449BC; *Quod Deus non est Auctor mali*, 6, *PG*, 31, 344BC, 345B.
[49] Cf. Philotheus, *PG*, 154, pp. 729–746.
[50] *Op. cit.*, pp. 36–39, 161–171.

in agreement with my understanding on how to begin a work, I lay it aside until I do find something."[51]

Basil writes similarly: "That every word or affair must be confirmed by the testimony from Divine Scripture in order to be persuaded to embrace only the good and to avoid the shame of evil."[52] The same insistence on reading the Holy Scriptures, in order to find the will of God, to resist the devil, to apply the best spiritual medicine to our wounded nature, is repated over and over by both authors. Basil makes the Holy Scriptures the one rule for the monk,[53] while Nil reiterates the same teaching with a literal simplicity that shocks us, used to a more juridical concept of monastic direction and obedience: "We have but one teacher, Our Lord Jesus Christ who gave us the Holy Scriptures . . ."[54] And again he stresses: "Study the Scriptures and you shall find eternal life in them." "Bind yourself to the laws of Divine Writings and follow the true Divine Writings . . ."[55]

As for the interpretation of the Holy Scriptures, we find a similar emphasis on the charismatic or prophetic quality in the teacher or interpreter. Both insist that only the man, who is guided by the Holy Spirit, possesses the same Spirit that wrote the Sacred Scriptures and so he is alone able to interpret them according to the mind of the same Holy Spirit. And above all, great care was to be exerted by the monk to choose a "pneumatic" guide.[56]

Basil's attitude against the anchorite life was the same as Nil's: a solitary hermit never corrected the faults or faulty tendencies in his nature due to the lack of guidance and from the nature of the solitary life which prevented social contact and hence the possibility of developing necessary virtues to off-set natural weaknesses of character. The life in a community, for Basil, a coenobitic community, for Nil, an idiorhythmic life of two or three, gave the opportunities for exercise of humility, patience, and charity, while the solitary life offered a snare of illusions coming from self-complaisance and even spiritual pride.[57]

But perhaps more in Basil's sense of moderation and "common sense" do we find the greatest indirect influence on Nil. We see this especially in the similarity of rules or counsels given in regard to mortification and

[51] Letter to Gurij, fol. 103A.
[52] *Mor.* 26, 1, *PG*, 31, 744CD.
[53] *Reg. Brev.* 1, *PG*, 31, 1080C–1081A.
[54] *Predanie*, p. 2.
[55] Letter to Gurij, fol. 102B.
[56] *PG*, 32, 296B; *Ustav*, pp. 13–14.
[57] *PG*, 31, 928C–933b. *Ustav*, p. 88.

fasting or temperance. All of the works of God are good and thus, in eating, a monk should partake of a bit of everything.[58] The golden mean of prudence is put into practice by both in not prescribing a set rule common to all in the amount of food to be taken. Each monk is to determine for himself what is in keeping with his physical needs in order to carry out his daily work.[59]

Basil was perhaps the first early spiritual writer to stress in a formal way that work done with a pure motive to please God was also a way to fulfill St. Paul's injunction to pray always. A monk could thus remain constantly in the presence of God by seeking only to please God as Nil expresses it in Basilian terminology in giving general rules of daily conduct: "We must continually keep our mind in a disposition of great reverence, piety and trust in God, and do all we can to please Him, and not for the sake of vainglory or to please men; for we have it for certain that God dwells within us, since He is everywhere and fills everything."[60] Basil's disposition of mind for doing good *(diathesis agathi)*[61] is repeated constantly by Nil to his followers. The repetition of the Jesus Prayer has the same end: not to produce any interior illumination of celestial (and physical at the same time, as the Palamists held) light, but to render the soul supple to the slightest inspiration of the Holy Spirit.

Isaac the Syrian is quoted by Nil, as we have already seen, sufficiently frequently. Nil clearly turns to him on matters touching temptations of the mind and the means to combat these, on constant prayer and higher forms of contemplation and very particularly in Nil's treatment of the gift of tears. Although Isaac was a Nestorian of the seventh century, his Christological errors did not enter into his spiritual treatises.[62] He wrote in Syrian but early his writings were translated into Greek and became most celebrated throughout the whole Byzantine world. Isaac in turn was influenced greatly in his theory of contemplation by the works of Evagrius Ponticus.[63] It would be safe to say that Nil is greatly indebted to Evagrius whom he comes to know through his knowledge of Isaac and more directly through his knowledge of Nil of Ancyra who is called by Nil Sorskij, Nil Sinaite, and to whom Nil attributed the treatise of

---

[58] *PG*, 31, 965B. *Ustav*, pp. 42–43.

[59] *Reg. Fusius Tract.*, *PG*, 31, 16, 958–959; 18–20, 966–970. *Ustav*, p. 41.

[60] *Ustav*, p. 36.

[61] *In Ps. 44*, 8, *PG*, 29, 405B.

[62] Cf. Viller M. and Rahner, K., *Aszese und Mystik in der Väterzeit* (Freiburg im Breisgau, 1939), pp. 245–246.

[63] Cf. Hausherr, I., "Evagre le Portique: 'Traité de l'oraison' ", in *RAM*, 14 (1933), pp. 196–198.

Evagrius, *De Oratione*.[64] Nil, in his letter to Kassian, seeking to comfort
him in his sufferings and persecutions, quotes extensively from Isaac
whom Nil calls "the child-loving Father Isaac the Syrian", "this heavenly Father", "this amazing Father",[65] thus indicating the great esteem
in which he held Isaac. But it is especially when Nil is searching for a
description, as so often happens in his second chapter of the *Ustav*,
of the higher, mystical forms of contemplation that he relies on Iaace
and quotes from him directly.

It is especially here also in the second chapter that Nil relies on Simeon the New Theologian to supply him with descriptions similar to those
offered by Isaac, of the mystical experiences accompanying the "prayer
of the heart". Simeon, abbot of the monastery of St. Mamas in Constantinople (†1022), had himself been greatly influenced by Mark the
Hermit and Diadochus of Photike with their "consciousness" of the
workings of the Holy Spirit in the soul as a sensible awareness. This
influence however reached an exaggerated point with Simeon insisting
that, if the Holy Spirit's operations were not felt in some physical way
in the soul, one was not in the state of sanctifying grace.[66] Mysticism
is for all, and his descriptions are graphically described so as to give the
ordinary lay man a burning desire to enjoy similar mystical experiences.

We must note, that, although Nil uses Simeon's descriptions of such
mystical raptures, depicted in most appealing and clear language, his
innate sense of proper measure and deep humility makes him use the
descriptions, not as something to be desired for by his followers to the
neglect of more solid virtue, but rather as a stimulus to greater humility
and compunction. After quoting Simeon's vision in his cell where he
beheld a "light which the world does not see..., while He (God) is in
heaven, He is at the same time in my heart, and I behold Him, here and
there", Nil reflects that he and his followers, so burdened with many sins
and a constant prey of passions, are unworthy even of hearing such
sublime words. Simeon and Isaac, with their mystical ravishments, were
spiritual giants, and for Nil their mystical flights serve to make him aware
of the degradation in which he wallows, of the waste of his precious time
with the trivialities of this world. He concludes that the way of the saints

---

[64] We have already made reference to Hausherr's work. *Les Lecons d'un Contemplatif.
Le Traité de l'Oraison d'Evagre le Pontique* (Paris, 1960), "Introd.", pp. 5–8, where
he shows Evagrius to be the true author of *De Oratione*. On the problem of Nil cf. also
Heussi, K., *Das Nilusproblem, Randglossen zu F. Degenharts neuen Beiträgen* (Leipzig,
1921).
[65] Letter to Kassian, Ms. 185, fol. 370B, 372A.
[66] Cf. Hausherr, I., "La Méthode...", *op. cit.*, pp. 121–123.

is opened to us, but it is God who favours those who seek this goal of higher contemplation with great love and fear, in obedience to His commandments and through a life of constant prayer.[67] Simeon, along with Isaac, furnishes Nil with his doctrine about the mystical gift of tears, above all, of the absolute necessity, as Simeon insisted always, of praying constantly to God for this gift.[68]

Just as in reality, Simeon the New Theologian during his lifetime did not succeed in creating a renaissance of hesychasm, but influenced greatly Gregory Sinaite and prepared the way for the great hesychastic revival of the 14th century on Mount Athos, so, too, it is Gregory Sinaite, who has the greatest influence on Nil in his doctrine about hesychasm. Next to Climacus and Isaac, Gregory Sinaite is quoted the most and referred by Nil always as "the blessed Gregory". The esteem Nil had for Gregory is seen, not only by these frequent and long quotations from Gregory's writings on hesychasm, but also by the *encomium* Nil pays him: "This blessed Father who so well understood the writings of all the "pneumaphoric" (spirit-bearing: *duxnonosyx*) Fathers and carried them out in his own life."[69]

We have already pointed out in the chapter treating of Nil as hesychast how dependent Nil was on Gregory, for his teaching on the Jesus Prayer, even for the formula used, for the very few mechanical aids suggested, especially the controlled breathing. But even here Nil shows his independence by not accepting completely all of Gregory's suggested mechanics, preferring only to suggest the one on controlled breathing and ignoring the others given by him. Also in the use of the Jesus Prayer, Gregory seems much more insistent than Nil on the exclusive use, even when fatigue and distractions overcome the monk, where Nil seems to see the Jesus Prayer more as a means, to be changed and other means to be substituted when fatigue or serious distractions overcome the monk.

Gregory, throughout all his writings, shows much more moderation than Simeon and perhaps for this reason Nil was attracted to him, not only as to a teacher of mystical contemplation but also as to a teacher of beginners, perturbed with fighting temptations. Gregory did not intend, as also Nil, to be original, but rather to collect together what the hesychastic Fathers, especially those of the Sinaite tradition, had to say on this hesychastic spirituality. Thus his works are full of quotations from the Fathers, yet produced in a clear, synthetic manner so as to be

[67] *Ustav*, pp. 30–31.
[68] Simeon the New Theologian, in *PG*, 120, 136, 672; 140, 676.
[69] *Ustav*, p. 23.

instructional and useful for all monks in the three spiritual stages leading to perfection. Undoubtedly it is this traditional link between Gregory and the earlier hesychast Fathers along with his clear instructions for all stages of the spiritual life that appealed to Nil and made him esteem Gregory so highly.

Another point of dependence is seen in a quotation attributed to Gregory by Nil and still more in the general "kenotic" spirit of deep humility that permeates Nil's writings, especially his letters. Nil's testament is a typical example of this debasement of the self in which Nil begs his followers to cast his body in the desert to be devoured by the beasts and birds, "for that body has greatly sinned against God and is unworthy to be buried..."[70] If they refuse him this, at least, he begs them to dig a pit in the ground and bury him in it with every sort of dishonour. Nil must have meditated long on the words of Gregory on how to develop humility:

Are there in the world sinners whose sins are equal to mine?... No, my soul, you and I are worse than all men, we are dust and ashes under their feet. How can I help considering myself the most despicable of all creatures, when they behave according to the order of their nature, whereas I, owing to my innumerable sins, have sunk below my nature... Truly I am the lowest of all, since I have brought myself down into hell and am lying there even before death...[71]

The influence is marked in Nil's words in Chapter 5 on pride: "Let us consider ourselves to be lower than everyone else, the least among men, the most perverse of all creatures, since we are addicted to unnatural vices, in a worse state than the devils who attack us by force..."[72]

Again this kenotic spirit of Gregory is seen admired and quoted by Nil when he deals in Chapter 3 with the means to repel evil thoughts. Debasement before God is the best means to insure God's continued assistence with His grace and to foster true compunction and humility before the attacks of the demons. When we are conscious of God's infusion of grace in our soul, says Nil, we should thank God and recall the numerous sins we have committed. One should recall the bestial condition that his nature is in, considering the impure images that rise up in the mind. Then Nil quotes directly Gregory on the necessity of crushing oneself before the almighty God.

---

[70] Ms. no. 188, from the Troice-Sergieva Lavra (now in the Lenin Public Library of Moscow).
[71] Gregory Sinaite, *PG*, 150, 1279C–D.
[72] *Ustav*, p. 57.

For, as blessed Gregory of Sinaite says: 'Until a man has experienced abandonment and failure, until he has been covered with wounds, enslaved by every passion, and conquered by the thoughts in his mind, so that he can find help, neither in turning to his own strength, nor in God, nor in anything else. When he is driven to the very edge of despair with no seeming way out, then only can man witness what true contrition is and then only can he understand that he is the least of slaves, more evil than the demons that attack him'.[73]

And very often one sees this attitude repeated by Nil in his *Ustav* and letters, showing his sincere conviction that he is an unworthy sinner, incapable of doing any good in himself, capable only of asking God pardon.[74]

These authors constitute the main source for Nil's ideas. The other authors whom Nil quotes less frequently offer him specific quotations, but do not provide him with the general hesychastic lines that he found in his favourite authors. One important point to note about these remaining Fathers who had an influence, at least in providing Nil with quoted ideas: all of them are well-known authors, such as John Chrysostom, Ephrem, Nil Sinaite, Philotheus, Hesychius, Maximus Confessor, Dorotheus, Macarius, Anthony, John Damascene, to quote only a few. No strange, rarely-heard of author enters Nil's writings.[75] And above all, Nil cuts clear from any dependency on authors prone to allegory genres, metaphorical speech, examples drawn from animal life and applied to man and so on. This shows Nil's sense of balance and moderation and also indicates his dependence by choice on those authors known for their solidity of doctrine. It is quite true Cassian, Climacus, and Nilus Sinaite abound in aphorisms and analogies drawn from animal life, but here precisely do we see that Nil's dependence never is slavish, but he depends on these Fathers for their ascetical and psychological ideas insofar as they fit in with his preconceived plan for his *Ustav*[76]

---

[73] *Ibid.*, p. 35.

[74] *Predanie*, pp. 2, 4. *Ustav*, pp. 14–15, 30, 31.

[75] Compare the list given by Spidlik, T., S. J., *op. cit.*, pp. 22–23, quoted by Joseph Volokolamsk, which includes such "Fathers" as George Hamartolos, Nicetas of Heraclea, Thalassios, Philon and even Josephus Flavius.

[76] Several points that touch on the dependency and originality of Nil as an author are developed at length by M. Borovkova-Majkova in her article: "K literatyrnoj dejatel'nosti Nila Sorskago" ("Concerning the Literary work of Nil Sorskij"), in *Pam. pis'm. i issk.*, 1911, CLXXVII. The author points out:

(1) Arxangel'skij in his work *(op. cit.)*, p. 72, attributes the letter "O inokax, kružaj uščix stjažanij radi" to Nil. But she prints the complete text from the ms. of the Kirill-Belozerskij Monastery alongside the text from Migne, *PG*, 79, 437 of Archimandrite Nikon. It is the identical text. Perhaps it is an exact translation of Nil of

The reader is referred to the many references made to the Fathers of the desert in the chapter on Nil's spirituality whom Nil usually groups under the general title of "Fathers" without any specific quotation from any individual. This means, in the mind of Nil, that he is passing on a doctrine that has its roots in the earliest times of Christian asceticism and monasticism, as one can check and find similar teaching in the *Apophthegmata Patrum*,[77] *Historia Aegyptiorum Monachorum*,[78] *Historia Lausiaca* of Palladius,[79] or the *Vitae Patrum*.[80]

Ancyra, done by Nil Sorskij and hence Nil is not really the author of this letter, but is only the translator. Cf. *Appendix*, I, ftnote no. 76.

(2) Arxangel'skij attributes to Nil as quite possibly the authorship of the composition: "nest' ubo dobro eže vsem čelovekom xoteti ugodnu byti" (*op. cit.*, p. 62), text reproduced by Arx. on p. 121), but Borovkova-Majkova suggests that as the first work is clearly not Nil's, but Nil Sinaite's, and that this same initial phrase beginning this composition follows in the Kirill-Belozerskij mss. with the same words as the above composition, i.e. "also Nil's", but we know that the first work was only his translation of Nil Sinaite's composition; thus most probably this work too is to be attributed to Nil Sinaite as author and Nil Sorskij as translator.

(3) Uvarov prints a work that he claims for Nil. But this same work is printed in *Čtenie moskov. obšč. ist. drev. ross.*, Moscow, 1847, part IV, p. 3, K, as a letter written by Joseph Volokolamsk. Therefore sometimes it is found as by Joseph's and at other times as Nil's.

But it might be explained in this way: oftentimes two authors' works will be joined together by a scribe or mutually mixed up inadvertently. But a comparison of the texts establishes it as a letter of Nil, expecially from the theme of the Greek Fathers in the second half of the letter and the utter lack of formal dogmatism that dominates all of Joseph's writings. We can only suggest, as often happens in the copying of manuscripts, that the copyist began a letter of Nil, inserted a few lines from Joseph's writings on the Novgorod heresy, and then continued the letter of Nil. Another suggestion: with loose sheaves of manuscripts, the least ones dealing with Joseph's letters on the Novgorod heresy, were mixed among those of Nil's letter and copied as a part of it. It would have been mixed among those of Nil's letter and copied as a part of it. It would seem right to deduce from the general tone of the letter (the inserted part) and the other writings of Nil that Joseph's work was accidently inserted into Nil's letter in the process of transcribing it.

It is interesting to note here that J. S. Lur'e, the Soviet authority on Nil Sorskij and his times, uses this letter with the insertion from Joseph's work against the Novgorod heretics to prove an absurd hypothesis that Nil Sorskij was of the same ilk as Joseph. Lur'e concluded after citing Borovkova-Majkova's article: "Whatever way we take it, one thing is clear: the use by Joseph of Nil's work in his struggle against the heretics shows the nearness between the two writers. Joseph saw in Nil a fellow-sympathizer in his struggle against heresy." Cf. Lur'e, J. S., "K voprosa ob ideologii Nila Sorskogo", ("Concerning the question of the ideology of Nil Sorskij"), Akad. Nauk, USSR, *Trudy Otd. drev. lit. instit. russkoj lit.*, T. XIII (1957), p. 194.

[77] *PG*, 65, 71–440.
[78] *PG*, 65, 442–456.
[79] *PG*, 34, 991–1278.
[80] *PL*, 73–74.

D. INDEPENDENCE IN THE USE OF THE PATRISTIC WRITINGS

In Nil's *Predanie* and *Ustav*, the Fathers are directly or indirectly quoted; the ideas are all patristic, for that is his very purpose. But even in these two works Nil manifests a great deal of independence and originality in the use of his sources. There is little doubt, especially in reading his letters, that Nil was a strong-willed personality. This trait, added to his intellectual acumen and practical knowledge of the Fathers' writings, makes his one purpose in writing stand out clearly before the reader and all other considerations are accidental and subordinated to the final end that he has in mind. His purpose in the *Ustav* is to present the doctrine of the Fathers on the mental battle, on the means necessary to conquer the devil in the individual's heart in order, through constant mental (interior) prayer, to live in permanent presence of God, supple to His holy will. With this single purpose in mind, Nil marshalls his patristic texts in an admirable unity and singleness of scope. Thus the *Ustav* appears to be a carefully laid out literary mosaic, producing a composite picture to the consternation of Levickij who takes Nil to task for the one-sided interpretation of the spiritual life with very little positive description of progressive moral growth leading to a clear image of perfection and the virtues.[81] Undoubtedly Nil shows his individuality in his interpretation of the spiritual life and the role of asceticism in his stress of the "battle" motif and he never cites the Fathers except insofar as they are witnesses to some phase of his master-idea.

Thus Nil shows a clear detachment from his sources, especially from his favourite authors as Climacus, Cassian (from whatever source he may have drawn Cassian's teachings) and Nil Sinaite, in the absence of any legendary elements, practically no cited example that these Fathers so abound in, no metaphors, utter lack of aphorisms and rhetorical figures of speech. He uses their psychological interpretation, as we have already seen, of temptation and the eight passions, but only as a practical means to an integrated "battle" against any obstacle to union with the Divine Will. One has the impression that not one quotation from the Fathers is superfluous. Nil shows a severe economy in his quotations due to the personal conviction of the central theme that he wants to convey to his readers. Thus we see that he has thought out for a very long time and

---

[81] Levickij, G., *op. cit.*, pp. 337–345.

has become thoroughly convinced about the necessity of his theme. No one could ever accuse Nil of being a mere compiler of patristic sayings. His ordering of these sayings is too original and too independent of his sources so that the final result is a new creation, and for Russian spirituality, a work of great value. Due to this originality in ordering his material, Filaret Gumilevskij does not hesitate to call Nil: "the great Father of the Russian Church".[82]

From Nil's letters we see his originality more as an author and one who must be rated as one of the best of the early authors in Russia before the 17th century. Here we find Nil using a style most spontaneous, a perfect command of language, with a sense for rhythmic flow of periods. The Fathers are quoted rarely directly, but he prefers to group their general teaching under some such general term as "the Fathers say". He reveals his own personality, his deep humility, sense of sin and compunction, his human tenderness towards his spiritual friends, his empathy in associating himself completely with the trials and difficulties of others. We see also his love and reverence of the Fathers and his desire, even in personal letters, not to veer one iota from their doctrine.[83] He has thoroughly steeped himself in their doctrine so that he needs no longer to refer to their works for direct quotations. He thinks in their language and thus one finds a symphony of his mind with their minds. He has practised well the advice he gave to Vassian "Learn some passages by heart from the Holy Scripture, concentrate your mind on this, for such passages turn back the attack of the devil."[84] Verses flow spontaneously from his pen from the New Testament, the Gospels and the Letters of St. Paul, plus the Psalms; never forced; always in harmony with the context.

At times he reaches sections in his letters that suggest a highly imaginative soul of high literary quality. In his letter to Kassian, wishing to give him motivation for bearing with patience and even joy the sufferings that have come to him, Nil writes:

The earthly angel, John, the Lord's Baptizer, did he not sit in prison? Did they not cut off his head with a sword? And then with tainted hands it was carried on a dish before the gluttonous feasters. O, holy head, that looked on God and saw the Light of Dawn. O, education in the desert even from swaddling clothes! Likewise the Prophet Elias suffered much and was carried in a flaming chariot to Heaven. About the Apostles, Holy Martyrs, our Confessors and Fathers, what is there to write? They all suffered many and diverse deaths,

[82] *Istorija russkoj cerkvi 3rd Period (1410–1588)*, (Černigov, 1862), p. 142.
[83] Letter to Gurij, fol. 107A–B.
[84] Letter to Vassian, fol. 96A.

misfortunes, slayings and imprisonments for the sake of the heavenly Kingdom, and all these in strange lands, among infidels and savage barbarians, they preached the name of Christ. Some of them were crucified, some pierced by a lance, others given over to fire or the sword, others, tied with stones, were drowned in the sea, others devoured by beasts as ground-up food. And what more can we quote? Did they not all rejoice in their sufferings of evils and sorrows?[85]

Another example of this deep sympathy towards the sufferings of others moving him to write in a very personal, moving manner is found in the same letter to Kassian:

For this reason, brother, am I moved deeply in soul, perplexed in conscience, interiorly rent as I recall even from your youth your many sufferings and misfortunes, your imprisonment and exile from your native land of birth and from your patria to a strange and unknown land with a foreign language and illiterate inhabitants and you moreover a son of most noble ancestors. How also the Lord delivered you in all these trials from many and diverse deaths; death from fire, from sword, from water; and He Himself all the time had a better plan in mind, for by these He led you to repentance and to a knowledge of the truth as God knows it. For this reason, namely, for our sins, has He inflicted on us temptations and sorrows and imprisonment. The Lord loves us and has mercy on us and wishes to instruct us with His wisdom by these trials. I rejoice over and over in the fact that the Lord still so loves us, that, not wishing to torture us in the future life, but here, He allows us to suffer in order to be purified from our sins.[86]

Besides showing an original spirit in ordering patristic thought to suit his over-all purpose, plus a command of language and a highly developed literary style for his times, Nil does show also much originality in the ideas he presents. Not that there are found ideas totally new and strange to patristic writings, but that Nil took what was often only in embryonic stage of development among certain Fathers and perfected the thought through his integrated synthesis that did not exist with the same build-up of accumulated ideas, one dependent on the other, prior to his time. Russian monks, before and even after Nil, had the Fathers, at least in Slavonic and Russian translations, but Nil's presentation of the patristic ideas would have a new and greater influence on the future Russian spirituality as we shall later see. Some of the key-ideas developed greater at length than had hitherto been known on Russian soil are:

(1) The emphasis on self-persuasion; rational, conscious activity; interior liberty. Nil cut through a labyrinthine maze of rules and canons

---

[85] Letter to Kassian, fol. 367B–368A.
[86] Ibid., fol. 365A–B.

that were stifling Russian monasticism through a dead formalism of obedience to the letter. Nil insisted with Basil the Great that man's greatest dignity was to be found in his intellect and will. These were the God-given faculties allowing man to perform actions worthy of an adopted son of God and heir of Heaven. But always the one condition for God-pleasing actions was that they flow from a free, conscious act of loving submission and obedience to the Divine Will.

(2) The guiding principle therefore for the spiritual life and for all moral actions was that of the interior spirit found in the Gospels and writings of the Apostles and as interpreted by the Holy Fathers and the apostolic tradition. Christ was the one teacher and His teachings were to be followed according to His mind which was found in the Church's tradition as recorded by the Holy Fathers.

(3) Thus he insists on a critical, scholarly approach to the sources of tradition in order to better understand the inner meaning of Holy Scriptures, in order to avoid the false and apocryphal writings, in order to sift the accidentals in Christianity from the essence. Seeking to get at the objective truth, the "mind of God", Nil avoids subjectivism as well as the dead formalism of the letter.

(4) Thus the exterior rules guiding the monk are always subordinated to the interior, spiritual perfection of the individual. They are reduced to a minimum in order to give maximum attention to self-perfection in the spiritual combat.

(5) This struggle for self-perfection Nil expresses in terms of a constant battle in this life against the forces of evil attacking principally the intellect and will. The counterattack consists in control of all thoughts through constant vigilance, climaxing in *hesychia* which is fostered and maintained by the spirit of *penthos* or lasting compunction for one's sins which in turn is nourished by thoughts of death, judgment and the gift of tears. Nil's insistence on constant prayer, but an interior prayer of intimate union of human intellect and will with the Divine, is in direct contrast with his times.

(6) Inflamed with this interior vision of spiritual perfection according to the spirit of the Gospels, Nil becomes a crusader for strict, monastic poverty, waging protest by his example and voice against the property-holdings of the Russian monasteries of his day. This is tied up fundamentally with his basic idea of what constitutes true monasticism. Nil was being faithful to the spirit of monasticism of the early Fathers of the desert whose spirit the Sinaite hesychast Fathers revived, where a monk's whole attention was given to his individual interior perfection. Cut off

completely from the world, such a monk had no need for property. He lived in the spiritual world and he practised fraternal charity in the same order, dispensing spiritual advice to those who came to seek it, but never immersing himself in charity which involved material possessions. Surely Nil was a strong reaction against the abuses brought about by an "active" form of monasticism which involved property-holdings. Necessarily Nil therefore exaggerated the strictly "spiritual" side of the hidden life. He does not show sufficient broadness on this point. He admits three types of legitimate monasticism, but even for the coenobitic life he would demand the same conditions of life and apostolate that he held out for his idiorhythmic or anchorite monks. Definitely on this point he is a most original reactionary on Russian soil as remains now to be shown.

VI

INFLUENCE OF NIL ON HIS CONTEMPORARIES

In the history of each nation there occur periods when the former existing order seems to have worn out its usefulness and new times demands radical changes. At such times Providence provides the leaders to effect such changes. Nil Sorskij and Joseph Volokolamsk were two of the leading actors in the drama that convulsed the latter part of the 15th and the beginning of the 16th century of Russia.

Historians, seeking to synthesize the complicated issues of this time, often content themselves with clear-cut, categories: Nil represents the interior, contemplative life, interior freedom, conscious persuasion; mercy towards heretics, evangelical poverty with violent protests against monastic possessions; while Joseph incarnates the antithesis, being for the social apostolate, external obedience to the letter of the law subject in all things to the Grand Prince, death penalty for heretics, absolute need of monastic holdings to carry on the religious vocation.[1] But history, as it unfolds, rarely falls into such clear-cut categories. It is therefore endangered, as J. S. Lur'e well points out in giving the picture of Nil as conceived by Russian historians in the past century, by false and incomplete interpretations.[2]

We do not intend to reproduce in all details the external events that took place in Russia of this time. As we are primarily interested in presenting the spirituality of Nil Sorskij, we must touch these historical events insofar as Nil's spirituality had an influential role to play in them.

Nil's writings and his own personal life bear witness to his conviction of the necessity of absolute separation from the world and its deceits.

---

[1] An example of over-simplification, cf. E. Behr-Sigel, *Priére et Sainteté dans l'Église russe, Collection Russie et Chrétienté* (Paris, 1950), Chapter 6: "Nil Sorsky et Joseph de Volokolamsk," pp. 76–88. Cf. also G. Fedotov: *Svjatye...*, *op. cit.*, pp. 166–175.
[2] Lur'e, J. S., *Ideologičeskaja bor'ba v russkoj publitcistike konca XV – načala XVI veka* ("Ideological Struggle in Russian Polemical Literature at the end of the 15th, Beginning of the 16th Century") (Moscow–Leningrad, 1960), pp. 285–296.

Nil's monk was to avoid as far as possible all contact with the world in order to avoid all possible distractions preventing the highest possible degree of contemplation and union with God in this life. But the times in which Nil lived and also his great love for fellow-men made contact with the world unavoidable.

Russia, under Ivan III, was seething with unrest and eager for unity and greatness as a nation. Ivan became officially "Tsar Ivan, Grand Prince, Autocrat of All-Russia".[3] His duties, after the fall of Constantinople in 1453 to the Turks, were "to care for all souls and all Orthodox Christendom".[4] The seeds of Moscow as Third Rome had been long ago planted and now were bursting forth in full fruit.[5] Backing the Tsar was the group of Moscow metropolitans such as Jonas, Phillip, Gerontius, Zosimus and Simon, eager to detach their ecclesiastical jurisdiction from that of Constantinople. Joseph Sanin (Volokolamsk, 1440–1515) was the leader of the monastic group ready to put all his forces behind the Tsar to bring about a centralized theocratic state. In his dynamic style Joseph formulated his theory of submission to the Tsar in these words: "He is the lord of all lords in the whole of Russia. God has given him all power and his name is the all-powerful One (vsederzitel'-pantokrator). God has placed him on the imperial throne, being of one mind with him in judgment and grace..."[6] But far from contributing to the Tsar's absolute power,[7] the same dramatic Joseph could write: "If there is found a tsar ruling over men who rules for himself, full of low passion and sin, avarice and anger, evil and injustice, pride and ire, most evil of men, unbelieving and corrupt, such a tsar is not a servant of God, but a devil, not a tsar but a tormentor..."[8] The limitations which Joseph was placing on the Tsar's power was that he rule always in conformity

---

[3] *SGGD* (*Sobranie Gosudarstvennyx Gramot i Dogovorov:* Collection of Governmental Degrees and Treaties), vol. II, no. 25, p. 27.

[4] *Ibid.*, p. 29.

[5] Cf. Denissoff, E., "Aux Origines de l'Église Russe autocéphale", in *Revue des Études Slaves*, 1947, pp. 66–88; Medlin, W., *Moscow and East Rome* (Geneva, 1952); Schaeder, H., *Moskau das Dritte Rom, Osteuropäische Studien*, Vol. 1 (Hamburg, 1929).

[6] "Epistle of Joseph to Tret'jakov", cf. Xruščov, *op. cit.*, p. 226. also in *Čtenija*, 1847, no. 8, "Smes".

[7] Zimin, A. A., "O političeskoj doktrine Iosifa Volockago", in, *TODL*, T. IX (1953), pp. 159–177. He divides the historians who treat Joseph's political theories into two classes: those who hold that Joseph favoured absolute authority for the tsar' and those who maintain that Joseph supported the monarch only insofar as the latter favoured Joseph's aspirations, especially his social apostolate. For a treatment on Joseph's relations with the Muscovite power see T. Spidlik, "Joseph...", *op. cit.*, pp. 139–144.

[8] *Prosvetitel'*, *ed. cit.*, pp. 324–5.

with the laws of God as interpreted by the canons and Church laws handed down through the centuries.

But, as Father G. Florovsky well points out (and often overlooked by historians), Joseph's religious ideal was motivated by his great desire to approach the masses, to elevate their economic, social and religious status.[9] Thus his whole political theory of Church and State relationship was moulded out of the needs he had for financial support and independence of action. This also determined the whole form he gave to his monastic Rule with its heavy emphasis on monastic possessions.

That Nil's ideal would clash sooner or later with Joseph's was merely a matter of time. There is not question merely of two men differing as to whether it were religiously more perfect to have or not to have monastic possessions, to persecute heretics or to show mercy. Here there was at stake two different concepts of monasticism and the means best adapted to attain personal perfection.[10]

Nil's spirituality exerted a quiet, subdued influence on his generation and on those of the future by his zeal in copying and spreading throughout Russia corrected versions of the writings of the Fathers and the Lives of the Saints. His loyalty to "divine writings "and the spirit of the Holy Fathers also provided a stronghold of conservatism in the Trans–Volga region. In his age, when so many of the hierarchy and the princes were desirous of breaking off from dependency on Constantinople, Nil favoured any and all Apostolic link with tradition.

Nil complains that his contemporaries find it "impossible to live according to the Scriptures and the precepts of the Fathers".[11] "Nowadays one does not see in the monasteries an observance of the laws of God according to Holy Writings and the Tradition of the Holy Fathers, but rather we act according to our own wills and human ways of thinking, and oftentimes we fall to the very seduction and do such things, all the while considering them as acts of virtue."[12] "Some of them do not even

---

[9] *Puti russkago bogoslovija* (Paris, 1937), p. 18. The same idea is expressed by J. Meyendorff: "Une Controverse sur le role social de l'Église. La querelle des biens ecclésiastique au XVIe siecle en Russie", in *Irénikon*, 1956, pp. 30, 162.

[10] Kadlubovskij delineates these two opposite views well in his book: *Očerki po istorii drevnerusskoj literatury zıtij svjatyx* (Warsaw, 1902), pp. 327–373.

[11] *Predanie*, p. 3.

[12] Letter to German, fol. 104A–B. See *Appendix*. Lur'e, *op. cit.*, p. 320, claims Nil's complaint here and a similar one against contemporary monasticism are directed against the monks exclusively of the Kirill-Belozerskij Monastery, but from the spirit expressed by Joseph and his later followers, we can safely claim that this was a universal tendency and that Nil actually was seeking in his modest way to set up a small skete monastery that would be as faithful as possible to ancient monastic traditions, as a reaction to a general laxity among his contemporaries.

wish these days to hear this for they would say: 'They were not written for us and it is impossible even for our present generation to observe them'."[13]

Perhaps he had already in mind Joseph and his counter-influence who only too readily repeated in his eclectic manner similar sayings culled from the Fathers, but his patristic tradition in practice became all too frequently local Russian tradition that he himself determined as the exigencies arose. Using strong language against those who preferred to interpret the Divine Writings for themselves, claiming that a superior had no right to do more than comment on the written word of the Fathers, Joseph replies in his *Rule* quoting Nikon Montenegro: "Thus in olden times it was so and even now it is becoming that each superior, as long as he is in his own monastery, is to formulate or to hand down teaching in conformity with the Divine Writings, and to give instruction in words and also in writing (Rules). The subjects must not be contentious or do anything or say anything to the contrary, but must do exactly what is said by the father (superior)."[14]

There was too much of Nil's freedom and spirit of individualism in the air to suit Joseph. The commandments of God must be observed, but as given by the Fathers in their writings, they remained too vague, too imprecise and too susceptible to conforming to one's own will. *Samocinie*, the following of one's own will, is the greatest evil to a monk's salvation.[15] This "rational" spirit of independence among the Novgorod heretics was one of the main reasons why Joseph could so readily link the Trans-Volga Starcy with the Judaizer heretics.[16] This same spirit that Nil propounded for his chosen ascetics, according to Joseph, was spreading among the masses an undesirable tendency to inquisitiveness, a yearning after knowledge so that "now in the houses and on the streets, in the market places, monks, laymen, all sorts of people are doubting, enquiring into and testing their faith".[17] Even if Nil wanted to remain hidden in his Sora hermitage, he and his followers were drawn into the Judaizer controversy, not only by their indulgent attitude towards the heretics, but also by their basic principles which oftentimes used the same formulae as the heretics.

---

[13] Letter to German, fol. 107B.
[14] *Velik. Čet'i Minei*, Vol. I, Sept. 15, col. 547.
[15] *Ibid.*, col. 530.
[16] Cf. Arxangel'skij, *Nil...*, *op. cit.*, pp. 277–281. Also, Fennell, *op. cit.*, p. 508.
[17] "Epistle to Nifont", in *Čtenija*, 1847, no. 1, "Smes".

In the famous letter "Pismo o neljubkax" (Letter on dislike between the Starcy of the Kirill monastery and those of Joseph's), the author[18] gives as the third cause of the lack of love between Joseph's and Nil's followers: "the heretics of Novgorod showed false repentance and were not sincere. The Starec Prince Vassian believed them and interceded on their behalf before the Grand Prince and with him other bishops and starcy. Hearing these things, Joseph wrote to the Grand Prince, telling him to believe their false repentance but to keep them permanently in prison so that they may not lead astray the others. And the Grand Prince yielded to Joseph. This was the third lack of love."[19] Here we have clearly Nil's followers pleading for clemency on behalf of the Novgorod heretics. What can be said of Nil's position this heretical sect?

From his writings and the spiritual image we have already assembled of Nil, it is safe to affirm that his general attitude to heretics, as to all sinners in error, was one of mercy and gentleness. His fidelity to the Apostolic traditions made him begin his *Predanie* with a Symbol of Faith, ending with his avowal: "I and all those with me reject the heretical teachings and traditions of false teachers; and may all heretics ever be foreign to us."[20]

He would be adamant about swerving one iota from the traditional teachings of the Holy Fathers and the Councils of the Church. But in his personal relationship to heretics he would seek to avoid them as much as possible, insofar as arguing with them destroyed the environment for proper prayer. He exhorts Gurij to break off such discussions: "But you, o man of God, do not have anything to do with such men; it is not fitting even to converse with such, not even to reprove or correct them. Let God do this, for God is powerful to correct them."[21]

But when one is forced to choose between truth or heresy, Nil exhorts heroism even to martyrdom in defence of the truth. "Prophets died for the truth, but false prophets spoke to please men and loved to gossip. For whatever you wish, choose: either be concerned for the truth and be ready to die for it and thus you will live forever, or seek to please men, to do all in order to be loved by them, but hated by God."[22]

---

[18] It is generally conceded by all that, from the tone of the letter, it was written by a Josephian. Lur'e says it was written at least not before the 30's or 40's in the 16th century. Cf. "K voprosu...", *op. cit.*, p. 195.

[19] *Loc. cit.*, p. 506.

[20] *Predanie*, p. 3.

[21] Letter to Gurij, fol. 101B, cf. *Appendix*.

[22] Letter VI of St. Nil, Elagin edition (St. Petersburg, 1864), pp. 197–8. Cf. *Appendix I* of this work.

In a composition on "How to overcome vanity", attributed to Nil, we find the same sentiments of Christ-like condescension towards sinners that we found reflected in his other writings:

Do not regard yourself in your heart as being of sharp intellect, nor hold yourself as holy or already saved. Do not correct another for some sin, not even if you see him doing such with your own eyes. Do not judge a sinner as guilty of judgment or torture, but attribute his sin to Satan. ...But rather think of yourself as the greatest sinner of all... They (certain mentioned saints) bore patiently all evils as though they were really not evil and prayed to God for those who inflicted on them insults. They did not reckon the sins of others as sins but as ignorance on their part.[23]

Christ as the only teacher and true model of kenotic forgiveness of enemies is held out by Nil for his followers' imitation:

Recall, brother, what great evil the Jews did to Our Lord Jesus Christ, but God, the Lover of mankind, still did not become angry with them, but prayed for them to the Father, saying: 'Father, forgive them this sin, for they know not what they do'. ...Recall the words of the Apostle Paul who said: 'Do not return evil with evil, but conquer evil with good works'. ...If you wish to be shown mercy by God and be forgiven, cease from anger and put off all enmity.[24]

This gives us a basis for judging Nil's mind from his writings in regard to heretics. These quotations show a passionate love for the truth which for Nil is found in the living traditions that come down through the Holy Scripture and the writings of the Holy Fathers. Contact with heretics is to be avoided as far as possible on two accounts: one, such discussions destroy the spirit of recollection and prayer; the other, their erroneous doctrine is a turning away from the Apostolic traditions and hence false to divine revelation.

But when charity demands direct contact with them, a monk should seek not to correct them, but to pray to God who alone can enlighten their minds to see the truth. The monk shows a spirit of Christ-like condescension and sympathy for the sinner, forgiving him any harm inflicted or any error promulgated, for a monk will be forgiven his own sins in proportion to his mercy and clemency shown to fellow-sinners. From these bits then we can proceed to examine Nil's actual contact with the Novgorod heretics as history has so sparingly recorded it for us.

[23] Letter VIII, *ibid.*, p. 201.
[24] *Ibid.*, pp. 204–5.

The heresy of the Judaizers burst out in Novgorod between 1470–1480. This northern region of Novgorod and Pskov was the highly developed commerce centre of Russia, due to the direct contacts with the West and also the spirit of initiative and individualism of its people. Here in the latter part of the 14th century arose the first important heresy in Russia, that of the *Strigol'niki*,[25] a rationalistic group which demanded moral reform from the churchleaders and from the monks.[26] The Judaizers who followed the *Strigol'niki* one century later thus had the way prepared, for both heresies revolted against the Church authorities and insisted on individual, subjective interpretations of the founts of revelation. Historians who treat the Judaizers are divided into three groups:[27] those who, relying entirely on Joseph's writings, see it as a clearcut form of Judaism against Christianity;[28] the second group, led by N. A. Rudnev,[29] modifies the Judaism as a *mélange* with Christian rationalism; while the third group links up the heresy with the culture movements that entered into Russia through the southern Slavic countries, especially from Bulgaria and Serbia.[30]

A view that embraces all three seems to be the right one if one is to judge from the assertions of Gennadij who saw not just one species of Judaism but a whole complexity with various shades of "Marcionism and

[25] Cf. Golubinskij, E., *op. cit.*, t. III (1900), p. 396; Panov I., "Eres' židovstvujuščix" ("The Judaizers' heresy"), in *Z.M.N.Pr.*, 1877, no. 3, pp. 40–41; Kazakova–Lur'e, *Antifeodal'nye...*, *op. cit.*, pp. 7–72.

[26] Cf. Bishop Stephan's composition against the Strigol'niki: *RIB*, T. VI, no. 25, col. 214, pp. 220–221, 223. Also the letter of Metropolitan Photius of Pskov against the Strigol'niki in: *RIB*, *ibid.*, no. 55, col. 476–479.

[27] Cf. Vilinskij, S. G., *Poslanija Starca Artemija* (Odessa, 1906), pp. 304–314.

[28] Makarij, *Istorija...*, *op. cit.*, T. VI, pp. 82, 83, 85; Golubinskij, *op. cit.* T. III p. 585; Ikonnikov, *Opyt issledovanija o kul'turnom značenii Vizantii v russkoj istorii* ("An Attempted Investigation on the Cultural Significance of Byzantium in Russian History") (Kiev, 1869), p. 406.

[29] *Rassuzdenie o eresjax i raskolax byvšix v russkoj cerkvi so vremeni Vladimira Velikago do Ioanna Groznago* ("A Critique on Heresies and Schisms Occurring in the Russian Church From the Time of Vladimir the Great Until Ivan the Terrible") (Moscow, 1838).

[30] The classical work on this heresy was written by Panov, I., *op. cit.*, appearing in *Z.M.N.Pr.* in three articles: 1877, no. 1, pp. 1–40; no. 2, pp. 253–295; no. 3, pp. 1–59. Lur'e brings it up to date in his *Ideologičeskaja...*, *op. cit.*, pp. 75–185. For English readers, an adequate summary of the leading events is found in J. Fennell's article: "The attitude of the Josephians and Trans-Volga Elders to the Heresy of the Judaizers", in *The Slavonic and East European Review*, vol. XXIX, no. 73 (1951), pp. 486–509. Denissoff, E., *op. cit.*, p. 75, well says: "L'on ne peut donc admettre la réunion simpliste des différents courants hétérodoxes sous une seule appéllation dont le choix du reste ne laisse pas d'être quelque peu tendencieux."

Messalianism",[31] while Joseph too speaks of "many heresies".[32] This would also make plausible the later accusations by the Josephians against the Trans-Volga followers of Nil as heretics.

But judging from the chief source of our doctrinal information, as given by Joseph in his *Prosvetitel'* ("The Enlightener") and in nine of his letters, we can summarize the chief tenets of the Jew Sxarija and his followers as: (1) denial of the Holy Trinity; (2) Jesus Christ is a mere man who never arose from the dead; (3) denial of a future life and a judgment hereafter; (4) denial of the Incarnation of the Son of God; (5) denial of all externals of a public religious cultus as sacraments, liturgy, churches, icons, relics; (6) denial of the intercession of the Blessed Virgin Mary and the Saints; and (7) a skeptical criticism of the patristic writings and even of some of the accepted books of Holy Scripture.[33]

The heresy began to take roots when the Western sympathizers in Novgorod called Prince Mixail Olel'kovič to defend their city's rights against the centralizing power of Moscow. "And with this Prince Mixail came to great Novgorod the Jew Sxarija."[34] Joseph describes the latter as the devil incarnate, who with his black magic and knowledge of astrology, astronomy and other sciences, converted two priests, Dionysius and Aleksej, who began a continuous campaign of conversions of other Christians to their beliefs.[35]

An event that cloaks the whole heresy with suspicion was the visit of Ivan III to Novgorod. Impressed by the two priests, Dionysius and Aleksj, he appointed them to key-positions in Moscow's leading churches (Uspenskij Cathedral and Arxangel'skij Cathedral). It was not long before Tsar Ivan's very household was accused of harbouring sympathizers to this heresy, especially in the person of Helene, his own daughter-in-law.[36]

---

[31] On various Byzantine and Bulgarian influences in Russian heretical thought, cf. Ikonnikov, *op. cit.*, pp. 396–7; Sobolevskij, A. I., "Perevodnaja literatura moskovskoj Russi XIV–XVII vv." ("Translated Literature of Moscow Russia, 14th–17th Century), in *Sbornik otdelenija jazyka i slovesnosti*, AN, Vol. LXXIV, no. 1 (St. Petersburg, 1903); Syrku, *op. cit.;* Radčenko, *op. cit.;* Iljinskij, F. M., "Russkie bogomili XV veka" (Russian Bogomils of the 15th Century), in *Bogoslovskij Vestnik*, 1905, July-Aug., pp. 436–460.

[32] Panov, *op. cit.*, 1877, no. 3; *Prosvetitel'*, p. 59.

[33] Cf. *Prosvetitel'*, Chapter 1–12, pp. 6–425.

[34] *Ibid.*, p. 44.

[35] *Ibid.*

[36] A certain monk named Zacharias was sent into exile by Gennadij but was set free and took off for Moscow where he received protection from friends surrounding Ivan III. Cf. AAE, I, no. 380; also the article in *Prav. Sob.*, April, 1963, pp. 476–481 and Xruščov, *Issledovanie o sočinenijax Iosifa Sanina* ("An Investigation of the Compositions of Joseph Sanin") (St. Petersburg, 1868), pp. 118–123.

Gennadij, appointed archbishop of Novgorod in 1484, threw himself into the fray with fanatical dedication, launching immediately with the assistance of a Croatian Dominican, Benjamim, an intellectual program of translating the entire Bible and other needed books to counteract the attack of the learned heretics.[37] He obtained an official charge from Ivan III in 1488 to seek out any heretics, to try them, to give adequate ecclesiastical punishment, and to hand over those deserving of civil punishment to civil authorities.[38]

Leaving no possibility untried, he turns in the next year with an appeal addressed to Joasaf, archbishop of Rostov, in whose diocese were living Nil and Paisij Jaroslavov: "Write to me if it is possible for Paisij and Nil to come to me and to discourse with me about the heretics (i.e. the Judaizers)."[39] In the preceding sentence of this same letter he registers his difficulty in answering the heretics on the problem of the end of the world and asks Ioasaf to speak seriously with Paisij and Nil about these difficulties and to write him their opinions.[40]

This shows that Nil was held in great esteem for his prudence and learning, plus also his orthodox views in the face of heretical difficulties. But the conclusion that Lur'e draws is to be rejected. He wishes to show that Nil and Joseph and hence Gennadij too all had the same views towards heretics[41] where most of his proof for this hinges on Gennadij's gift to the Kirill monastery of a book of St..Athanasius, proof, he claims, that relations between Gennadij and Nil became stronger after his letter of 1489 to Ioasaf. The most reasonable deduction to explain the lack of an answer of Nil to Gennadij's request is that either Nil and Paisij refused to help him or that they had different views towards heretics and the means to correct them and merely kept silent.[42]

Gennadij made known his dissatisfaction with the indecisiveness of Ivan III and the Metropolitan of Moscow. "May they (the prayers of the

---

[37] Cf. Florovsky, op. cit., pp. 14–16, who implies that Gennadij had been greatly influenced by Latin translators who aided him in making a complete Bible translation and in making available to him many other Latin works of a politico-religious nature.

[38] Found in RIB, T. VI, no. 114 and also reproduced by Kazakova-Lur'e, using the Ms. no. 341 from the F. Tolstoj Collection, fol. 167–170. Cf. Antifeodal'nye..., op. cit., no. 14–15, pp. 313–315.

[39] Feb. 1489, "Letter of Archbishop Gennadij to Ioasaf, Archbishop of Rostov", Ms. of Troickaja Lavra, no. 730, fol. 246 and foll. now found in the Lenin Public Library. It is reproduced by Kazakova-Lur'e, op. cit., pp. 315–320. This cited quotation is on p. 320.

[40] Ibid., p. 320.

[41] Lur'e, "K voprosu...", op. cit., p. 192.

[42] Cf. Arxangel'skij, op. cit., pp. 30–31, 282; Kologrivov, op. cit., p. 194.

Mother of God and the Tsar's threats and his boyars) all clearly teach his Majesty, the Grand Prince, also his Metropolitan and also you, my brother, archbishop and bishop. And it seems to me that you have now conceived the affair as though it seemed to you that Novgorod and Moscow were not of the same orthodoxy."[43] Ivan III stirred to action and on October 17, 1490, called a synod to judge some captured heretics and to elect a new bishop. Among the members attending, perhaps at the personal request of Ivan III, were Paisij and Nil, as the chronicler reports.[44] Gennadij, fearing that the Fathers would show too much mercy, sent a letter to the Metropolitan Zosima and again a separate letter to all the bishops gathered at this synod, urging them not to hesitate to sentence the heretics to be hanged and burned alive.[45]

Lur'e again insists that the lenient decision against the nine heretics was indicative only of the mind of Ivan III and not of the Fathers who assisted.[46] But recalling Gennadij's fears about the attitude of the Fathers before the synod began and the fact that the Tsar called Nil and Paisij the distance from their Trans-Volga hermitage to Moscow, Ivan III must have seen in them men of a similar attitude of leniency. Again, the consistent attitude Nil shows in his writings coupled with the leniency of his followers would be sufficient to refute the above assertion.

This is the last official mention of Nil's participation in the heresy affair. The continued war against the heretics by Gennadij and Joseph need not detain us further. But let us go on to show how Nil's predominant attitude towards heretics influenced the writings and practices of his followers.

Nil's attitude towards the treatment of heretics came from his Gospel-permeated spirituality. If we hear nothing more directly from himself about his expression of this Gospel of gentleness and clemency towards those in error, we can nevertheless trace his evident influence among his followers who remained after Nil's death to apply his evangelical teaching to the practical situation.

---

[43] "Letter of Gennadij to Ioasaf", loc. cit., p. 317.

[44] PSRL, T. IV, p. 158.

[45] "Letter to Zosima" and "Letter to the Bishops of the Oct. 1490 Synod", from two mss. namely, Q. XVII, no. 15, fol. 377–380, the F. Tolstoj Collection, II, no. 254 and the other ms. no. 962/852, fol. 331; 341–342 of the Soloveckij Collection, both mss. found in the Saltykov-Ščedrin National Public Library of Leningrad and reproduced by Kazakova–Lur'e, op. cit., pp. 374–382. On Gennadij's admiration for the Latins and especially for the Spanish inquisitional methods, cf. Kazakova–Lur'e, ibid., p. 114.

[46] Lur'e, "K voprosu...", op. cit., pp. 192–193; also Kazakova-Lur'e, op. cit., pp. 129–130, and Arxangel'skij, op. cit., pp. 31–33.

The chief disciple of Nil's school of thought who engaged directly in this struggle with Joseph and his followers, Vassian Patrikeev, the prince forced to take the tonsure by order of Ivan III, after having been complicated in a political scandal.[47]

From the polemic writings of Vassian against Joseph, in an effort to win the support of the ruling Prince Vasilij Ivanovič, we can see the outstanding influence that Nil's spirit had on his disciple Vassian. The fundamental principle that Vassian insisted on in the governmental and ecclesiastical dealings with heretics was Nil's accentuation of the mercy of God. In the dialogue form used by Vassian to summarize Joseph's teaching on heretics and monastic holdings and to present his own position and that of the entire Trans-Volga school, followers of Nil,[48] he insists that the mercy of God posits the universal will of God to save all sinners by bringing them to repentance[49]. There is no sin that cannot be pardoned if the sinner repents, but he argues, "those who put the heretics to death without a chance to repent, make of them martyrs".[50] Basing his attitude towards heretics on the Word of the New Testament which is founded on the infinite Mercy of God rather than on the Old Testament Law alone, Vassian, in words similar to those already quoted of Nil, affirms:

If you had a sound mind and just sense of judgment, you would decide not to attack with force this heretical evil, but taking your lead from the Saviour's commands, from the proper canonical teachings, you would sentence them, but not with the death penalty as you now wish because you interpret the instructions of the Holy Fathers according to your passions (*creva*, literally: stomach) and not from Holy Scripture. You do not understand correctly the

[47] Vassian was sent on a mission along with other boyar leaders, including the Josephian denounced heretic Ivan Kurcyn along with Vasilij and Simeon Rjapolovskij to arrange the marriage of Ivan III's daughter Helena to Alexander, Grand Prince of Lithuania. Cf. *PSRL*, vol. IV, 164; VI, 39, 240; VIII, 228. The whole affair indicates a boyar clash against a centralized Moscow with the boyars eager to make an alliance with the West. In January, 1499, he and his noble family became involved in a political move to elevate the nephew of Ivan III, Dimitrij, to the throne in preference to Vasilij, Ivan's son. When Vasilij, backed by his mother Sophie, came into power, the opposition was either put to death or tonsured by force. Cf. *PSRL*, vol. VII, pp. 254–255. Also Solov'eev, S. M., *Istorija...*, *op. cit.*, bk. I, part V, pp. 1409–1410.
[48] A summary article of Vassian's chief polemical compositions which presents: (1) Vassian's introduction to his compositions against Joseph; (2) A composition about monastic life and ecclesiastical structure; (3) A collection against Joseph gathered chiefly from Nikon Montenegro; and (4) A shortened version of all his polemics from a probable book of more than ten chapters against Joseph in a dialogue form, is found in *Prav. Sob.*, III (1863), pp. 95–112, 180–210.
[49] *Ibid.*, p. 203.
[50] *Ibid.*, p. 204.

Gospel's parable about letting the servants of the Lord not separate the evil cockle from the good wheat, but letting both grow together until the harvest time.[51]

Vassian with his practical mind for society and the necessity of lawful authority to judge existing evils in that society insisted, contrary to the general advice of Nil and his more spiritual followers among the Trans-Volga Starcy, insisted on the need for bringing the heretics to ecclesiastical and civil trial; but with Nil, he insisted that they be given a chance to reform; hence no death penalty. Vassian however remained more a boyar than a faithful follower of the kenotic spirituality of Nil as is shown in his use of force and torture methods with the priest whom the two Josephian monks, Dionysius and Nil Polev, had sent with a report to the Grand Prince of a discovered heresy among the nothern Trans-Volga hermits with whom the Judaizer heretics took refuge. When questioning did not avail, Vassian suggested torture, but unfortunately the torturers overdid their zeal in carrying out Vassian's suggestion and the priest died.[52]

The so-called Trans-Volga Starcy, as a group, penned a strong rebuttal to Joseph's letter sent to Tsar Vasilij Ivanovič, probably about 1504-1505.[53] Joseph had proposed new examples to enforce his position that the Church had the duty to try and to condemn heretics, even to death. To this, the Trans-Volga Starcy, still during the time of Nil, answered in Nil's same language.[54] Nil's influence, in the evangelical language and references used, is more strongly felt than in most of the polemic works of Vassian; still, it is possible, as Xruščov maintains,[55] that Vassian was the author or the main force behind it.[56] It was probably written during

---

[51] *Ibid.*, p. 198–199.
[52] Panov, "Otnošenija inokov...", *op. cit.*, p. 506.
[53] Cf. Hruščov, *op. cit.*, pp. 188–189. Kazakova–Lur'e reproduce this letter from the best manuscripts available, *op. cit.*, appendix, no. 29: *Slovo ob osuzdenii eretikov* ("Discourse About Judging Heretics"), pp. 488–498, with a discussion of the Mss. that distinguish this from or intermingle it with Chapter 11 of Joseph's *Prosvetitel'*, *ibid.*, pp. 486–488. The *Slovo...* is found also in *DRB*, vol. XVI, p. 424.
[54] "Otvet Kirillovskix starcev na poslanie Iosifa Volockogo o nakazanii eretikov" ("Letter of the Trans-Volga Starcy"), cf. note 57 that here follows.
[55] *Op. cit.*, p. 188.
[56] There are many similar passages that coincide with Vassian's dialogue-polemic with Joseph, e.g. quoting Joseph as saying it is the same thing to kill the heretics by weapons as by prayers *(Prab. Sob., op. cit.*, p. 202); the mercy of God towards all sinners (*ibid.*, p. 203); Joseph follows the Old Testament and the Holy Fathers with their interpretation of Holy Scripture, as found in the seven councils and in the local synods (*ibid.*, p. 202).

the lifetime of Nil, Xruščov,Panov and Žmakin maintaining that it was written before the 1504 Synod which gave the victory over the heretics clearly to the Josephians and to their general method of treating the offenders.[57]

This Trans-Volga letter begins by refuting Joseph's remark in his letter to Tsar Vasilij that "to kill a sinner or a heretic with one's own hands or by prayer is the same thing".[58] The Starcy from the Kirill Monastery and all the other Trans-Volga hermits agree that Joseph's letter goes against the Holy Writings and the very essence of the Church which was founded by Christ, the Son of God Incarnate, to seek out the sinners and save those perishing.[59] Against Joseph's example of Moses using force against the Israelites when he found them adoring the golden calf, they point to the example of the same Moses begging God to take his own life rather than to destroy Israel. "See, lord, how love and zeal towards sinners are powerful to dissolve the anger of God."[60]

Even if the Old Testament did so decree, we have received the New Covenant of love from Christ and the command not to judge another's brother, but to let only God judge a sinful man, for He said: "Judge not that you may not be judged" (Mt. 7, 1). Nil had early written to Gurij Tusin not to seek to reprove or correct those in sin, but "let God do this, for He is powerful to correct them".[61]

They cite the example of Our Lord, reproving the accusing Pharisees who sought to judge the woman taken in adultery: "He who is without sin, let him cast the first stone." Again they appeal to the New Testament examples of sinners who showed repentance and were granted forgiveness by Christ: the Good Thief; the Publican (Zaccheus) who by his alms was cleansed; the adulteress weeping obtained forgiveness. True, Paul blinded the Magus by his prayer, but only because he sought to turn away Antipater from the faith. "The Apostle Paul himself wrote: 'I would be anathema from my Christ, if only my brother Israelites would be

---

[57] Xruščov, op. cit., pp. 188–197; Panov, op. cit., 1877, no. 2, p. 276, footnote 1, pp. 282–285; Žmakin, V., op. cit., pp. 66–69.
[58] We follow the more critical text as reproduced by Kazakova-Lur'e, op. cit., Appendix, no. 32, pp. 511–513. This letter also can be found in DRB, vol. XVI, pp. 424–428. Cf. Climacus on prayer as the weapon used against heretics. Gradus 28, PG, 88, 1129B.
[59] Kazakova–Lur'e text, p. 512.
[60] Ibid.
[61] Letter to Gurij, fol. 101B, cf. Appendix of this work. The same Trans-Volga sentiments are expressed in the treatise attributed to Nil on overcoming evil thoughts: Elagin ed., (1864), op. cit., p. 205; also translated in Appendix of this work, Letter IX.

thus saved.' Don't you see, Lord, that he is laying down his own soul for the erring brethren in order that they may be saved, and he does not pray that they be given over to the fire to be burnt or that they be swallowed up by the earth, but that they may be received by God."[62] And the letter ends with a moving plea for Christ-like mercy to all sinners, forgiving a sinful brother not seven times but seventy times seven.[63]

The literal interpretation of the Gospels with the rather otherworldly detachment of these Trans-Volga Starcy in their attitude towards the heretics shows the influence of Nil's spirituality on a large scale, for this letter itself, written most probably before Nil's death, claims that the sentiments expressed therein were those of all the Starcy of the Trans-Volga area, plus those of the Kirill-Belozerskij Monastery. By 1531 most of their hermitages were wiped out and many of these monks suffered imprisonment and death for their clemency shown towards the heretics.[64]

One of their typical representatives and one of the faithful disciples of Nil, the recipient of one of his longer letters,[65] was German, one of the Starcy in the Podol'nyj Monastery. The disciple of Joseph, Nil Polev, who left the Volokolamsk Monastery to live among the hermits of Trans-Volga along with his fellow Josephian, Dionisij Zvenigorodskij, wrote German a letter of protest for not giving Holy Communion to the Josephians, due to the excommunication ordered by the Metropolitan Serapion, a sympathizer of the Trans-Volga Starcy against the Josephians. (This excommunication was later lifted by the new Josephian Metropolitan Simon). Nil Polev complains about the widespread conviction among these northern Starcy of showing mercy to heretics and of not bringing them to judgment and proper punishment. He writes to German: "You say, concerning the enemies and those apostates of the true faith, that it is not right to judge them nor to put them in prison, but only to pray for them..."[66]

---

[62] Letter of the Trans-Volga Starcy, p. 512.
[63] *Ibid.*, p. 512. The *BAN* Ms. *(Biblioteka Akademii Nauk SSSR:* Library of the Academy of Sciences, USSR), Arxangel'skoe D. 221, fol. 146, ends with the evangelic scene of the Apostles asking Christ to send down fire from Heaven on the Samarians who refused to received them. Christ answers the Apostles and Joseph Volokolamsk: "You know not of what spirit you speak. The Son of God came not to destroy the souls of men, but to save them." Kazakova-Lur'e, *op. cit.*, p. 513, ftnote no. 13.
[64] Meyendorff, *op. cit.*, in *Irénikon*, 1956, p. 156.
[65] Letter to German Podol'nyj, Troick Ms. now in the Lenin Public Library, no. 188, fol. 104–108. Cf. the *Appendix* of this present work, Letter III.
[66] Volokolamsk Ms. no. 235/661 in the Lenin Public Library, fol. 128. Xruščov, *op. cit.*, XXXI and pp. 238–9. Cf. also Žmakin, V., "Nil Polev", in *Z.M.N.Pr.*, Part CCXVI, Aug. 1881, p. 194.

The war between such Trans-Volga Starcy as German and the Josephians, including Archbishop Gennadij, hinged around the dispute concerning the adamant, almost ruthless, unbending attitude of Joseph and his followers in not accepting the penitence of heretics. Those who pleaded mercy for the heretics were the equivalent of heretics.[67] Gennadij pleads in his letter to Zosima that he and the other bishops are to curse the heretics and those also who agree on any point with them or anyone who might intercede for them; "all these should be anathematised as heretics".[68] Joseph uses the common doctrine of Nil Sorskij, German and other Trans-Volga Starcy as the title of his 13th chapter in the *Prosvetitel'*: "Against the heresy of the Novgorod heretics who say that it is not proper to judge either a heretic or an apostate."[69]

If it is true that heretics and boyars not only infiltrated into these northern hermitages seeking refuge from the inquisitional methods of the Josephians, and even entering such a monastic life similar to that proposed by Nil's *Ustav*,[70] it is also true that Nil's basic view of the spiritual life and of the end of monasticism was again in direct conflict with that of Joseph's. In these northern expanses monks, bent on seeking true spiritual perfection, found here Nil's tradition as dominating all other spiritual teaching. S. Ševyrev insists that the spirit of Nil, as expressed in the letter of the Trans-Volga Starcy, is the expression of Christian charity at its highest in contrast to an exaggerated fanaticism of Joseph and his followers.[71]

But not all of the monks of these northern regions reached the deeper, inner spirit of Christianity that Nil taught. That his principles of criticism of holy writings, of personal freedom, of revolt against the predominant externalization in religious practice, especially among monks, contained

---

[67] Cf. the article by J. Fennell, *op. cit.*, in which the author shows some of the interrelationships between the Judaizers and the Trans-Volga Starcy. He implies however more than he actually proves by his stattement: "And likewise the Trans-Volga Elders, in pleading for leniency on behalf of the heretics and, where possible, interceding for them personally, were surely prompted by something more than a feeling of purely moral obligation." (P. 508.)

[68] "Letter of Gennadij to the Bishops of the 1490 Sobor", Kazakova–Lur'e, *op. cit.*, p. 381.

[69] *Ed. cit.*, p. 526.

[70] Rybakov, B. A., "Voinstvujuščie cerkovniki XVI v." ("Belligerent Churchmen of the 16th Century"), in *Antireligioznik*, 1934, no. 3, p. 24. He exaggeratedly claims that one had only to lift the monastic habit slightly of these Trans-Volga monks and one would find the boyar's silk *kaftan* underneath.

[71] *Istorija russkoj slovesnosti* (Moscow, 1860), vol. 4, conf. 19, p. 174.

the seeds for real heresies, this cannot be doubted.[72] This is evident from the history of Artemij, one of Nil's most faithful followers, although perhaps the last and most removed from Nil's lifetime to come under his strong influence.[73]

Not only in his own earlier life does he seem to indicate a somewhat heretical position, as he himself admits,[74] but two heretics claim him as their master. Matvej Baškin, a wealthy Moscow inhabitant, pushed the evangelical doctrine of the Trans-Volga Starcy too far and began insisting on radical reforms in the State and Church. Artemij was summoned to refute him, but when Baškin insisted that he had the support of the Trans-Volga Starcy and that Artemij was saying the same doctrine, Artemij was subjected to a complete examination. He was found guilty on eight charges of heretical tendencies,[75] but, rather than defend himself, he fled to the northern White Lake Area. He was brought back to Moscow and sentenced in 1554 to imprisonment in the northern monastery of Soloveckij. From here he escaped and fled to Lithuania.

The other true heretic who was openly Artemij's disciple, not only before the Moscow Synod of 1554 while Artemij was still higoumen of Troice-Sergieva Lavra, but who followed him to Lithuania, was Theodosius Kosoj. He serves as an example of what heresies a weak intellect, mingled with pride, and the basic principles of Nil and Artemij about rational criticism are capable of conjuring up. Artemij cites the identical words of Nil Sorskij:

Bind yourself to the commands of the Holy Scripture and follow them for they are the true and Divine Writings; for there are many writings, but not all are Divine. Search the truth with that which is already known, from the reading of them (the Holy Writings) and through conversations with spiritual and

---

[72] "At that level of enlightenment and popular freedom, the direction of Nil easily could lead to heresy while the tendency of Joseph, his antagonist, would seem the hopeful means to preserve someone from heresy and self-willed deception. Strict observance of the rule and unconditional submission, here is the ideal which was proposed to Russian society by the Volokolamsk Monastery and Russian society of this time very quickly and thoroughly understood this direction... The tendency of Joseph overruled while that of Nil quickly disappeared." Kojalovič, M. O., cited by Kalugin, *Zinovij Inok otenskij* (St. Pet., 1894), p. 55.

[73] Grečev, B., *op. cit.*, 1908, no. 3, p. 333. Kalugin, op. *cit.*, p. 58.

[74] *RIB*, vol. IV, col. 1420. Cf. also 1372, 1394, 1399.

[75] *AAE*, vol. I., no. 239, p. 250–255. Kalugin, *op. cit.*, p. 61, ftnote 19, gives all eight of the charges. Zimin, A. A., "Delo eretika Artemija", in *Voprosy istorii religii i ateizma*, no. 5 (Moscow, 1958), pp. 213-232, produces an excellent work in re-establishing Artemij's reputation against the unjust charges of heresy leveled at him in the Synod of 1553. Cf. also Vilinskij on Artemij's "heresy", pp. 82–85.

discerning men, because not all, but only the discerning, have true understanding...[76]

...Every understanding which is not based on faith in the Divine Gospels is carnal wisdom.[77]

All the things examined by the actions of the Fathers or written down by them is not worthy of our acceptance, but only the written commands, I mean, the Holy Gospels, the Letters of the Apostles and the Acts. The wicked gospel-writer and the patristic writings that follow such, even the Apostolic canons and conciliar canons which are based on the Holy Writings, if these contain something that is contrary to Divine Writings, do not accept anything of these because there are many deceivers of the intellect and self-legislators who ought not to teach, for they know not what they do.[78]

Such a vast principle of Artemij given to Theodosius Kosoj soon led the pupil to the conviction that the only fount of revelation was the Holy Scripture. In contact with Protestantism in Lithuania, he left the Orthodox faith completely.[79] With such personal contacts with heretics and his own admitted heterodox past, it is understandable why Artemij, more than any of Nil's followers, formulated a sympathetic doctrine of the origin and nature of heresy. Vilinskij gives three leading tendencies in Russia of the 16th century: (1) A movement to unite the religious life with the temporal power of the Moscow Tsar, emphasizing a continuous lineage from the other two Romes which gave the basis for the doctrine of the Moscow Third Rome; (2) Freedom from Byzantine influence and an inclination to Western, Latin or Protestant influence, which showed itself mostly in opposition to the centralization power of the Moscow Prince, in a rationalistic criticism of traditions, and even to the point of heresies; (3) A mystical character which tried to live strictly according to the precepts and counsels of the Gospels and the spiritual writings of the Sinaite and Mount Athos hesychasts.[80] The same author maintains that Artemij passed through all three stages in his personal life. In the latter one, especially in his exile in Lithuania, he manifests his dependence on Nil, above all in his attitude towards heretics.

He defines heresy as essentially not stemming from passions but of a perverted will.[81] This distorted will is to be changed and no amount of force will ever effect a conversion of such an obstinate error. Christians, or true followers of Christ, have the obligation to show meekness in teaching

---

[76] Letter of Nil to Gurij, fol. 102B; cf. *Appendix.*
[77] *RIB*, col. 1406.
[78] *Ibid.*, 1419, 1399.
[79] Cf. Vilinskij, *op. cit.*, p. 101.
[80] *Ibid.*, pp. 297–8.
[81] *RIB*, col, 1213.

heretics the truth. They must pray that God grant the heretics repentance and bring them to an understanding of the truth, and thus free them from the snare of the devil.[82]

The influence of Nil and the Trans-Volga Starcy is evident. But it stands out especially in his attack against the use of torture in dealing with heretics. There may be a basis, as the Josephians argued, in the Old Testament for such methods, but the New Testament of Christ-like charity towards sinners allows no place for such misdirected zeal. Artemij cites the examples from the Lives of the Apostles and the teaching of the New Testament on Christian liberty and the submission to one law only, that of the love of the neighbour. The Apostles, in their supposed zeal for God's glory, wanted to order down fire, but Christ rebuked their spirit as that of the devil.[83]

St. Paul had used such methods before succumbing to the charity of Christ. But afterwards, he preaches only the fulfillment of mercy and evangelical love as the distinguishing marks of Christians. Artemij follows Vassian in the parable of the wheat and the cockle with Christ's implicit command not to cut the harmful element from society until the harvest or last judgment.[84]

In his second letter Artemij repeats the doctrine of Nil as given by the Trans-Volga Starcy in their letter that Christians should give over heretics to God's judgment alone.[85] If they take upon themselves the duty of judging, they show a lack of faith in the permanence of the Church, that such enemies of the Mystical Body of Christ, the seething waves on the sea of the world, could harm the boat of Christ. He promulgates a more human, personal treatment of heretics, teaching them truth in meekness, but not using means of torture, as he mentions in his letter to Tsar Ivan the Terrible.[86]

Also in the same letter, as well as in several others, Artemij reiterates over and over, along with Nil Sorskij, the necessity of studying Holy Scripture as the necessary condition for a virtuous life. In order to fulfill the Will of God, it is necessary to know it and perfect knowledge is impossible without a careful searching of the Holy Writings where this Divine Will is hidden. He sees this as the reason for every heresy: a mis-

---

[82] *Ibid.*, 1213, 1275, 1385.
[83] *Ibid.*, 1214. Cf. also *supra*, ftnote no. 62.
[84] Cf. the polemical works of Vassian, *op. cit.*, *Prav. Sob.*, III (1963), pp. 199–200.
[85] *RIB*, col. 1378. For Nil's doctrine, cf. his letter to Gurij, fol. 101B. Vd. *Appendix*. Cf. also Xruščov, *op. cit.*, pp. 238–9.
[86] *RIB*, col. 1437. Vilinskij, *op. cit.*, p. 151.

understanding of the Divine Writings. The heresy does not lie in the writings which retain always their divinely designated saving force, but rather it lies in the person who reads the writings with erroneous inter-pretations. Nil himself insisted that monks in his own days either did not want to follow commands found in the Holy Writings or they mis-interpreted them according to their passionate inclinations.[87] Nil does not go into the meaning of "understanding" *(razum)*, but from Artemij we get a better insight into what Nil probably taught either in other works unknown to us or verbally handed down to his followers. Artemij follows chiefly, as Nil did, the teaching of Isaac the Syrian, but he works out in detail, and not only as hinted vaguely by Nil, the doctrine of Isaac into a careful gradation of spiritual perfection. Building his doctrine of understanding Holy Scripture on the threefold distinction given by Isaac the Syrian of body, soul and spirit, with the corresponding knowl-edge of corporal, sense-knowledge, natural intellection and true, super-natural faith,[88] Artemij insists that each Christian must learn to read the Holy Writings to discover the mind of God; this means not merely reading words, but feeding on the inner Spirit, "for the letter kills, while the spirit gives life".[89] Salvation comes from obeying the commands of Christ, which are very simple and are not meant to be complicated. They are reduced to the one commandment of the love of God and the love of the neighbour. But the person who seeks to interpret the Holy Writ-ings with only the corporal sense-knowledge is bound to fall. The source of all internal illumination of grace which allows the individual to come into direct contact through faith with the mind and will of God is humil-ity.[90] The proud can never hear the meek Teacher Christ who invites men to come to "learn from Me, for I am meek and humble of heart." Heretics are those proud souls who have separated themselves from the true source of spiritual enlightenment by their lack of humility which is the necessary step to faith. Like rays of the sun falling on a blind man and having no illuminating effect on his inner eye, so the words of Our Lord in the Holy Scripture fall on the eyes of a heretic and have no salu-tary effect.[91]

Where Artemij shows a return to Nil's doctrine on the Christian attitude towards heretics in opposition to the predominant views of the

---

[87] Nil's Letter to German, fol. 104B, 107B, 106B. Vd. *Appendix.*
[88] Vilinskij, *op. cit.*, pp. 190–193, 323–329. *RIB*, Col. 1232.
[89] *RIB*, col. 1218.
[90] *Ibid.*, 1301.
[91] *Ibid.*, 1275.

Trans-Volga Starcy is in his teaching on total separation from any contact
with the heretics. We have seen Nil advising total flight in order to
escape not only dissipation through angry discussions, but also to avoid
scandal and a threat to one's faith and convictions of the true doctrine of
the Church. Artemij in the third stage of his life, when he finds himself in
Lithuania where there were communities of German Protestants, repeats
fairly exactly Nil's advice: "It is not proper for us to take alarm nor to
attack the position of those who lack true vision and have gone astray;
but rather we should pray for them until God will give them true contrition."[92] If there is any unavoidable contact with them, the proper
attitude of a Christian should be one of teaching them the truth in a
spirit of meekness and never using force.[93] But in general, relying on
St. John the Evangelist's teaching: "If you are visited by one who does
not bring this teaching with him, you must not receive him into your
houses or bid him welcome,"[94] and on the teaching of St. John Chrysostom, Artemij insists: "Let no Orthodox believer, even under pretext of
virtuous acts, make contact in any way with the Lutherans and other
heretics, and let them not even listen to their words. They are not to
meet with them, as St. John Crysostom says, 'not in eating or drinking or
forming family bonds or friendships'."[95]

Thus, among all of those who came after Nil, Artemij seems to reflect
most closely the attitude of Nil in relationship with heretics. We went
into detail on this point of Nil's influence on the general thinking in
Russia towards heretics because it was felt that in this sphere of influence
the literal following of the Gospel spirit by Nil and his true followers is
most clearly seen. It also gives us the fundamental kenosism of Nil
which flows through all of his writings, a Christ-like condescension to all
sinners, and for a monk whose exclusive preoccupation, as Nil conceived
it, was to pray for the conversion of such, without taking the initiative to
correct them.

The other question that divided the religious leaders of Russia in the
latter part of the 15th and first half of the 16th centuries was the complex
problem about monastic possession. We need not repeat what we have
already given on the historical development of this problem in Russian
history,[96] nor need we to repeat again Nil's strict views on monastic

---

[92] *Ibid.*, 1275; also 1213.
[93] *Ibid.*, 1437.
[94] Second Epistle of John 10
[95] Col. 1324–5.
[96] Cf. *supra*, Part I, Chapter I, B.

poverty.[97] Nil insisted too much on strict, absolute poverty as a corollary to his total absorption in the one preoccupation of a monk: contemplation of God. Creature attachments disturbed the soul's union with God, therefore only the extreme necessities of life were allowed Nil's monks. Naturally this ideal would conflict with the predominant view of his time. It becomes a conflict more of interpretation of the monastic state of life than one of "possessors" *versus* "non-possessors".[98] The earliest Russian monks, as Theodosius Pečerskij, favoured strict poverty as the highest ideal of monasticism, but circumstances did not always permit its perfect practice, especially in Russia, with the unique relationship of princes to monasticism through which means they exercised their social obligations to the poor and sick of society, plus the highly complicated but exact legislation on stipends and benefices for prayers said for the living and the dead. "Many are the monasteries founded by the rulers and the boyars and from riches, but they are not such as those founded by tears, fasting, prayer and watching," complained Theodosius.[99] He gave advice on keeping strict, evangelical poverty, but reluctantly had to accept money and land benefices from the various princes.[100] Budovnic traces the current among the early Russian monks to react instinctively against monastic possessions; especially strong protests come from those influenced by the hesychastic writers of Sinai and Mount Athos, such as the Metropolitan Kliment Smoljatič, Abraham Smolensk (the author compares him to St. Francis of Assisi),[101] Metropolitan Kiprian,[102] Paul Obnora and Kirill of Belozerskij, or rather from Pachomius Logothete, his biographer who had lived, as Nil did, for many years on Mount Athos.[103] With the growing of monastic possessions to enormous proportions at the end of the 15th century, the peasant poor were gradually losing their reverence for their holy monks of whom many were mere overseers of large landed estates. The opinion that one third of all useful land in Russia at this time belonged to the Church seems a bit

---

[97] Part II, Chapter IV, B.

[98] Florovsky, G., *op. cit.*, p. 17.

[99] *Povest' vremennyx let*, edited by Adrianova-Peretc, V. P., T. I (Moscow–Leningrad, 1950), p. 107.

[100] Budovnic, I. U., "Pervye russkie nestjažateli", in *Voprosy istorii religii i ateizma*, no. 5 (Moscow, 1958), pp. 264–5.

[101] *Ibid.*, pp. 267–281.

[102] *RIB*, T. VI, no. 32, pp. 263–265. Kiprian writes to Higoumen Athanasius giving rules and norms for monastic possessions, but, above all, he gives the ideal to which monks should strive, as he himself saw it lived on Mount Athos.

[103] Nikol'skij, N. K., "Obščinnaja...", *op. cit.*, p. 161.

exaggerated,[104] but a mere glance at the research done by A. I. Kopanev[105] would be sufficient to allay any doubts that the affair had assumed gigantic proportions.

Added to this general discontent among the poor classes at seeing those who voluntarily vowed to follow Christ poor, the rich lords ruling over large landed estates, villages and peasants often numbering in the thousands, the boyars and those "newly arrived" functionaries and military service-men whom the Tsar was wont to reward for services rendered to the throne with land grants, were quick to raise their voice of protest against the best lands held by the Church.[106] The issue became even more complicated when the heretics used abuse as one of their rallying points of popular appeal against the traditional religion. It is therefore not to be wondered that Nil, though never wanting to start a "movement", above all, one mixed with political issues, found the air charged with tension when he made his formal protest in the Moscow Synod of 1503 against the monasteries holding properties. Had there not been the third group, (besides the strictly ascetical view of those monks influenced by Sinaite and Mount Athos hesychasm and the view of the Josephians favouring corporate monastic possessions as a necessary means to carry on their social works of mercy) those ready to use the ascetical arguments of Nil's spiritual teaching to further their own economic and political aims, it is doubtful that Nil's complaint would have even been recorded in Russian history.

But it is an undeniable fact that Nil's doctrine did start a polemic struggle that lasted for centuries. He had clearly outlined his ideal of monasticism in his writings, especially in his *Ustav* where he favours the "middle way" of skete type of monasticism but he does not disparage the other two forms, the eremitical and the coenobitical life, as evils. Nil's views on poverty touch only the individual monk and his complete dedication to self-perfection. There could be no place for possessions, at least for landed property of vast proportions, because such a way of

---

[104] "Plurima ibi exstruuntur Basilianorum coenobia; his magni sunt agrorum reditus nam tertian fundorum partes totius imperii tenent monachi," reported Adam Climent after a visit to Moscow in 1553, in *Rerum Moscoviticarum scriptores varii* (Frankfurt, 1600), p. 152, cited by I. Smolitsch, *op. cit.*, p. 79. Ključevskij, *op. cit.*, p. 345, gives the same opinion of one third of the land in the hands of the Church as expressed by the Englishman Fletcher. But Nikol'skij, *op. cit.*, p. 178, says it is impossible to accept this. Cf. Pavlov, *op. cit.*, pp. 17–24.

[105] Kopanev, A. I., *Istorija zemlevladenija belozerskogo kraja XV–XVI vv.* ("The History of Landownership in the White Lake Region in the 15–16th Centuries") (Moscow-Leningrad, 1951).

[106] Pavlov, *op. cit.*, pp. 17–18.

life, for Nil, was inconsistent with the very fundamental self-dedication to the interior life, which demanded complete detachment from the world or from any created things that could distract the soul. When Nil was called to participate in the Synod of Moscow in 1503, just five years before his death one wonders whether Ivan III did not see in Nil a means to bring about a political move to secularize some of the vast church lands. The primary aim of the synod was to decide the fate of widowed priests and deacons, whether they should be forced to take up the monastic life after the death of the wife or whether a second marriage would be permitted them, a question that does not seem to have much to do with Nil. Lur'e insists that it was not Nil who, as most historians paint the scene, dramatically, as the synod was disbanding, pronounced his philippic against monastic possessions, but, rather, it was Ivan III who brought up the topic for general discussion.[107] The "Pis'mo o neljubkax" (Letter on Lack of Love) records it thus: "And when there was held the council about widowed priests and deacons, the Starec Nil got up and said that monasteries should not have villages, but monks should live in solitude and be fed by the fruit of the work of their own hands. And with him were all the hermits of the Belozerskij region..."[108] The letter, after presenting Joseph's rebuttal, goes on to say that Nil and his disciple Vassian Patrikeev did not agree with Joseph; and the others, who had been on Mount Athos and other similar thinking starcy, along with the Grand Prince Ivan III, were in agreement with them. Nil retired to his solitude in the Sorskij hermitage and we hear nothing more from him. But the wound had been opened and the painful polemics for and against monasteries having property began. It would be too long and beyond the scope of this present work to give a history of this controversy, especially as it developed through the compositions of Vassian and his opponents, Joseph and the Metropolitan Daniel.[109] We must be content to indicate,

[107] Lur'e, "K voprosu...", op. cit., p. 195. Cf. Vassian's polemical dialogue with Joseph, Prav. Sob., op. cit., p. 206, where Joseph says "...the Grand Prince of All-Russia, Ivan Vasil'evič, ordered to come to Moscow as consultors both Nil and Joseph, in regard to the married priests and, after this was discussed, then he (the Tsar) said, 'I would want to take away the villages from the holy churches and monasteries'." Ikonnikov, op. cit., p. 435, insists that Nil and Paisij had proposed this to Ivan III.
[108] Op. cit., p. 505.
[109] The classic work is that of Pavlov, A. S., Istoričeskij očerk..., op. cit. An adequate summary of the main events including the history after the 16th century controversy is given by J. Meyendorff, "Une controverse sur le rôle...", op. cit., in Irénikon, 1955, pp. 396–405; 1956, pp. 28–46, 151–164. This is also found in a special number edited separately by Irénikon-Chevetogne. Cf. also Žmakin, Metropolit Daniil, op. cit., where there is found a complete history of the polemic between Vassian and Joseph's follower, Daniil.

however, some of the followers of Nil's doctrine of strict poverty, without going into great detail about their doctrine or the role they played in Russian history; our aim will be to indicate some lines of Nil's influence in their thinking.

The ardent exponents of the non-possession theory for monasteries split into three groups; oftentimes it is difficult to classify any given personality into one of the three categories: the strictly ascetical, hesychastic ideal of monasticism, not rejecting coenobitic life but reducing the monasteries in size and in social apostolate and in general favouring the skete type of monasticism; the boyar-monks who mixed this religious ideal with political aspirations in their war against Moscow centralization; and finally the heretics, who, stressing always reform in the Church, focused attention on this, the biggest source of contemporary abuse.

The most evident follower of Nil in his doctrine of non-possession is Vassian Patrikeev.[110] After the Synod of 1503 Vassian remained at Moscow where he had regained the favour of Ivan III and his successor Vasilij III. Relying on his sense of scholarship and spirit of criticism which he learned from Nil, he set out to refute Joseph and his followers on their theory of the necessity of the Church to have possessions and of the inalienability of the same against the power of the State. Using the same founts often as Joseph, e.g. Nikon of Montenegro and his *Pandectes*, or quoting from the Holy Scripture or the Holy Fathers, more often from the canonical legislation of the Church and State, he proves his point with a satire and ironical tone Nil's humility would never have approved of.

Vassian's views as a reflection of Nil's can be seen in his answer to Joseph's attack that "Nil and his disciple Vassian say and write that it is not proper to decorate the divine churches and the all-honorable icons with gold and silver and likewise not right to have in church holy vessels made of gold and silver." Vassian answers:

It is St. John Chrysostom who writes that it is not becoming to decorate churches, while depriving the poor and the needy, but it is better to give to them rather than decorate the churches. Another reason is that church decorations are consumed by fire and the barbarians and Tartars steal them; but if you give them to the poor, then not even the devil can steal them away. If there will be alms left over, there should be a committee that takes care of the Church's riches in providing for the poor, either the bishop or a lay person at

---

[110] Filaret, *Obzor russkoj duxovnoj literatury*, ed. III, (St. Petersburg, 1884), pp. 129–30, claims that Vassian preached one doctrine, faithful to Nil and practised another, living like a boyar when he returned to Moscow. "He erred in much, especially in demanding in vain that all monks embrace the skete life. He spoke of the coenobitic life without having had any personal experience."

the head, but not a monk in the monasteries. But a monk should live in the strictest poverty and need and without refinements, without amassing wealth. He should not have even disposable alms but he should have only the mere necessities for the Church and those should be without embellishments; for himself he should be fed and clothed only with the necessaries. On this account it is sufficient to refer to Nikon's book *(Pandectes)*, Chapter 21.[111]

In 1517 he began a correction of the *Nomocanon* or *Kormcaja Kniga* or, rather, he composed a new *Kormcaja Kniga* from which all the texts allowing monasteries to own land were omitted. Using Nil Sorskij's criterion of Holy Scripture as the guide in all moral life, he solved apparent contradictions found in various canons by admitting only those in accordance with the Gospels and Epistles.[112] Most of the feuding between the followers of Nil and the Josephians came about from their mutual citing of Russian canons on this matter, so Vassian omitted any such references, relying entirely on non-Russian legislation.[113]

Vassian found a great support for his non-possession views in the brilliant thinker and monk from Mount Athos, Maksim the Greek. He had been called to Russia by Vasilij III to translate Greek works into Slavonic and to correct other already translated works. His various works against monastic property repeat the same pure, ascetical views of Nil, but as far I could find, there is no direct influence or citation from Nil. Rather, both he and Nil agree only because they draw their ideal from hesychastic, scriptural monasticism.[114] Here we find among Maksim's writings the same stress as we found in those of Nil: monasteries must not possess any wealth or property but all should be distributed to the poor,[115] a condescension to the poor classes, a criticism of the abuses in contemporary monasticism with pleas for reform and a return to a more intense ascetical life,[116] whose ideal was the skete form of monasticism, the stress on a monk's complete dedication to self-perfection, em-

---

[111] *Prav. Sob., op. cit.,* 1863, p. 209.

[112] Pavlov, *op. cit.,* pp. 71–72.

[113] Cf. the work done on the Kormčaja kniga published Ivan Zuzek, S. J. of the Pontifical Oriental Institute of Rome: *The Kormčaja kniga: The Main Lines of the Origin, the History, the Juridical Value and the Use of the Kormčaja kniga in the Russian Church,* in the Series *Orientalia Christiana Analecta,* Rome, 19.

[114] Cf. Pypin, *Istorija russkoj lit . . . , op. cit.,* vol. 2, pp. 108–120, expecially pp. 119–120.

[115] *Sočinenija prepodobnago Maksima Greka,* Kazanskaja duxovnaja Akademia ("The Compositions of St. Maksim the Greek, Kazan Ecclesiastical Akademy"), 3 vols. (Kazan', 1859–60). Vol. 2: *Stjazanie o izvestnom zitel'stve lica ze stjazujuščixsja: Filoktimon da Aktimon sireč' ljubostjazatel'nyj da nestjazatel'nyj* (P. 89.) ("The Dialogue Between Filoktimon, the Advocator of Possessions, and Aktimon, the Advocator of Strict Poverty").

[116] *Ibid.,* p. 95. Also discourse no. 1, p. 5 and foll.

phasis on the interior with a rejection of dead formalism and ritualism,[117] and, lastly, a high esteem for scholarly, literary research and a critical spirit against all error, phantasy and heresy in the holy writings.[118] For this spirit, similar to that of Vassian and later of Artemij, he was accused of heresy twice, in 1525 and in 1531, and imprisoned.

Metropolitan Daniel, Joseph's successor in counteracting these "rational" ideas sown by Nil and cultivated by his successors, labels Vassian, because of his rejection of monastic possesions, as a heretic (and thus along with him his starec Nil), because he contradicts the sacred tradition of the miracle-workers who maintained the right of monasteries to have possessions as they proved by their own example. "You call the miracle-workers troublemakers, because they had in their monasteries' possession villages and peasants."[119] In Maksim's trial Daniel makes the same accusation: "Yes, you also, Maksim, blaspheme and calumniate the holy miracle-workers, Peter and Aleksej and Iona, metropolitans of All-Russia and the saintly miracle-workers, Sergej and Varlaam and Kirill and Paphnuntius and Makarij, saying 'Because they maintained towns and villages and peasants and had much wealth, for this reason they could not have been miracle-workers'."[120]

The official Church was strong enough to condemn Vassian and Maksim as heretics and one of the main charges as we have seen was Nil's position, clearly seen in his writings and in his protest in the Synod of 1503.

On this subject of Nil's influence in the polemic that by this time, the time of Vassian's and Maksim's trials, had engaged the whole of Russian society, we must mention yet Nil's influence on an important document concerning the polemic about monastic possession, that is, the Beseda prep. Sergija i Germana, Valaamskix Čudotvorcev ("Discourse of SS. Sergej and German, the Valaam miracle-workers").[121] It has never been

---

[117] *Ibid.*, p. 7; discourse no. 4, p. 127 and foll. also vol. 3, pp. 271–2.
[118] *Ibid.*, vol. 3, discourse no. 1, p. 5 and foll.; discourse 9, p. 60 and foll.; discourse 10, p. 79 and foll.
[119] "Prenie M. Daniila s Vassianom Patrikeevim", edited by O. Bodjanskij in *Čtenija*, no. 9 (1847), p. 3. ("Accusation of Metropolitan Daniel against Vassian Patrikeev".)
[120] "Prenie M. Daniila s Maksimom Grekom" in *Čtenija*, no. 7 (1847), p. 6. ("Accusation of Metropolitan Daniel Against Maksim the Greek".)
[121] O. Bodjanskij edits the text but calls it "Rassuždenie inoka-knjazja Vassiana o nepriličii monastyrjam vladet' otčinami" ("Argument of the Prince-monk Vassian on the Unsuitability for Monasteries to Exercise Power over Property"), in *Čtenija*, 1859, III, pp. 1–16. S. Avaliani, in his treatment of it is a source of history: "Beseda prep. Sergija i Germana valaamskix čudotvorcev kak istoričeskij istočnik" ("Discourse of SS. Sergej and German, Miracle-Workers of Valaam Considered as an Historical Source), gives a fairly complete bibliography of authors who treat this document. In *Bogosl. Vestnik*, 1909, III, p. 368.

decided conclusively who the author of this work was. Bodjanskij, Ikonnikov, Nevostruev, Xruščov, Žmakin claim Vassian Patrikeev as the author, while Pavlov, Ključevskij, Golubinskij, D'jakonov and Družinin rule him out as author, claiming it was written later than 1545, the death of Vassian, probably by a learned layman from Novgorod or at least written by one of the opposition to the possessors of the Josephian camp[122]

We are confronted here with a document in which Nil's attitude towards monasticism and poverty is most evidently a direct source of inspiration. The author writes with a fiery conviction, a genuine type of crusader who seems to have much more at stake than religious convictions. He shows us that the quarrel about monastic possessions at the time of its writing had become of universal interest to all classes of society. The basic idea is that of the irreconciliability of the monastic ideal and religious vows with monastic possessions which are the root cause of all evil in right government and in the common good of that society. Ideas repeated from Nil are those touching abuses in monasteries stemming from riches, plus the evil certain monks cause by their false interpretation of the "Holy Writings". After complaining that in times past monks fled the world and all riches in order to save their souls, the author paints a similar picture as Nil did.

In this present century there are men who love the great possessions that come from being monks and they embrace the habit as a spouse goes to meet his wife at the wedding, and not for the sake of humility and the salvation of his soul, but rather for high renown of the monastery's fame and its possessions...[123]

The Holy Fathers built monasteries and churches for the salvation of the human race and not for high learning and not for increasing the wealth of the monks; monasteries in the eyes of Christians were not for gathering up landed property but for never-ending singing and prayers sent up to the Lord in His praise and honour and adoration unceasing.[124]

The monks should live the life they vow which means to live according "to the teachings of the Gospel, the writings and Lives of the Holy

---

[122] Cf. Avaliani, S., op. cit., p. 369 and foll. Also Pypin, A. N., op. cit., II, pp. 121–9. Ikonnikov, V. S., Maksim Grek i ego vremja ("Maksim the Greek and His Times"), 2nd ed. (Kiev, 1915), pp. 404–408. From the internal and external evidence which Avaliani, op. cit., assembles, I would favour his conclusion and attribute it to Vassian; thus placing its composition after the condemnation of Vassian in the Synod of 1531 and not later than 1535.
[123] Text given by Bodjanskij, O. in Čtenija, loc. cit., p. 3. Nil's Ustav, p. 59.
[124] Čtenija, ibid., p. 4.

Fathers... to be guided by all the commands of God and to be monks manifesting every virtue instead of vice".[125] The good monk leaves to the Tsar and the civil authority the business of handling finances while he focuses all his attention on the interior battle, keeping ever in mind, like a good soldier, his dying hour and arming himself with purity in every virtue pleasing to God and the faith of the Orthodox Christianity.[126]

Like Nil, the author complains about the vast number of "false" writings and false interpretations of the Holy Writings, due to false monks being guided by passions rather than by love of virtue.

Because of the Tsar's naiveté, many monks, had they not in copying left out or suppressed from books containing the genuine writing of the Holy Fathers and had they not written in place of these passages things governing food and other things pleasing to themselves, then the Tsars and the Grand Princes would not, along with all the people, have been so naive, but rather they would have known what was genuine in all of the writings of the holy and saintly Fathers.[127]

It follows that these monks, having changed the writings of the Holy Fathers and their biographies, forced their falsifications as law in the synods. "There are many, and their number increases all the more in the world and among the learned advisers of the Tsar; but mostly they cite from books about invented facts; and there will be few who can discern among these and come to the aid of the secular Tsar with the holy, divine books."[128]

Such are some of the citations from this strange document that indicate an intimate connexion with Nil Sorskij, but in language and style, fire of conviction, worldly *savoir faire* and familiarity with princes, show a most direct dependence on the writings of Vassian, if the author be truly not he himself.

The last person we wish to cite as indicative of Nil's continuing influence on his disciples in the matter of strict monastic poverty is again Artemij. Artemij follows Nil's strict views on the monastic asceticism. He preaches Nil's totality and dedication to the contemplative life with absolute detachment from the "world". "If anyone loves this world, there is not the love of the Father in him."[129] He favours, as did Nil, the

[125] *Ibid.*, p. 7.
[126] *Ibid.*, p. 14.
[127] *Ibid.*
[128] *Ibid.*, p. 15.
[129] *RIB*, vol. IV, col. 1237.

skete form of monasticism.[130] Criticizing also the state of monasticism in his day, he laments the sad plight of those Josephian monasteries which introduced abuses of all sorts by allowing monastic possession. In this section he literally transcribes, as Vilinskij points out, a direct passage from Nil's Ustav[131].

That there were other followers of Nil's doctrine on monastic non-possession but who were greatly removed in time from Nil's direct influence and who were influenced by other infiltrations into Nil's purely ascetical ideal is clearly typified by the example of Prince Andrej Mixajlovič Kurbskij. This nobleman, faithful military leader of Ivan IV's campaign in Kazan' against the Tatars, exiled by flight into Lithuania, and known to posterity through his vivid writings, especially his pungent letter to the Tsar,[132] had other reasons than Nil had in battling against the rich monasteries. He was a devoted pupil of Maksim the Greek and from him he drew inspiration to devote the last part of his life in exile to learn Latin in order to translate the patristic heritage that was not available but in Latin translations. "True spirituality," in Kurbskij's eyes, "was to be found among the non-possessors,"[133] although the cited author goes on to give his true motive: Kurbskij, as so many other boyars of the generation after Nil's death favoured the same cause but in order "that more land would become available for the nobility." Still a passage from Kurbskij's second letter to V. Muromcev has much of Nil's protest in it: "As for the monks who have willingly renounced the good things of this world ... they are seduced by the very cunning serpent to forget their vows, they are choked by their many riches and their vast property and the many villages which they own, from which they gather great wealth, which they lock up in strong repositories."[134]

Again he shows the same zeal of Nil and Maksim the Greek in searching from among the many patristic writings for the false, erroneous, apocryphal and extirpating them from the Russian religious literature. In his first letter to Muromcev he shows his critical attitude towards such apocryphal writings as the Gospel of Nicodemus and the need to avoid

---

[130] Ibid., 1261, 1426. Cf. Vilinskij, op. cit., p. 347.
[131] Ibid., 1236. Ustav of Nil, p. 59. Vilinskij, op. cit., 348.
[132] In RIB, vol. XXXI (St. Petersburg, 1914). J. Fennell has made available in English in a critical edition his correspondence with Ivan IV: The Correspondence between Prince A. M. Kurbsky and Tsar Ivan IV of Russia. 1564–1579 (Cambridge, 1955).
[133] Andreyev, N., "Kurbsky's Letters to Vas'yan Muromtsev", in The Slavonic and East European Review, vol. XXXIII, no. 81, June, 1955, p. 425.
[134] Ibid., p. 431.

such as they contradict the true founts of revelation, especially the four
Gospels. In the second letter he elucidates his conviction on the necessity
to study the writings of the Fathers and to avoid such exaggerated fantasies as the Gospel of Nicodemus, which the devil uses to stir up heresies
in the minds of the simple believers.[135]

Thus we see Nil's influence extending into the public life of Russia in
this question of monastic possessions especially, which would have
lasting effects for the Church and State in Russia. In the *Stoglav* Council
called by Ivan IV in 1551 to legislate against the great abuses prevalent
at that time, the Tsar asked the opinion of Ioasaf, the retired metropolitan
before Makarij, on monastic possessions. He replied in the 100th Chapter
that the Synod of 1503 and other consequent ones, together with Ivan's
grandfather, Ivan III, and his father Vasilij III, canonized the opinion
of Joseph and his followers, while they forgot that of the holy monks
who had assisted at that first Synod, to the everlasting injury to the
Russian Church. The names of Nil Sorskij and his teacher, Paisij Jaroslavov, are not mentioned but his reference to them is clear.[136]

The doctrine of Joseph becomes canon-law by Chapter 101 of *Stoglav*
while the eremitic life as conceived by Nil in his *Ustav* and as lived by
his many faithful followers, the Trans-Volga Starcy, now becomes
tabooed, or at least difficult to live as forbidden by law. [137] Still Nil's
influence continues as we see by the numerous manuscripts copied out
by the hands of monks eager to realize the Kingdom of God in their
souls.

But if by now it is difficult to point out the clear influence of Nil in
these public issues that touched Russian society of the second half of
the 16th century, there is however another source that shows more
conclusively and on more solid ground Nil's continued influence after his
death and with this we can close this section. This is the large number of
monks who sanctified themselves in the Trans-Volga region during the
15th and first half of the 16th centuries. From the Lives of the earlier
Saints which they themselves wrote or from their own spiritual writings or
their biographies written by disciples we can see an undeniable influence
of Nil's spirituality. Nil's *Ustav* had had a great impact in forming,
first, as we have already shown, a vocal reaction against the stilted

---

[135] *Ibid.*, p. 429; found in *RIB*, XXXI, pp. 377–81 (the first letter). The second letter
is found *ibid.*, pp. 383–404.
[136] *Stoglav, op. cit.*, Chapter 100, p. 200.
[137] *Ibid.*, pp. 201–2; Pavlov, *op. cit.*, p. 116.

formalism of the times, then a hidden influence that is difficult to measure, but strong enough to divide the spirituality of this period into two decisive tendencies. From the written Lives of the Saints of this period we can see two distinct lines. But before these characteristics it would be better to present those saints who manifest clearly a similar spirituality to that of Nil. Then we can in summary show more clearly the two different spiritual accents.

The first great saint of this Trans-Volga region was Paul Obnora (†1429). His biography was written in the first half of the 16th century, shortly after the death of Nil,[138] and we see here terminology that is evidently taken from Nil and could not have been current in the time of St. Paul Obnora. Here, as in Nil's *Ustav*, we find solitude and silence stressed, love of prayer, meekness and obedience to the spiritual guide, a constant striving to obtain tranquillity or *hesychia*, emphasis on purification of the mind from all thoughts in order to give all attention to God through constant prayer. Fear of God, manual work, struggle against the thoughts that develop passionate desires, fasting, watching, tears are ideas repeated as in Nil's writings.[139] In an instruction of Paul to novices on prayer, found in the 16th century biography, we find for the first time the clear mention of the Jesus Prayer in the hesychastic terms used by Nil but with the recommendation to use the monk's *četki* or beads.

The same hesychastic terminology and stress on interior prayer and purifications is found in the life of St. Ioasaf, the Prince Andrej Zaozerskij who left his inheritance to become a simple monk and after five years died in the fame of a mystic, a Russian St. Aloysius Gonzaga. "He gave himself to the exercise of purifying the light of his intelligence, holding it concentrated in his heart and contemplating there the glory of the Lord."[140] It seems just to deduce that the authors of these biographies, writing in the time shortly after Nil's lifetime and in the geographical area where Nil's followers were living out his *Ustav*, came under his

---

[138] Kadlubovskij, A., *Očerki po istorii drevnerusskoj literatury zitij svjatyx* ("Sketches on the History of Ancient Russian Literature: Lives of the Saints") (Warsaw, 1902), pp. 202–3. Konoplev, N., "Svjatye volgodskago kraja" ("Saints of the Trans-Volga Region"), in: *Čtenija*, 1895, IV, pp. 68–69. Ključevskij, V. *Drevnerusskija zitija svjatyx, kak istoričeskij istočnik* ("Ancient Russian Lives of Saints as an Historical Fount") (Moscow, 1871), p. 271.

[139] From the citations made by Kadlubovskij, using mainly the Ms. Udol'skij, no. 309, and Graf Uvapov, no. 1247, *op. cit.*, pp. 203–7.

[140] Ključevskij, *op. cit.*, p. 275; Konoplev, pp. 56–7; Kadlubovskij, pp. 268–273.

influence and used his hesychastic terminology in their biographies of the saints who had lived before Nil.[141]

Kadlubovskij points out other Trans-Volga saints who lived several decades before Nil, but whose Lives were written during Nil's lifetime or shortly after his death and in which we find similar ideas to those expressed by Nil in his *Ustav*. Such are Dmitrij Priluckij (†1392) with his accent on spiritual alms to the neighbour, detachment and pilgrim wandering, manual work and constant thought of death;[142] Dionisij Glušickij (†1437) with his rigourous non-possession doctrine, love of solitude, love of the brethren, purification of evil thoughts in order to attain *hesychia*, meekness and self-abasement, forgiveness of enemies;[143] Gregory Pel'šemskij (†1449), the disciple of Dionisij, who stressed similarly solitude, complete detachment from the world, examination of the mind and heart, purification of all bad thoughts, directing every thought and action to God.[144] Again we see the strong similarity of stress on the hesychastic spirituality that Nil sought to bring to Russia from the Sinaite and Mount Athos hesychasts.

But those saints, who lived during Nil's own lifetime and who were avowed disciples of him or who were formed by Nil's followers, show without a doubt the great esteem and love that the monks of the Trans-Volga region had for Nil. An outstanding example of one of Nil's direct disciples who spread Nil's doctrine by copying out his writings and even writing a long introduction to the *Ustav*[145] of Nil is Innokentij Oxlevini (†1491) of the Komel'skij Monastery which he founded, after having left Nil's skete along the bank of the Sora. Little information about Innokentij is left us because, as with Nil, his writings and biography were burned. F. Byčkov gives us the few facts we know of him from the remains of a fragmentary biography.[146]

---

[141] Kologrivov, *op. cit.*, p. 152: "Ce n'est que dans des cas fort rares que cette action intérieure est décrite en termes techniques empruntés à la pratique des hésychastes. Leur vrai sens n'est vraiment intelligible qu'à la lumière de cette doctrine, dont Nil Sorskij (1433-1508) promulguera les fondements et développera les principes. C'est précisément la raison pour laquelle on ne peut rien déduire que nous fasse connaître l'état d'âme des vies comme celle de Paul d'Obnora où de saint Joasaph, ou les larmes hésychastes semblent manifestes, car ces vies furent écrites au XVIème siècle, comme on l'a dit, c'est-à-dire après la parution des ouvrages de Nil Sorskij. Elles parlent en termes qui ne correspondent pas nécessairement à la réalité."

[142] Kadlubovskij, *op. cit.*, pp. 189-193. Cf. also Konoplev, pp. 34-38.

[143] Kadlubovskij, pp. 194-199; Konoplev, pp. 43-53.

[144] Kadlubovskij, pp. 199-202; Konoplev, pp. 60-64.

[145] Cf. Part II, Ch. 5, ftnote, no. 40.

[146] Filaret, *Ist. russk. Cerkvi, op. cit.*, T. I, pp. 379-381. Konoplev, pp. 76-85.

From this we learn that Innokentij modelled his monastery on Nil's skete. "What concerns the practices in our hermitage in regard to prayer and singing, and what we eat and when it is fitting to leave the hermitage for the sake of manual labour, all these are set down in the writings of our lord and teacher, my Starec Nil."[147] In the ms. containing his *Nadslovie* or introduction to Nil's *Ustav*,[148] we find repeated the same doctrine as well as the exact terms used by Nil on "mental activity", plus the difference that Nil's pupil, writing after Nil's *Ustav* had already been circulated in the northern regions of the Trans-Volga, takes a polemic tone in stressing the superiority of interior prayer over mere external piety; evidently a hint that at this time there were developing the two diverse tendencies between the followers of Joseph and those of Nil.[149] Konoplev, using the Optyna-edition of the *Nadslovie*, summarizes the two parts of this work of Innokentij, the first, giving a synopsis of Nil's doctrine as contained in his *Ustav* and in the second, a discussion of the three monastic types, with strong arguments for the skete type.[150]

Other monks from the Komel' area who showed evident favour towards Nil's type of spirituality were Arsenij (†1550), Kornilij (†1537) and Stephan (†1542). Kornilij is one of the leading Trans-Volga ascetics and, due to his life written in 1589 in a most simple, unartificial style,[151] had a great influence on his contemporaries. From the evidence offered in this biography written so shortly after Kornilij's death and from his own *Ustav*[152] we see the great influence, which Nil's *Ustav* had on him. Konoplev, citing from the unedited manuscript of this biography,[153] and Kadlubovskij, citing from another,[154] summarize Kornilij's main lines of emphasis in such a way as to leave little doubt as to Nil's influence. His own personal life in the coenobitic monastery that he found-

---

[147] Byčkov, F., *Opisanie slavjanskix i russkix rukopisej sbornikov imperatorskoj publičnoj biblioteki*" ("A Description of the Manuscripts of the Imperial Public Library"), Part I, no. 4 and 27, pp. 15–16, 96–98. Ključevskij, *op. cit.*, p. 304, published his book before Byčkov and knew of only one ms. giving any biographical data of Innokentij: Collection of A. S. Uvarov, no. 107, fol. 64. Cf. Arxangel'skij, *op. cit.*, "Nil...", p. 60, ftnote, 40, 42.

[148] Arxangel'skij, *ibid.*, ftnote 42, p. 60.

[149] Konoplev, *op. cit.*, pp. 81–2.

[150] *Ibid.*, pp. 82–84.

[151] *Ibid.*, pp. 85–94. Ključevskij, *op. cit.*, p. 303.

[152] Edited by Bishop Amvrosij in *Istorija russkoj ierarxii*, vol. IV, pp. 661–704. Also it can be found in Murav'ev's work *Russ. Fivaida na severe, op. cit.*, pp. 41–50.

[153] Ms. from the collection of Spaso-Priluckij Monastery, no. 37/36, fol. 202–247. Konoplev, pp. 85–90.

[154] Ms., no. 608, fol. from the Moscow Synodal Library. Kadlubovskij, *op. cit.*, pp. 299–306.

ed show his love for prayer, interior self-perfection, his struggle against sinful thoughts, his striving ever to attain *hesychia*, a profound love for neighbour and forgiveness of all, especially those who offend oneself (illustrated by his readiness to forgive the robbers who took all he had) and an independence from all civil authority. Although he constructs his coenobitic monastery along the lines of the official Josephian policy, yet, as Konoplev points out after analyzing carefully the *Ustav* of Kornilij: "All this brings us to the conclusion that the influence of Nil Sorskij's views on St. Kornilij was much stronger than the influence of Abbot Joseph."[155]

Nil's spirituality gives the interior spirit of Kornilij while he takes from Joseph's *Ustav* those coenobitic regulations touching common prayer, food and drink, clothing, in a word, all those things touching the external side and discipline of the monks. As an example of Kornilij's dependence, besides the points given from his biography, Konoplev makes a comparison between a passage of Nil's introduction to his *Ustav* and that of Kornilij's introduction to his own *Ustav* and the words are practically identical.[156]

That Kornilij was evidently influenced by the spirit of Nil's *Predanie* and *Ustav* is seen by a comparison we can make with similar passages, especially corresponding to the *Predanie* where Nil had the same scope as Kornilij, to give principles and rules to their followers which would guide them in their external discipline.

Nil's *Predanie*	Kornilij's *Ustav*[157]	Similarity in terminology or ideas expressed.
P. 6	Pp. 684, 697–699	No money accepted from others nor asked; if direly needed, one could ask, but never more in excess of necessity.
Pp. 6, 8	Pp. 701–2	No property possessed.
P. 3	Pp. 662, 664, 668	Live according to God's commands and the traditions of the Fathers.
Pp. 3–4	P. 663	Drive out such as do not keep the same traditions.
P. 2	P. 663	The writer is an unworthy and sinful monk.

[155] *Op. cit.*, p. 101.
[156] *Ibid.*
[157] The citations are given according to the text reproduced by Bishop Amvrosij, *IRI, op. cit.*, pp. 661–704.

P. 5	P. 695	Confession to the Superior of any violations of the tradition of the Fathers.
P. 6	Pp. 693–696	No one is to leave the monastery except for grave reasons and with permission of the superior.
Pp. 8 and 37 *Ustav*	P. 693	Conversation with the brethren only on spiritual subjects.
P. 8	P. 662	Criterion: that which is helpful to souls.[158]
P. 9	Pp. 688–690 685–688	Strict poverty, possessing nothing personal.
Nil's *Ustav* Pp. 62–63	Pp. 666–668	Thought of death, last judgment.
P. 36	Pp. 691–693	Silence and prayer during manual work.

The list of saints of the Trans-Volga region, faithful to Nil's spirit could be extended but what has been already presented suffices to show that the majority of saints of this period come from this geographical area and represent a uniformity in their spirituality. Another point worth mentioning is the large number of noblemen who left their possessions and eagerly sought the solitude and silence that Nil had so insisted on in his writings. The contrast is striking, as Meyendorff points out, between the lack of great intellectuals among the Josephians and, on the contrary, the many brilliant followers of Nil.[159] Those who antedated Nil but whose written Lives were done by Trans-Volga followers of Nil and who belonged to the rich and distinguished families of Russia at that time were Prince Ioasaf Zaozerskij, Ignatij Priluckij (Ugličskij), Galaktion Vologodskij (Bel'skij), Dmitrij Priluckij, Paul Obnorskij, Gregory Pel'semskij. Direct followers who stemmed from leading families were the Knjaz'-monk, Vassian Patrikeev, Prince Kassian Mavnukskij, Innokentij Oxlevinin, Arsenij Komel'skij and Kornilij Komel'skij.[160]

From the ranks of these northern Trans-Volga monks of the 15th and early 16th centuries came the greater proportion of Russia's canonized saints of this period.[161] The northern Thebaid was the refuge of Russian monks in an unsettled time where they were able to keep alive the true traditions of Russian monasticism as canonized in the life of Sergej

[158] "Polezno dušam".
[159] "Les Biens Eccl...", *op. cit.*, *Irénikon*, Part II, 1956, p. 41. Cf. Kadlubovskij, *op. cit.*, p. 338.
[160] Konoplev, *op. cit.*, p. 110.
[161] Fedotov, G., *A Treasury of Russian Spirituality*, *op. cit.*, p. 85.

Radonež and passed on down through his followers who were in general the founders of these northern monasteries and the writers of the various *ustavs* which preserved the early Russian spirit. In outlining Nil's spirituality, we have stressed his dependence on the spirituality of the Fathers of the Desert and of the Sinaite and Mount Athos hesychastic fathers, but in the basic fundamentals that formed the spirituality of Sergej, Paul Obnora, Kirill Belozerskij, there was complete agreement.[162] We can safely affirm with Fedotov that there was an uninterrupted line of spiritual, ascetical and mystical tradition from Sergej Radonež to Nil Sorskij.[163] These characteristics that are found, not so much as principles formulated by Sergej, but rather as incarnated in his living example, are the same as the principles outlined by Nil in his *Ustav* with greater precision and order.

These characteristics common to Sergej, to Nil, and to the whole Trans-Volga "Thebaid" of the 15–16th century saints can be thus summarized:[164] (1) All exterior asceticism, all monastic discipline has meaning only in relation to the interior perfection of each monk. To this end he gives all his attention. (2) Thus this interior perfection is conceived as a gradual purification of the mind,[165] a constant struggle with thoughts that distract one from the "mental activity" or the constant living in prayerful union with God. (3) Striving to attain *hesychia* by avoiding passionate thoughts, contact with the "world", attachment to riches, by developing a deep spirit of humility, meekness, self-abasement and charity towards the neighbour as the outstanding virtues taught by Our Lord in the New Testament. (4) Stress on the literal obedience to the

---

[162] Kadlubovskij, *op. cit.*, p. 355.

[163] *Svjatye drevnej Rusi, op. cit.*, p. 165.

[164] Kadlubovskij, using manuscripts unavailable in the West and for the most part unedited, gives general tendencies deduced from the Lives of the Trans-Volga Saints, *op. cit.*, pp. 327–369. From our exposition of Nil's spirituality, it seems useless to point out the evident similarity.

[165] It must be pointed out that the English word "mind" does not render exactly what the Byzantines wanted to say by *nous* and the Russians by the equivalent *um*. Kologrivov gives an indication as to the breadth of this term in saying: "Il désigne non pas l'intellect au sens étroit du terme, mais l'ensemble des facultés cognitives et contemplatives, la lumière de la raison et de la conscience qui fait de l'homme un être personnel et libre... Les 'Startsi' russes identifient très souvent l'esprit avec l'image de Dieu en l'homme. En employant une terminologie plus moderne, nous pourrions l'appeler la conscience personnelle illuminant toutes les sphères de la vie humaine, elle-même conçue comme un écheveau complexe de rapports avec divers ordres de réalités. Quant au coeur, il désigne dans la tradition orientale le centre de l'être humain, la racine des facultés actives de l'intellect et de la volonté, le point d'où provient et vers lequel converge toute la vie spirituelle." *Op. cit.*, p. 152. Cf. Lossky, V., *La Théologie mystique de l'Église d'Orient* (Paris, 1944), pp. 197–8.

"commands" of the Lord in the New Testament. This means, above all, the strictest poverty, no possessions of large, landed properties. (5) In regard to civil authorities, a reverence and respect, but a preservation of monastic independence. (6) Lastly, the whole ascetical life is directed by a moderation, that is intelligent, that can reason and choose the necessary means in the necessary proportion to attain the one and only end desired: love and union with God. This moderation, besides showing itself in prudent mortification, in conscious self-motivation in opposition to a blind following of a written rule, also manifests itself in the avoidance in their writings of exaggerated, rhetorical language, legends, fables, weird accounts of demonical phenomena.

Nil was not starting a new spirituality, nor bringing anything new to Russian monasticism that could not have been found on Russian soil before his time. He wanted to formulate in an orderly manner that same tradition that his favourite hesychastic Fathers of the Sinaite and Mount Athos tradition had passed on to the early saints of Russian monasticism. Anthony and Theodosius Pečerskij, Abraham of Smolensk, Metropolitan Kiprian, Sergej Radonež, Paul Obnora and Kirill Belozerskij, with so many other hidden names who had lived this same teaching, lacked the patristic learning to synthesize all in an orderly composition. The followers who had imbibed Nil's ideas had put them down in an incarnated form in the saintly biographies which they wrote and thus passed on these ideas to the Russian masses.

But Nil's direct influence would always come from his *Predanie* and *Ustav*, copied out by hand and passed on from monastery to monastery, from house to house. When Joseph's ideal of a symphony between Church and State came crashing down under the autocratic secular fist of Peter the Great, there were still monks in Russia and abroad who were influenced by Nil's writings. Nikodim of Mount Athos collected in his *Philokalia* the hesychastic writings of the Holy Fathers who formed Nil's spirituality and Paisij Veličkovskij of Moldavia translated the *Philokalia* into Slavonic, calling it the *Dobrotoljubie* ("Love of the Good"). Nil's writings complemented the selections found in the *Dobrotoljubie* so that Nil's name was always revered by the Russian monks in subsequent centuries and also by the simple people, while St. Joseph Volokolamsk was a name in history books relegated to the 15–16th centuries.

That Nil's personal example of sanctity and his writings, plus his direct influence on his followers who handed down his tradition, had an influence that lasted beyond any Josephian attempt to do away with his type of monasticism by legislation can be seen clearly in the case of Nil's influence exerted on Paisij Veličkovskij. Paisij can be called the father of modern Russian contemplation for he started a renaissance of Nil's hesychasm, indirectly in Russia, due to circumstances that forced him to stay in Moldavia where he directly launched a revival of Nil's skete form of monasticism. Through his translation of the *Philokalia* he gave a great impetus to interior prayer and hesychastic spirituality in Russia.[166]

Paisij wrote an *ustav* which comprises 18 parts, many of which contain texts and ideas quoted from Nil and his sources. M. S. Borovkova-Majkova gives a critical comparison of these two *ustavs* and concludes:

> The repetition of ideas and even of exact words of Nil, the remembrance of him, all taken together, give us the impression not only of the influence of Nil on his near successors, but also on a man who lived 200 years later and thousands of miles away. Both strove to renovate monasticism. Naturally we do not deny the immediate influence of Athos on Paisij, but we say that the striking resemblance in the two compositions and the close acquaintance through writings of the young man with the Starets Nil and his evident interest in the latter give us the right to think that the ifluence of Nil was more than that of Athos.[167]

The author also quotes a manuscript containing Nil's *ustav*, his letters and a foreword written by Paisij's disciple, Vasilij, again showing Nil's influence even beyond the confines of Russia itself 200 years after his death.[168]

It is impossible to know what influence Nil's writings still have on monasticism in Soviet Russia today. But one last example will indicate to us the love and devotion for Nil and the appreciation of the timeliness of his spirituality for Russian *émigrés* abroad, not only for monks, but lay persons as well. In 1958 the Pochaevsky Press in Montreal, Canada[169] reprinted the edition of Bishop Justin's life of Nil and a summation of his *Ustav*.[170] Bishop Vitalij, in a very short preface, stresses how the

---

[166] Cf. the article written by Ieromanax Leonid, "Paisij Veličkovskij", in *Zurnal Moskovskogo Patriarxata*, October, 1954, pp. 53–59.

[167] "Nil Sorskij i Paisij Veličkovskij", in the *Collection dedicated to S. F. Platonov* (St. Petersburg, 1911), pp. 27–31.

[168] *Ibid.*, p. 32.

[169] Belonging to the Russian Synodal Émigré Church (Karlovtsy).

[170] *Zitie i tvorenija prepodobnago i bogonosnago otca našego Nila Sorskago* ("Life and Compositions of our Saintly and God-Bearing Father Nil Sorskij"). But curiously no mention is made that this is the work of Bishop Justin. The two editions of his work with the same title, Moscow, 1892 and Berlin, 1939, which I could check, are identical with this new edition of 1958. In presenting Nil's *Ustav*, the author gives substantially the whole composition, but it was not meant to be a literal translation.

modern world is in need of the sane spritual principles that Nil's *Ustav* outlined.

Instead of understanding the significance of the Gospels and going to Him who with a single word healed the possessed boy of Gerasa, there has appeared an innumerable quantity of psycho-analysts who, by means of very doubtful principles based on the half-atheistic philosopher Freud, attempt to substitute for the Holy Sacrament of Confession. . . . In the following composition of St. Nil Sorskij there is unfolded the simplest teaching of Christ's Church about the development of every kind of sin. By this teaching each person can, with surprising clarity, see how sin, the cause of all unhappiness in general and of all sufferings, of all mental disturbances and abnormalities, is conceived. One can follow the path it takes in the human soul and, most important of all, each person, in this unfolding of wisdom, can see his own personal relationship to the truth, to the God-Man who gave us an eternal example of the only genuine norm.[171]

[171] *Ibid.*, pp. 1–2, Foreword.

EPILOGUE

We have attempted to trace the general lines of Nil Sorskij's spirituality. Perforce, it must always remain an incomplete presentation, for there are only extant Nil's *Predanie* and *Ustav* with a handful of personal letters from which to draw. There is no existing autobiography or biography that can help us with missing details about Nil's personal sanctity. The task at first would have seemed as futile as trying to work out St. Basil the Great's spirituality from his *Regulae fusius tractatae* and a few personal letters. One could rightly ask if such an attempt indicates the whole gamut of Nil's spirituality or rather is not the spiritual doctrine contained in these few extant writings mere phases of a more complete and more complex spirituality? We have already quoted G. Levickij's objection that Nil's conception of the spiritual life as a constant battle to get rid of bad thoughts was too negative and left us with no positive, progressive teaching on the virtues.[1]

We do not know whether Nil had written other instructions similar to his *Ustav* for his disciples. But it is my belief that the spiritual doctrine contained in the *Ustav* is a true reflection of what Nil held and taught, and, had we any other writings, more letters, other instructions, I believe they would repeat the same basic teaching that we already see. This seems to be confirmed from Nil's letters which are still extant and which rarely give us anything new that was not already presented in his *Predanie* and *Ustav*. Also Nil's primary aim in presenting the traditional teaching of the Fathers on the spiritual life would lead us to the conclusion that the spirituality presented in these extant writings do give us his basic principles as he conceived the spiritual life.

Nil's Holy Writings from which he drew his spirituality were, as we have already pointed out, the Gospels and Epistles of the Apostles, the commentaries of the Fathers on these sacred writings, the other writings

---

[1] Levickij, G., *op. cit.*, pp. 339–344.

of the Fathers insofar as they conformed to the written Scriptures as
we know them to-day or to the oral traditions as handed down generation after generation by the teaching Church, and finally the Lives of the
Saints. It can justly be objected that Nil's views were too narrow, leaving
whole areas of the spiritual life untouched. His ideas on the social apostolate and "practical" fraternal charity towards all men, especially the
poor and sick, seem to indicate a spirituality that not only leaves the
"world" behind in the monk's flight into the desert, but goes so far as
even to forget its very existence. That Nil speaks rarely or not at all of
the sacraments, the chief means of receiving divine grace, of the Church
as a visible, hierarchical society, of the various virtues and the means to
develop these, does not mean of course that he denied them nor that he
had little use for them. It means that Nil was presenting a primitive spirituality. His sources, the Fathers of the Desert, did not speak much of
these. Evagrius, Climacus, Isaac the Syrian, Philotheus and Hesychius
of Sinai, Simeon the New Theologian, Gregory Sinaite, all took these
for granted. Their instructions were concerned with the one great obses-
sion – how to overcome the obstacles that impeded continual contemplation and union with God. Nil was presenting what he considered their
traditional teaching on this matter and his readers were disciples eager
to return to that primitive type of Christianity as depicted by the early
hesychastic Fathers.

The one conclusion that forces itself on us is that Nil faithfully transmitted in orderly, synthetic instructions the teaching of these early
Fathers. Nowhere does Nil cite local Russian saints or writers. At Mount
Athos, Constantinople (and possibly even in Palestine), he learned this
patristic spirituality and he was determined to build his whole spiritual
life and that of his disciples around it. The struggle for self-perfection
thus never loses its internal battle against the evil demons and the passionate thoughts. The psychology of thoughts and how they develop
into the eight passions is investigated only enough to give the battling
monk means to overcome them in their initial stage. Solitude and silence,
the emptying of the mind of all irrelevant thoughts in an effort to attain
tranquillity or *hesychia*, vigilance and sobriety, the constant thought of
death and the last judgment, tears of compunction, these form the basic
spirituality of Nil as they did for the early Fathers of the desert and for
those who later followed their spirituality. The Jesus Prayer, so biblical,
so full of tender love for Christ the Saviour and of compunction towards
one self, gave Nil, along with Climacus, Isaac, Philotheus, Hesychius,
Simeon and Gregory Sinaite, the basic means to combat the evil

thoughts, to gain purity of heart and to prepare the soul for higher contemplation.

These, to my mind, reflect the basic spirituality of Nil Sorskij, a reflection of the true hesychastic Fathers. If many points of their mutual teaching were not too clear or developed, it was due to their conviction of the absolute importance of their one aim – to pray always. If Nil fled from the world, feared to mingle with the world except in giving "spiritual" alms, seemed to favour a more "angelic" life than "human", it was because he was preaching a special vocation – that of a monk who professionally strove at every moment of his life to live only for God. Was he condemning the others who did not follow him? No, there were various gifts of grace, various vocations. "The work of silence is one and that of a coenobite another; but each abiding in that to which he has been called, shall be saved."[2]

Nil's spirituality must be always judged and evaluated in the light of the special vocation that he was advocating, one of "hesychasm" in the true sense of the word as the early ascetical Fathers conceived it with no overtones of neo-hesychasm or Palamism and no immoderate stress of physical method divorced from a solid, *penthos* asceticism.

Presupposing a basic preparation already in the coenobitic life, his followers were invited to a lifetime, not of enjoying selfish spiritual delights, but rather of fighting a more intense battle with the enemy in order that God be greater glorified in their divesting themselves of any inordinate affections by conforming their own will to God's.

Nil never wanted to start a "movement", unless it were to stir up among his Russian fellow-monks a greater desire for interior perfection by a return to a purer Christian asceticism. Yet Nil, in his hidden hermitage near the swampy Sora, through the disciples he formed and the few writings he left us, especially his *Predanie* and *Ustav*, has given his people the spiritual foundation for all that is praiseworthy in the phrase "Holy Russia". At a time when his contemporaries were stressing a dead ritualism, the strict letter of the law with very little interior persuasion or understanding, Nil recalled to them the need for interior perfection built upon an intelligent and truthful understanding of the revealed Word of God in Holy Scripture and Tradition.

His spirit of criticism sifted the falsity from the truth; his spirit of compunction, self-depreciation, Christ-like meekness, gave them a dis-

[2] *Ustav*, p. 26.

trust of their own will and subjected it to the delicate operations of the
Holy Spirit's grace in order to know and do always God's will.

At a time when Russia was becoming a nation and a world-power,
when the official Russian Church and the State both saw advantages in
developing the doctrine of the Third Rome, Nil quietly preached a Messianism that was above chauvinism, that was universal and that embraced
all nations destined to be saved through the merits and grace of the one
human and divine Messias, Jesus Christ. When monks were obedient
to the letter, but forgot to sacrifice to God their complete judgment, Nil
stressed absolute obedience to the commands of God, as interpreted by
the spiritual *Starec*. With his emphasis on the Kingdom of Heaven
within man, he laid the foundation for the *Starec*-tradition that in the
18th and 19th centuries would produce saints like Serafim of Rostov
and the Starcy of the Optyna-hermitage made famous by the writings
of Dostojevskij and I. Kireevskij.

Thus it can be said that Nil was no original thinker, no abstract spec-
ulator. His ideas came from the Fathers whom his contemporaries also
knew, but Nil shows originality by his synthesis and emphasis of certain
faucets that hitherto had been found only in embryonic development
among the early Russian Saints. Nil bequeathed the beginning of a new
intellectual development in Russia by his emphasis on the development
of the full human personality by submitting the intellect and will of man
to the interior liberty that comes from a delicate cooperation with grace.
Not just blind piety or external obedience but self-persuasion and interior conviction, based on reason and faith, would be his distinguishing
trait. To an age and a people that tended to embrace extremes in lines
of human conduct, Nil preached human discretion and a proportioned
moderation which distinguished clearly between the essence and accidentals, between the end and the means in the spiritual life.

The sad part of Russian history is that the 16th century insisted that
a choice had to be made between the pure evangelical spirituality of Nil
Sorskij and the accommodated Christianity of Joseph Volokolamsk.
And it chose to follow the aegis of Joseph with his emphasis on external
ritualism, monastic possessions and the Church in submission to the
Tsar, the Christian Prince who not only guided the destinies of All-Russia, but of the Third Rome. When the Tsar, as Peter the Great, forgot
his Christian duties, he found little opposition in wiping away the Patri-
archate and setting up his own autocratic Synod to guide the Church
as he saw fit. When the God-fearing Tsar was removed and replaced by
the God-hating Communists, Third Rome came tumbling down and the

chauvinistic Messianism of the Slavophiles disappeared among the rubble. One wonders whether the destiny of Russia would have been different had no choice been made, but rather the spirituality of Nil would have been allowed to continue to develop hermitages faithful to his principle, alongside with the more social-slanted spirituality of Joseph.

APPENDIX I

LETTER I[1]

Letter of the Great Starec Hermit to a Brother Asking about Temptations[2]

You have stirred up a praiseworthy desire, dearest friend, to hear the word of God, seeking to gain assurance for yourself. You are desirous to keep yourself from all evil and to learn how to do only good. But how much better it would have been for you to seek that from good and intelligent persons, instead of asking it of me, an irrational sinner. For I cannot claim to be among the ranks of learned men.[3] For this reason

93   I declined and postponed for a long time, not because I was unwilling to be of assistence in fulfilling your good wishes, but rather on account of my lack of intelligence and my sinfulness. What indeed can I say, when I myself do not do anything good? What sort of understanding does a sinner have, besides that of his sin? But because you have so strongly insisted that I write you a letter on acquiring virtues (I know it is presumption on my part to do that which is beyond my capacity),

94   I cannot ignore your request, otherwise you will be greatly offended. You asked about the temptations that have been occurring to you about your former worldly life. You yourself, reflect from your own past experience; how many sorrows and how much seduction does this fleeting world contain. And what evil it rewards those who are enamoured by it. How it laughs when those who served it must finally depart. Seemingly sweet, even caressing with pleasant things during life, how bitter it becomes in the last moments. For in proportion as they think the goods of the world are coming to them in ever increasing abundance and at the same time they bind themselves all the more to them, so in that degree do they increase their own sorrows. The goods of the world seem

---

[1] This letter is addressed to the Prince-monk Vassian Patrikeev. I follow in this translation the Troick. Ms. 188, fol. 93–98, now found in the Lenin Public Library. The numbering in the margin corresponds to the *folia* of the ms. As these letters do not exist as yet in English, it was thought necessary to append a translation. The references in the main body of this work are given to the folia of the mss. and not to these pages.
[2] Filaret in "*Obzor...*", *op. cit.*, footnote no. 116, claims this letter was sent by Nil to the Prince-monk Kassian Mavnukskij and many subsequent authors repeat this opinion, but we hold with Gorskij *(Pribav. k Tvor.*, vol. VI, 1848, pp. 143–144) and Arxangel'skij, *Nil...*, *op. cit.*, p. 58, on the basis of this Troick. Ms. 188 which we have before us, that it was addressed to Vassian as can be seen from the top of fol. 93.
[3] Surely a sign of Nil's self-abasement and not an indication that he was of a peasant class and not well-educated.

evidently good, but interiorly they are full of much evil. For this reason those who have a truly sane understanding should not become attached to that which proves itself to be only ephemeral.

At the end of this life, what usually happens? Think very seriously about this statement: "Of what profit is the world to those who have bound themselves to it?"[4] Even if one has much praise, honours, riches, are not all these as nothing? For is it not indeed like a passing shadow and as smoke that soon disappears?[5] And many of these men, immersed in and moved by the attractions of the things of this world, while enjoying youthful happiness, were harvested by death as flowers of the fields, in full bloom, are cut down.[6] Even though they were unwilling, they had to depart from here. But when they were living yet in this world, they could not be bothered with reflections on its corrupting stench, but they busied themselves with beautifying the body and in seeking physical comforts. They were able to make their intellects apt for making worldly gains and they passed their time in studies, crowning the body in this fleeting time as the be-all and the end-all. Even if they attained all their desires, nevertheless, they could not be preoccupied about the future and unending happiness. What is to be thought of such persons? Are they not, as a certain wise saint said, the most foolish persons in the whole world?

Some of them, being more pious, turned their minds to thoughts about the desire to save their souls. They had the courage to wage war against the passions and live, as far as was possible, a virtuous life. They wanted to be freed and to cut themselves off from this world, but they were not able to detach themselves from its knot of snares and its evil cunning. The all-loving God has taken you from this world and placed you in His service by His mercy and design. For this you must give great thanks for His mercy and do all in your power to do all that will please Him and that will serve for the salvation of your soul. Forget the past as not being profitable and strive for future virtue, which leads to eternal life.[7] Rejoicing, go on in the honour of such a noble calling which is bestowed upon those who seriously seek the heavenly *patria*. In regard to your question about impure thoughts which the devil implants in our souls, do not be too overwhelmed by this trial, nor be frightened. Because not only to us, so weak and passionate, does such opposition come, so the Fathers say, but also to those who have already progressed by a praiseworthy life and enjoy particular, spiritual graces; even they have a bitter struggle with such thoughts.[8] They undergo great feats of asceticism and by the grace of God barely manage to drive them away, being always conscientious to get rid of them. And you ought to be consoled by this, but care-

95

---

[4] Matt. 16, 26.
[5] Wisdom 2, 2–5.
[6] Ps. 102, 15.
[7] Fil. 3, 13.
[8] *Ustav*, p. 34.

fully cut away all such evil temptations. Have at hand the constant, victorious prayer against them. Call on Our Lord Jesus. With this cry you will drive away such thoughts which quickly enough will flee away, as John Climacus said: "Fight the enemy with the name of Jesus; there is no more powerful weapon."[9]

If these evil thoughts become more powerful in their attack against you, then rise up and with eyes toward Heaven and arms stretched out, sincerely say with compunction: "Have mercy on me, Lord, for I am weak.[10] You, Lord, are powerful and success is yours; fight for us and conquer, O Lord."[11] And if you will do so diligently with experience you will learn in many ways how these thoughts are to be conquered by

96   the power of the All-High. Do also some hand-work, for such drives away evil thoughts. Such is the angelic tradition given to one of the great saints.[12] Learn something by heart from Holy Scripture, concentrate your mind on this, for such passages turn back the onslaught of the devil. So have the Holy Fathers found it to be. Keep yourself from hearing conversations and seeing impure things for such stir up the passions and strengthen unclean thoughts.[13] God will help you.

You also mention fear. Fear is a trait of children and not for matured souls. But for you it should not have a place. When such thoughts occur, fight manfully so that they do not overcome you and make your heart resolute in a deep trust in God, saying the following: "I have a God who is watching over me. Without His will nobody can harm me in anything. Even if He allows something to happen to me which would make me suffer, I would not take that for evil, because I do not wish to make His will ineffective, because the Lord knows much more than I and wishes only my profit. So I am thankful for all because of His clemency." Thus with the grace of God, you will be firm in doing good. Arm yourself always with prayer and when in whatever places such thoughts occur, be all the more careful in going there. Stretch out your hands in the form of a cross; call out to the Lord Jesus[14] and, with the help of the Most High, do not be frightened "from the night's fear and from the arrows flying during the day".[15]

So much for these. In all other things as far as is praiseworthy, honourable and virtuous, think about them and do, be courageous in good;

97   hating all evil; give obedience to your superior and other Fathers in the Lord in regard to every good work. You have now been given a responsible position, or you will receive such a one. Fulfill it with brilliance

[9] Climacus, *PG*, 88, *Gradus 21*, 945C. *Ustav*, p. 23.
[10] Climacus, *op. cit.*, *Gradus 15*, 900D. Letter to Gurij, fol. 100.
[11] Already quoted in Nil's earlier letter to Gurij, fol. 100 where Nil takes his citation from Isaac, *Logos 54*, *op. cit.*, p. 320.
[12] *Ustav*, pp. 32–33 where Nil quotes the tradition as given in the *Vita S. Antonii, PG*, 65–76A–B.
[13] Advice given also to Gurij, fol. 102.
[14] Climacus, *Gradus 15*, 900D.
[15] Ps. 90, 5.

and a devoted diligence, as serving Christ Himself. Hold every brother as a saint.[16] If you must speak, ask a question, or give an answer to anyone, do it with a pleasant tone and gentle speech, showing spiritual love and true humility, and not an indifferent, superficial manner. Do not offend any brother. Stay close to a devout Father and this at the proper time and in the proper measure. Do not mingle with those who are not so. Keep yourself under control, not losing your temper. Do not judge anyone in anything, even if his actions appear not good, but consider yourself as sinful and utterly useless. If from the superior or any other Father so appointed, you have need of anything, first pray over it, reflecting whether this is truly useful and then ask for it. If a thing does not turn out as you would have wished, do not be dejected; no need to be angry simply because it did not turn out according to your wishing, even if a thing seemed good to you. But with patience go on and with calmness and, taking your time, do all things. If you will so conduct yourself as to seek to please God and to save your soul, then God, knowing in all ways how to help and knowing also the exact time to do so for that end, will give you help according to your needs. Be sincerely bent on obeying the Divine Writings. With their sayings your soul will be refreshed as with living water. Be careful as far as your strength permits to live according to them.

So to such as have an understanding of Divine Writings and a spiritual wisdom and a life mirroring the virtues, to such, I say, strive to give yourself under obedience, and be an imitator of their way of life, showing
98 patience in sorrows and praying for those who offend you. Consider those as your benefactors. Understand that this which I am telling you is wisdom from Divine Writings, which tell us the wish of God to do good. The saints of all times are those who "having served the cause of right, received the fulfillment of promises".[17] Those, who walked in the paths of virtue, not only bore hardships and sorrows, but even endured the cross and death and this is a sign of the love of God, that sufferings are granted to the one doing what is right. This is called a gift of God, according to the Apostle Paul in his writings. This has been given us from God, not only to believe in Christ, but also to suffer for Him. This makes a man a participator in the Passion of Christ[18] and like to the saints who bore hardships for His Name. God blesses such in His Name who love Him in no other way but by sending them temptations in the form of sufferings. And by this are the lovers of God distinguished from the others, that the first live in sorrows and hardships while the lovers of the world rejoice in food and comforts. And this is the true way, to bear trials of sufferings because of virtue. Teaching them to follow

[16] Probably Nil is here quoting from Simeon the New Theologian who has the same thought, *PG*, 120, no. 123, 669D.
[17] Heb. 11, 33.
[18] 2 Corin. 1, 5.

this path, God will lead His sufferers to eternal life.[19] For this reason it is becoming that we travel along this path with joy, keeping the commandments of the Lord and thanking Him with all our heart for having sent us this blessing and grace out of His love for us. We must pray incessantly for His grace, recalling the end of this life of sorrows and the unending happiness of the future life. And God will comfort your heart with every joy and consolation and will keep you in His fear, by the prayers of the most Pure Mother of God and all the Saints. Do not forget me before the Lord; remember me a sinner in your prayers, for I tell you what good you must do while I myself do not do it. May God deliver me from the swirling flood of passions and lead me out of the darkness of my sins.

LETTER II

Of the Same Starec Nil to Someone Seeking Help[20]

Even as in your pious conversation with me, most reverend Father, so also in your letter which you sent me, you ask me, so utterly incapable, to send you some useful, written discourse both pleasing to God and profitable to the soul. But I am a sinful man and unintelligent, overcome by every passion an so I feared to begin such a thing. For this reason I have declined and put it off. But because your spiritual love ordains me, even forces me beyond my capacity, to write you something edifying, for this reason I persuaded myself to do it.

Your first question: how to combat impure, carnal thoughts? About this not only must you have care and perform works of asceticism, but your whole being must fight the battle along with God, because this is a great struggle, the Fathers say, having a double conflict (to wage) in the soul as well as in the body. There is nothing more necessary for your very existence than this. For this reason one must be powerfully careful and diligent and courageous to keep one's heart from such thoughts. Having the fear of God before our eyes, we must remember our vows, which we have professed to live in chastity and purity. Chastity and purity not only look to external things of life, but also it means a man is chaste and pure when he protects his heart from polluting thoughts, by cutting out with

---

[19] I Corin. 1, 18 and foll.

[20] Letter written to Gurij Tušin. Again in our Troick. Ms. no. 188, there is written on top by hand the name of the receiver: "Gurij Tuš" (fol. 99A). Gurij was a noble of the Kvašnin-Tušin family, son of the boyar Michael Aleksandrovič. Bishop Amvrosij in his listing of higoumens of the Kirill-Belozerskij Monastery indicates Gurij as the tenth after the founder St. Kirill, holding office in 1461–1462 for nine months. Cf. *IRI, op. cit.*, vol. IV, p. 497. He enjoyed a reputation as a spiritual director and also followed Nil's example in the literary editing of critical Lives of the Saints. Nikol'skij, "Obščinnaja...", *op. cit.*, p. 174, ftnote 2, gives an extensive list of works that Gurij copied out by hand. He died July 8, 1526. Cf. Nikol'skij, *op. cit.*, p. 187.

great diligence all such thoughts. To gain this great victory over such thoughts it is necessary to pray to God. This was the constant tradition of the Holy Fathers, expressed in various ways but always the same thing understood. David is said to have prayed in this fashion: "My enemies now have surrounded me; my Joy, deliver me from those who have besieged me."[21] And another passage from his psalms says: "God, attend to my help"[22] and others similar. Again another, "Judge, Lord, those insulting me and impede those who struggle against me"[23] and other psalms. Call on the help of those about whose great exploits to preserve chastity and purity we read in their lives.[24] When the battle becomes very intense, then rise up and with eyes to Heaven and arms outstretched, pray thus: "You are powerful, O Lord, and Yours is success. Fight on our behalf and be victorious in this battle, O Lord."[25] And cry out to the All-Powerfull for help with the humble words: "Have mercy on me, Lord, for I am powerless."[26] For such is the teaching handed down by the Saints. And if you will so conduct yourself in these struggles you will learn from experience, that by the grace of God, these (i.e. bad thoughts) are more easily conquered. "Always flog the enemies with the weapon of the name of Jesus"[27] than which there is no more powerful way to attain victory. Keep yourself from seeing persons and hearing such conversations for these stir up the passions and provide unclean thoughts and God will keep you from these.

In regard to your second question about blasphemous thought, this is indeed a shameless and cruel evil; it attacks with great force and at intervals; such is not only the case now, but was also in ancient times. So the Great Fathers and Holy Martyrs found it and at the very moment when the tormentors wanted to inflict on their bodies wounds and bitter death, because they professed faith in Our Lord Jesus Christ. And against this temptation they secured victory thus: they did not blame their own soul for this thought but accused the wretched demon, saying against the blasphemous spirit: "Get behind me, Satan: I worship the Lord my God and Him alone I serve."[28] "On you let your blasphemy be again heaped.[29] The Lord also writes thus: 'Depart from Me!'[30] God who created me according to His image and likeness,[31] may He destroy you." If after such a prayer the shameless thought still lingers on, turn your thought

---

[21] Ps. 21, 13; 107, 10–14.
[22] Ps. 21, 20; 39, 14; 70, 12.
[23] Ps. 30, 16; 34, 1, 22 and foll.
[24] *Ustav*, p. 44.
[25] Nil already quoted this from Isaac the Syrian in his *Ustav* in treating the vice of fornication, p. 45. Isaac, *Logos 54*, p. 320.
[26] Ps. 6, 3; Climacus, *Gradus 15, op. cit.*, 900D.
[27] Climacus, *Gradus 21*, 945C.
[28] Matt. 4, 10.
[29] Ps. 7, 17. Climacus, *Gradus 23*, 977B–C.
[30] Matt. 16, 23.
[31] Gen. 1, 26.

101 to something else, divine or human, if something proper can be found. Keep yourself from pride and take care to walk the path of humility. For the Fathers said: "Indeed, pride gives birth to blasphemous thoughts."[32] They happen out of the devil's envy for us. If from him or another source they come, like a deer bitten by a poisonous, wild beast, nevertheless humility is capable of destroying this passion and not only this, but also others, so the Holy Fathers said.[33]

In your third question you seek how to abandon the world and this shows your good diligence. Strive concretely to accomplish the following in your life, for this is the golden road to eternal life. Having understood in their clear wisdom, the blessed Fathers travelled along this way. For if one does not cut himself completely from the world, he will be like one who habitually has intercourse with the world, for certain images and worldly habits, formerly acquired by him from hearing and seeing worldly things, again are renewed and one cannot carefully persist in prayer and learn to find always God's will. One wishing to learn how to please God must leave the world. Do not desire the pleasant conversations of your ordinary friends and of worldly wise men and of those absorbed in unending worries, as the posessing of monastery wealth and properties, which they consider under the guise of generosity and from an ignorance of Divine Writings or from conducting themselves according to their own passionate ways which they consider as virtues.[34]

102 But you, o man of God, do not have anything to do with such; it is not fitting even to converse with such, not even to reprove or correct them, but let God do this, for God is powerful to correct them. Keep control of yourself in all ways with courageous boldness, for self-control is, as is written, like a great fire: "all things flee from its face".

And turn away from hearing and seeing the affairs of the brethren and from their secrets and their actions. For that empties the soul of every good and makes one focus attention on the failings of the neighbour, while one leaves off weeping for his own sins. And do not be concerned to be engaged quickly in conversations with the brethren, even if they may appear to be helpful conversations. But if some brother wants to know something from us and truly seeks the word of Good and if we have something to give him, we even are obliged to give to him not only the word of God, but according to the testimony of the Apostles, even our own soul. Give attention to such and wish them well in their labours, for they have spiritual wisdom and such are the children possessing the secrets of God. But conversations with others who are not of this type, even if few, tend to dry up the flowers of virtues. The garden of the soul, not long ago in full flower from the seclusion of *hesychia* and immersion

---

[32] Climacus, *Gradus 23*, 965C; 969B–C; 976B–C.
[33] Climacus, *Gradus 25*, 1004A.
[34] A clear reference to Joseph and his school of followers.

in meekness and childlikeness, was planted by the flowing waters of penitence, as a wise Saint said.[35]

In your fourth question you also ask: how not to wander from the true path? About this I will give you good advice. Bind yourself to the laws of Divine Writings and follow them, the True Writings, Divinely inspired. For there are many writings but not all are Divine. You, seeking the true from the various readings, stick to it and converse with prudent and spiritual men, because not all, but only the intelligent, understand these and without proof from such writings, do not do anything. Thus have I always done;[36] see, your love for God makes me senseless even to the point of speaking about myself. But as it has been said: "My secrets I open to those who love me;"[37] for this reason do I tell you this. For I do not act without testimony from the Divine Writings, but finding something in Them, I do it as far as in me lies. For when I must do something, first I search the Divine Writings and if I do not find something in agreement with my understanding on how to begin a thing, I lay it aside until I do find something.[38] When I betake myself, by the grace of God, to the task, I do with tenacity that which is known. Of myself I do not dare to do such because I am an ignoramus and a peasant.[39] In this way, if you also wish, act according to the Holy Writings and according to your understanding of them; be diligent in keeping the commands of God and the traditions of the Holy Fathers. And if the agitations of worldly things should disturb your heart, do not be alarmed. We rely on the unmovable rock of the Lord's commandments.[40] And we take defense by means of the traditions of the Holy Fathers. Be zealous towards those whom you hear and see bearing witness by their living and wisdom to the same as is found in the Holy Writings, for their way is the right ways of journeying. And writing this deep in your heart, continue unswervingly in the way of the Lord and you will not err, by the grace of God, from the truth. For it is written that it is impossible for a wise man, knowing the right and living in virtue, to perish. But those who with a distorted mind do God's work transgress from the right path. Travelling without turning back, "having put your hand to the plow of the Lord and not looking back, you will be ushered into the Kingdom of God".[41] And take care, that, having received the seed of the word of God, you do not turn your heart into a path of stone, nor thorns, but into fertile earth, bringing forth manifold fruit for the salvation of your

103

---

[35] Gregory Sinaite, *PG*, 150, 1333D; but Gregory is evidently borrowing from Climacus, *Gradus 28*, 1129B.
[36] Nil repeats in this paragraph exactly what he had said to German. Cf. 105B.
[37] Letter to German, 104A.
[38] *Ibid.*, 105B–106A.
[39] *Poseljanin* in the Slavonic. For this reason Arxangel'skij and Grečev believed Nil to have been of the peasant class, but it is evidently an expression of this self-abasement and humility.
[40] I Corin. 10, 4.
[41] Lk. 9, 62.

soul.[42] Indeed, I rejoice, seeing your wisdom in hearing the word of God and I praise worthily the things found in you and corrected by virtue; I give thanks to God, seeing in you one who, having heard the word of God, kept it. I beg you, for the sake of Our Lord, pray for me a sinner, preaching what good must be done, but not doing any of it ever myself. God, the Creator, praising exceedingly and giving in every way gifts to those who graciously do His will, may He give you intelligence and assurance to do His Holy will, by the prayers of our Most Pure Queen, Mother of God and all the Saints, for He is blessed forever. Amen

LETTER III

Of the Same Great Starec Nil to a Brother Requesting Him to Write Something of Profit to his Soul[43]

Your letter, Father, which you wrote me, requested me to write you something useful to you and at the same time to tell you something of myself. (You write) that you think I grieve because of the conversation

[42] Lk. 8, 5 and foll.; Mk. 4, 26 and foll.

[43] We follow again the Troick. Ms. no. 188, fol. 104–108, now in the Lenin Public Library. It is found also, as the other letters of Nil, in an uncritical edition (at times a faulty transposition of the text) of the Elagin Edition, *op. cit.*, (St. Petersburg, 1864), pp. 178–183. We place it here as the third of Nil's letters because this is the order found in Ms. 188, but from the content it is clear that it was written quite shortly after Nil's arrival from the East, for he mentions his withdrawal from the Kirill-Belozerskij Monastery as a recent event. On the top of this ms. are found the words: "German pustoj". Arxhangel'skij, *op. cit.*, p. 49, cites another ms. of the Novgorod-Sophia Collection, no. 1460, fol. 326–327, where this letter is also attributed to the recipient German: "Letter of Starec Nil of Trans-Volga hermitage and skete of Sora to the Starec German Podol'nyj". The opinion of Gorskij (expressed in his article in *Pribav. k Tvor.*, T. VI, 1848, p. 142) and that of Makarij (*Istorija...*, *op. cit.*, T. VII, p. 262) that this letter was written to Innokentij is clearly to be rejected, for Nil would not tell of his pilgrimage and return to his fellow-traveller to the East. This is the same German who was the recipient of two stern letters of protest written by Nil Polev, Joseph's follower, in evident protest against the Trans-Volga position taken by German in the Joseph–Archbishop Serapion dispute. We have already quoted German's position as criticized by Nil Polev: "You say that it is not right either to judge or send the enemies of the faith and the apostates to prison, but only to pray for them." Cf. Xruščov, *op. cit.*, p. 239. He is further criticized by the Josephians because he openly expressed the opinion that "the patriarch and the whole Synod fear the Tsar and proceed with weakness and judge falsely". Cf. Žmakin's edition of these letters, in *Ž.M.N.Pr.*, Sept. 1881, pp. 185–199. German was of noble birth (Nikol'skij: "Obščinnaja...", *op. cit.*, p. 181) and entered the Kirill-Belozerskij Monastery where he must have come in contact with Nil. From the letter he is referred to as the "hermit", so at this time, between his stay in the Kirill Monastery and his stay in the Podol'nyj Monastery, 1509–10, from where he gets his last name (Cf. Nikol'skij: "Opisanie...", *op. cit.*, p. XXXIX) he was probably living a hermit's type of life. He died April 30, 1533. Cf. Arxangel'skij, *op. cit.*, p. 51, ftnote, no. 9.

which we had with you when you were still here; for this (you ask me)
104   to pardon you. I give advice to myself and also to you as to my former,
dear friend, recalling to the mind what is written: "I open my secrets
to my sons of my house."[44]

We should not do things simply nor in a way only that seems best to
us, but according to the Divine Writings and according to the tradition
of the Holy Fathers. Before we left the monastery, was it not only for
spiritual benefits and not for any other reason that we were guided in
our actions? Nowadays one does not see in the monasteries an observance of the laws of God according to the Holy Writings and the tradition of the Holy Fathers, but rather we act according to our own wills
and human ways of thinking and often we fall to the very seduction and
do such things, all the while considering them as acts of virtue.

This happens from our ignorance of Holy Writings because we are not
diligent to search the Holy Writings with fear of God and humility, but
in our carelessness, we make them void by our human way of thinking.
I spoke to you thus for this reason, because it is true, and because you
are one who does not wish to hear and keep the word of God in a phari-
saical manner. I, not pandering you nor keeping from you the difficulty
of the narrow and sorrow-ladened path, proposed to you a subject of
this nature, but to others I speak in a different way about this same
matter.

105   You know my utter incapability, right from the beginning, for you
were my dear spiritual friend from the start. For that reason I now write
you, speaking frankly about myself because your love for God forces
me and makes me irrational even to the point of writing you about myself.
When we lived in the monastery together,[45] you know how I removed
myself from worldly enticements and I have always acted as far as I have
strength according to the Divine Writings, even if I am incapable of
that because of my laziness and ignorance. Thus, after I returned from
my pilgrimage,[46] I came to the monastery, but I fixed for myself a cell
outside and near the monastery and so I lived as far as my strength permitted. Now I have moved farther from the monastery, because, by the
grace of God, I found a place suited to my thinking, where worldly
people rarely come, as you yourself have seen; chiefly, here I search the
Divine Writings, first the commandments of the Lord along with a
commentary, and the Apostolic traditions, then the Lives and teachings
of the Holy Fathers. To these I attend and what is in agreement with my
understanding as to what would be pleasing to God and the good of my
soul, I prescribe for myself. On such I meditate and in such I have my life

[44] Cf. Jn. 17, 26.
[45] Kirill-Belozerskij Monastery where Nil was first tonsured and as we learn in this
letter to which monastery he returned after his pilgrimage to the East.
[46] The only ms. giving any authentic biographical data about Nil is that no. 212,
found in the Ščukin Moscow Museum, 17th cent. Mss., cited by Borovkova-Majkova,
in *Russ. Fil. Vestnik, op. cit.*, T. LXIV (1910), pp. 62–64.

and my very breath. But I abandoned all my inability and laziness and ignorance to God and the Most Pure Mother of God, and if it happens that I have something to do and if I do not find any solution in the Holy Writings, I lay it aside for the time being until I do find (in them, i.e. the writings) something; because I do not dare to act according to my own will and intellect. And if anyone approaches me out of spiritual love, in this manner also I advise him, above all, you, because from the very beginning you came to me out of spiritual love for advice. For this reason in preparing a discourse for you, I am advising you as to what good is to be done, as I would advise my own soul; as I myself am conscientious to do, so also I have spoken to you. If we are now physically separated, yet we are united by our spiritual love and form a unity and as I then addressed you by way of explaining the monastery's rules with Divine Love, so now I write you, seeking only (your) soul's salvation. And you, as you heard from me and you yourself see in these writings, if there is someting here that pleases you, strive to be a son by imitation (it) and an heir of the inheritance bequeathed by the Holy Fathers; keep the Lord's commands and the traditions of the Holy Fathers. Tell also the brethren living with you. If you are alone in your cell (as a hermit) or in the monastery with the brethren, give your attention to the Holy Writings and walk in the footsteps of the Holy Fathers, because the Divine Writings so command us. Or give yourself in obedience to such a person who will prove himself spiritual in thought, word and deed. So St. Basil the Great wrote in one discourse which begins with the words, "Come to me all you who labour."[47] If such a guide is not found, then give yourself in obedience directly to God through Divine Writings and not so stupidly as some when they are in the monastery with the brethren and think they are obeying, yet they are fed innanely on their own self-will and they then leave and foolishly take up the anchoret life, guiding themselves by their own carnal will and imprudent judgment, "For they know not what they do."[48] Those things apply to them John Climacus says in his discourse on various kinds of "tranquillity": "There are some who out of conceit prefer to sail by their own discretion rather than under the guide and direction of another."[49] Let it not be for us; but you, acting according to the Holy Writings and the way the Saints lived, by the Grace of Christ, will not sin. Now, indeed, I would be offended should you be sorrowful. For this very reason I was forced to write you, so you would not be so overwhelmed with sorrows. May the God of all joy and consolation console your heart and may He make known to you our love for you. If I have expressed this sentiment to you somewhat crudely,

[47] The ms. at this point is not clear and I was unable to locate this composition of St. Basil. Passages similar to this cited one are: St. Basil's, Ep. 188, 15–16, *PG*, 32, 681C–684B; Ep. 204, *PG*, 34, 744–756; Hom. in. Princ. Prov., 8, *PG*, 31, 404A, and *PG*, 31, 1149A–B. Cf. Gribomont, J., "Obéissance et Évangile selon St. Basile le Grand", *op. cit.*, pp. 192–215.
[48] Lk. 23, 34.
[49] Climacus, *Gradus 27*, 1105A.

I did not wish to ignore your request. I hope that you will take this with charity and not look too much on my lack of intelligence. For our affairs and for those for which I begged your holy help, you have diligently and well arranged them, for which I am reverently grateful.

107   (it was) not to any other, but to you, my beloved friend from so long ago; May God grant you a great reward for your labour. Still I beg of your holiness one thing – that you do not take these words sorrowfully which I have spoken above. For if outwardly they seem harsh, they are nevertheless interiorly full of profit because they are not my own words but they have been taken from the Holy Writings. They are truly harsh for those who do not wish sincerely to humble themselves in the fear of God and to abandon the (false) wisdom of the carnal world, but who insist on living according to their own passionate wills and not according to Holy Writings. Such do not search the Holy Writings with spiritual humility. Some of them do not even wish these days to hear this for they would say, "They were not written for us and it is impossible even for our present generation to observe them." But to the true labourers, in ancient and in present times and for all times, the words of the Lord are pure as purified silver and furbished seven times and His commands are illuminating and more desired than gold and precious gems. They please them better than honey and the honeycomb and they keep them. And they always will keep them and thus they will receive great rewards.

108   Greetings in the Lord, reverend Father, and pray for us sinners. We hold your sanctity in great respect.

LETTER IV[50]

From the Divine Writings of the Fathers to a Suffering Brother[51]

For my brother in Christ, I, the least of our brethren (monks), fulfill your request because I am forced from a sense of obligation to write and send to you that which we promised, so that you may know by

[50] Letter to Kassian. We follow Ms. no. 185, fol. 363–375, earlier found in the Moscow Ecclesiastical Academy, now in the Lenin Public Library. This is the longest letter that we have of Nil and due to the subject matter it reveals better than any other of his works Nil's literary style, plus his intimate knowledge of St. Paul.
[51] Kassian, before becoming a monk, was Prince Konstantin Mavnukskij (Mankupskij) who came to Russia in the cortège of Sofija Paleolog. He was born in Amorea (Arxangel'skij, *op. cit.*, p. 55). He had intimate relations with the Russian hierarchy and was in the service of Archbishop Ioasaf of Rostov. Ioasaf was stripped of his office for some unclear clash with Ivan III. (Cf. Lur'e, "Nil...", *op. cit.*, p. 194.) With him fell also in disgrace Prince Konstantin who was forced against his will to be tonsured in the Ferapont Monastery near to Nil Sorskij's hermitage, taking the name of Kassian. He died Oct. 2, 1504 and is honoured on the same day as a saint. Cf. Filaret, *Russkie Svjatye, Oktjabr'* (Černigov, 1965), pp. 184–189.

means of that which I have written how much faith and love I have for
you. I cannot bear, o my loved one,[52] to keep my secret in silence but I
364   become foolish[53] and lose my head[54] when there is question of helping
a brother, because this is true love: that one does not hide any secret
from one's loved ones.[55] For a long time when I began to write these
lines, my hand paused over the paper and I could not bear to move my
sinful right hand without shedding sincere tears, recalling God's mercy
and pity towards you. For He called you out of the land of Egypt[56] and
led you into the land of Israel and showed you the knowledge of our one,
true God, Jesus Christ who became flesh. By His Baptism you were
baptized. Then He deemed you worthy to receive the angelic, monastic
365   habit and with us you began your monastic life of the vows in our poor
cell.

For this reason, brother, am I moved deeply in soul, perplexed in conscience, interiorly rent as I recall even from your youth your many sufferings and misfortunes, your imprisonment and exile from your native
land of birth and from your patria to a strange and unknown land with a
foreign language and there to live among illiterate and you, moreover,
a son of most noble ancestors. How also the Lord delivered you in all
these trials from many and diverse deaths; death from fire, from, sword
from water;[57] and He Himself all the time had a better plan in mind for
by these He led you to repentance and to a knowledge of the truth as
God knows it. For this reason, namely, for our sins, has He inflicted on
us temptations and sorrows and imprisonment. The Lord loves us and
has mercy on us and wishes to instruct us with His wisdom by these
trials. And I again rejoice in the fact that the Lord still so loves us, that,
not wishing to torture us in that future life, but here, He allows us to
suffer in order to be purified from our sins.

366   Thus I am going to write for love of you from the Holy Writings to show
you that these sorrows the Lord sends to those who love Him and who
are able to bear for His sake every sort of evil, for the Lord will never
allow any evil to exceed our strength according to the Apostle Paul.[58]
And if He allows them, it is to be for the profit of the one tempted. But
again and again for this reason, as was the case with those before us, all
the saints of former times, prophets and apostles and martyrs were
saved and are still being saved by sorrows, misfortunes and persecutions.
Let us recall first of all the just Job; did he not rue the day he was born?[59]

[52] 'Ljubimče moj" which indicates Nil's intimate, personal warmth that permeates his
letters and that is so absent from his strictly "patristic" teaching in the *Ustav*.
[53] *bezumen.*
[54] *jurod.*
[55] Jn. 14, 21. Letter to German, 104A.
[56] Osee, 11, 1; Matt. 2, 15.
[57] Heb. 11, 34.
[58] I Corin. 10, 13.
[59] Iob 3, 3.

Likewise Jeremias the prophet said, "Woe is me, why my mother was ever born? Cursed be the night in which I was born."[60] And Moses, the great law-giver of God, said, "Lord, if I ever found grace before You, take away my soul from me, for I cannot bear the burden of these people; rather would that they beat me with stones."[61] Habacuc the Prophet complained: "Why did you send me labours and sicknesses?"[62]

Thus all the just suffered; the same is seen in the lives of the saints. May you model yourself on their example, because they were not fed during the time they lived their holy lives on any other than suffering such disturbing evils. What about the just David? Was he not persecuted all 367 the days of his life, guarded, deprived of food; did he not await death from Saul each hour in a strange land? Did not Abraham the just one suffer in a foreign land among infidels and barbarians and there was his wife not snatched away from him? So also his son Isaac and his grandson Jacob. Even Our Lord Jesus Christ, was He not led to the Cross? Was He not pierced with a lance? Was He not buffeted in the face by slaps from the soldiers' hands? He was reckoned among criminals by the ungodly Jews. All these the Lord suffered for our salvation in order to free us from the oath of God.[63]

The earthly angel, John, the Lord's Baptizer, did he not sit in prison? Did they not cut off his head with a sword? And then with tainted hands it was carried on a dish before the gluttonous feasters. O, holy head that looked on God and saw the Light of Dawn. O education in the desert from the cradle! Likewise the Prophet Elias suffered much and was carried in a flaming chariot to Heaven. About the apostles, holy martyrs, our confessors and fathers, what is there to write?[64] They all suffered many and diverse deaths, misfortunes, slaying, and imprisonments for the sake of the heavenly Kingdom and all these in strange lands, among infidels and savage barbarians, preached the name of Christ. Some of them were crucified, some pierced by a lance, others given over to fire or the sword, others tied with stones were drowned in the sea, others devoured by beasts as food. And what more can we quote? Did they not rejoice in their sufferings of evils and sorrows? Joseph the fair, the son of the just Jacob of Israel and the favourite child of holy Rachel, was he not sold by his brother into the bondage and service of his master Putiphar in the strange land of Egypt? I propose for you just one more account. O what a terrible and fearsome fulfillment! I speak about the great orator and prophet Isaias who was put to death by the ungodly Jewish race by being cut in two by a wooden saw, right through his insides and his limbs, as if they were sawing through an inanimate log.

[60] Jerem. 20, 14.
[61] Num. 11, 11.
[62] Hab. 1, 3.
[63] Gal. 3, 13.
[64] Heb. 11, 32 and foll.

All suffered these abuses from infidel barbarians in strange lands for the name of Christ. My brother, the all-seeing eye, God Our Lord, foresaw
368 you before your birth and loved you above all things, formed you from the womb of your mother, snatched you from the hellish mouths, from your own native land and beliefs and brought you to a land to which you did not wish to come and did not even hope for such. He signed you with the seal of His Kingdom in the Baptism of the Father and the Son and the Holy Spirit and adorned you as with a crown with the angelic habit. He led you to us to this unpopulated hermitage.

He wishes you to suffer all sorrows, misfortunes, nakedness for the name of Christ and He allows such sorrows to befall us because He loves us, Our Creator. "Whom the Lord loves, him will He chastise."[65] And if sorrows happen to us, greater than our being can support seemingly, let us rejoice in the hope of the future good; let us strengthen one another looking on all these saintly models and lives and their achievements who have gone before us. What patient suffering for Christ as they poured out their very own blood! And if they, the just and holy, so suffered in whom the Holy Spirit dwelled and worked (for their miracles and great wonders we cannot sufficiently read through, nor describe them adequately), how much more it befits us to suffer for our innumerable sins. We ought not to become discouraged. But ought we not to strengthen one another to take courage in our mutual ascetical battle? The saints suffered for love of Christ; we should (at least) suffer for our sins. For this reason let us recall, o my favourite one, our crimes, as seen by our Creator, committed from our youth. How we have angered Him; how we have
370 violated His lifegiving commandments, and still how long He bears with us, waiting for our repentance and our return from our evil ways!

Recalling such mercy and unlimited forgiveness on the part of God, let us inflame our conscience, let us pour out tears and sighs and similar acts of compunction. Henceforth with all strength let us not bother about carnal preoccupations but present to God both our souls and bodies and let us diligently attend to the efficacy of the Name of the Lord in fighting temptations. Let us, with all our members, sail through them (the temptations). Let us fill our eyes with spiritual tears and our hearts with deep sight that accompany us to bed and arise with us in the morning. We have our guardian angel who will never forsake us. For this reason, God drives away the bitterness of these sorrows, not even allowing them to get near us. The enemy is weakened at the sight of our guardian angel protecting us. This God does for those loving Him and those preparing themselves for death with great sincerity, for those who do not turn their backs to the enemy. Concerning this struggle and most bitter temptation, the child-loving Father, Isaac the Syrian, wishing to strengthen the weak souls who take a wavering attitude towards asceticism, says the following: "Let there be among us that zeal in our souls against

[65] Heb. 12, 6; I Corin. 11, 32; Apoc. 3, 19.

the devil and his helpers as the Maccabees and the holy prophets, apostles and martyrs, confessors and all the justified had; they suffered in their
371   truth and were not filled with fear at such terrible sufferings surrounding their souls and bodies; but they conquered them manfully and put their (the devils') enticements and deceits behind them. Their stories and lives were written down as inspired and living models. How they endured, not yielding to the tender entreaties and allurements of evil-minded men, but with joy and sincerity they entered into the struggle with temptations and sorrows.

If it were not for sufferings, the Providence of God would not be seen as operative in mankind; it would be impossible to approach God with boldness; impossible to learn the wisdom of the Spirit and to be assured of the divine love in the Soul. Before sufferings come to a person, he prays to God as if he himself were a stranger to Him; but if he constantly struggles out of His love, soon he undergoes a change. Before, he held God as a task-master, but now he becomes a sincere friend of God. Do you see, brother, what a child-loving soul this heavenly Father (Isaac) possessed? Among his virtues he himself suffered and was tempted and
372   thus he helps us in our temptations by strengthening our weak spirit and overcoming our incapability for asceticism, with the words of the St. Paul, "for the present time of suffering will give way to future reward".[66]

Note, dear one, how pleasing to God is the prayer of a person suffering under temptations according to the words of this amazing saint where he speaks above about a person holding God as a taskmaster, but when he has to bear sorrows, he becomes a sincere friend of God. Continuing, he (Isaac) says: "God does not bless those, even though they are chosen ones, who honour Him, but still remain attached to carnal affections, but rather He blesses those who, as long as they were in the world, bore sorrows, difficulties, labours, deprivations, loneliness, lack of necessities, sicknesses and poverty, humiliations, insults, shame, harms from men and devils. They fostered sincere sorrow, harnessed the body, were cut off from compatriots and from their homeland and even from this earth.
373   Thus they attained the wisdom of the compunction and embraced the monastic state and solitude, preferring the invisible world to the visible one of men. These weep, while the world laughs; these do penance while the world anoints itself with oil; these fast while the world seeks only pleasures. During the day they work and at night they devote themselves to asceticism in seclusion and in labours; some suffer with sicknesses; others in labours going against their passions; still others are persecuted by men; some in woes and sorrows produced by the devils and other evil men; others are persecuted by them; some even beaten; others according to St. Paul: "experienced mockery and scourging, chains, too, and imprisonment; they were stoned, they were cut in pieces, they were

[66] Rom. 8, 18.

tortured, they were put to the sword; they wandered about, dressed in sheepskins and goatskins, amidst want and distress and ill-usage; men whom the world was unworthy to contain, living a hunted life in desert and on mountain-sides, in rock-fastnesses and caverns underground."[67] The Lord knows how impossible it is to remain in His love in tranquillity as long as one is in this flesh and for this reason He prevents those enemies from disturbing His peace and sweet consolations. This God enjoins on those who love Him and who wish to bear all evil for His name's sake. The word of God is fulfilled in them which says: "As you accept sorrows in this present life and do not become too enthralled by the world, for

374   the world will hate you, know that it has hated me first."[68] Do you not see, o brother, that from former times all who ever were found pleasing to God reached salvation by means of sorrows and troubles and difficulties and entered into eternal joy. Of them it is written that the former type (those of this world) were powerful while the latter (the beloved of Christ) were weak and powerless,[69] about this the ancient skete Fathers prophesied, that the last class would be called before the former because they pleased God more by their sorrows and misfortunes. See, that God does not wish that those who love and honour Him in this present life should have peace and neither should the former type (persons of this world). You, o lover of Christ, engrave all this on your heart and bear without weakening all sorrows.

Recall your initial faith at all times; your first fervour in undertaking the path of perfection, your ardent, burning thoughts with which you came to me in my poverty, in the uninhabited solitude, keeping solitary vigil and working only for my God from my youth. Recall also how you then were so careful about small transgressions even which you did not commit. It is the devil's wont, when he sees one beginning with an ardent faith to lead a good life, to make him suffer by various, passionate

375   temptations, which arise from demons and from human beings, in order to bring him finally to fear. Having reached this weakness by means of suggested thought, the person destroys any good intention and never conceives in himself further the ardour to approach a harsh life full of suffering. And for these reasons, let us not weaken under these thoughts but recall our sins from our youthful past, the terrible torments of Hell for sinners and the rewards for the just. When we find ourselves strongly tempted, let us unflinchingly bear the temptations. A traveller, falling suddenly into such temptations, finds his liberation in the words of the Prophet: for "many sorrows befall the just and from all of them the Lord will deliver them",[70] because they trust in Him with every breath. "And they called to Him and He heard them and protected them,"[71] and "He

[67] Heb. 11, 36.
[68] Jn. 15, 18.
[69] I Corin. 1, 18 and foll.
[70] Ps. 33, 20.
[71] Ps. 106, 6, 13.

is with them in sorrows."[72] He delivers them and glorifies them and is
their salvation according to His promise as He said, "I will not depart
from you nor leave you."[73] He saved Joseph in Egypt and also Daniel,
keeping him without harm in the den of the lions. The three youths
in the blazing furnace also did not suffer harm. He delivered Jeremias
from the den of darkness and led Peter out of prison when the doors were
376   closed; He saved Paul from the Jewish mob. Thus, in all this, the wonderful and merciful God, everywhere present and all powerful, will direct
us and free us if it be for the good of our souls. But only let us place all
our hope and confidence and aspiration in Him with all fervour. Let
376   us bear as from the Lord these present gifts of sorrows, be they justified
or unjustified; purified by them, we will stand without guilt before the
judgment seat of Christ. To Him praise and power for ever and ever.
Amen.

LETTER V[74]

Of Nil Sorskij on the remembrance of Death[75]

Dearly beloved: Remember the day decreed for your death and you will
thus never allow any weakness to overcome you. Let there be always
196   and everywhere with you a sickness of soul over your sins and a sorrowing
in body along with silence in poverty of the things of this passing world
through faithful observance of all your monastic rules. Never leave your
cell, but sit in it as in your coffin.

Clean your cell and the poverty of your possessions will teach you restraint
because when we possess a great many things we may have a sufficiency,
but we are unable to control our desires. If you wish to have tears, love
lowliness, poverty and humility and do not strive to have fine things in
your cell. For when your soul seeks something and does not obtain it,
197   then it sighs and is humbled. And again then God comforts it and gives
it much compunction. When the soul experiences the sweetness of God,
then it hates to bear even the monastic habit and even laments being tied
to the body. If at times temptations and the devils attack you as so many
buzzing bees while you are sitting in your cell, then arise, pray and in a
little while they will leave you.

[72] Ps. 32, 18 and foll.; 33, 18–21.
[73] Heb. 13, 5; Ps. 117, 6.
[74] I present these letters or compositions V–IX in an English translation, but there is
no conclusive proof that anyone of these came from the pen of Nil Sorskij.
[75] I use the Ms. no. 409, fol. 217–218 (Roumanian Museum) in the collection of 17th–
18th century Mss. in the Lenin Public Library. Arxangel'skij, *op. cit.*, p. 61, attributes
this to Nil.

LETTER VI

Of St. Nil[76]

197
198
For there is no good which is able to please all men. For it is written: "Woe, when all men say to you, well done."[77] Prophets died for the truth, but false prophets spoke to please men and loved to gossip. For whatever you wish, choose: either be concerned for the truth and b, ready to die for it, and thus you will live for ever; or seek to please mene to do all in order to be loved by them, but hated by God.

LETTER VII

On the Proper Way to Examine Oneself[78]

198
199
Each day we must examine ourselves in the following way to see how we have passed the day. So one must inquire the self first of all how he passed the night: whether he rose with diligence for services or whether he complained at the one awakening him or whether he showed a lack of generosity towards him. One must look upon the one appointed to awaken him for services as upon one performing a great favour for him; for he awakens him in order to speak with God, to pray over one's sins, to become enlightened, to profit for oneself. How should one not be obliged to thank such a person? Truly he ought to regard him as though his very salvation were coming from him. And I will tell you something amazing told by a man who heard it from a great starec who could read the future. For while standing in the church while the brethren were beginning to sing, he saw someone, carrying a light, leave the altar. He was carrying a certain box, radiantly lighted and an anointing rod. He dipped the rod into the bowl and went up to all the brothers, signing each of them on the forehead. Of those who were not in their places, some he signed, others he passed by their places. When they were about to leave, he saw this person leave the altar and do the very same thing again. Only the starec halted him and, falling at his knees, he asked to see what he was doing and to know who he was. This light-

---

[76] Elagin Ed., pp. 197–198. This is without a doubt not Nil Sorskij's original work, but a work of Nil Sinaite copied by Nil's hand. Cf. Borovkova-Majkova, M. S., *K literaturnoj...*, *op. cit.*, p. 3, cf. for exact text *PG*, 79, 437.

[77] Ps. 69, 4.

[78] Elagin Ed., pp. 198–200. We can in no way ascertain whether Nil actually wrote this. The long narration of the edifying story to illustrate does not indicate Nil's usual style. This selection is most probably a section of a translation work (or at least copied by hand) done by Nil of a coenobitic "*ustav*", for the mention of communal, liturgical singing of the office was not a regular feature of Nil's skete life.

bearer told him, "I am the angel of God and I was ordered to make a sign over those found in church at the beginning of the singing and then on those persevering right up to the end, for their diligence and care and good will." And the starec asked him: "How is it you sign the places of some who are not there?" The holy angel answered him saying: "These are those brothers who are conscious and of good will, but for some necessitating cause they are unable to be present and so are excused with the blessing of the Fathers, or for some command of obedience imposed on them and for this reason they are absent. But such, even though absent from the church, receive their anointing because by their good will they are present with the other singers. Only to those able to come and from laziness are not present, I am commanded not to give the signing because they prove themselves unworthy."

200   See what gifts he brings his brother who awakens him for the church services. For be diligent, brothers, so as not to be deprived of so great a blessing by the holy angel. If it happens that one becomes lazy and another calls his attention to his duty, one should be grateful. Looking on the good, he must give thanks to the one reminding him regardless of whoever it be.

LETTER VIII

How to overcome vanity[79]

200   S. Nil says: If you wish to overcome vanity, do not love the praises of men, not to be honoured; do not seek fine clothing nor ambition to exercise authority over your brethren. Do not appear as one among those doing good deeds, do not pose before the popular crowd as a thinker whose advice-answers the world eagerly seeks. Do not seek to be preferred before others, nor to sit in the front seats in assembly. Do not regard yourself in your heart as being of sharp intellect, nor hold yourself

201   as holy or already saved. Do not correct another for some sin, not even if you see him doing such with your own eyes.[80]
Do not judge a sinner as guilty of judgment or torture, but attribute his sin to Satan;[81] because it is Satan who so zealously seeks to lead your brother to shame, wishing to separate us from the goodness of God. But rather think of yourself as the greatest sinner of all, meditate on

---

[79] Elagin Ed., pp. 200–202. This seems to be at most a collection of Nil's sayings but definitely no proof can be found that it came from Nil's pen. The evident citations from Nil's other works, the general tone of Nil's spirituality, the citing of local Russian saints, plus the final quotation of Rufinus, would indicate rather a later disciple of Nil.

[80] Letter to Gurij, fol. 102.

[81] The typical attitude of the Trans-Volga followers of Nil towards the Judaiser heretics.

your own salvation; do good secretly as our holy Father Vitaly[82] did or as Simeon the Fool for Christ's sake did[83] or as St. Andrew of Constantinople.[84] And love their moral attainments. May they be your admonisher and judge. They will not flatter you, but will treat you as Our Lord, so that by such you will be led to give up evil doing. They bore patiently all evils as though they were really not evil and prayed to God for those who inflicted on them insults. They did not reckon the sins of others as sins, but as ignorance on their part. With all sorts of such suggestions
202 the devil forces on us his own crimes. For the lovers of sin he arranges all sorts of sinister deceits as snares and by such means he stirs up agitating thoughts in their intellect. He is eagerly bent on bringing to destruction by pride and vanity those wishing to be saved. We must despise all of his clever cunning. If we do something hidden, we seek to reject vanity by so doing, protesting that we want to honour the All-High, yet we will not be freed ever from this temptation, for the enemy corrupts all human works by vanity.

For in fasting I am vain; then I relax the fast so that I will be known as one already saved and in no need more of fasting and again I am vain. Dressed in brightly coloured clothes, I am conquered by vanity; dressed in poor, simple clothes because I do not have any good clothes; again I am vainly seeking the praise of others. I am conquered in conversation by vanity so I keep silence of tongue and become puffed up in thought, again I am overcome.[85] O my stupidity! The rewards of all labour are taken away by one's own foolishness. You, brethren, hold fast with humble wisdom and ascetical practices so that your labour does not vainly perish as with me. Rufinus said: "There are four virtues most
202 necessary for a monk: silence, observance of God's commands, humility, and poverty." This is how a monk should battle against the world, the flesh and the devil: against the world by standing firm; against the flesh by mortification; against the devil by fast and prayer.

[82] Filaret in his collection of Saints honoured in the Russian Church (*Russkija Svjatye*, *op. cit.*, vol. XII, 1900), in the index, gives no Russian Saint Vitalij. Three other Vitalijs are given but as non-Russians. The lack of the usual title of saint accompanying the name, the mere title of Father, would seem to indicate a holy monk of that monastery, known to the writer and the reader, but nothing more implied by way of official cult.

[83] The only *jurodovyj*-saint or fool-for-Christ's-sake (Filaret, *op. cit.*, pp. 221–222), with a similar name is St. Simon but he died in 1584. If this is the saint the author refers to, then it is a clear proof that Nil is not the author, but this composition is a later compilation of Nil's thoughts done by a much later admirer of Nil.

[84] It is not clear whether this St. Andrew is the *jurodovyj* († 10th cent., feast day celebrated October 2) or the Martyr Andrew (†767, feast day October 17) for both of them are of Constantinople.

[85] Climacus, *Gradus 22*, 949C.

LETTER IX

Treatise of St. Nil on overcoming Evil Thoughts[86]

If you wish, child, to gain victory over the devil of gluttony,[87] love restraint; that is to say, regulate for yourself your food and drink according to a fixed, modest measure and have before the eyes of your heart the fear of God and you will conquer the temptation of the greedy devil.
203 If you desire victory over fornication, love hunger and do not drink except only your fixed daily quantity, and this taken during your meal at table. Recall the hour of your death when suddenly the awful messengers of God will stand before you to take away your soul, when your adversaries will come to reveal you. Represent to your heart that awful last judgment and how you will have to give an answer before God.

To conquer this temptation do not in any whatsoever converse with women, nor look even on their clothing, nor attend to their personal goodness, but flee ever from women and youth. And so doing you will conquer the passion of the devil of fornication. If you seek to conquer avarice, love strict poverty and poor clothing and simple food and drink; and you will thus be victorious over the suggestions of the devil of avarice.

If you want to overcome anger, that is to say, the habit of strong, hardhearted anger, love to imitate the meekness of Our Lord and His longsuffering patience. For He said, "Take up my yoke and learn of me for I am meek and humble of heart and you will find rest for your souls."[88] It is the riches possessed only by the just in this world. As the Apostle Paul says: "This is perfect love, that the sincere person does no evil."[89] Do not seek to do your own will, nor to obtain honour, nor to harbour in yourself any evil revenge. But seek to bear all, to be merciful of heart, not to envy, not to be lifted up, nor to be proud, not to be disobedient; not to be filled with anger, not to retain in oneself any evil remembrance.[90] This also Peter, the primate of all, teaches us by saying: "If for the sake of God's command, one bears sorrows, unjust sufferings, this is pleasing before God. To this were you also called, to show patience in doing good. For even before, Christ suffered for us, leaving us an example that we should follow in His footsteps."[91]

---

[86] This is a short summary of Nil's ideas as expresses in his Chapter 5 of the *Ustav*. We include it here for the ideas and style are quite faithful to Nil's.
[87] On the Oriental custom of assigning a special virtue for each capital vice, cf. Pourrat, P., *La Spiritualité Chrétienne, op. cit.*, vol. I, p. 208.
[88] Matt. 11, 29.
[89] Rom. 13, 10.
[90] I Corin. 13, 4–7.
[91] I Pet. 2, 20–21.

Recall, brother, what great evil the Jews did to Our Lord Jesus Christ,
204 but still God, the lover of mankind, did not become angry with them,
but prayed for them to the Father saying: "Father, forgive them this sin
for they know not what they do."[92] Do so also and you will conquer
anger.

If the evil enemy suggests the following to you concerning thoughts: he
causes me much harm and I have driven him away but he still does not
stop. I ask that he may not cause you any evil. Recall the words of the
205 Apostle Paul who said: "Do not return evil with evil, but conquer
evil with good works."[93] If, finally, Satan inflames you with anger,
moving you to revenge, then recall the words of the Lord: "If you do
not forgive others their trespasses, then neither will your Heavenly Father
forgive you yours. If however you forgive with all your heart your brethren all their sins, then also God will forgive you yours."[94] Just recall
yourself, how many sins you have committed against God and, still
not ceasing in your sinning, you constantly call out: "Have mercy on
me, Lord, and forgive me." If you wish to be shown mercy by God and
forgiven, cease from anger and put off all enmity.

Never will an angry man because of enmity be forgiven by God and
without His help he can do no good. Anger is the arrow of Satan, evil
remembrance is the snare and net of the enemy. Angry rage is the chain
206 of the devil. An angry, impetuous man is his own ruination and does
harm to others. For an impetuous person, the devil is as living in a hut;
for an angry person, the devil is as the owner of the entire house. Both
are slaves to the adverse spirit. Bold, demanding, proud, a destroyer,
such names are given the one who harbours evil, the hard of heart, the
lawless and the image of evil.

And God's words do not dwell in them and soon they bring themselves
to ruin. About these the Scripture bears testimony.

LETTER TO A BROTHER IN AN EASTERN COUNTRY: KASSIAN[95]

So this seems to us to be a thing useful to you in the Lord, that is, be
22 nourished on bodily penances insofar as your strength permits and to
undertake nothing beyond the proper measure. But devote yourself to
the study of Divine Writing and to the learning of some manual work.

[92] Lk. 23, 34.
[93] Rom. 12, 21.
[94] Matt. 6, 14–15. Mk. 11, 26.
[95] This letter is found only in one ms., that which we have used for this translation of
the Volokolamskij collection of the 16th century mss., formerly of the Moscow Ecclesiastical Academy, no. 577, now, no. 189/577 of the Lenin Public Library, fol. 22–23.
Arxangel'skij, *op. cit.*, p. 56, says it is probably Kassian Mavnukskij, the Prince-Monk.
Cf. footnote 51, *supra*.

Love solitude. If God wishes that we should see each other, then we shall speak about everything more in detail.

23 Gregory the Theologi ansays: "It is[96] better to be separated for piety's sake than to be united but at the same time an occasion for giving in to the passions." The same one says that the better thing is the praiseworthy spurning of the world which is ever trying to separate us from God.

Another author says that it is better to lead a life among those having little intelligence, yet who observe the commands of God, than to live among many disordered persons, who violate the laws of the Holy Spirit and who spurn the rules written by the Holy Fathers.

[96] Gregory Nazianzen but I was unable to locate the source of this quotation.

APPENDIX II

THE HESYCHASTIC METHOD

In presenting a rapid survey of Hesychasm, one cannot leave out of discussion its method, be it for profit or abuse. But as it does not enter into the true essence of Hesychasm, we relegate the discussion of it to this appendix.

Various historical factors in the evolution of Hesychasm prepared the way for a more materialistic, mechanical method. The most fundamental was to take the physical, material heart as the place of "return" to God. The Old and New Testament as in other Semitic writings, conceived the heart, that organ so indispensable for the life of the body, as also the centre of all psychological and moral life, as the centre of the very interior life.[1] It is physiologically the centre of reaction for emotions and sentiments, so naturally it became the seat of all sensible and affective life. Mixing metaphorical language with psychological and physiological phenomena, the heart became the place where the individual person was most an individual. That which made him most typically himself and not another person, the heart, for here he "thinks", deliberates, determines his way of conduct towards God and other men.

The spiritual writer who remotely prepared the way for the Byzantine mysticism of the heart was Diadochus of Photike.[2] What the body along with the five senses is for the exterior life, the heart is for the interior life of man. Through the sin of Adam, a schism resulted in man, destroying the simplicity that existed in him with the godlike *nous* in complete hegemony over all the other subordinated faculties and senses.[3] This image of God resides in the intimate recesses of the heart, but con-

---

[1] Cf. Guillaumont, A., "Le sens du nom de coeur dans l'antiquité", in *Ètudes Carmélitaines*, 1950, pp. 42–50.
[2] Cf. Hausherr, I., S. J., "Noms du Christ", *OCA*, 157, (Roma, 1960), pp. 202–210. Also Popov, K., "Učenie o molitve iisusovoj blažennago Diadoxa 5-ogo veka", in *Trudy*, Eccles. Academy of Kiev (1902), tome 3, pp. 651–676.
[3] Diadochus, in *Philokalia, op. cit.*, T. I., ch. 25, p. 241.

stantly is being besieged by the inordinate activities of the exterior senses. The heart has a "sense" which permits it to "feel" God, to become aware of His presence in the heart.[4] This conscious awareness is brought about by meditation and constant remembrance of the Lord Jesus and by living according to God's commandments.[5]

We already pointed out that Simeon the New Theologian had read the 100 Chapters of Diadochus and tended to emphasize the conscious awareness of divine activity in the soul that Diadochus insisted on. Like Diadochus, who placed his "one natural sense of the soul"[6] in the intellectual faculty of *nous*, Simeon also posits the interior "one sense". "He who gives us that which is above the senses, also endows us, through the grace of the Holy Spirit, with another sense which is above the senses, in order that we may clearly and purely apprehend His gifts and blessings, which are above the senses."[7] But he stresses more than any of his predecessors the importance of mystical gifts, visions, and the confirmation of the activity of the Holy Spirit by sensible repercussions, especially by the highest and surest sign of His presence, a material light.

If Simeon did not actually write *The Method of Hesychast Prayer*[8] he at least prepared the way. The *Method*, which Nil Sorskij certainly knew

---

[4] *Ibid.*, ch. 29, pp. 242–243; ch. 30, p. 243.

[5] *Ibid.*, ch. 88, p. 265. As to whether Diadochus was the first to use the Jesus Prayer, see I. Hausherr, *supra cit.*, p. 208. Among other things he says: "Diadoque ne donne nulle part, même d'une façon approximative, la formule classique de la prière de Jésus. Il ne la connaît même pas. Sa spiritualité se rattache à celle du "souvenir de Dieu", telle que nous l'avons rencontrée chez saint Basile, saint Grégoire de Nazianze, Marc l'Ermite, etc.; mais plus systématiquement que ces théologiens, Diadoque a tiré les conséquences d'un principe qu'il admettainet tous: l'unité spirituelle de l'homme."

[6] *Ibid.*, ch. 29, pp. 242–243.

[7] Simeon the New Theologian, *Dobrotoljubie, op. cit.*, tome 5, pp. 49–50, no. 136.

[8] This will remain one of the unsolved problems. D. Holl, *Enthusiasmus und Bussgewalt beim griechischen Mönchtum* (Leipzig, 1898), p. 128, and I. Hausherr, "La Méthode...", *op. cit.*, maintain that Simeon is not the correct author, but a later author (according to Fr. Hausherr in "Note sur l'invention de la méthode hésychaste", *OC*, vol. XX, 1930, p. 180), Nicephorus, monk of the 14th century and master of Gregory Palamas, is the author. Hausherr's arguments, besides the manuscript arguments against which M. Jugie levels a dissenting voice (in his "Les origines de la méthode d'oraison hésychaste", *Èchos d'Orient*, vol. 30 (1931), p. 184 and foll.), are: (a) Simeon, whose profound doctrines are based solidly on Holy Scripture especially on the mystical doctrine of St. John and St. Paul, could not have invented a method "short and easy, physical and scientific" without sweat and fatigue to arrive at the same end for which he declared during all his lifetime the utmost necessity of possessing the perfection of all the Christian virtues; (b) about this infallible means to arrive at such a necessary end, he does not breathe a whisper in his other 100 discourses, "hymns of divine love", and more than 200 chapters on practical and theological precepts. Cf. *op. cit.*, "La Méthode...", p. 114.

and attributed to Simeon, presents an innovation on the general doctrine of Simeon which would indicate strongly that a later admirer of Simeon used his reputation to promulgate innovations. A definite technique is recommended and with an assurance that if the instructions are carried through, one would surely see the divine light in his soul. "Sit in a peaceful cell, in a corner and do that which I tell you: close the door and raise your mind above any vain and temporal object. Then, letting your beard rest on your chest, turn your bodily eyes with your whole mind concentrating on the middle of the stomach, on the so-called navel. Suppress the breathing of the air which passes through the nose in a way so as not to breathe too often. Explore with the mind inside the entrails to find there the place of the heart where all the powers of the soul are wont to gather. In the beginning, you will find a darkness and a dogged heaviness, but in persevering and practicing this occupation day and night, you will find, o marvel, a happiness without limit. As soon as in fact the mind finds the place of the heart, it perceives suddenly that which it never knew; for it perceives the air as existing at the centre of the heart and it sees itself all immersed in light and full of discernment. Before, when besieged by a stinging temptation, the mind was not able to combat successfully; now through the invocation of Jesus Christ, it drives out and destroys it utterly."[9]

The similarity, as I. Hausherr points out[10] between this method and that proposed by Nicephorus, monk of Mount Athos, could not be mere accident. The accent is stronger now for exact observation of a material technique with more assurance to a greater public of mystical experiences. Nicephorus warns of the necessity of having an undeluded director, but if, after a search for such a director, one is not found, "after calling upon God in contrition of spirit and with tears, and after praying to Him earnestly with humility, do what I tell you. You are aware that our breathing by which we live is an inhaling and exhaling of air. The organs that serve for this purpose are the lungs which surround the heart. They pass air through themselves and flood the heart with it. Thus breathing is the natural way to the heart. And so collect your mind and conduct it by way of your breathing by which air passes to the heart and together with the inhaled air force it to descend into the heart and to stay there. And train it not to come out of there quickly; for at first this inner

---

[9] Cf. the text of the three methods of attention and prayer, edited by I. Hausherr, *OC*, vol. IX (1927), pp. 164–165.

[10] *Ibid.*, p. 133; cf. also *OC*, vol. XX (1930), p. 180.

enclosure and restraint is very wearisome, but when it becomes accus-
tomed to it, then on the contrary it does not like whirling without,
because it is there filled with joy and happiness. ...And you should also
know that when your mind is established in the heart, it must not remain
there silent and idle, but must unceasingly make the prayer: 'Lord Jesus
Christ, Son of God, have mercy on me!' This prayer, by holding the
mind without dreaming, renders it inaccessible and immune to the appeals of the enemy and daily leads it more and more into love and
longing for God."[11]

It is Gregory of Sinaite who must be credited with having started the
Hesychasm Renaissance of the 14th century on Mount Athos. He is
known as the teacher of holy sobriety and of the active method of the
prayer of mind-in-heart.[12] In his *Texts on Commandments and Dogmas*
we find the traditional, solid teaching of the Sinaite Fathers on asceticism and prayer. But in his *Instructio ad Hesychastas*[13] he sets down in
exact detail instructions on "How to sit in the cell", "How to say the
Jesus Prayer", "How to hold the mind", "How to drive away thoughts".
We have already quoted his method on how to sit and say the Prayer
which shows the evident influence of Nicephor's method.

No doubt the attraction of the unknown with the descriptions of the
mystical exaltation contributed much to rapid diffusion of this method.
Nicephorus Gregoras, Byzantine historian of this period, writes that
Athos was infested at this time with the error of Messalianism and
Bogomilism.[14] This heretical teaching was strongly developed in Bulgaria and could have been easily, according to Nicephorus Gregoras'
account, introduced into Athos by the number of monks who at this
time migrated there from Bulgaria. J. Bois, in speaking of Gregory
Sinaite's method, says: "We can presume that this method was developed further with great aberrations. Recruits, illiterate persons coming
from the hills and Balkan mountains, already filled with extravagant

[11] Nicephor, *De cordis custodia, PG*, 147, 963B–965A. N.B.: Nicephor, according to
the data in the *Philokalia*, died about 1340 and was the master of Gregory Palamas.
This is not universally accepted by all. Cf. M. Jugie, "Les Origines de la méthode
d'oraison hésychaste", *op. cit.*, p. 184: "Nicephor lived in the 12th century or at the
latest in the beginning of the 13th because Gregory Palamas lists him among the
ancient Fathers."

[12] Cf. *Dobrotoljubie*, "Introduction to Gregory of Sinaite", tome 5, p. 195.

[13] Gregory of Sinaite: *Praecepta ad Hesychastes, PG*, 150, 1329–1346.

[14] *Byzantinae Historiae, PG*, 147, Lib. XIV, ch. 948B.

theories of Messalianism and Bogomilianism... each followed his own tastes with changes, not always successful, nor orthodox, leading to great absurdities and extravagances."[15]

Timothy of Constantinople[16] gives a list of Messalian propositions which manifest the leading tendency to be at the same time quietistic and pelagianistic. Its quietism rejects all efficacy to asceticism and combat against passions. The body was delivered from passions through prayer. In the soul was a demon, chased out by prayer and then the Holy Spirit descended with His light, a visible mark of His working presence and assurance that the body was now safely delivered from the demon or from the control of the passions. No longer were mortifications or fasting necessary. The human nature, through prayer, had been transformed into a divine nature. The soul saw the Holy Trinity with corporal eyes. Barlaam of Calabria,[17] in railing against the excesses of hesychasts on Mount Athos shortly after the time of Gregory Sinaite (†1360), accuses the Athos hesychasts of excesses in eating and drinking. Its pelagianism is evident in the exaggerated efficacy of human prayer, of the -οιοψολ/sd gical and physical elements. Violence was to be exerted on superior faculties, for Messalians believed that they, by their own force and will-power, could reach the heights of contemplations. Receiving mystical experiences soon became synonymous with sanctity.[18]

In his treatise *On the Blessed Hesychasts*[19] Gregory Palamas (†1359) gives a defence of the method and places it in its true subservient relation with the essence of hesychasm. This would prove to be the canonization of the hesychast spirituality for Orthodoxy, not only as having been always the true, traditional spirituality of the Christian, Byzantine Orient, but as being the only spirituality for future Orthodox generations.

[15] Bois, J., *op. cit.*, pp. 71–72. Another writing, influenced greatly by Messalian materialization is the pseudo-Chrysostom method which M. Jugie places as written in the 12th century. Cf. *op. cit.*, pp. 184–185. Also I. Hausherr, "Les noms...", pp. 200–202, who treats in detail the spiritual letter to some monks, falsely attributed to Chrysostom.

[16] *PG*, 86, 45C–52C.

[17] Syrku, P., *K istorii ispravlenija knig v Bolgarii v XIV v.* ("Concerning a History of Correction of Books in Bulgaria in the 14th Cent.") (St. Petersburg, 1898), T. I., pp. 95–100.

[18] On this point cf. I. Hausherr, "Contemplation et Sainteté...", *op. cit.*, pp. 193–194, and also his thorough treatment on this subject in: "L'erreur fondamentale et la logique du messalianisme", *OCP*, vol. I (1935), pp. 328–360.

[19] *PG*, 150, 1101 and foll.

Through sobriety, self-mastery, the mind must be held within the body so that the whole can partake of the greatness of the mind. But how can the mind be controlled unless it be collected and confined within the body and not be allowed to be dispersed into multiplicity through the senses. By returning into oneself, man is permitted to ascend to God.[20] "No one who thinks logically would be against those who have not yet attained contemplation, using certain methods to lead the mind into itself. ...Hence some advise them to refrain from breathing rapidly, but to restrain their breath somewhat, so that, together with their breath, they may also hold the mind inside, until, with God's help, through training, they accustom the mind not to go out into its surroundings and mingle with them, and make it strong enough to concentrate upon one thing."[21]

The *Century* of Callistus and Ignatius of Kanthopoulos is a collection of the teaching of the traditional "neptic" Fathers on hesychasm. It is a synthesis, the first *Philokalia* composed, if we wish to view so this work and its solid, ascetical teaching, as the source of reading and learning for succeeding monks. But unduly stressed is the *lumen thaboricum*, the Taboric light, as the be-all and the end-all of the whole process.

At times it becomes evident that the two authors are joining in the polemics raised by Barlaam and Greek historians and theologians as Nicephorus Gregoras, Gregory Acyndinos, Demetrius and Prochorus Cydonios against the abuses of the method. "It can in no way be achieved solely by this natural method of descent into the heart by way of breathing or by seclusion in a quiet and dimly lit place. This can never be.[22] In Chapter 58 the reader is given a clear break from the traditional hesychast Fathers' teachings to be enlightened as to the details of what we can call Palamitic hesychasm, with its emphasis on the Taboric *lumen* as the goal of contemplation.[23] It is not without foundation that A.

[20] *Ibid.*, no. 4–5, 1105D–1108A.
[21] *Ibid.*, no. 9, 1109C.
[22] *Century*, ch. 24, p. 73. N.B. Page-references are given according to A. Ammann's text, *op. cit.*
[23] "Wir aber reden jetzt von dem vollendeten wesenhaften Augleuchten, in welchem die Auserwählten unter den Aposteln, nämlich die, welche mit Jesus auf den Berg Tabor gestiegen, unaussprechlicherweise die schöne und in Wahrheit selige Entäusserung erlitten haben und gewürdigt wurden mit ihren sinnlichen, zu etwas Göttlicherem verwandelten Augen. – Sie waren ja unter der Rechten des Ganz Heiligen Geistig geworden – die unschaubare Herrlichkeit der Gottheit zu sehen... Die andere aber,

Ammann calls his book on the Century *Die Gottesschau im palamitischen Hesychasmus.*[24]

With the lack of expert spiritual guides to keep ever the material aids subordinated to the final end of union with God through solid virtues and prayer it is easy to understand that abuses would creep in. This is undoubtedly the reason for the evident moving away since the last century from psycho-physiological techniques.[25] In the 1905 edition of the *Dobrotoljubie* the Russian editor gives a caution in presenting the "Three Methods of Attention and Prayer" which is attributed to Simeon the New Theologian. "Here St. Simeon describes certain external methods by which some fall into temptation and relinquish their work, and others distort the work itself. Since, owing to scarcity of instructors, these methods may lead to evil effects, while in themselves they are nothing more than external adaptations for inner doing and have no essential value, we omit them. The essential thing is to acquire the habit of making the mind stand on guard in the heart – in this physical heart, but not physically. It is necessary to bring the mind down from the head to the heart and to establish it there or, as one of the Fathers said, to join the mind with the heart. How to attain this? Seek and you will find. The best way is by walking in God's presence and by the work of prayer, especially by going to church. But it should be remembered that ours is only the labour. But the thing itself, i.e. keeping the mind concentrated in the heart, is a supernatural gift, given when and how the Lord wishes. The best example is Maxim Causokalivit."[26]

As for abuses resulting from exaggerated use of a material technique, we need only quote from the warnings of two later witnesses. In the ano-

---

nämlich die Betätigung aus der empfangenden Entgegennahme, pfleget unmittelbar von Gott selbst im Herzen zu entstehen, manchmal entsteht sie auch von aussen her und gibt dem Leibe deutlich über die Erkenntnisskraft hinaus Anteil an der eigenen Heiligkeit und dem göttlichen Lichte... 'Denn mit dem einem Auge sehen wir das, was in den Geschöpfen verborgen ist: nämlich die Macht Gottes, seine Weisheit, seine Obsorge für uns, die wir aus der Heiligkeit seiner Mühewaltung um uns erfassen. Mit dem andern Auge schauen wir die Herrlichkeit seines heiligen Wesens, wenn es Gott gefallen wird uns in seine geistlichen Geheimnisse einzuführen' (Hl. Isaak)." Ch. 68, pp. 120–121.

[24] But he cautions: "...also in Falle unserer beiden Verfasser palamitisch gesehen und ausgewertet haben ganz anders vielleicht, als es die wirkliche Absicht der angezogenen Schriftsteller war" (p. 22).

[25] Un Moine de l'Église d'Orient, "La Prière de Jésus" Chevetogne, 1951, p. 80.

[26] *Dobrotoljubie, op. cit.*, tome 5, p. 507.

nymous text quoted by J. Gouillard,[27] a warning of certain physiological, fake consequences coming from an imprudent use of material aids
leading to erotic sins of lust is sounded to the followers of this method,
along with a denunciation of Islamic fakes and their methods of *dhikr*[28]
and a general lamentation against the general neglect of the hesychast
method. "Because of inexperience many suffer and fall into sins instead
of acquiring sobriety and attention of the mind", the text says, "through
the continuous thought of death and tears of compunction. They fall
into the error of false prophets, into the unnatural and unholy operations
as taught by the pseudo-Mohammedan monks."[29]

The other later witness to excesses and dangers to avoid is the Russian
Bishop Ignatius Brianchaninov, writing on the Jesus Prayer in 1865.
He too laments the almost universal disuse of hesychastic spirituality in
Russia, gives a detailed description of the heart, relying on Basil of
Moldavia and Theophilact of Philadelphia (example: the power of speech
(reason) or spirit of man is present in the breast or in the upper part of
the heart; the power of fervour in the middle part; and the power of
desire or natural cupidity in the lower part of the heart) and he warns
strongly against misuse of the material aids designed to help and not to

[27] This is from a codex of the 18th or 19th century, but the author believes it must
be dated earlier. J. Gouillard, "Petite Philocalie..." *op. cit.*, pp. 300-316.
[28] *Ibid.*, pp. 300-310. No one can deny the evident similarity between the physiological
and psychological methods of latter hesychasm and Islamic mysticism. Cf. M. L.
Gardet, "La mention du nom divin en mystique musulmane", in *Revue Thomiste*,
1952, pp. 642-646, and the text of the cheikh Muhammad Amin (†1332) as given by
J. Gouillard, *op. cit.*, appendix, pp. 317-336. Here we find similar notions on the
physiology of the heart, on breathing technique, repetition of a set prayer formula,
rapture with blinding light, constant recall of the thought of death and the necessity
of having a master to guide one in this method. Swami Siddheswarananda, of the
Hindu religious order of Ramakrishna, exposes the Hindu technique of meditation
and gives some striking similarities with the hesychast method: the meditation *(dhyana)*
constituting the principal part of *yoga* or union with the divine principle, use of
breathing-control, posture, entering into the heart, repetition of the Divine name (the
mantra), guidance of a *guru* or spiritual director, purification, union with the Infinite,
the realization of the Infinite, *samadhi*. Cf. "La technique Hindoue de la Méditation",
in *Ètudes Carmélitaines: Technique et Contemplation* (Paris, 1949), pp. 17-35. For this
reason Prof. George Wunderle concludes: "On peut vrai semblablement supposer qu'après le grand Siméon le Nouveau Théologien il ya a eu dans sa technique psychologique
des infiltrations d'éléments empruntés à l'Extrême-Orient (ou mieux encore au Brah-
manisme)." Cf. "La Technique de l'Hésychasme", in *Ètudes Carmélitaines: Nuit
Mystique* (Paris, 1938), p. 62. Cf. also his "Zur Psychologie des hesychastischen
Gebets", in the series, *Das östliche Christentum*, Würzburg, 1949, p. 20.
[29] J. Gouillard, "Petite Philocalie...", *op. cit.*, pp. 305-306.

hinder union with God. "Of those who have used with special diligence the material aids very few have attained success, but very many have deranged and harmed themselves. With an experienced director the use of the material aids incurs little danger; but with the guidance of books it is very dangerous since it is so easy, through ignorance and imprudence to fall into delusion and other kinds of spiritual and bodily disorder. Thus some, on seeing the harmful consequences of indiscreet labour and having only a superficial and confused idea of the prayer of Jesus and the circumstances that accompany it, attributed these consequences not to ignorance and imprudence but to the most holy Prayer of Jesus Himself. Can anything be sadder and more disastrous than this blasphemy, this delusion?"[30]

These two sources above have been quoted to show how easily secondary means to aid prayer can be turned into abuse or an end in itself when wise directors are not available. On the other hand, one must strive to see the good in such a physical help to concentrate the mind in interior prayer. There is no reason why one should not use the good found in natural religions to aid prayer.[31]

But in using a technique, one must always keep in mind that it is a mere, simple preparation, not adequate in itself to attain mystical union with God.[32] As a means, it can be dispensed with or used insofar as it helps; and in general the best Byzantine hesychastic writers always insisted on this.[33] Abuses enter and do great harm to hesychastic spirituality and the Jesus Prayer with its suggested aids when it is demanded of a material technique a quick and sure method of attaining mystical union.

We can evaluate the merit of any technique only in relation to these essential characteristics outlined by Fr. J. Maréchal,[34] that must accompany always true Christian mysticism:

---

[30] Bishop Ignatius Brianchaninov, *On the Prayer of Jesus* (London, 1952), pp. 83–88. Cf. also *Besedy o molitve iisusovoj. Čto takoe molitva iisusova po predanijam pravoslavnoj cerkvi* (Serdobol', 1938), pp. 405–433.

[31] Cf. Poucel, Victor, S. J., "Pour que votre âme respire", in *Art Catholique*, 1936, p. 13, as quoted by I. Hausherr, "A propos de spiritualité hesychaste: Controverse sans contradicteur", *OCP*, 1937, vol. III, pp. 271–272.

[32] Gardet, Louis: "Recherches sur la 'Mystique Naturelle' ", in *Revue Thomiste*, no. 1–2 (1948), p. 103.

[33] Cf. E. Behr-Sigel, "La prière à Jésus", in *Dieu Vivant*, no. 8, p. 82.

[34] J. Maréchal, S. J., "Études sur la psychologie des mystiques" (Paris, 1937), I, pp. 252–258.

(1) Supernatural grace, because of its ontological character, is inaccessible to direct, human experiences. Here we can readily discern the basic difference between natural and supernatural mysticism.[35] Exteriorly the same manifestations and phenomena may be in evidence, but interiorly there is a radical difference of value and finality. In the supernatural mystical state the human faculties are elevated to a state that makes operations possible, through God's operations, that would, naturally speaking, be impossible. The finality is a prefiguring of the intimate union with God in the beatific vision of the next life and this prefiguring can also be the basis of meriting an increase in the future vision. It must be noted that, in saying grace is not the object of direct sensible experience, it is not denying that grace can and does have sensible, experienced effects.

(2) That God, in a mystical experience, communicates Himself through an immediate intuition, but the communication is made to a "man" and not just to a soul separated. Hence there is a necessity for ascetical preparation to bring the whole "being" to a point of aptability by persevering and progressive ascesis, recollected prayer, and moral acts. With the increase in intensity of God's self-revelation, there will be an increase in ascesis and prayer and virtuous acts.

(3) All these preparatory acts of ascesis, of self-renouncement, of prayer are prerequisite, *necessary* conditions for a state of mystical union. But in the ultimate analysis man's best efforts leave him absolutely impotent to reach such a union by his own force. Mystical union with God is a free and gratuitous gift of God, a favour bestowed on man, and whose bestowal cannot ultimately be dictated by a human will, nor be foreseen as bestowed after so long a time of preparation.

In natural mysticism, pantheistic or Buddhistic, ascesis is also considered as necessary, but also as *sufficient* condition for ecstasy. For Christian mysticism, ascesis is necessary but never sufficient in itself for mystical states.

(4) If true Christian mystical activity is informed by grace and is meant by God to be a superior step to supernatural destiny, negatively it must conform to the whole plan of supernatural salvation. It must be in complete accord with revealed dogma and Christian morals based on the natural law of God and the doctrine of the Gospels.

---

[35] Cf. Maritain, Jacques, *Quatre essais sur l'esprit dans sa condition charnelle* (Paris, 1939), especially ch. III: "L'expérience mystique naturelle et vie", pp. 131–177.

It is this last characteristic which gives us a norm, even though a negative one, to judge whether a mystic is experiencing purely natural mysticism brought on by physiological factors prepared by intense ascesis and intellectual concentration or whether he is being moved by supernatural grace. "By their fruits shall you know them." If it is God working in this person, He will work in harmony always with His revealed Will. And the mystic will lead a life of virtue according to God's revealed word, especially as Incarnated in the Divine Word, Jesus Christ. And he will accept, preach and live according to the revealed truths as proposed by God to men through the two living founts of Holy Scripture and Tradition.

SOURCES

EDITIONS OF NIL SORSKIJ'S WRITINGS CONSULTED

Akty Istoričeskie (St. Petersburg, 1841).

Amvrosij Episkop, *Istorija Rossijskoj Ierarchii*, vol. V (Moscow, 1813), pp. 210–336.

Beseda prepodobnyx Sergija i Germana Valaamskix čudotvorcev. Apokrifičeskij pamjatnik XVI-go veka, in *AAE* (St. Petersburg, 1889).

Borovkova-Majkova, M. A., * " Nila Sorskago Predanie i Ustav s vstupitel'noj statej", in *PDP*, no. 179 (St. Pet. 1912).

"Daniel of Scete", Ed. by M. Leon-Clugnet, in *ROC*, 5 (1900), p. 65 and foll (in Greek).

Dobrotoljubie, Ed. by Bishop Theophan the Recluse. T. I (1895), T. II (1884), T. III, ed. 2 and 3 (Moscow, 1888), T. IV (1889), T. V (1889).

Dopolnenija k Aktam Istoričeskim (St. Petersburg, 1849).

Elagin Edition,** *Prepodobnyj Nil Sorskii pervoosnovatel' skitskago žitija v Rossii, i Ustav ego o žitel'stve skitskom* (St. Pet., 1864).

Justin Episkop, *Prepodobnyj i bogonosnyj otec naš Nil, podvižnik Sorskij* (Moscow, 1892; Berlin, 1939; Toronto, 1958).

Kassian, *Conferences:* vol. 1, bk. I–VII: Sources Chrétiennes, no. 42 (Paris, 1955); vol. 2, bk. VIII–XVII, *ibid.*, no. 54 (1958); vol. 3, XVIII–, *ibid.*

De Institutis Coenobiorum et de Octo Principalium Vitiorum Remediis, Corpus Scriptorum Ecclesiasticorum Latinorum, ed. Petschenig, M. (Prague–Vienna, 1838).

Lenin Public Library of Moscow. *Manuscripts of Nil's Letters:* a. Letter to Vassian Patrikeev, Troick. Ms. no. 188, fol. 93–98; b. Letter to Guri Tušin, same Ms. no. 188, fol. 99–103; c. Letter to German Podol'nyj, *ibid.*, fol. 104–108; d. Leter to Kassian Mavnukskij, Moscow Ecclesiastical Seminary, no. 185, fol. 363–375; e. Letter to a Brother in an Eastern Country, Volokolamsk Ms. 189/577, fol. 22–23.

TRANSLATIONS

"Prenie M. Daniila s Maksimom Grekom", in *Čtenija*, ed. by O. Bodjanskij, no. 7 (1847), p. 6.

"Prenie M. Daniila s Vassianom Patrikeevim", in *ibid.*, no. 8, (1847), p. 3 and foll.

Synodal Edition, *Prepodobnogo otca našego Nila Sorskago predanie učenikom svoim o žitel'stve skitskom* (St. Pet., 1852).

* This is the critical edition and text I have used in this work for all citations (unless I have otherwise indicated) from the *Ustav* and the *Predanie*.

** This edition contains the text of Nil's *Predanie* and *Ustav* in question and answer form. There are also given several letters of Nil and compositions attributed to him, at times inaccurately. Cf. the *Appendix I* of this work.

Fedotov, G. P., *A Treasury of Russian Spirituality* (N. Y., 1948) (Abridgement).
Lilienfeld, Fairy von, *Nil Sorskij und seine Schriften – Die Krise der Tradition im Russland Ivans III*, II Teil: *Die Schriften Nil Sorskijs in Deutscher Übertragung* (Berlin 1963).

OTHER RELATED SOURCES CONSULTED

Smolitsch, I., *Leben und Lehre der Starzen*, 2nd ed. (Cologne-Olten, 1952).
Akty Arxeografičeskoj Komissii (St. Petersburg, 1836 and foll.).
Drevnerossijskaja Biblioteka, 2nd ed. (Moscow, 1788–91).
Evergetinos, Paulos, *Synagoge* (Constantinople, 1861).
Gennadij, Bishop of Novgorod, "Letter to Ioasaf", Troickaja-Lavra Ms. no. 730, fol. 246 and foll., reproduced by Kazakova-Lur'e, in *Antifeodal'nye eretičeskie dviženija na Rusi XIV načhala XVI v.* (Mosc.–Len., 1955), no. 16, pp. 315–320.
–, "Letter to Nifont", edited by Kaz.-Lur'e, *op. cit.*, pp. 419–433. Also found in *Čtenija*, 1847, part IV, no. 1, "Smes".
–, "Letter to Zosima", Q. XVII Ms., no. 15, fol. 372–77, and Tolstoj Ms., no. 962/852, fol. 331–341, edited by Kaz.-Lur'e, *op. cit.*, no. 18, pp. 373–379.
–, "Letter to the Bishops of the Oct. 1490 Synod", edited by Kaz.-Lur'e, *op. cit.*, pp. 379–382 from the two above Mss. fol. 377–380 and fol. 341–342 respectively.
Gregory Sinaite, *Žitie ize vo svjatyx otca našego Grigorija Sinaita*, ed. by Pomjalovskij, I, in *Zapiski ist.-fil. fak. St. Pet. Univ.*, vol. XXXV (text in Greek) (St. Pet. 1894–96).
Isaac the Syrian, *De Perfectione Religiosa*, ed. by P. Bedjan (Paris, 1909).
–, *Tou osiou patros imon Isaak . . . ta eurethenta Askitika*, ed. by Nikephoros Theotokis (Leipzig, 1770).
Istorija Rossijskoj Ierarchii (IRI), Ed. by Episkop Amvrosij, vol. IV, 1812, vol. V (Moscow, 1813).
Izdanie Obščestva ljubitel'nej drevnej pis'mennosti (St. Pet., 1878–1911).
Joseph Volokolamsk, *Prosvetitel'* (Kazan', 1857).
–, *Ustav* or *Duxovanaja Gramota*, in *Velikija Čet'i-Minei*, ed. by Metropolit Makarij, *Pamjatniki slavjano-russkoj pis'mennosti, izdanie Arxeografičeskoj komissii*, Sept. 1–15, col. 499–615 (St. Pet. 1868).
–, "Žitie prepodobnago Iosifa Volokolamskogo", *Velik. Čet'i-Minei*, Sept., col. 453–485.
–, "Slovo ob osuždenii eretikov" (Joseph the probable author), ms. edited by Kazak.-Lur'e, *op. cit.*, no. 29, pp. 488–498. Also found in *DRB*, vol. XVI, p. 424.
Kurbskij Prince, "Poslanie Kurbskago", in *Prav. Sob.*, 1863, June, p. 571 and foll.
Maksim the Greek *Sočinenija Prep. Maksima Greka*, ed. Kazan's Eccl. Academy, Kazan', 3 vols. (1859–62).
Paisij Jaroslavov "Skazanie o Spaso-Kamenni", in *Prav. Sob.*, 1861, I, pp. 203–211.
Pamjatniki drenej pis'mennosti (PDP) (St. Petersburg, 1817–1925).
Pamjatniki drevnerusskago kanoničeskago prava, 2nd ed. (1906–8). The first tome is the same as tome VI of *RIB* and continues in the same edition.
Patrologiae Cursus Completus, Series Graeca, Ed. by Migne (Paris).
Patrologiae Cursus Completus, Series Latina, ibid.
Philokalia ton ieron neptikon, 3rd ed. (Athens, 1957–8), 3 vols.
"Pis'mo o neljubkax starcev Kirillova-Iosifova monastyrja", Ed. by Panov, in *Otnošenija inokov Kirillova i Iosifova monastyrej*, in *Prib. k Tvor.*, T. X, p. 505 and foll.
Polnoe Sobranie Russkix Letopisej (PSRL) (St. Petersburg, 1841 and foll.).
Povest' Vremennyx Let, Ed. by D. S. Lixačev (Mosc.–Len., 1950).
Russkaja Istoričeskaja Biblioteka (RIB), Izd. Arxeografičeskoj Komissii (St. Pet., 1879 and foll.).

Simeon the New Theologian (Pseudo), "La méthode d'oraison hesychaste", ed. by I. Hausherr, S. J., in *OC*, vol. IX, no. 36 (1927).

Sobranie Gosudarstvennyx Gramot i Dogovorov, 5 tomes (Moscow, 1813–1894).

Stoglav, 3rd ed. (Kazan', 1911).

Theodosius Pečerskij, "Žitie Prep. Feodosija" by Nestor, Ms. edited by O. Bodjanskij, in *Čtenija*, 1879, I.

Trans-Volga Starcy. "Letter of the Trans-Volga Starcy", ms. edited by Kazak.-Lur'e, *op. cit.*, pp. 511–513; also found in *DRB*, vol. XVI, pp. 424–428.

Vassian Patrikeev, "Polemičeskija sočinenija Vassiana Patrikeeva", in *Prav. Sob.*, T. III (1863), p. 208 and foll.

–, "Rassuždenie inoka-knjazija Vassiana o nepriličii monastyrjam vladet' otčinami", in *Čtenija*, 1859, III, pp. 1–16.

PARTICULAR BIBLIOGRAPHY DEALING WITH NIL SORSKIJ

Arxangel'skij, A. S., *Nil Sorskij i Vassian Patrikeev, ix literaturnye trudy i idei v drevrej Rusi. Istoriko-literaturnyj očerk*, Part I: *Prepodobnyj Nil Sorskij* (St. Pet., 1882), in *PDP*, no. 25.

Barsukov, N., "Istočnik russkoj agiografii", in *Izdanija obščestva ljubitelej drevnej pis'mennosti*, no. 81, col. 406–7 (St. Pet., 1882).

-, Slovar' istoričeskij o byvšix v Rossii pisat'eljax duxovnago čina greko-rossijskoj cerkvi, T. 2 (St. Pet., 1827).

Behr-Sigel, E., "Prière et Sainteté dans l'Église russe", in Collection: *Russie et Chrétienté* (Paris, 1950).

Borovkova-Majkova, M. S., "Velikij Starec Nil, Pustynnik Sorskij", in *Russkij Filogičeskij Vestnik*, vol. LXIV (1910), pp. 62–78.

-, "Nil Sorskij i Paisij Veličkovskij", in *Sbornik statej posvjaščennyx S. F. Platonovu* (St. Pet., 1911).

-, "K literaturnoj dejatel'nosti Nil Sorskogo", in *PDP*, 177 (St. Pet., 1910).

Fedotov, G., *Svjatye Drevnej Rusi* (Paris, 1931).

-, *Treasury of Russian Spirituality* (N. Y., 1948).

Fennell, J. L. G., "The Attitude of the Josephians and Trans-Volga Elders to the Heresy of the Judaizers", in *The Slavonic and East European Review*, vol. XXIX (1951), pp. 486–509.

Florovsky, G., *Puti russkogo bogoslovija* (Paris, 1937).

Gorskij, A., "Otnošenija inokov Kirillova-Belozerskago i Iosifova-Volokolamskago monastyrej v XVI veke", in *Prib. k Tvor.*, vol. X (1851), p. 502 and foll.

Grečev, B., "Zavolžskie starcy v literaturnom rešenii spornyx voprosov russko-obščestvennoj žizni konca XV–XVI vv.", in *BV*, 1907, p. 477 and foll.

-, "Prepodobnyj Nil Sorskij i Zavolžskie Starcy", published in *BV*, 1908, no. 5, pp. 57–82; no. 9, pp. 49–66; no. 11, pp. 327–343; 1909, no. 5, pp. 42–56.

Grunwald, Constantin de, *Quand la Russie avait des Saints*, p. 94 and foll.

Ikonnikov, V. S., *Maksim Grek i ego vremja*, 2nd ed. (Kiev, 1915).

-, *Opyt izsledovanija o kul'turnom značenii Vizantii v russkoj istorii* (Kiev, 1869).

Kadloubovskij, A., *Očerki po istorii drevnerusskoj literatury žitij svjatyx* (Warsaw, 1902), pp. 231–258.

Kalestinov, K., *Velikij Starec. Očerk žizni prepodobnogo Nila Sorskogo* (St. Pet., 1907).

Kazakova, N. A., and Lur'e, J. S., *Antifeodal'nye eretičeskie dviženija na Rusi XIV – načala XVI v.* (Mosc–Len., 1955).

Kologrivov, I., *Essai sur la Sainteté en Russie* (Bruges, 1953), pp. 187–213.

Levickij, G., "Otčet professorskogo stipendiata G. Levickago o zanjatijax v 1889–90 g.", in *Xrist. Čtenie*, 1895, part 2–3, pp. 332–335.

Lilienfeld, F. von "Josif Volockij und Nil Sorskij, ihre sogenannten "Schulen" und ihre Stellung im gesellschaftlichen und politischen Leben ihrer Zeit", in *Zeitschr. f. S.*, 3 (1958), pp. 786–801.

–, "Der athonitische Hesychasmus des 14. und 15. Jahrhs. im Spiegel zeitgenossischer Quellen", in *Jbb. GO*, vol. 6 (1958), pp. 436–448.

–, *Nil Sorskij und seine Schriften – Die Krise der Tradition im Russland Ivans III* (Dissertation der theologischen Fakultät der Martin Luther Universität) (Berlin, 1963).

Lur'e, S. J., K voprosu ob ideologii Nila Sorskogo, in *TODL*, vol. XIII (1957), pp. 182–212.

–, *Ideologičeskaja bor'ba v russkoj publicistike konca XV – načala XVI veka* (Mosc.–Len., 1960). Cf. V: *Napravlenie Nila Sorskogo v ideologičeskoj bor'be konca XV v.* pp. 285–346.

Meyendorff, J., *Une controverse sur le rôle social de l'Église. La querelle des biens ecclésiastiques au XVIe siècle en Russie*, in *Irénikon*, Chevetogne, 1956.

Murav'ev, A. N., *Russkaja Fivaida na Severe* (St. Pet., 1894).

Nikolaevskij, P. F., "Russkaja propoved' v XV–XVI vv.", in *Ž.M.N.Pr.*, no. 4, 1868, pp. 268–388.

Nikol'skij, N. K., *Kirillo-Belozerskij monastyr'*, 2 vols. (St. Pet., 1897, 1910).

–, "Obščinnaja i kelejnaja Zizn' v Kirillo-Belozerskom monastyre, v XV i XVI vekax i v načale XVII v.", in *Xrist. Čtenie*, 1907, Aug., pp. 153–189.

–, "Materialy dlja istorii drevnerusskoj duxovnoj pis'mennosti", in *Izvestija Otdelenija russkago jazyka i slovesnosti Akademii Nauk*, XXIII, no. 1 (St. Pet., 1907).

–, "Opisanie rukopisej Kirillo-Belozerskogo monastyrja sostavlennoe v konce", Izd. *OLDP*, no. 113 (St. Pet., 1897).

–, "O vlijanii vizantijskix učenij na Nila Sorskago", in *Visantijskij Vremennik*, III (1895), pp. 192–5.

P-ov "Iz istorii russkogo monašestva v XVI v. (O Nile Sorskom, ego ustave i sočinenijax)", in *Čtenija*, 1872, no. 9, pp. 138–149; no. 11–12, pp. 349–357.

Panov, I., "Eres' Židovstvujuščix", in *Ž.M.N.Pr.*, 1877, no. 1, pp. 1–40; no. 2, pp. 253–295; no. 3, pp. 1–59.

Pavlov, A. St., *Istoričeskij očerk sekuljarizacii cerkovnyx zemel' v Rossii*. Part I: *Popytki k obraščeniju v gosudarstvennuju sobstvennosť pozemel'nyx vladenij russkoj cerkvi v XVI veke (1503–80)* (Odessa, 1871), ed. *Zapiski Novorossijskogo Universiteta*, Part 4, vol. VIII, 18.

Filaret, Arxiepiskop Xar'kovskij, *Obzor russkoj duxovnoj literatury* (Xar'kov, 1859), pp. 173–181.

–, *Russkie svjatye*, T. 4, April (Černigov, 1862), pp. 15–23.

Pokrovskij, K. V., "K literaturnoj dejatel'nosti Nila Sorskogo", in *Drevnosti, Trudy slavjanskoj komiissi Mosk. arx. obšč.*, Vol. V, Protokol 103 (Moscow, 1911).

Pravdin, A., "Prepodobnyj Nil Sorskij i Ustav ego skitskoj žizni", in *Xrist. Čtenie*, 1877, Jan., pp. 114–157.

Pypin, A., *Istorija russkoj literatury*, T. 2 (St. Pet., 1916), pp. 75–87.

Ševyrev, S., *Istorija russkoj slovesnosti, Lekcii*, vol. 4 (Moscow, 1860), pp. 177–196.

–, *Poezdka v Kirillo-Belozerskij monastyr'*, 2 vols. (Moscow, 1850).

Smolitsch, I., "Velikij Starec Nil Sorskij", in *Put'*, no. 19, Nov. 1929, Paris.

–, "Studien zum Klosterwesen Russlands, II. Zum Problem des Klosterbesitzes im 15. u. 16. Jh.", in *Kyrios*, 4 (1939), pp. 29–30.

–, "Das Altrussische Mönchtum (11.–16. Jahrhundert)", in *Das östliche Christentum*, Würzburg, 1940.

–, *Leben und Lehre der Starzen*, 2nd ed. (Cologne-Olten, 1952).

–, "Das Russisches Mönchtum, Entstehung, Entwicklung und Wesen, 988–1917", in *Das östliche Christentum*, 10/11 (Wurzburg, 1953).

Stroev, P., *Xronologičeskij ukazatel' materialov otečestvennoj istorii literatury i pravovedenija* (St. Pet., 1834).

–, *Slovar' istoričeskij o svjatyx proslavlennyx v rossijskoj cerkvi i o nekotoryx podvižnikax blagočestija mestno čtimyx* (St. Pet., 1836).

Uspenskij, F., *Očerki po istorii Vizantijskoj obrazovannosti* (St. Pet., 1892).

Žmakin, V., *Mitropolit Daniil i ego sočinenija*, Ch. I–II (Moscow, 1881).

GENERAL BIBLIOGRAPHY

Amand de Mendieta, E., *Le Mont-Athos, la presqu' île des caloyers* (Bruges, 1955).
Ammann, A. M., S. J., "Die Gottesschau im palamitischen Hesychasmus", in *Das östliche Christentum*, vol. 6–7 (Würzburg, 1938).
--, *La Storia della Chiesa Russa* (Turin, 1948).
Andreyev, N., "Kurbsky's Letters to Vas'yan Muromtsev", in *The Slavonic and East European Review*, Vol. XXXIII, no. 81 (June, 1955), pp. 414–436.
Arxangel'skij, A., *K izučeniju drevnerusskoj literatury. Tvorenija otcov cerkvi v drevnerusskoj pis'mennosti* (St. Petersburg, 1888).
--, *Tvorenija otcov cerkvi v drevnerusskoj pis'mennosti* (Kazan', 1889–1891).
Arseniev, N., *Ostkirche und Mystik* (Münich, 1943).
Avaliani, S., "Beseda prepodobnyx Sergija i Germana Valaamskix čudotvorcev kak istoričeskij istočnik", in *BV*, vol. III (1909), p. 368 and foll.
Bacht, H., "Das 'Jesus-Gebet'. Seine Geschichte und seine Problematik", in *Geist u. Leben*, 24 (1951), pp. 326–338.
--, " 'Meditari' in den ältesten Mönchsquellen", in *Geist u. Leben*, 28 (1955), pp. 360–373.
Balthasar, H. U. von, "Aktion und Kontemplation", in *Geist u. Leben*, 21 (1949), pp. 361–370.
Barsukov, N., "Istočniki russkoj Agiografii", *Izdanije Obščestva ljubitelej drevnej pis'mennosti*, no. 81 (St. Petersburg, 1882).
Bauer, F., "Die Heilige Schrift bei den Mönchen des christlichen Altertums nach den Schriften des Johannes Cassianus", in *Theologie und Glaube*, 17 (1925), pp. 512–32.
Behr-Sigel, E., "La Prière à Jésus", in *Dieu Vivant*, no. 8, 1947, pp. 69–94.
Belov, E., *Ob istoričeskom značenii russkago bojarstva do konca XVII veka* (St. Petersburg, 1886).
Beneševič, V. N., "Taktikon Nikona Černogora", in *Zapiski ist. filol. fakul'teta Petrogradskago Universiteta*, CXXXIX vol. I. (St. Pet., 1917).
Benz, E., *Russische Heiligenlegenden* (Zürich, 1953).
Bettencourt St., "Doctrina Ascetica Origenis", in *Studia Anselmiana*, 16 (Roma, 1945).
Biedermann, H., OESA, "Das Menschenbild bei Symeon dem Jüngeren dem Theologen (949–1022)", in *Das östliche Christentum*, no. 9 (Würzburg, 1949).
Bloom, Antoine, "Contemplation et Ascèse", in *Études Carmélitaines* (1949).
--, "L'Hesychasme et Yoga Chrétien" in: *Cahiers du Sud* (Paris, 1953).
Bloomfield, M. W., "The Origin of the Concept of the Seven Cardinal Sins", in *Harvard Theol. Review*, 34 (1941), pp. 121–128.
Bois, J., "Les Hésychastes avant le XIVe siècle", in *È. d'Or.*, V (1902), pp. 1–11.
--, "Grégoire le Sinaïte et l'hésychasma à Athos au XIVe siècle", in *È. d'Or.*, V (1902), pp. 65–73.
--, "Les debuts de la controverse hésychaste", in *É. d'Or.*, V (1902), pp. 353–362.
Bolshakoff, S., *Russian Nonconformity* (Philadelphia, 1950).

Bolshakoff, S., "Influence of Patristic Studies on Modern Russian Mystics", Paper presented to the 2nd International Conference on Patristic Studies, Oxford, England, 1955, in *One Church*. vol. XII, no. 3–4, March-April, 1958.

Bousset, W., *Apophthegmata: Studien zur Geschichte des ältesten Mönchtums* (Tübingen, 1923).

Bouyer, L., *Le sens de la vie monastique* (Turnhout, 1950).

–, *Histoire de la Spiritualité chrétienne*, vol. 1 and 2 (Paris, 1960).

Brianchaninov, Bishop Ignatius, *On the Prayer of Jesus, from the Ascetic Essays*, transl. by Fr. Lazarus (London, 1952).

Bremond, H., "Les Pères du Désert", vol. 1 and 2, in Collection: *Les Moralistes Chrétiens* (Paris, 1927–29).

Budovnic, I., *Russkaja publicistika XVI veka* (Mosc.–Len., 1947).

–, "Pervye russkie nestjažateli", in *Voprosy istorii religii i ateizma*, vol. 5 (Moscow, 1958), pp. 264–282.

Bulgakov, S., *L'Orthodoxie* (Paris, 1932).

Buslaev, Ø. I., *Istoričeskie očerki russkoj narodnoj slovesnosti i iskusstva*, II, 4th ed. (Moscow, 1888).

Byčkov, A. F., *Opisanie slavjanskix i russkix rukopisej sbornikov Imp. publičnoj biblioteki*, vol. 1 (St. Pet., 1882).

Casey, R. P., "Early Russian Monasticism", in *OCP*, 19 (1953), p. 372–423.

Cayre, F., *Spirituali e Mistici dei primi tempi* (Catania, 1957).

Chenu, M. D., "Moines, clercs au carrefour de la vie évangelique", in *RHE*, T. 49, 1 (1954), p. 59–89.

Crainic, N., "Das Jesusgebet", transl. from Rumanian by W. Biemel, in *Zeitschr. f. Kirch.*, 60 (1941), p. 341–353.

Cuttat, J. A., *La rencontre des religions avec une étude sur la spiritualité de l'Orient Chrétien* (Paris, 1957).

Dalmais, J. H., O. P., "Prière du Coeur et Prière de Jésus", in *Vie Sp.*, 1952, Jan., p. 95 and foll.

De Clercq, C., *Les Textes Juridiques dans les Pandectes de Nicon de la Montagne Noire* (Venice, 1942), in *S. Congreg. per la Chiesa Or. Codificazione Canonica Or. Fonti*, Serie II, Fasc. XXX.

Denisoff, E., "Aux origines de l'Eglise russe autocéphale", in *RES*, vol. XXIII (1947).

Dimitrievskij, A., *Bogosluž, enie v russkoj Cerkvi v XVI veke*, part I (Kazan', 1884).

Dörr, *Diadochus von Photike und die Messalianer. Ein Kampf zwischen wahrer und falscher Mystik im fünften Jahrhundert* (Fribourg en B., 1937).

–, "Drevnija pustyni i pustynnožiteli na severo-vostoke Rossii", in *Prav. Sob.*, 1860, III, p. 202 and foll.

Fedotov, G., *The Russian Religious Mind*, Harvard Univ. Press (Cambridge, Mass., 1946).

Festugière, A. J., O. P., *Les Moines d'Orient, I, Culture ou Sainteté, Introduction au Monachisme Orientale* (Paris, 1961).

Filaret Bishop, *Russkie Svjatye*, 12 vols. (St. Pet , 1882).

Florinsky, M., *Russia: a History and an Interpretation* (N. Y., 1953).

Florovsky, G., "St. Gregory Palamas and the Tradition of the Fathers", in *Sobornost'*, p. 165 and foll. (Winter-Spring, 1961).

–, *Puti Russkogo Bogoslovija* (Paris, 1937).

Gardet, L., "Un problème de mystique comparée: la mention du Nom divin-dhikr-dans la mystique musulmane", in *Revue Thomiste*, III (1952), pp. 642–79; I (1953), pp. 197–216.

–, Recherches sur la mystique naturelle, in *Revue Thomiste*, 1948, no. 1–2, pp. 76–112.

Gauvain, Jean, *Récits d'un pèlerin russe* (Neuchâtel, 1943).

Gillet, Lev., The Gift of Tears, in *Sobornost'*, 1937, p. 5 and foll.

Godet, P., "Jean Cassian", article in *DTC* II² (1910), col. 1823–29.

Golubinskij, E., *Istorija russkoj cerkvi*, vol. I, 2nd ed. (1901); vol. II (Moscow, 1904).

Gorodetsky, N., *The Humiliated Christ in Modern Russian Thought* (London, 1938).

Gorskij, A. V., "O snošenijax russkoj cerkvi s svjatogorskimi obiteljami", in *Prib. k. Tvor.*, VI, pp. 123–168.

–, "Maksim Grek, svjatogorec", in *Prib. k. Tvor.*, XVIII (1859).

–, *Zizn' i istoričeskoe značenie Kn. A. M. Kurbskago* (Kazan', 1854).

Gorskij, A. V., and Nevostruev, K. I., *Opisanie slavjanskix rukopisej moskovskoj sinodal'noj biblioteki* (Moscow, 1855).

Gouillard, J., "La Centurie", Review of Ammann's book: *Gottesschau...*, in *É. d'Or.*, 37, 1938, pp. 456–460.

–, "Petite Philocalie de la Prière du Coeur", in *Documents Spirituels*, 5 (Paris, 1953).

–, "Syméon le Jeune ou le Nouveau Théologien", in *DTC*, vol. XIV, 1 (1941), col. 2945–2946.

Gribomont, J., "Obéissance et Évangile selon St. Basile le Grand", in *Vie Sp.*, Suppl. VI (1952), pp. 192–215.

Guillaumont, A., "Le sens du nom de coeur dans l'antiquité", in *Études Carmélitaines* (1950), p. 77 and foll.

Hausherr, I., S. J., "Un pèlerin russe de la prière intérieure", in *OC*, vol. VI (1926), pp. 174–76.

–, "La méthode d'oraison hésychaste", in *OC*, vol. IX, no. 36 (Roma, 1927), pp. 109–210.

–, "Vie de Syméon le Nouveau Théologien (949–1022) par Nicetas Stethatos. Texte grec inédit", in *OC*, vol. XII (1928), no. 45.

–, "Note sur l'inventeur de la méthode d'oraison hésychaste", in *OC*, vol. XX (Dec. 1930), pp. 179–182.

–, "Les Versions syriaques et arméniques d'Evagre le Pontique", in *OC*, vol. XXII, no. 69 (1931).

–, "Par delà l'oraison pure grace à une coquille. À propos d'un texte d'Evagre", in *RAM*, 1932, pp. 184–188.

–, "L'origine de la théorie orientale des huit péchés capitaux", in *OC*, vol. XXX, no. 86 (1933), pp. 164–175.

–, "Evagre le Pontique: 'Traité de l'oraison', trad. et commenté" in *RAM*, XV (1934), pp.

–, "Les grands courants de la spiritualité orientale", in *OCP*, 1 (1935), pp. 114–138.

–, "L'erreur fondamentale et la logique du Messalinisme", in *OCP*, 1 (1935), pp. 328–360.

–, "L'ignorance infinie", in *OCP*, 2 (1936), pp. 351–362.

–, "À propos de la spiritualité hésychaste: Controverse sans contradicteur", in *OCP*, 3 (1937), pp. 260–272.

–, "Penthos, La doctrine de la compunction dans L'Orient chrétien", in *OCA*, no. 132 (Roma, 1944).

–, "Les Orientaux, connaîssent-ils les 'nuits' de saint Jean de la Croix?", in *OCP*, 12 (1946), pp. 5–46.

–, "Opus Dei", in *OCP*, 13 (1947), *Miscellanea a Guillaume de Jerphanion*, pp. 195–218.

–, "L'imitation de Jésus-Christ dans la spiritualité byzantine", in *Mélanges offerts au R. P. Ferdinand Cavallera* (Toulouse, 1948), pp. 231–259.

–, "Variations récentes dans le jugement sur la méthode d'oraison des hésychastes", in *OCP*, 19 (1953), pp. 424–428.

–, "Les exercices spirituels de Saint Ignace et la méthode d'oraison hésychaste", in *OCP*, 20 (1954), pp. 7–26.

– "Direction spirituelle en Orient autrefois", in *OCA*, no. 144 (Roma, 1955).

Hausherr, I., S. J., "Direction spirituelle chez les chrétiens Orientaux", in *Dict. Sp. A. M.*, III, pp. 1008–1060.

–, "L'hésychasme, Étude de spiritualité", in *OCP*, 22 (1956), pp. 5–40, 247–285.

–, "Comment priaient les Pères", in *RAM*, 1956 (Jan.-Mar.), pp. 33–56, 284–296.

–, "Les noms du Christ", in *OCA*, no. 157 (Roma, 1960).

–, *Les leçons d'un contemplatif. Le Traité de l'oraison d'Evagre le Pontique* (Paris, 1960).

–, "La Théologie du Monachisme chez S. Jean Climaque", in Collection: *Théologie de la vie monastique* (Paris, 1961), p. 405 and foll.

–, "Contemplation et Sainteté-Philoxène de Mabboug", in *RAM*, XIV (1933), p. 190 and foll.

–, "Spiritualité Monacale et Unité Chrétienne", in *OCA*, no. 153, *Il Monachesimo Orientale* (Roma, 1958).

H. de B., "La Prière du Coeur", in *Messager de l'Exarchat du Patriarche Russe en Europe Occidentale*, no. 4, 1953, pp. 13–40.

Heppell, M., "Slavonic Translation of Early Byzantine Ascetical Literature. A Bibliographical Note", in *Journal of Ecclesiastical History*, vol. 5 (1954), pp. 86–100.

–, *(Das) Herzensgebet Mystik und Yoga der Ostkirche. Die Centurie der Mönche Kallistus und Ignatius* (München, 1955).

Heussi, K., *Der Ursprung des Mönchtums* (Tübingen, 1936).

–, "Untersuchungen zu Nilus dem Asketen", *Texte und Untersuchungen*, No. 42, vol. 2 (Leipzig, 1917).

Holl, D., *Enthusiasmus und Bussgewalt beim griechischen Mönchtum. Eine Studie zu Symeon dem Neuen Theologen* (Leipzig, 1898).

Ikonnikov, I., *Issledovanie o glavnyx napravlenijax v nauke russkoj istorii* (Kiev, 1869) (2).

Ilinskij, G., "Značenie Afona v istorii slavjanskoj pis'mennosti", in *Ž.M.N.Pr.*, vol. XVIII (1908), pp. 1–41.

Ilinsky, Th. M., "Russkie Bogomili XV veka", in *BV*, July-Aug., 1905, pp. 436–460.

–, "Izučenie i upotreblenie Biblii v Rossii", in *Prav. Sob.*, no. 11, 1868, p. 268 and foll.

Ivanka E. "Palamismus und Vätertradition", in *1054–1954. L'Église et les églises. Neuf siècles de douloureuse séparation entre l'Orient e l'Occident*, vol. II (Chevetogne, 1954), pp. 29–46.

Jugie, M., A. A., *Theologia dogmatica Christianorum in Eccl. Cath. dissidentium: theol. dogm. graeco-russorum*, vol. 1 (1926). (Dealing with Hesychasm, p. 432 and foll.).

–, "Palamas (Controverse)", in *DTC* T. XI, 1735–1817 (Paris, 1931).

–, "Les origines de la méthode d'oraison des hésychastes", in *É. d'Or.*, 30 (1931), pp. 179–185.

–, "Note sur le moine hésychaste Nicephore et sa méthode d'oraison", in *É. d'Or.*, 35 (1936), pp. 409–412.

Kadloubovsky., E., and Palmer, G., *Writings from the Philokalia on "Prayer of the Heart"* (London, 1951).

Kalugin, F., *Zinovij inok Otenskij i ego bogoslovsko-polemičeskija i cerkovno-učitel'nyja proizvedenija* (St. Pet., 1894).

Karamzin, N. M., *Istorija gosudarstva rossijskogo*, t. 8, 5th ed. (St. Pet., 1842).

Kazakova, N. A., "Ideologija strigol'ničestva – pervogo eretičeskogo dviženija na Rusi", in *TODL*, vol. XI (1955), pp. 103–117.

–, "Bor'ba protiv monastyrskogo zemlevladenija na Rusi v konce XV načale XVI v.", edited in *Eżegodnik muzeja ist. religii i ateizma* (Mos.-Len., 1958).

Kazanskij, P., *Istorija pravoslavnogo monašestva na vostoke*, 2 vols. (Moscow, 1854, 1856).

–, "Prepodobnyj Iosif Volokolamskij", in *Prib. k Tvor.*, vol. V (1858), pp. 225–270.

Ključevskij, V. O., *Kurs russkoj istorii*, vol. 2 (St. Pet., 1918).

Ključevskij, V. O., Drevnerusskija žitija svjatyx kak istoričeskij istočnik (Moscow, 1871).

–, Bojarskaja duma drevnej Rusi (St. Pet., 1919).

Klibanov, A. I., Reformacionnye dviženija v Rossii v XIV – pervoj polovine XV veka (Moscow, 1960).

Kologrivov, I., Essai sur la sainteté en Russie (Bruges, 1953).

Konople, N., "Svjatye vologodskago kraja", in Čtenija, vol. 4 (1895), pp. 73–130.

Kopanev, A. I., Istorija zemlevladenija belozerskogo kraja XV–XVI vv. (Mosk.-Len., 1951).

Kostomarov, Russkaja istorija v žizneopisanijax eja glavnejšix dejatelej 4th ed., 2 t. (St. Pet., 1896, 1892–5).

Kovalevsky, Pierre, St. Serge et la spiritualité russe (Paris, 1958).

Krivosheine, Basil, "Ascetic and theological teaching of S. Gregory Palamas", in Eastern Churches Quarterly, vol. III (1938–9), p. 26 and foll., p. 138 and foll., and p. 192 and foll. Also in Russian: Seminarium Kondakovianum, VIII (Prague, 1936); and in German: "Die asketische und theologische Lehre des hl. Gregorius Palamas", in Das östliche Christentum, Heft 8 (1939).

–, "The Writings of St. Symeon the New Theologian", in OCP, 20 (1954), pp. 298–328.

–, "The Most Enthusaistic Zealot. S. Symeon the New Theologian as Abbot and Spiritual Instructor", in Ostkirchliche Studien, 4 (1955), pp. 108–128.

–, "Date du texte traditionnel de la 'Prière de Jésus' (given at the 1st Patristic Congress at Oxford, Eng.), in Vestnik Russkogo Zapadno-Evropejskogo Èksarxata, no. 7–8, 1951, pp. 55–59.

Leclerq, H., Article: "Hésychastes", in Dict. Arch. et Liturg, vol. VI, pp. 2362–2365.

Leonid, Arximandrit, "Afon i russkoje monašestvo", in Ž.M.P., 8, 1958, pp. 60–64.

–, "Paisij Veličkovskij", in Z.M.P., Oct., 1954, pp. 53–59.

Lossky, V., Essai sur la théologie mystique de l'Église d'Orient (Paris, 1944).

–, "Le problème de la "Vision face à face" et la tradition patristique de Byzance", in Studia Patristica, vol. II (Berlin, 1957), pp. 512–537.

Lot-Borodine, M., "La doctrine de la déification dans l'église grecque jusqu'au XIe siècle", in Revue d'histoire des religions, 1932.

–, "Le mystère du 'don des larmes' dans l'Orient chrétien", in Vie Sp., 18, col. XLVIII, supplément (1936), pp. 65–110.

Lur'e, J. S., "Kratkaja redakcija 'ustava' Iosifa Volockogo – pamjatnika ideologii rannego iosifljanstva", in TODL, vol. 1958, pp. 219–228.

–, Bor'ba cerkvi s velikoknjažeskoj vlast'ju v konce 70x – pervoj polovine 80x godov XV v.; in TODL, vol. XIV (1958), pp. 219–228.

Makarij (Bulgakov), Istorija russkoj cerkvi, ed. 1–3, 12 tomes in 8 vols. (St. Pet., 1879–98).

–, "Kritičeskij ocherk istrui russkago raskola izvestnago pod imenem staro obrjadčestva", in Xrist. Čtenie, 1853–4, p. 161 and foll.

Maréchal, J., S. J., Études sur la psychologie des mystiques, I (Paris, 1937).

Marsili, S., O. S. B., "Résumé de Cassien sous le nom de St. Nil", in RAM, 15 (1934), pp. 241–245.

Marx, M. J., O. S. B., Incessant Prayer in Ancient Monastic Literature (Città del Vaticano, 1947).

Medlin, W. K., Moscow and East Rome: a political study of the relations of church and state in Muscovite Russia (Geneve, 1952).

Ménager, A., "La doctrine spirituelle de Cassien: la contemplation", in Vie Sp., 4, (1923), pp. 183–212.

Mercier, Eugène, La spiritualité byzantine (Paris, 1933).

Meyendorff, J., Triades pour la défense des saints hésychastes, translation of the text of Gregory Palamas (Louvain, 1954).

Meyendorff, J., "Introduction à l'étude de Grégoire Palamas", vol. 3 in Collection: *Patristica Sorbonencia* (Paris, 1959).

–, *St. Grégoire Palamas et la mystique orthodoxe* (Bourges, 1959).

–, "Le thème du 'retour en soi' dans la doctrine palamite du XIVe siècle", in *Revue d'histoire des religions*, no. 145, 1954, pp. 188–206.

Meyer, Ph., *Die Haupturkunden für die Geschichte des Athoskloster* (Leipzig, 1894).

Miller, O., "Vopros o napravlenii Iosifa Volokolamskago", in *Ž.M.N.Pr.*, no. 2, 1868, pp. 527–545.

–, Review of Arxangel'skij's book, *op. cit.*, "Nil Sorskij…" in: *Istor. V.*, T. IX (August, 1882), p. 430 and foll.

Moine de l'Église d'Orient, *La priére de Jésus, Sa genèse et son dévelopement dans la tradition religieuse byzantino-slave*, in Collection: *Irénikon*, 4 (1951, Chevetogne).

–, "L'invocation du Nom de Jésus dans la tradition byzantine", in *Vie Sp.*, 1952, Jan., pp. 38–45.

–, "Sur l'usage de la Prière de Jésus", Collection: *Irénikon* (Chevetogne, 1952).

Monk of the Eastern Church, *Orthodox Spirituality* (London, 1946).

Mošin, V., "Russkie na Afone i russko-vizantijskie otnošenia, in *Byzantinoslavica*, 9 (1947), pp. 55–85; 11, 1959, pp. 32–71.

Nikol'skij, N. *Materialy dlja povremennago spiska russkix pisatelej i ix sočinenij* (St. Pet., 1906).

–, "O Čtenii knig v drevnija v vremena Rossii", in *Prav. Sob.* II (1858), pp. 173–198.

Olphe-Galliard, M., S. J., "Vie Contemplative et vie active d'après Cassien", in *RAM*,

–, "La Science spirituelle d'après Cassien", in *RAM*, 18 (1937), pp. 141–160.

–, "La pureté de coeur d'après Cassien", in *RAM*, 17 (1936), pp. 28–60.

–, "Cassien, Jean" article in *Dict. Sp. A. M.*, 2 (1953), pp. 214–276.

Orlov, A. S., "Iisusova molitva na Rusi v 16 veke", in *PDP* (St. Pet., 1914), pp. 1–32.

Pomjalovskij, Ivan, V., *Zitie iže vo svjatxy otca našego Gregorija Sinaita* (text in Greek) (St. Pet., 1894).

Popov, K., "Učenie o molitve iisusovoj blažennago Diadoxa (5-ogo veka)", in *Trudy* (Eccl. Academy of Kiev), t. 3 (1902), pp. 651–676.

Porfir'ev, I., "O domostroe", in *Prav. Sob.*, III (1860), pp. 279–331.

Porfirij, Arximandrit: "Ob avtoritete sv. otcov cerkvi i važnosti ix pisanij, in *Prib. k Tvor.*, 1863, pp. 1–59.

–, " 'Prosvetitel' ' Josifa Volokolamskago", in *Prav. Sob.*, 1859.

Radčenko, K., *Religioznoe i literaturnoe dviženie v Bolgarii v epoxu pred tureckim zavoevaniem* (Kiev, 1898).

Ranke-Heinemann, N., "Zum Ideal der vita angelica im frühen Mönchtum", in *Geist u. Leben*, 29 (1956), pp. 347–57.

Recheis, A., "Das Jesusgebet", in *Una Sancta*, 9 (1954), pp. 1–24.

Resch, P., *La doctrine ascétique des premiers maîtres égyptiens du IVe siècle* (Paris, 1931).

Rezac, J., S. J., *De Monachismo secundum recentiorem legislationem Russicam* (Roma, 1952).

Rouët de Journel, M. J., S. J., *Monachisme et monastères russes* (Paris, 1952).

–, "Russkie inoki na Sv. Gore Afonskoj ot perexoda X veka do poloviny XIX v.", in *Xrist. Čtenie*, t. II (1853).

Rousseau, Oliver, O. S. B., "Le rôle important du monachisme dans l'Église d'Orient", in *OCA*, 153, vol: *Il Monachesimo Orientale* (Roma, 1958).

Schoelle R., and Kroll, G., *Corpus Legum Justiniani*, vol. III, ed. 2 (Berlin, 1899).

Schaeder, H., *Moskau – das Dritte Rom. Studien zur Geschichte der politischen Theorien in der slavischen Welt* (Hamburg, 1929).

Schultze, B., S. J., "Untersuchungen über das Jesus-Gebet", in *OCP*, XVIII (1952), pp. 319–343.

Schultze B., S. J,, "Der Streit um die Göttlichheit des Namens Jesu in der Russischen Theologie", in *OCP*, XVII (1951), pp. 321–394.

Ševyrev, ?., *Istorija russkoj slovesnosti*, 4 parts (Moscow, 1860).

Šumakov, S., *Obzor gramot kollegii ekonomii* (Moscow, 1900).

Siddhenswaranada, "La Technique Hindoue de la meditation", in *Études Carmélitanes: Technique et contemplation* (Bruges, 1949).

Smirnov, S. I., *Kak služili miru podvižniki drevnej Rusi?* (Sergiev-Posad, 1903).

–, *Duxovnyj otec v drevnej vostočnoj cerkve* (Sergiev-Posad, 1906).

–, "Snošenija Rossii s vostokom po delam cerkovnym", in *Ž.M.N.Pr.*, 1858, p. 15 and foll.

Sobolevskij, A., "Perevodnaja literatura Moskovskoj Rusi, XIV–XVII vekov", in *Sbornik otdelenija russkago jazika i slovesnosti*, Imp. Akad. Nauk, 74, 1 (St. Pet., 1903).

Sokolov, I., "Vnutrennee sostojanie monašestva v vizantijskoj cerkve s poloviny IX i do načala XIII veka (842–1204)", in *Prav. Sob.*, III (1893).

Sokol'skij, V., *Učastie russkago duxovenstva i monašestva v razvitii edinoderžavija i samoderžavija v moskovskom gosudarstve v konce XV i pervoj polov. XVI vv.* (Kiev, 1902).

Solov'ev, S. M., *Istorija Rossii*, 2nd ed., T. IV (St. Pet., 1894, 1897).

Sophrony Hieromoine, *Des fondements de l'ascèse orthodoxe* (Paris, 1954).

Speranskij, M. N., *Istorija drevnej russkoj literatury*, vol. 2 (Moscow, 1920–21).

Spidlik, Thomas, S. J., "Joseph de Volokolamsk. Un chapitre de la spiritualité russe", in *OCA*, no. 146 (Roma, 1956).

–, "La sophiologie de S. Basile", in *OCA*, no. 162 (Roma, 1961).

–, "L'autorità del Libro per il Monachesimo Russo", in *OCA*, no. 153 (Roma, 1958), pp. 159–179.

Sreznevskij, E., *Svedenija i zametki o maloizvestniyx i neizvestnyx pamjatnikax* (St. Pet., 1874).

–, *Drev. Pam. Russk. pism. i jazyka* (St. Pet., 1863).

Steidle, B., O. S. B., "Die Tränen, ein mystiches Problem im alten Mönchtum", in *Benediktinische Monatschrift*, 20 (1938), pp. 181–187.

Stroev, Pavel, *Spiski ierarxov i nastojatelej monastyrej rossijskija cerkvi* (St. Pet., 1877).

Subbotitina, N. I., "Ob otnošenijax duxovenstva russkago k knjaz'jam s XI do poloviny XV veka", in *Prib. k Tvor.*, XVII (1858), pp. 327–403.

–, "Svedenija o soborax byvšix v X–XVI stoletijax", in *Xrist. Čtenie*, I (1852), pp. 301–353; 1871, II, pp. 529 and foll.

Syrku, P., *Vremja i Žizn' patriarxa Evfimija Ternovskogo* (St. Pet., 1896).

Tyszkiewicz, S., S. J., "Spiritualité et sainteté russe pravoslave", in *Gregorianum*, vol. XV, no. 3 (1934), pp. 349–376.

–, "Moralistes de Russie", in *OCP*, 1949, pp. 341–367; 1950, pp. 377–439.

–, "Église", article in *Dict. Sp. A. M.*

–, "Le visage de l'Orthodoxie", in *NRT*, Juin, 1954.

–, "Platonisme et Plotinisme dans l'ecclésiologie russe orthodoxe", in *NRT*, Mars, 1954.

–, *Tserkov' bogocheloveka* (Roma, 1958).

Tyszkiewicz, S., S. J., and Dom. Th. Belpaire, O.S.B., *Ascètes russes. Ecrits d'ascètes russes* (Namur, 1957).

Uspenskij, T. I. "Očerki po istorii Vizantijskoj obrazovannosti", in *Ž.M.N.Pr.*, 1891, 1892; separately, St. Pet., 1891.

Vilinskij, S. G., *Poslanija Starca Artemija* (Odessa, 1906).

Viller, M., "Aux Sources de la Spiritualité de St. Maxime, les oeuvres d'Evagre le Pontique", in *RAM*, T. XI (avril-juillet, 1930), pp. 156–184, 239–268.

–, *La spiritualité des premiers siècles chrétiens* (Paris, 1930).

Viller, M., and Rahner, K., *Aszese und Mystik der Väterzeit* (Freiburg. Br., 1939).
Vyšeslavcev, B., *Serdce v xristianskoj i indijskoj mistike* (Paris, 1929).
Vogtle, A., "Woher stammt das Schema der Hauptsünden?", in *Theologische Quartal-schrift*, 122 (1941), pp. 217-237.
Wunderle, G., "Zur Psychologie des hésychastischen Gebets", 2nd edit. in *Das östliche Christentum*, no. 2, Würzburg, 1949.
–, "La Technique de l'hésychasme", in *Études Carmélitaines-Nuit Mystique* (Paris, 1938).
Xariton Igoumen, *Umnoe delanie o molitve iisusovoj* (Sortavalassa [Valaam], 1936).
Xruščov, Ivan P. *Izsledovanie o sočinenijax Iosifa Sanina* (St. Pet., 1868).
Ždanovyj, I. M., *Očerk umstvennoj žizni Rossii v XVI–XVII vekax* (St. Pet., 1890).
Žmakin, V., "Nil Polev", in *Ž.M.N.Pr.*, Part CCXVI (Aug., 1881), p. 194 and foll.
Zimin, A. A., "O političeskoj doktrine Iosifa Volockogo" in *TODL*, vol. IX (1953), pp. 159-177.
–, "Delo eretika Artemija", in *Voprosy istorii religii i ateizma*, vol. 5 (Moscow, 1958), pp. 213-232.

INDEX

Abraham Smolensk, 219
abstinence, 107
acedia, 83, 95–97, 139, 152, 158, 181
acceptance, 80
Adam, 269
adaptibility, 86
adultery, 97, 114, 140
Agathon, St., 77
Aleksej, 206
Alexander, 209
amerimnia, 103
Ammann, A., 274–275
Amvrosij, 33, 231, 232, 249
anchoret, 149, 152, 159
Andrew, 265
Andreyev, N., 227
angelic, 88, 89, 111
anger, 83, 92–93, 163–164, 181, 266
Antony, see *Life*
apatheia, 76, 104, 106, 109, 117, 145, 175, 181
Apocalypse, 27
apocryphal, 66
Apophthegmata patrum, 192
apostasis, see *emptying*, 113
Apostles, 57, 59, 65, 77, 123
apostolate, 160, 161–171
Apostolic tradition, 9, 10, 40, 59, 61
Arsenij, 231, 233
Arsenius the Great, 111
Artemij, 214, 218, 226
Arxangel'skij, A., 11, 68, 70, 167, 173, 183, 192, 202, 207, 245, 252, 256, 262, 267
ascesis, 145
asceticism, 11, 25, 27, 28, 31, 34, 35, 42, 51–54, 63, 64, 74, 83, 86, 88, 104–107, 110, 113, 115, 117, 118, 127, 129, 132, 144, 145, 146, 152, 158, 161, 165, 177, 182, 184

Athanasius, 185, 207
attention, 104
Avaliani, S., 225
avarice, 91–92, 156, 181

Baptism, 47, 133
Barlaam, 273–274
Barsanuphius, 85
Basil, 56, 57, 86, 87, 99, 112, 152–153, 156, 174, 175, 185–187, 196, 239, 255, 270
Baškin, M., 214
Behr-Sigel, E., 198, 277
Benjamin, 207
Bible, 207
Bodjanskij, O., 224–225
body, 85–86, 88
Body of Christ, 169–170
Bogomilism, 272, 273
Bois, J., 272–273
Borovkova-Majkova, M., 11, 13, 192, 236, 254, 263
Budovnic, I., 219
Bulgaria, 205, 272–273
Byčkov, F., 230, 231
Byzantine, 269, 273

Callistus, 108, 109, 274
canonization, 46
captivity, 81
cares, see *amerimnia*, 103
Cassian, 91, 95, 96, 98, 173, 174, 183–185, 191, 193
Century, 274–275
charity, 93, 110, 161, 166–168, 204
chastity, 88–89
Christ, see *Jesus*
Chrysostom, 191, 218, 222, 273
Church, Russian, 19, 20–31, 66, 153

Climacus, 62–63, 73, 78, 88, 90, 96, 98, 101, 103, 106, 109, 112, 114–116, 128, 131, 133, 141, 145, 163, 165, 173–176, 180–183, 185, 189, 191, 193, 211, 240, 247, 250, 251, 255, 263
Climent, A., 220
coenobitic, 29, 36, 140, 149, 151–153, 157–159
commandments, 111, 113, 118, 121–124, 133, 143–145, 150, 158, 170
community, 149–152
concupisences, 86
consolations, 110
consciousness, 80, 105
Constantinople, 200, 201
contemplation, 9, 10, 37, 38, 40, 101, 104, 105, 107, 109, 113, 114, 117, 122, 129, 135, 140

Damascene, John, 191
Daniel, Metrop., 221, 224
death, 104, 124–126, 128, 131, 145–146, 156, 181, 262
decoration of churches, 156–157
Demetrius, 274
demons, 73, 75, 99, 100, 138
Denissoff, E., 200
desert, 75, 112
desire, 117, 136
despair, 95, 96
detachment, 52, 104, 112, 115
devil, 74, 77–79, 80–84, 88, 90, 91, 95–99, 100, 101, 122, 123, 136, 140, 145, 158, 175
Devos, P., 72
Diadochus of Photike, 105, 109, 137, 142, 144, 175, 188, 269, 270
Dimitrij, 209
Dionisij, 67, 206, 210, 212
disposition, 99, 104
divinization, 104
D'jakanov, 225
Dobrotoljubie, 235, 272, 275
doctrine, 57
Dorotheus, 169, 175, 191
Dostojevskij, 9, 242

ecstasy, 142
effort, 146, 152
ejaculation, 104

emptying (of thoughts), 113–117
enlightenment, 114, 118, 142, 143
Ephrem, 191
Evagrius, 101, 103–106, 109, 113–115, 120–123, 129, 131, 133, 136, 142, 144–145, 152, 175, 187–188, 240
Evangelic tradition, 10, 12
evil, 81–83, 91, 93, 95, 99, 121, 135, 138, 139, 158, 163, 266

fasts, 84–87, 107, 265
Fathers, Holy, 10, 12, 27–28, 37, 40–41, 47, 55–72, 76, 79, 80–81, 83–89, 108, 119, 122, 124, 125, 128, 129, 130, 134, 144, 150, 152, 165, 173–174, 196, 201, 215, 222, 225, 226, 228, 239, 250, 254
Fathers of desert, 11, 73, 103, 130–131, 136, 152, 158, 165, 171, 192, 203, 234, 240
fear, 96, 121, 125, 126; of God, 88, 91
Fedotov, G., 233
Fennell, 202, 205, 213
Filaret, G., 194, 222, 230, 245, 256, 265
flexibility, 146
flight, 111, 112
Florovsky, G., 201, 207, 219
food, 84, 87
forgiveness, 92, 133, 163–164, 168
formalism, 77, 152
fornication, 83–84, 88–91, 96
fortitude, 111
freedom, 104, 146

Gardet, L., 277
Gennadij, 43, 44, 205, 207, 220
German, 202, 212–213, 217, 252, 253, 257
gift of tears, 104 (see tears)
glory of God, 117
Glusickij, D., 230
gluttony, 83, 87
Golubinskij, E., 205, 225
Gorskij, 253
Gouillard, J., 276
grace, 76, 80, 82, 104–105, 111, 113, 117–118, 126–127, 130, 133, 141–146, 152, 161, 164
Grečev, B., 214
Gregory Acyndinos, 274
Gregory Nazianzen, 268, 270
Gregory Palamas, 108, 173, 270, 273
Gregory, the Sinaite, 38–39, 73, 79, 95–96, 99–101, 106–108, 117, 135, 138–

Gregory, *continued*
139, 140–141, 174–181, 189–191, 240, 252, 272–273
Gribomont, J., 255
Guillaumont, A., 269
guilty, 81–82
Gurij, 194, 203, 211, 215, 247, 249, 264

Hausherr, I., 115, 117, 188, 269–271, 273, 277
heart, 104, 106–108, 112–118, 120, 124–125, 134–140, 142–143, 145–146, 156, 269
heart activity, 76, 89, 120, 272
Helena, 209
Hell, 125–126
hermitic, 29, 36, 39
hermits, 96, 110, 111, 130, 168, 171
heresy, 93, 168, 204
heretics, 43–44, 66–67, 205, 217
hesychasm, 103–147, 151–153, 159–160, 169, 177, 181, 234, 240, 269, 272, 274
hesychastic, 37, 38, 39, 47, 57, 183
hesychia, 196, 229, 230, 232, 240, 251
Hesychius of Jerusalem, 74, 114, 119, 120
Hesychius of Sinai, 103, 119, 120, 123, 136, 138, 146, 175, 183, 191, 240
higoumen, 39, 45, 154
Holl, D., 270
Holy Name, 137–138, 146
Holy Spirit, 57–61, 63, 75, 97, 105, 112, 118, 119, 123, 124, 127, 133, 141, 144, 242
humility, 107, 141, 144, 156, 158, 165, 181

ideal, 9, 30, 37, 136
idiorhythmic, 186
Ignatius, 109, 274, 276, 277
Ikonnikov, 205–206, 225
Iljinskij, 206
illiteracy, 20–24
image, 78, 79, 80, 113
imagination, 137–140, 146
impurity, 84, 88, 91
individualism, 42, 63
Innokentij, 185, 230, 231, 233
inspiration, 57–59, 124, 149
Ioannikij, 72
Ioasaf, 207–208, 228
Isaac, 52, 73, 94–95, 97, 101, 109, 111, 118, 129, 130, 132, 141, 142, 145, 240, 247

Ivan Kurcyn, 209
Ivan III, 200, 206–209, 221, 228
Ivan Terrible, 216, 227

Jaroslavov, P., 37, 44, 207
Jesus Christ, 56, 58–59, 67, 78–79, 93, 104–105, 113, 118–119, 124, 126–127
Jesus Prayer, 103, 106, 107, 109–110, 128, 134–147, 187, 189, 240, 271
Joseph Volokolamsk, 30, 39, 44–45, 56, 58, 63, 68, 69, 71, 153, 168, 171, 174, 177, 198, 200, 202–203, 206–207, 209, 210, 212–214, 221–222, 228, 232, 235, 242–243, 251
joy, 94, 118, 134, 142, 163–164
Judaism, 205, 267
Judaizers, 202, 205, 207, 210
judgment, 104, 125–126 128, 131, 133, 144, 145, 150

Kadlubovskij, 201, 229, 230, 231, 233
Kalugin, 214
Kassian, 37, 188, 194, 195, 233, 256, 267
Kazakova, 207, 208, 211–213
Kazan, 227
kelliotai, 41
kenotic, 45, 92, 141, 143, 156, 164, 180, 190
kingdom of God, 104
Kiprian, 219, 235
Kireevskij, I., 242
Kirill, 219, 235, 249
Kirill Monastery, 36, 37, 39, 41, 165, 207
Kirillo-Belozerskij Monastery, 37, 39, 40, 69, 70, 71, 151, 153, 157, 167, 203, 212, 249, 253, 254
Kliment, S., 219
Ključevskij, 28, 220, 225, 229
koinonia, 169
Kojalovič, M., 214
Kologrivov, I., 207, 230
Konoplev, 231, 233
Kopanev, A., 220
Kormcaja Kniga, 223
Kornilij, 231–233
Kurbskij, A., 227

Levickij, G., 193, 239
liberation, 64
Life of St. Antony, 75, 175, 191

light, 142–143
Lilienfeld, von F., 11, 13
Lithuania, 209, 214, 218, 227
Liturgy, 21, 23, 24, 42, 154, 155
lives of Saints, 68
love of fellow man, 161–171
love of God, 121–124
Lur'e, J., 13, 70–72, 192, 198, 203, 207, 208, 221
lust, 81, 88, 91

Macarius, 75, 79, 109, 142, 144, 145, 162, 173, 191
Makarij, 205, 228, 253
Marcionism, 205
Marechal, J., 277
Maritain, J., 278
Maksim Causokalivit, 275
Maksim Greek, 223–224, 227
Mark, 188
materialism, 105
Maximus, 109, 191
meditation, 84, 124–128, 159
memory, 137
mental activity, 9, 12, 37, 76, 77, 119, 120, 125, 137, 141, 144, 146, 154
mental prayer, 41, 140
Messalians, 105–106, 206, 272–273
Messianism, 242, 243
method, 269, 270
Meyendorff, J., 212, 221
middle way, 149
mind, 137–138, 140–146, 152, 156, 160
moderation, 88
Moldavia, 236
Moscow Synod, 44, 45, 67, 92, 220, 221
monasteries, 23, 101, 150, 153, 155
monastic, 10, 12, 35, 36, 52–55, 86, 112
monasticism, 25–31, 149, 153, 170, 184
monk, 65, 73, 76, 84, 85, 86–88, 91, 92, 94, 96–100, 105, 110–118, 128, 141–166, 171–177
Mount Athos, 37, 38, 41, 53, 106, 108, 110, 144, 151, 152, 153, 154, 173, 177, 178, 184, 185, 219, 221, 223, 230, 240, 271–272
Muromcev, V., 227
Murav'ev, 231
mystical, 105; mysticism, 106, 110, 112, 127, 130, 132, 142, 143, 146, 278

nationalism, 9, 10
nepsis, 109, 111, 118, 120–122, 124, 137, 145, 183
neptic, 108
Nevostruev, 225
Nicephorus, 271, 272
Nicephorus Gregoras, 272, 274
Nikol'skij, N., 219, 249, 253
Nikon of Montenegro, 177, 178, 202, 209, 223
Nil Polev, 210, 212, 253
Nilus, 73, 103
Nilus of Sinai, 114, 185, 187, 193
Nomocanon, see Kormcaja Kniga, 223
Novgorod, 43, 204, 205–207, 225

obedience, 149
Old Testament, 211, 216, 269
Olel'kovic, P., 206
Orient, 273
Origen, 103, 104, 160, 165
Orthodoxy, 106, 273

Pachomius, 157, 185
Paisij, 207
Paisij, V., 235, 236
Palamas, see Gregory
Palamism, 241
Palamists, 187, 274
Palladius, 192
Pandectes, 223
Panov, I., 205, 206, 210, 211
passion, 78, 81, 82, 91, 101, 104, 106, 109, 136, 137, 142, 143–145, 184
passions, 118, 125, 132, 133, 141, 149, 155–157, 161, 181, 193
passivity, 162, 163, 166
Pateriki, 25, 27
patience, 107, 125, 158
patriarch, 66
patristic, 193
Paul, St., 73–75, 95, 107, 158, 169, 194, 204, 211, 267
Paul Obnora, 219, 229, 233, 235
Pavlov, 220, 221, 223, 225
Paxomij, 36, 219
peace, 81
Pel'semskij, G., 230
penance, 23, 80, 144
penthos, 104, 109, 110, 124–134, 145, 181, 196, 241

Peter, St., 74, 266
Peter the Great, 242
Philokalia, 235, 269
Philotheus of Sinai, 122, 123, 185, 191, 240
pilgrimage, 38
plenenie, 78
Pokrouskij, K., 69, 70
Popov, K., 269
possessions, 43, 115, 155–158
Poucel, V., 277
Pourrat, P., 266
poverty, 30, 36–37, 91–92, 116, 155–158, 181, 218–219, 222–223
practica, 104, 145
praxis, 121, 122, 133
prayer, 23, 58, 76, 77, 81, 83, 84, 89, 91, 92, 93, 95, 96, 98, 101, 103, 107–122, 126, 128, 129, 130, 134, 135–147, 154
Predanie, 9, 11, 12, 41, 42, 51, 154, 165, 175, 178, 180, 183, 203
presence of God, 136, 137, 139, 145, 150, 155, 175, 183
presence to neighbor, 162, 168
pride, 83, 98, 99–101, 110, 152, 156, 181
priests, 20, 21, 22
prilog, 78
Priluckij, D., 230
Prochorus, 274
prosoche, see *attention*, 104
Providence, Divine, 94, 96, 116
prudence, 67, 86, 144, 180
Pskov, 205
psychological process, 82, 83
psychology, 137
purification, 105, 106, 109, 110, 114, 120, 124, 132, 133, 146, 182
purity, 58, 88, 104
purity of heart, 76, 101, 110, 112, 116, 119, 122, 124, 132, 133, 137, 145, 152, 155
Pypin, A., 223, 225

Radčenko, 206
renunciation, 116
repentance, 81–82, 95, 129, 144
respiration, 103, 107, 109, 136, 137, 146
revelation, 57
riches, 30, 36, 37
ritual, 22, 23, 66
Russia, 19, 31, 149, 151, 153, 159, 177, 178, 194, 198, 200, 201, 218, 242

Rudnev, N., 205
rule, 149–171, 177, 178
Rybakov, B., 213

sadness, 83, 94–95, 116
salvation, 55, 82, 111, 116, 133, 169
sanctification, 52, 96, 170
Scriptures, Holy, 40, 41, 42, 54–72, 75, 84, 93, 105, 117, 119, 122, 124, 126, 143, 150, 151, 152, 153, 159, 160, 167, 169, 176, 185, 210, 216, 222, 223, 240
sentiment, 105
Serafim, 242
Serbia, 205
Sergej Radonež, 233, 235
service, 116, 161–171
Sevyrev, S., 213
silence, 62–63, 107–108, 111–114, 117, 134, 137, 168–169, 175, 181
Simeon the New Theologian, 38–39, 58, 73, 79, 103, 105–106, 114, 129, 130, 132, 133, 136, 139, 140, 141, 142, 144, 151, 175, 180, 183, 188–189, 240, 248, 270–271, 275
sin, 23, 54, 59, 80, 82, 97, 99, 100, 101, 115–119, 126–129, 130–133, 145, 163–165
singing, 139, 147
Skete, 29, 39, 42, 45, 53, 62, 149, 151, 153–155, 158, 160, 161, 169–171, 173, 178
Slavic, 205
Slavonic, 185, 195, 223
Slavophiles, 243
složenie, 78
sobriety, 84, 109, 111, 118–119, 121–122
Sobolevskij, A., 206
Solitude, 40, 62, 75, 76, 83, 103, 105, 109, 111, 113, 115, 117, 145, 149, 152, 159, 166, 168, 169, 171, 175
Soloveckij, 214
Sophie, 209
Sora, 12, 202, 221, 241
sorrow, 95, 104, 271
soul, 81, 82, 84, 86, 91, 97, 99, 104–107, 111, 113, 116–121, 123–127, 130–133, 138, 140–145
Soviet Russia, 236
Spidlik, T., 55, 185, 200
Stephan, 231
Stoglav, 67, 228
strast', 78

Strigol'niki, 43, 205
struggle, 182
sufferings, 94, 95, 97, 116, 128, 164, 168
sunduasmos, 78
Sxarija, 206
Syrku, 206, 273

Taboric Light, 271
teach, 165, 168
tears (see *gift*), 107, 109, 124, 125, 127, 128, 129–134, 145, 168, 169, 175, 181
temptation, 80, 82, 83, 87, 89, 94, 96, 97, 101, 116, 117, 123, 125, 134, 139, 140, 143, 146, 181, 182
Theodore Studite, 152–153
Theodosius Kosoj, 214, 215
Theodosius Pečerskij, 219
theoria, 103, 104, 106
Third Rome, 200, 215, 242
thought, 81, 82, 101, 104, 109, 111, 113–117, 120–121, 125, 134–138, 140–142, 145, 158, 175, 181, 182, 183, 266–267
tonsure, 28, 29
Tradition, 201, 204
tranquility, 111, 118, 140, 155, 183
translations, 176, 177, 178, 179
Trans-Volga, 185, 201, 206, 208, 209, 211, 212, 228, 230, 231, 233
Trans-Volga Starcy, 202
Trebnik, 67
Trifon, 36–37
Trinity, 104, 106, 118, 147
trust, 121

union of God, 136, 137, 138, 140, 141, 142, 143, 145, 170
universality, 9, 10
Ustav, 9, 11, 12, 33, 34, 37, 42, 51, 56, 64, 66, 67, 119, 120, 125, 134, 141

vainglory, 83, 97–99, 157, 163, 181
vanity, 97–99, 100, 118, 121, 143, 163, 170, 204
Vasilij, Prince, 209
Vasilij, Tsar, 211, 223, 228
Vassian, 194, 203, 209, 210, 216, 221, 222, 223, 224, 225, 226, 233, 245
Veličkovskij, P., 33
Velikaja Cet'e Minei, 71
vice, 83–110, 116
vigil, 107
vigilance, 111, 118, 119, 121, 145
Vilinskij, S., 205, 214, 215, 227
Vitae Patrum, 192
vocation, 140
Volokolamsk (see *Joseph*)

waiting, 138
will, 104, 122, 124, 137, 149, 150 – 152
wisdom, 149
women, 90, 155
work, 97, 100, 147, 154, 156, 158–161, 163, 170, 171
world, 162, 175
Writings (Holy), 201, 211, 214, 216, 217, 225, 239, 252, 254, 255, 256, (see *Scriptures*)
Wunderle, G., 276

Xruščov, 206, 210, 211, 216, 225, 253

Zaorzerskij, A., 229, 233
zeal, 119
Zimin, A., 200
Zmakin, 68, 211, 212, 221, 225, 253
Zosima, 208, 213
Zuzek, I., 223

SLAVISTIC PRINTINGS AND REPRINTINGS

Edited by C.H. van Schooneveld

f

38. George Y. Shevelov, *The Syntax of Modern Literary Ukrainian: the Simple Sentence.* 319 pp.   62,—
39. Alexander M. Schenker, *Polish Declension: a Descriptive Analysis.* 105 pp.   22,—
40. Milada Součkova, *The Parnassian: Jaroslav Vrchlicky.* 151 pp.   28,—
42. Charles A. Moser, *Antinihilism in the Russian Novel of the 1860's.* 215 pp.   29,—
44. Hongor Oulanoff, *The Serapion Brothers: Theory and Practice.* 186 pp.   32,—
45. *Dutch Contributions to the 5th International Congress of Slavicists, Sofia, 1963.* 162 pp.   48,—
46. *American Contributions to the 5th International Congress of Slavists, Sofia, 1963, I: Linguistic Contributions.* 383 pp.   98,—
49. Edward Stankiewicz/Dean S. Worth, *A Selected Bibiliography of Slavic Linguistics, I: General, Old Church Slavonic, South Slavic* (General), *Bulgarian, Macedonian, Serbo-Croation, and Slovenian.* 315 pp.   54,—
50. *American Contributions to the 5th International Congress of Slavists, Sofia, 1963, II: Literary Contributions.* 341 pp.   98,—
51. Roman Jakobson/Dean S. Worth (ed.), *Sofonija's Tale of the Russian-Tartar Battle on the Kulikovo Field.* 71 pp., 49 plates   26,—
52. Waclaw Lednicki, *Tolstoy between War and Peace.* 169 pp.   30,—
53. Tatjana Čiževska, *Glossary of the Igor' Tale.* 405 pp.   78,—
54. A. V. Florovskij (ed.), *Georgius David, S. J.: Status modernus Magnae Russiae seu Moscoviae* (1690). 135 pp. –   34,—
55. Frances De Draaff, *Sergej Esenin: a Biographical Sketch.* 178 pp.   42,—
56. N. S. Trubetzkoy, *Dostoevskij als Künstler.* 178 pp.   35,—
57. F. C. Driessen, *Gogol as a Short-Story Writer: a Study of his Technique of Composition.* 243 pp.   44,—
58. V. Zirmunskij, *Introduction to Metrics: the Theory of Verse* 245. pp. 36,—
59. Dale L. Plank, *Pasternak's Lyric: a Study of Sound and Imagery.* 123. pp.   24,—
60. Henry M. Nebel, Jr., N. M. *Karamzin: a Russian Sentimentalist.* 190 pp.   36,—
61. Kazimierz Polánski/James A. Sehnert (ed.), *Polabian-English Dictionary.* 239 pp.   55,—
62. Carl R. Proffer, *The Simile in Gogol's "Deand Sould".* 208 pp.   32,—
63. Julius M. Blum, *Konstantin Fedin: a Descriptive and Analytic Study.* 235 pp.   36,—
65. David J. Welsh, *Russian Comedy, 1765—1823.* 133 pp.   24,—

66. *Poètika: Sobrnik statej* Leningrad, 1926   29,—
67. P. A. Lavrov, *Materialy po istorii vozniknovenija drevnejšej slavanskoj pis'
mennosti* Leningrad, 1930. 258 pp.   38,—
70. Howard I. Aronson, *Bulgarian Inflectional Morphophonology.* 189 pp.
35,—
72. Robert L. Belknap, *The Structure of "The Brothers Karamazov".* 122 pp.
24,—
73. Maria Zagórska Brooks, *Nasal Vowels in Contemporary Standard Polish:
an Acoustic-Phonetic Analysis.* 55 pp., 8 plates   18,—
74. Sigmund S. Birkenmayer, *Nikolaj Nekrasov: his Life and Poetic Art.*
205 pp.   38,—
80. Henry Kučera (ed.), *American Contributions to the 6th International Congress of Slavists,* Prague, 1968, I: *Linguistic Contributions.* 427 pp. 98,—
81.   William E. Harkins (ed.), *American Contributions to the 6th International
Congress of Slavists,* Prague, 1968, II: *Literary Contributions.* 381 pp. 98,—
82. Krystyna Pomorska, *Russian Formalist Theory and its Poetic Ambiance.*
127 pp.   24,—
83. Jacques Veyrenc, *La Forme poétique de Serge Esenin: Les rythmes.* 222.pp.
42,—
91. M. Geršenzon, *P. Ja. Čaadaev: Žizn i myslenie* [St. Petersburg, 1908].
329 pp.   45,—
92. A. N. Pypin. *Istorija russkoj literatury,* I-IV [2nd edition, St. Petersburg,
1902]. 4 vols. 2,347 pp.   315,—
94. Byloe: *Zurnal posvjascennyj istorii osvoboditeľnago dviženija,* Volume I,
1-6 [St. Petersburg, 1906]. 3 vols. 2,054 pp.   570,—
99. Alexandre Eck, *Le Moyen-Age russe* [2nd edition, Paris 1933]. 610 pp.
70,—
100. A. Romanovic-Slavatinskij, *Dvorstjanstvo v Rossii ot načala XVIII veka
do otmeny krpostnogo prava* [2nd edition, Kiev, 1912]. 596 pp.   82,—
101. Serge Kryzytski, *The Works of Ivan Bunin* 283 pp., 1 plate   56,—
108. Thomas F. Rogers, '*Superfluour Men*' *and the Post-Stalin 'Thaw'* 410 pp.
84,—
112. Charles A. Moser, *A History of Bulgarian Literature* 865—1944 282pp.
60,—
116. J. G. Garrard, *Mixail Čulkov: An Introduction to his Prose and Verse*
162 pp., 1 plate   28,—
254. A. A. Fokker, and Emilia Smolikowska, *Anatomy of a World-Class:
A Chapter of Polish Grammar* 108 pp.   32,—
264. Alexander F. Zweers, *Grown-Up Narrator and Childlike Hero: An Analysis
of the Literary Devices Employed in Tolstoy's Trilogy Childhood, Boyhood
and Youth* 165 pp.   32,—
Waclaw Lednicki, *Reminiscences, The Adventures of a Modern Gil Blas
During the Last War* 278 pp.   54,—

MOUTON · PUBLISHERS · THE HAGUE